Unhomely Empire

Empire's Other Histories

Series Editors: Victoria Haskins (University of Newcastle, Australia), Emily Manktelow (Royal Holloway, University of London, UK), Jonathan Saha (University of Leeds, UK) and Fae Dussart (University of Sussex, UK)

Empire's Other Histories is an innovative series devoted to the shared and diverse experiences of the marginalised, dispossessed and disenfranchised in modern imperial and colonial histories. It responds to an ever-growing academic and popular interest in the histories of those erased, dismissed, or ignored in traditional historiographies of empire. It will elaborate on and analyse new questions of perspective, identity, agency, motilities, intersectionality and power relations.

Published:
Extreme Violence and the 'British Way' Michelle Gordon

Forthcoming:
In the Service of Empire, Fae Dussart
Spiritual Colonialism in a Globalizing World, Christina Petterson
Unexpected Voices in Imperial Parliaments, Josep M. Fradera, José María Portillo, Teresa Segura-Garcia

Unhomely Empire

Whiteness and Belonging, c.1760–1830

Onni Gust

BLOOMSBURY ACADEMIC
LONDON • NEW YORK • OXFORD • NEW DELHI • SYDNEY

BLOOMSBURY ACADEMIC
Bloomsbury Publishing Plc
50 Bedford Square, London, WC1B 3DP, UK
1385 Broadway, New York, NY 10018, USA
29 Earlsfort Terrace, Dublin 2, Ireland

BLOOMSBURY, BLOOMSBURY ACADEMIC and the Diana logo
are trademarks of Bloomsbury Publishing Plc

First published in Great Britain 2021
This paperback edition published in 2022

Copyright © Onni Gust, 2021

Onni Gust has asserted their right under the Copyright, Designs
and Patents Act, 1988, to be identified as Author of this work.

For legal purposes the Acknowledgements on p. vii constitute
an extension of this copyright page.

Cover Image: Colonel Blair with his Family and an Indian Ayah.
Johann Zoffany (1733–1810). Photo © Tate

All rights reserved. No part of this publication may be reproduced or transmitted in
any form or by any means, electronic or mechanical, including photocopying,
recording, or any information storage or retrieval system, without prior
permission in writing from the publishers.

Bloomsbury Publishing Plc does not have any control over, or responsibility for,
any third-party websites referred to or in this book. All internet addresses given in
this book were correct at the time of going to press. The author and publisher
regret any inconvenience caused if addresses have changed or sites have
ceased to exist, but can accept no responsibility for any such changes.

A catalogue record for this book is available from the British Library.

Library of Congress Cataloging-in-Publication Data
Names: Gust, Onni, author.
Title: Unhomely empire : whiteness and belonging, from the Scottish Enlightenment
to liberal imperialism / Onni Gust.
Description: London ; New York : Bloomsbury Academic, 2020. | Series: Empire's other
histories | Includes bibliographical references and index.
Identifiers: LCCN 2020027575 (print) | LCCN 2020027576 (ebook) | ISBN 9781350128514
(hardback) | ISBN 9781350192737 (paperback) | ISBN 9781350128521 (ebook) | ISBN 9781350128538 (epub)
Subjects: LCSH: Great Britain–Colonies–Intellectual life. | Home in literature. |
Whites–Race identity–Great Britain–Colonies–History–18th century. | Race
awareness–Great Britain–Colonies–History–18th century. | Belonging
(Social psychology) | Exile in literature. | Enlightenment. | Imperialism in literature. |
Great Britain–Colonies–In literature. | Emigration and immigration in literature.
Classification: LCC DA480 .G87 2020 (print) | LCC DA480 (ebook) | DDC 909/.0971206–dc23
LC record available at https://lccn.loc.gov/2020027575
LC ebook record available at https://lccn.loc.gov/2020027576

ISBN: HB: 978-1-3501-2851-4
       PB: 978-1-3501-9273-7
       ePDF: 978-1-3501-2852-1
       eBook: 978-1-3501-2853-8

Typeset by Integra Software Services Pvt. Ltd.

To find out more about our authors and books visit www.bloomsbury.com
and sign up for our newsletters.

Contents

Map	vi
Acknowledgements	vii
Introduction	1
1 The racialization of belonging in Adam Smith's *The Theory of Moral Sentiments*	19
2 Dugald Stewart and the colour of progress	37
3 The role of 'home' in Edgeworth and Graham's critiques of slavery	59
4 Belonging and exile in the debate over Scottish Highland emigration	79
5 Colonial knowledge and the making of white masculinity in Bombay	103
6 'A hothouse of weeds': reproducing white womanhood in colonial India	127
Conclusion	151
Notes	156
Bibliography	198
Index	220

Map

Map 1 Thomas Kitchen Jnr and John Evans, 'A New Map of the World: With all the new discoveries by Capt. Cook and other navigators: Ornamented with the Solar System, the eclipses of the Sun, moon & planets' (London: I. Evans, 1799), https://www.loc.gov/item/2003630537/ x

Acknowledgements

This book has sat heavily on my shoulders for nearly a decade. I am deeply indebted to those friends and colleagues who have shared with me their enthusiasm for historical research and for anti-racist, feminist scholarship. I am even more indebted to the many people – from workers in cafes, to librarians, archivists, therapists and friends – who have supported me through the existential angst that has been the writing process.

The origins of this book lie in my PhD research at University College London, which was made possible by the support of the AHRC, the Scoloudi foundation and a Simeon Shoul bursary. In 2011, the Five College Women's Studies Centre, Massachussetts provided me with a visa and a collegial space from which to begin re-envisaging that initial project. My research has also been supported by a Mellon fellowship at the Illinois Program for Research in the Humanities at the University of Illinois, Urbana-Champaign. A semester-long sabbatical at the University of Nottingham, as well as a writing retreat funded by the Rights and Justice RPA, gave me the space and time to finish this book. For this financial and institutional support, I am incredibly grateful.

The support I have received from the publishing team at Bloomsbury, especially from Maddie Holder and Abigail Lane, has been exceptional. The two anonymous reviewers made excellent suggestions that significantly improved the clarity of my arguments. I am thankful for Kellee Weinhold's 'Unstuck: The Art of Productivity' course that enabled me to overcome a chronic case of writer's block. Parts of Chapters 5 and 6 were previously published as 'The Perilous Territory of Not Belonging: Exile and Empire in Sir James Mackintosh's Letters from Early Nineteenth-Century Bombay' in *History Workshop Journal*, 86 (2018).

I am incredibly fortunate to have been supported and encouraged by a group of intellectually formidable women who have provided me with a model of feminist scholarship and mentorship to which I can only hope to aspire. My PhD supervisor, Catherine Hall, has given her time, enthusiasm and intellectual rigour from the very beginning of the project. Since they examined my thesis, Jane Rendall and Margot Finn have provided feedback on draft articles and chapters, and written countless references. Barbara Taylor's passion for making the past relevant to the social, political and emotional world of our present opened up ways for me to envisage the relevance of my research. Finally, Antoinette Burton and Dana Rabin made my year surrounded by corn fields in Urbana-Champaign one of the most intellectually exciting of my academic career so far. Their support, intellectual engagement and friendship have kept me focused and motivated to finally finish this book.

I have been extremely lucky to have an increasingly wide circle of academic friends and colleagues who reject competitiveness and embrace compassion and mutual support: Karen Adler, Ibtisam Ahmed, Sascha Auerbach, Jayadev Athreya, Ross Balzaretti, Hongwei Bao, Shahanna Battacharya, Justin Bengry, Toby Beauchamp, Rachel Berger, Dean Blackburn, Rosi Carr, Esmé Cleall, Kavita Datla (much missed), Kate Donington, Catherine Fletcher, Radhika Govindrajan, Daniel Grey, Katharine Jenkins, Rachel Johnson, Aparna Kapadia, Arun Kumar, Zoe Laidlaw, Steve Legg, Emily Manktelow, Mario da Penha, Silas Moon Cassinelli, Durba Mitra, Shipra Nigam, Eleanor Newbigin, Simin Patel, Humaira Saeed, Jonathan Saha, Karen Salt, Aditya Sarkar, Uditi Sen, Falgani Seth, Krupa Shandilya, Nitin Sinha, Ella Simpson, Taylor Sherman, Carole Spary, Amina Steinfels, Sanjukta Sunderason, T.J. Tallie, Clare Tebbut and Erica Wald. Zirwat Chowdhury, Richard Hornsey and Laura Ishiguro have been particularly wonderful interlocutors and sources of intellectual support. Thank you for your friendship, insights and encouragement.

My trans-national queer and trans community has sustained me throughout a very difficult decade. Thank you especially to Anamika, Danielle Chynoweth, Silas Moon Cassinelli, Maryam Din, Briar Dunn, Robin Edwards, Dee Fairchild, Sam Hope, Rowan Hyde, Beth Metz, Sonny Nordmarken, Marco Pino, Cherise Richardson, Nyx Zierhut, Angie Willey, Sage Wolf and Dov Zeller.

My students, especially my Gender and Sexuality Studies students at Smith College, Amherst College, and the Universities of Massachusetts (Amherst) and Illinois (Urbana-Champaign) shared their enthusiasm and insights. I am deeply impressed by their intelligence, and proud of their achievements. My final-year Special Subject students at the University of Nottingham will see our discussions of racism and the Enlightenment reflected here. Their willingness to engage and think critically about the legacies of the Enlightenment in the world we live in today has made this book possible.

Nearly nine years ago, my sister taught my then three-year-old nephew to ask me, 'Have you finished your book yet?' He's too cool and grown up to care now, but I am grateful to all the Edgers – Nicola, Rob, Benjamin, Toby and Susannah – for providing fun and distraction. To my parents, Trudy and Bob: thank you for all your support, for the reminders to switch off occasionally, as well as for the numerous tea and biscuit breaks during some wonderful home-from-home writing retreats. Tipton has kept me fit, muddy and laughing.

My partner, Uditi Sen, is my rock. Thank you for your love, support and belief in me. This book was finished just in time for the birth of our baby, Maayan Ari. Her arrival serves as a powerful reminder of the need to dismantle white supremacy and to embrace difference in order to make a better world for our children. This book is my tiny contribution to that project.

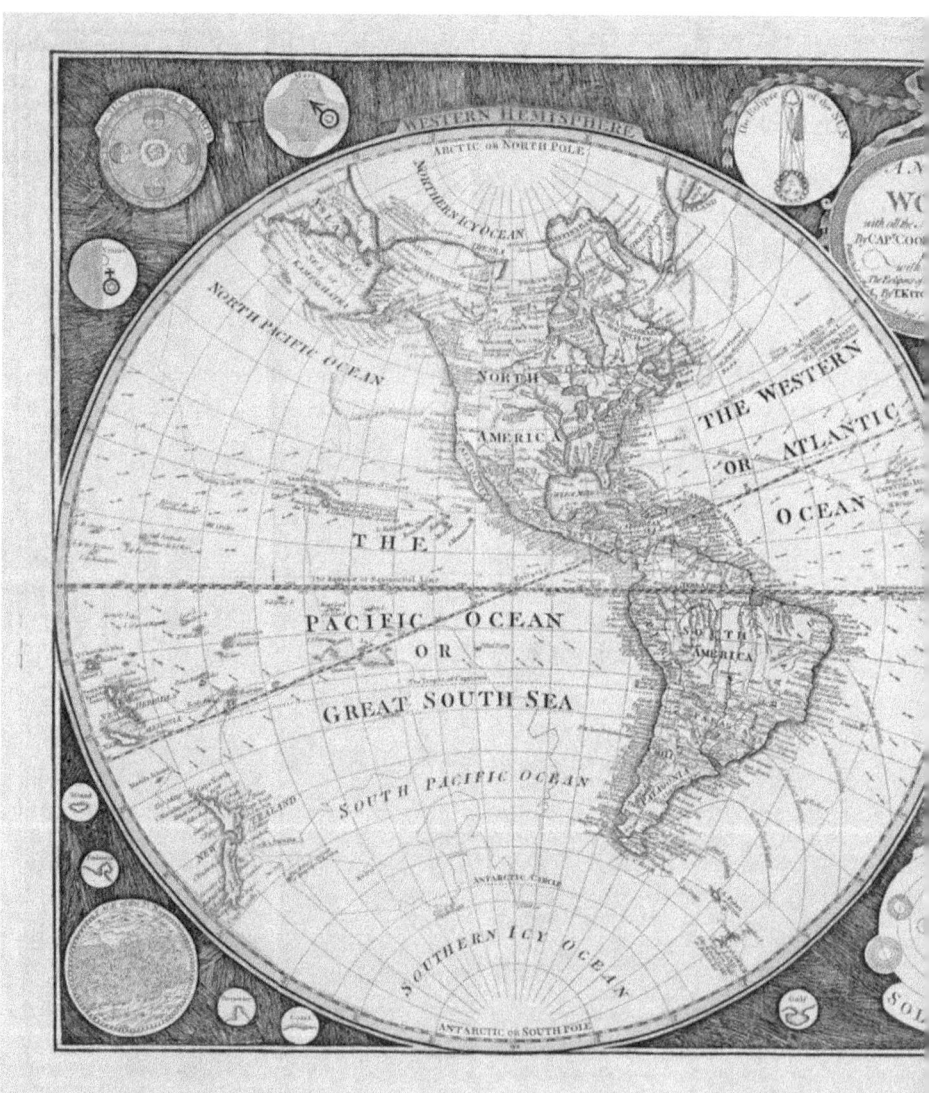

Map 1 Thomas Kitchen Jnr and John Evans, 'A New Map of the World: With all the new discoveries by Capt. Cook and other navigators: Ornamented with the Solar System, the eclipses of the Sun, moon & planets' (London: I. Evans, 1799), https://www.loc.gov/item/2003630537/

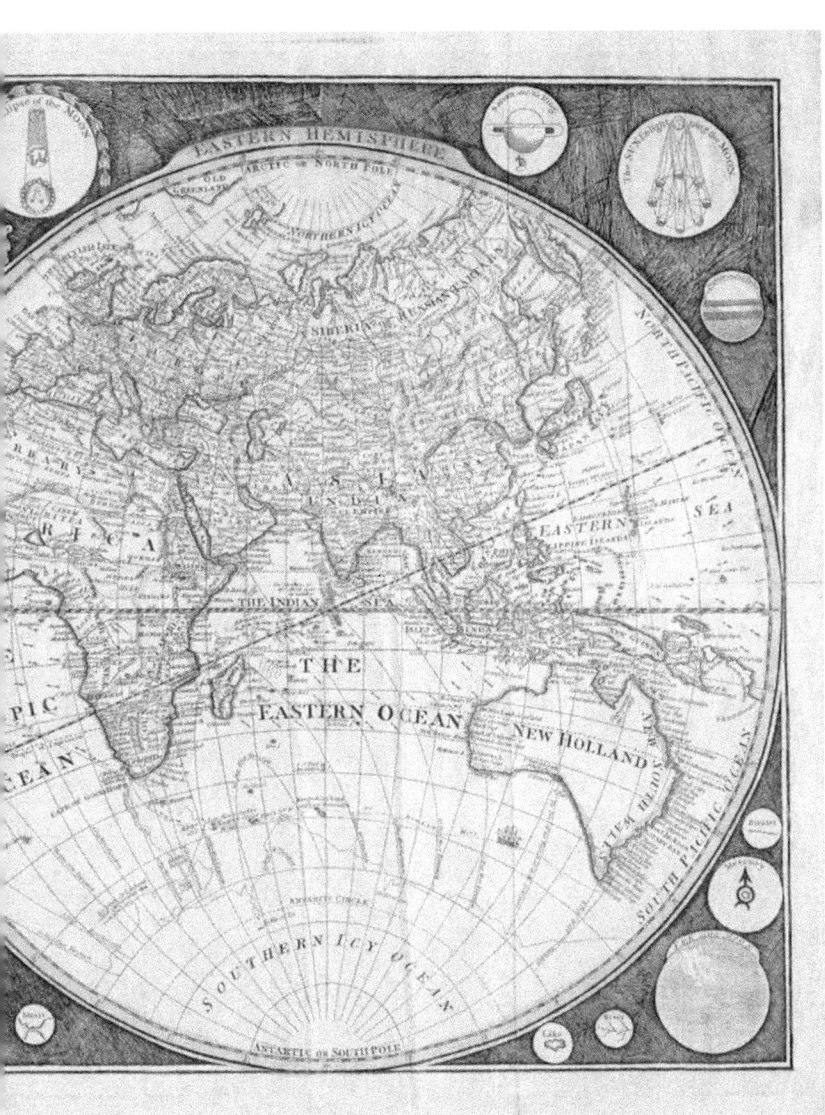

Introduction

> Oh blest are they whose eyes have ne'er
> Seen smoke of stranger's dwelling!
> And happy those who still have found
> Their father's feasts excelling!

In 1809 or early 1810, Maria Graham wrote a poem to her friend and confidant, William Gordon Mackenzie, a lieutenant-colonel in the East India Company based in Calcutta. Entitled 'Atala in the Wilderness', the poem follows a wanderer as he roams across an unfamiliar landscape in search of a bed for the night.[1] The theme would have resonated with both the author and recipient. Like thousands of their contemporaries from all ranks of society, Graham and Mackenzie were of Scottish heritage but looked to the British Empire to secure their livelihoods. Graham's highly successful imperial career as a travel writer, first in India and then in South America and Italy, was launched when she accompanied her father, a naval officer, to India in 1809. Her correspondent, William Gordon Mackenzie, served as an East India Company officer in the Bengal Army in Calcutta and as Political Agent on the South West frontier; he died in South Africa in 1842. Graham's poem forms part of a collection of William Gordon Mackenzie's private letters from Calcutta, held in the National Library of Scotland in Edinburgh. The small collection of Graham's letters to Mackenzie, of which this poem forms a part, suggests an intimacy borne of the shared experience of imperial travel, the ambivalences of their involvement in the project of empire building and their sense of absence of a place to call home. 'Atala in the Wilderness' articulates that absence in verse. Despite the abundant crops and 'groves to exclude the noontide beams', the wanderer's progress is impeded by a lack of emotional connection. Turned away from a stranger's cottage, he retraces his steps through a hostile and unfamiliar landscape. In the final two stanzas, Graham contrasts the wanderer's rejection and despair with the friendship and love that abounds amongst those who remain in their native land and who retain 'their father's ways'. As the refrain quoted above suggests, Graham's lament for those who are forced to leave their 'native land' in search of economic security configured 'home' as the settled site of patriarchal inheritance, as well as the ultimate space of emotional fulfilment.

Graham was not alone in her expression of desire for 'home'. From the late eighteenth century, the desire to belong – articulated through the discourse of 'home' – gained increasing currency in British-imperial discourse. The popular song, 'Home, Sweet Home!' (1823), written by John Howard Payne, contrasts the material riches encountered whilst 'roaming' through the world with the emotional richness of the humble cottage as 'home'.[2] Like Graham's poem, 'Home, Sweet Home!' represented mobility and migration as necessarily accompanied by intense, emotional loss. Although neither Graham nor Payne uses the word 'homesickness', the emergence of the concept in the mid-eighteenth century, and its greater prevalence by the mid-nineteenth century, provides further evidence of the growing importance of emotional attachment to 'home'.[3] In 1782, Josiah Wedgwood articulated this sentiment in a pamphlet to his workers in his Staffordshire potteries warning of the threat that migration posed to emotional health: 'There is a disease of the mind, peculiar to people in a strange land; a kind of heart-sickness and despair, with an unspeakable longing after their native country.'[4] The idea that migration led inevitably to despair was accompanied by a new reverence for 'home', which is reflected in the changing meaning of the adjective 'homely': where previously 'homely' was a derogatory term meaning 'plain', 'coarse' or 'rude', by the mid-nineteenth century it was also used as a positive attribute to refer to emotional warmth and material simplicity.[5] At the same time, home's antonym, 'exile', took on increasing emotional and social significance. Whereas early-eighteenth-century writers such as Defoe, Swift and Voltaire used 'exile' only in the narrow sense of 'expulsion', later-eighteenth-century writers employed 'exile' in a much wider sense to include socio-economic displacement. 'Exile' thus became associated with a much wider range of migration and mobility, a generalized marker of uprooting and the loss, even if only temporary, of 'home'.

Unhomely Empire is an examination of the changing meaning of 'home' and 'exile' in the context of mass mobility and displacement engendered by European, and particularly British, imperial expansion. It makes three, interrelated arguments. Firstly, it argues that the emotional capacity to belong played a central role in Scottish Enlightenment ideas of human difference and development. As later-eighteenth-century Scottish thinkers turned away from materialist explanations and towards a more essentialist understanding of human difference, emotional attachment took on increasing significance as a primary marker of moral superiority and, in some cases, humanity itself. By the late eighteenth century, to lack an attachment to 'home' – to be rootless and wandering – was to lack the fundamental emotional capacity that served as a signifier for humanity. This idea did not derive exclusively from, nor was it confined to, the philosophical debates of the 'high' Scottish Enlightenment. The second argument of this book is that to trace the emergence of a hegemonic configuration of belonging, through the discourse of 'home' and 'exile', it is necessary to read across different genres, which were written and intended for different, but often intersecting, audiences. *Unhomely Empire* shows how ideas of belonging became consolidated into the common-sense of British-imperial thought as a result of their articulation and re-articulation in philosophy, travel writing, novels, political pamphlets, imperial policy, letters and diaries. These different types of literature circulated amongst a relatively wide imperial elite who themselves spent much of their lives travelling across different sites of the British Empire, the ideas within them informed imperial policy and provided the justifications for the assertion of imperial power, often through violence. How those ideas were received and interpreted by subalterns both in metropolitan Britain and in the colonies is far beyond the scope of this book, rather the aim is to show how elite imperial imaginaries of 'home' structured the meaning of 'humanity'. As an ideology, 'home' is inseparable from the consolidation of norms of heterosexual reproduction, patriarchal authority, class and national formation during this period; a process that has been well-documented by historians.[6] The final argument of this book is that British-imperial configurations of 'home' were constituted in relationship to ideas of racial difference and white supremacy. *Unhomely Empire* argues that whiteness was central to nineteenth-century liberal imperialism's understanding of belonging, whilst emotional attachment and the perceived ability, or inability, to belong were key concepts in constructions of racial difference.

Mobility, displacement and empire in the eighteenth century

It is no coincidence that the growing significance of 'home' in Anglo-imperial thought took place at the same time that more and more people were moving around the British Empire. Between 1730 and 1830, the expansion of European empires radically increased population mobility as new trade routes, war, disease, and the expropriation of land and labour displaced people across the world. From enslaved Africans trafficked across the Atlantic, to Indian lascars manning East India Company ships, to peasants fleeing famine and eviction, millions were on the move. Exact numbers are, of course, impossible to tell. This period saw an estimated 7.5 million enslaved African men, women and children transported in European slave ships from the Western coast of Africa to the Americas, primarily to work on plantations.[7] In different circumstances, well over a million Europeans emigrated to North America and the Caribbean, settling on indigenous lands, enslaving indigenous and African peoples, and tapping into trade routes.[8] Many of those emigrant-settlers were from the peripheries of Britain's internal empire, including Ireland and the Highlands of Scotland, where the expansion of the English state disrupted older allegiances and ways of life. For them, emigration offered a potential escape from political repression, as well as poverty. In India, the British East India Company's dominance over Bengal led to a radical increase in the population of Calcutta, which filled up with merchants from across the subcontinent, as well as from Europe.[9] At the same time, the devastating famine of 1770, caused by the Company's excessive revenue demands, led to mass migration of peasants from the countryside to the city.[10] Almost-constant war in Europe, South Asia and North America saw thousands of young men from all ranks of society serving in the military. Many spent years on the seas on board merchant or navy ships bound for China, via the Cape of Good Hope, Bombay and Calcutta; some settled in India, still others bought plantations in the Caribbean. Amongst the British-imperial elite who are the subject of this book, their own mobility, as well as that of friends, family, material and capital across the British Empire, was a constant feature of their lives and letters.

Although European-imperial expansion certainly affected the volume of people on the move and the routes through which they circulated, there was nothing new about population mobility. For many societies the world over, moving across the land as the seasons changed, manipulating animal migration and navigating environments to ensure a constant supply of food, was the norm.[11] In nominally 'settled' societies, political and economic opportunities, which were themselves dictated by the seasons, had long informed migratory patterns. For centuries, Highland Scots had served as mercenary soldiers in overseas armies, often returning to the Highlands to help with harvesting in the summer and autumn months.[12] Similarly, Indian men and women found employment in the military labour market, moving from one battleground to another across the Indian subcontinent.[13] Trade routes zigzagged over land and across continents. Long before European ships dominated the Indian Ocean, the

Parsis – Zoroastrians from Persia, living in India – were master ship-builders who traded between the Middle East, India and China.[14] Although they certainly did not perceive themselves to be a 'wandering tribe', Britain's elite was also a highly itinerant group of people. Moving from countryside to city residences for politics and sociability, from northern to southern climates in search of health, and on tours of Europe in search of culture, the upper ranks of British society were almost constantly on the move.

It was not the fact of mobility, therefore, but the meaning of mobility, and its intersection with ideas of belonging, that underwent a transformation during late eighteenth and early nineteenth centuries. The association between mobility and feelings of sadness and loss, and the idealization of 'home', took place in constitutive relationship to wider, socio-economic transitions. Industrialization and urbanization in parts of Britain during the course of the eighteenth century reconfigured material life and social relationships. New methods of tapping mineral resources, particularly coal, led to the greater availability of energy that literally fuelled the economy. A better food supply, medical advances, higher levels of fertility and lower rates of infant mortality engendered a population boom. The development of manufacturing and agricultural technologies redistributed people from countryside to town, radically changing lifestyles as well as lifecycles. Increasing prosperity saw a rise in the numbers of people who occupied what contemporaries referred to as the 'middling ranks' of society; those whose livelihoods rested on trade and commerce, rather than from inherited wealth in land.[15] Their demands for a say in the running of the country and for the redistribution of political power reached fever-pitch during this period, culminating in the compromise of the 1832 'Great Reform' Act.[16] What historians refer to as the 'age of reform' was not restricted to political change. As Joanna Innes and Arthur Burns have noted, 'reform' was a broad and contested term, applicable to a wide variety of institutions from the Church to the East India Company, from law to prisons, schools and hospitals.[17] Those institutions and practices that have long been associated with the 'age of reform' were often developed in, and circulated around, Britain's colonies before being exported 'home' to Britain.[18]

The British Empire was key, economically, socially and conceptually, to British peoples' sense of themselves as a national community who, as part of a wider community white, European Christians, understood themselves as the torch-bearers of 'progress'.[19] The period covered by this book marks a broad transition in the structural orientation of the British Empire, from its focus on the American colonies as part of the triangular trade based on plantation slavery, to an empire that was increasingly geographically oriented towards trade and the exploitation of resources in India.[20] These transformations were themselves premised on the actions of people in European colonies as well as changing power relations between European states. In North America indigenous peoples who fought for and against the British, often in alliance with France as well as Scottish Highland emigrant settlers, played a fundamental role in expanding the trade routes into the North-West.[21] In the Caribbean, rebellion by enslaved Africans, particularly in Jamaica, posed a constant threat to both economic production and social relations that were based on white supremacy. Rebellion reached a peak in the Haitian revolutionary wars of 1791 to 1804, which fundamentally reoriented economic production and European-imperial political power across the Americas.[22] In South Asia, it was the waning power of the Mughals and the rise of regional powers that enabled the British to extend its own dominance over parts of India. Since the early eighteenth century, the Mughal Empire's centralized power-base in Delhi had been undermined by alliances of more localized powers, including Maratha, Rajput and Jat rulers. Like the French and Dutch, but with considerably more success, the British East India Company took advantage of political fragmentation, forming protection alliances with local rulers in return for access to land and trade resources.[23]

Imperial expansion rested on the labour of a vast number of people, the majority of whom were from the regions of conquest (or, in the case of the Americas, from Africa) rather than from the British Isles. They played a critical role in meeting increasing demand for luxury produce, including tea, chinaware and calicoes from China and India and for the sugar, tobacco and coffee manufactured by enslaved Africans in the Caribbean. At the same time, the wealth gained from trade and plunder that British men (and some women) sent or brought 'home' to Britain from the West and East Indies enabled British families to purchase luxury goods. The lack of inherited status amongst those who returned from empire with vast wealth made conspicuous consumption more important for their aspirations to belong to the upper echelons of British society. As historians of material culture and empire have illustrated, many of the manors that dot the British countryside were purchased and built on the wealth of slavery in the Caribbean.[24] Many of Britain's stately homes remain filled with the fabrics, designs and artefacts of colonial India, their furnishings and décor literally bring the legacy of imperial rule in India 'home' to Britain.[25] Imperial produce – the tea-sets and tea leaves that accompanied games of cards, the tobacco that smoothed out evenings spent debating politics and the coffee that fuelled conversation – and metropolitan social aspirations combined to fuel the 'polite sociability' that has been credited with the reformation of manners and the reconfiguration of social hierarchies. Consumption of addictive substances – tea, coffee, opium, tobacco and sugar – underpinned the material culture of this new 'commercial society'.[26] If 'commercial society' made a virtue out of material consumption, it was simultaneously concerned about the implications of that consumption on the morals of society. As Chapters 1 and 3 discuss in greater depth, humanitarian sentiment emerged out of the combination an awareness of exploitation – whether of children in factories or enslaved Africans on plantations – and of an emergent sense of individual and subsequently national responsibility for embodying 'civilized' values.[27] Situated at the intersection of material, social and emotional structures, 'home' offers an insight into the tensions and contradictions of a society in the midst of a far-reaching change.

Race, whiteness and belonging

One of the foundational transformations during this period was the emergence of 'race' as a key marker of human difference, alongside what we would today call 'racism' as a means of justifying oppressive hierarchies. Hume's infamous footnote in 'Of National Characters', in which he stated that 'I am apt to suspect the negroes and in general all other species of men (for there are four or five different kinds) to be naturally inferior to whites', provides one of the clearest examples of Enlightenment constructions of human difference along a 'racial' hierarchy in which 'whites' were deemed superior.[28] His statement must be situated in the context of a wide-ranging debate over human origins, which was broadly split between philosophers who believed that all humans derived from one, original human couple (monogenists), and those who argued that human variation was the result of multiple origins, akin to different species (polygenists). Although the latter tended towards more extreme condemnations of non-European peoples, there is no easy correlation between eighteenth-century 'racism' and polygenesism.[29] Indeed, it is the subtle aspects of Enlightenment theorization of the human mind – supposedly 'universal' but imagined to be always already white, European and male – that embedded exclusion and prejudice. The concept of 'reason', which went to the very heart of definitions of 'the Enlightenment', was premised on the spectre of the inherently 'irrational' and emotionally unstable nature of non-European men and all women. As Emmanuel Eze has argued, this configuration justified the exclusion of non-European people from 'civilization' and governance, and, in some cases, from the category of 'human' altogether.³⁰ Building on the work of Eze, this book shows how Scottish Enlightenment Moral Philosophy – one of the key means of theorizing belonging and the self – was fundamentally racialized. It argues that the shifting discourse of belonging intersected with debates over human variation and 'racial' difference to establish a collective 'white' identity that became increasingly associated with 'civilization' and 'progress'.

In an essay entitled 'Subjects in History: Making Diasporic Identities', Stuart Hall explained the importance of thinking about 'race' not as a 'biological referent' but as a 'discursive logic', which functioned to constitute subjects in place at a particular historical juncture. 'Race', Hall argued, is always a question of interpellation – of being called into subject-hood through relationships of representation and power – and of identification, rather than of any essential nature of being, waiting to be found.³¹ Several excellent studies of 'race' in Enlightenment thought have shown how ideas and representations of 'blackness' developed across the eighteenth century, from a relatively malleable conceptualization of human difference based on climate, to biologically essentialist notions of 'race' by the mid-nineteenth century. Andrew Curran's work, for example, documents the changing ways in which French travel writers and *philosophes* understood the differences between African and European bodies to illustrate the shifting construction of blackness in French Enlightenment thought.³² As Jennifer Morgan argues, these European ideas about African difference transformed alongside the changing nature of power from a fascinated and admiring objectification of African women to abhorrence and debasement. 'Confronted with an Africa they needed to exploit, European writers turned to African women as evidence of a cultural inferiority that ultimately became encoded as racial difference.'³³ It was this racism – the coming together of power and prejudice on the basis of skin colour and other anatomical markers of difference – that defined European imperialism and slavery. 'Racism' needs to be carefully defined; there was nothing new, or uniquely European, about prejudice towards different groups of people.³⁴ Yet if the use of 'racism' can be contested for the Early Modern period, by the mid-nineteenth century it served as one of the defining features of European-imperial modernity. Tracing the hardening of racial categories over the course of the eighteenth century, Roxann Wheeler has argued that at the beginning of the century complexion was just one among many fluid markers that served to define the self in opposition to others; religion was far more important. It was not until the nineteenth century that 'race', the combination of phenotypical and anatomical traits, became the over-determining signs of difference.³⁵

This book builds on this research but focuses less on Enlightenment constructions of blackness or other forms of racialized alterity, and more on the ways in which Enlightenment thought consolidated notions of whiteness and white supremacy through the discourse of 'home'. Drawing on Hall's seminal insights on 'race' and difference, I examine the production of subjects as 'white', and the role of 'home' in consolidating one's belonging to, or exclusion from 'whiteness'. Critical race scholars have defined 'whiteness' as the product of relationships and as itself relational.[36] As Sara Ahmed argues, 'whiteness' is not an ontological state, but a form of orientation, a means by which bodies take on meaning in space.[37] For Cheryl Harris, whiteness derives from the socio-economic privilege that originated in the right of people, legally defined as 'white' to own property, including property in Black people. In early American society, the ability to own property was the key marker that distinguished Black from white, and as such became the critical marker of freedom from commodification.[38] In Britain, this distinction was clarified through the Somerset ruling of 1772, which determined the right of the enslaved African, James Somerset, to his freedom in Britain, but not in Virginia. Dana Rabin argues that this ruling constructed a legal distinction between forms of un-freedom, whereby villeinage, marked as white, pertained (historically) to Britain, whilst chattel slavery was marked as black and confined to the colonies.[39] As Rabin notes in her conclusion, this construction of a legal binary represented an attempt by imperial law-makers to define the boundaries of freedom and un-freedom at the intersection of race and place: 'Freedom and whiteness were metropolitan attributes while slavery and blackness were colonial.'[40] Taken together, Ahmed, Rabin and Harris's arguments suggest a definition of whiteness in which property ownership, upon which notions of individual selfhood were contingent, converges with belonging in space.

Historiography

Historians have long understood the eighteenth century as a period in European history in which the idea of the self was significantly reconfigured to reflect 'modern' notions of interiority and individuality. In *The Autobiographical Subject*, Felicity Nussbaum argues that the impetus to 'know oneself' developed out of the material and discursive practices that produced a middle class in England. Autobiography, borne in part out of philosophical debates on the self, enabled the appearance of a 'free, whole and rational' subject, which was coded as white, male and middle class.[41] Dror Wahrman, in *The Making of the Modern Self*, concurs with this general argument, that the idea of a whole self came about at the turn of the nineteenth century in relationship to changing notions of class and gender, as well as of race. Wahrman notes a fundamental shift in understandings of the self, from the self as fluid, malleable and potentially deceptive, to the self as 'innate and even congenital, which was supposedly stamped on each and every individual'.[42] These discussions of new forms of self necessarily intersect with ideas of both race and feeling, what Enlightenment philosophers referred to as 'sensibility'. Indeed, in the poem with which this introduction began, Maria Graham's characterization of longing for 'native land' as 'home' drew on the 'sentimental project' of the eighteenth century, which understood the relationship between self and society as intimately connected to feeling. 'Sensibility' referred to both a physiognomic and a moral response to the social world; the more emotionally perceptive an individual was to their surroundings, the more refined and 'exquisite' their sensibility.[43] Few captured this figure more precisely than William Gordon Mackenzie's own father, Henry Mackenzie, whose *Man of Feeling* (1771) became the archetype of the sentimental novel, whilst his protagonist, Harley, became the model of white, male sensibility. Whilst Graham herself certainly inherited this eighteenth-century genre, her poem also encapsulates an emergent configuration of selfhood in relationship to space, in which 'home' became an increasingly significant marker of 'civilization', which could be used to construct the boundaries of belonging at different political registers, from the whole of humanity to particular groups of individuals.

This book illustrates how sensibility, self and whiteness come together in Scottish Enlightenment assumptions about, and debates over, the capacity of people to feel a sense of belonging to 'home', and the dissemination of those ideas in different imperial contexts. To examine belonging through the discourse of 'home' is to bring together material and social practices, geographical imaginaries, and emotional and embodied norms. During the eighteenth century, the transformation of material and social life throughout large parts of the British Isles reconfigured 'home' as a material formation and a social relationship. As Catherine Hall and Leonore Davidoff argued in *Family Fortunes*, the home became an increasingly important site for the configuration and performance of middle-class English identity and ideology. The home as a space of familial harmony, in which an angelic wife and dutiful children awaited the patriarch's return from the 'public' sphere of work, politics and masculine sociability, has become a key feature of capitalist 'modernity'.[44] Imperial expansion played a fundamental role in the emergence and consolidation of this ideology. Recent cultural and literary historians have shown how British emigrants and imperialists living across the empire used the 'home' to demarcate the boundaries between themselves and the 'natives' amongst whom they lived. In their letters and diaries, their articulations of 'home', and particularly of not feeling 'at home' in the colonies, reinforced their claims to belong to Britain and played a constitutive role imperialists' self-fashioning as white, British subjects.[45] Furthermore, 'home' from the perspective of empire illustrates the metaphorical connection between domestic space and nation-space, through which the idea of 'Britain' itself was configured and reconfigured. Ideologies of 'home' in British-imperial imaginings thus offer cultural historians an insight into ways that belonging operated through gendered, racial and class-based exclusions.

For cultural historians of the British Empire, the idea that racism – and its intersections with class and gender – is embedded in 'everyday' life in Britain, as well as the very meaning of 'Britain' as a nation has been well established. In *Island Race: Englishness, Empire and Gender in the Eighteenth Century*, Kathleen Wilson argued that English national identity formation took place and was performed in constitutive relationship to imperial encounter with non-European peoples, whose ways of expressing and enacting gender and sexuality informed ideas of English masculinity.[46] Ironically, it was Scottish thinkers and historians who played a major role in advancing the idea of English exceptionalism, a process that Colin Kidd described as the configuration of an 'Anglo-British' identity, which undermined Scottish history and traditions and looked, instead, to emulate 'English' 'achievements'.[47] As this book illustrates, 'English' and 'white' were not distinct categories, rather it was increasingly assumed that to be 'English' was to be 'white', whilst both identity markers became associated with civilizational superiority. Saree Makdisi has discussed the literary process of demarcating 'the West' is a specific site of meaning, one that was marked by racial and, within it, national superiority. Makdisi's *Making England Western* argues that Romantic writing, with its obsession with 'the East', played a fundamental role in constructing England as a part of a putative 'West'. By representing Occidentalism as a specific set of attitudes and practices, Romantic writers were teaching the English not only to imagine themselves as part of a 'superior' nation but to internalize that imaginary and to behave in ways that performed that superiority. The construction of 'racial' difference, Makdisi argues, played a constitutive role in this process of homogenizing the nation.[48] This book develops this argument, showing how the idea of England as 'home' became a moral imperative that was inextricably linked to the emergence of both a new socio-economic system and new forms of racialized difference.

Unhomely Empire covers the period from the high-point of the Scottish Enlightenment, which is usually associated with the works of Adam Smith and David Hume in the mid-eighteenth century, to around the 1830s, when the key precepts of liberalism were established in metropolitan British governance. In doing so, it follows the chronology put forward by Jennifer Pitts and Sankar Muthu in their important discussions of the relationship between Enlightenment and European imperialism. Responding to the critiques of 'the Enlightenment' by the Frankfurt School, both Muthu and Pitts focus primarily on the political, economic and historical texts of thinkers such as Adam Smith, Denis Diderot and the Abbé Raynal and examine their vocal critiques of the brutal suppression and exploitation of indigenous peoples, along with the notion of the inherent superiority of European societies. Arguing for a fundamental transition in thinking across the 'long' eighteenth century, Pitts and Muthu illustrate the transformation from a more tolerant and pluralist cosmopolitanism that characterizes the Enlightenment, to the hardening of racial categories and belief in European superiority of nineteenth-century liberalism.[49] Although less concerned with chronological change, Uday Singh Mehta's *Liberalism and Empire* maps a similar transition, representing Edmund Burke's thinking as embedded in, and the epitome of, Enlightenment notions of pluralism and respect for difference compared to the high liberalism of the nineteenth century.[50] Although this book shows how the hardening of racial categories intersected with a more concrete and rigid notion of 'home', it is less interested in plotting a fundamental transition between Enlightenment and liberal ideas and more interested in the subtle shifts and layers of white supremacist thinking across this period.

Methodology: imperial and discursive networks

As the historiographical discussion above suggests, this book bridges intellectual history, literary studies and cultural histories of the British Empire. It shows how the motifs of 'wandering', 'exile' and nostalgia for 'home', which are usually the focus of Romantic literary studies, entered into philosophical works and political tracts, and were used in everyday letters and diaries of a British-imperialist elite. In doing so, this book endeavours to show how 'home' travelled between nominally 'private' and 'public' realms, between intimate family letters and acts of public policy in order to constitute a particular mode of being in relationship to people and place became the 'common sense' of belonging. It draws on the actor-network theory put forward by Bruno Latour and Donna Harraway, which understands ideas that come to be accepted as universal 'laws' or as 'reality' to be constituted as such through the ever-widening extension of networks of knowledge.[51] Over the last fifteen years, historians of the British Empire have increasingly conceptualized the British Empire as an expanding network that spread across imperial space, connecting vastly different regions and peoples, often through practices of violence, appropriation and subordination.[52] As Alan Lester has argued, the circulation of peoples, newspapers, publications and correspondence, alongside the material commodities that provided the raison d'être of empire, configured the meaning and practices of empire.[53] This book draws on the concept of imperial networks to trace the configuration, circulation and consolidation of a racialized idea of 'home' in the writings of what I refer to as a 'British-imperial *literati*'. Much like the 'republic of letters' of a slightly earlier period, this *literati* comprised white men and women who were connected intellectually, socially, politically and culturally across British, European and imperial geographies. Socio-economically and politically privileged in contrast to the majority of people in the societies in which they lived, their cultural power lay in the transmission and preservation of their ideas. By looking at letters, diaries, philosophy, political pamphlets, travel writing and novels, this book shows not only how the discourse of 'home' circulated between genres and across imperial sites, but how the repetition of those ideas constituted the only-possible 'reality' of what it meant to be 'at home'.

This process of consolidating meaning through networks is encapsulated in a letter, written in 1805, from Richard 'Conversation' Sharp to Sir James Mackintosh in Bombay. Describing his daily ritual of locating his absent friends, as well as his merchant fleet on the map that hung on the wall of his office in Mark Lane, London, Sharp wrote that 'I become minutely acquainted with the Eastern and Western coasts of Africa in consequence of my daily visits to the great map which hangs in the room where I generally write'.[54] Sharp's tracing of his friends and fortune on his 'great map' of the world provides a visual imagery of the dispersed and interconnected nature of empire. Both he and Mackintosh were members of the British elite, closely affiliated with the whiggism of Holland House, and active participants in the clubs and societies that characterized the 'polite' sociability of the period. Indeed, Sharp's middle nick-name, 'Conversation', derived from his reputation as a socialite and conversationalist amongst London's high society. They were friends and correspondents with some of the key thinkers and writers of age, including Madame de Staël, the Scottish Enlightenment philosopher, Dugald Stewart, the diarist James Boswell, the political-economists David Ricardo, Jeremy Bentham and Thomas Malthus.

Yet both men originally hailed from the peripheries of the British Empire: Mackintosh was born into a petty gentry family in the Highlands of Scotland in 1765, whilst Sharp was born in Newfoundland in British North America in 1759. As a young man, he was sent to London to learn his grandfather's hatting trade, a trade which relied on the felt made from beaver pelts found primarily in North West British America. At the time of writing his letter, Sharp was based in London, a partner in the merchants, Boddington and Co, whose profits derived from exporting the sugar produced by enslaved labour on their plantations on St Kitts in the West Indies.[55]

Sharp's act of visiting, re-visiting and becoming acquainted with routes is itself a tracing of those routes, an inscribing and a forging of connections between people, capital and emotions across space. His concern for his friend's safety on the high seas serves as a reminder of the ways that material and affective economies are entangled. His letter points to a key theme of this book: the ways in which belonging – as an emotional relationship to place, a longing to be in place – was configured in and through the circulation of people and ideas around the British Empire. Those ideas and expressions of belonging were conveyed in letters and diaries – shared amongst relatives and friends – which provided the key means through which to retain a presence in absence.[56] In an earlier letter to Mackintosh, Sharp wrote that 'the poor thin paper has had a more troublesome journey in my pocket book about London, than it had in crossing deserts and seas.'[57] Yet the expressions of belonging in those nominally 'private' letters were not constructed in a void. Rather, they gained meaning in relationship to a wider discourse of belonging that circulated across space, time and genres. In this context, the 'colonial archive' is more than one fixed location, usually in a former colony, rather, it becomes an assemblage of texts that span and connect metropolitan and colonial sites. Drawing on archives and libraries in Edinburgh, Kolkata, London and Mumbai, this book traces the discourse of 'belonging' through different types of writing, both published and unpublished, including philosophy, poetry, political pamphlets, travel writing, short stories, letters and diaries. These writings were powerful tools for configuring the meaning of 'the world', which together shaped the parameters of belonging. Empire and whiteness, this book argues, were fundamental to that imagining.

Structure of book

Unhomely Empire is an intellectual and cultural history of belonging in the 'long' eighteenth-century British Empire. It maps the transformation of ideas of 'home' and 'exile' in elite British-imperial thought from the high period of the Scottish Enlightenment to the consolidation of liberal-imperialist thought by the 1830s. The title itself draws on Freud's notion of the *unheimlich*, usually translated as 'uncanny', which he defines as the resurfacing of that which was once familiar but has been repressed and disavowed.[58] To understand empire as 'unhomely' is to open up a space to explore the many ways in which the imperial expansion was contingent upon longing and loss, as well as the fantasy of wholeness that is embedded in the idea of 'home'. Here, 'unhomely' is not so much about the discomfort or anxieties of British imperialists, rather it is to point to the ways in which empire was profoundly disorienting; out of place and yet integral to, the narrative of national belonging and the idea of Britain as 'home'. Interrogating the changing meaning of 'home' in the 'long' eighteenth century, this book argues that the idea of belonging was itself historically constituted in relationship to imperial expansion. It traces the process by which the feeling of belonging to 'home' became understood as a universal attribute of human nature, whilst being simultaneously mobilized to exclude certain peoples from definitions of 'Britain', 'civilization' and even 'humanity'.

This book begins by situating Enlightenment philosophies of human 'nature', 'civilization' and 'progress' in the context of European-imperial encounters with non-European peoples. Chapters 1 and 2 show how Scottish Enlightenment philosophers relied heavily on travel narratives and missionary reports of non-European peoples, particularly in the Americas. Although neither Smith nor Hume participated directly in debates over human variation, both employed stereotypes of non-European peoples, especially Africans, to construct their philosophical theories. Smith posited a generalized binary between 'civilized' and 'savage', which mapped onto the colour-line dividing white Europeans from non-Europeans. This division became one of the axes of difference upon which he developed his theory of sympathy. In *The Theory of Moral Sentiments*, the exclusion of non-European 'savages' from sympathy undermined the universalist argument that all humans relied on sympathy to live as part of society. Instead, he represented 'savages', as a result of material hardship, as incapable of forming affective attachments and thereby lacking a sense of belonging. In this context, sympathy, which was integral to moral virtue and progress, became a particular attribute of whiteness. Thus, although Smith was deeply critical of the worst excesses of European conquest, of slavery and of imperial monopolies, his philosophy was white supremacist in its construction of non-European societies as morally, materially and emotionally inferior.

By the time Dugald Stewart was teaching Moral Philosophy to the next generation of young men at the University of Edinburgh, Enlightenment philosophers had a greater awareness of the nuances of, and differences between, non-European societies. Stewart had a strong interest in Indian history and culture, corresponded with imperial travellers and colonists, and had almost certainly met a number of servants of African heritage. Nonetheless, he too used 'the Negro' as a symbol of alterity, which served his philosophies of human difference and progress. Chapter 2 examines Stewart's rejection of Smith's materialist analysis and his idea of sympathy. Stewart contended for the existence of moral truths and general laws that he claimed could be discovered through sustained, philosophical analysis. Those innate moral qualities included the idea that all humans possessed a sense of belonging and attachment to 'home'. Indeed, Stewart, following John Millar, argued that 'the Hottentot', living at a more primitive stage of societal development, was particularly attached to 'his' native land. Theoretically, this belief in innate human qualities and the capacity of all humans to feel a sense of belonging, as well as to advance through reason, represented a less racially divisive worldview. Yet in practice Stewart's philosophical arguments were, like Smith's, founded on the assumption of the superiority of white, European men. Indeed, the combination of moral certainty and white supremacist thinking contributed towards the narrowing definition of the meaning of 'home' and its ideological imperative. The idea that *all* human beings felt a sense of belonging to, and desire for, 'native land' naturalized and universalized the idea of 'home' as part of a patriarchal order in which fixed settlement on land was paramount. At the same time, the naturalization of attachment to 'native land' led 'wandering' to become increasingly associated with immorality and 'barbarity'.

The ideology of 'home' was by no means confined to, or derived exclusively from, Moral Philosophy. Like the majority of Scottish Enlightenment philosophers, Stewart borrowed extensively from travel narratives, quoted the works of poets, including Oliver Goldsmith, and drew on imagery from fictional literature. In this respect, Moral Philosophy must be considered as part of a wider literary movement in the Anglophone world, which consolidated and disseminated patriarchal land ownership as the only morally acceptable form of attachment and belonging. By reading the discourse of 'home' and 'exile' across different literary genres, this book shows how the ideology of belonging, which was developed in constitutive relationship to Scottish Enlightenment theories of difference, became hegemonic. The four case studies that comprise Chapters 3 to 6 each illustrate the ways in which the discourse of 'home' and 'exile' was mobilized in very different contexts. Focusing on Maria Edgeworth's short story, 'The Grateful Negro' and Maria Graham's *Journal of a Voyage to Brazil*,

Chapter 3 shows how the image of the home-loving enslaved African served as a reassurance to their readers that the abolition or amelioration of slavery did not pose a threat to white supremacy. The idea that African men would limit their aspirations to the governance of a wife, children and a small plot of land, whilst paying deference to their white master, was articulated through the discourse of 'home'. In contrast, those who dismissed the abolitionist campaign argued that Africans were 'savages' whose lack of identification with 'home' was a sign of inherent immorality, rendering them unfit for freedom. The idea that an attachment to 'native land' as 'home' was a sign of innate morality, whilst wandering suggested immorality is also evident in the debate over the meaning of Scottish Highland emigration to British North America, discussed in Chapter 4.

Compared to enslaved Africans, Scottish Highlanders occupied a very different position vis-à-vis white supremacy. As both colonized and colonizers, their location in relationship to whiteness was conditional upon their performance of belonging as well as their usefulness, to Britain. Here, too, the discourse of 'home' and 'exile' played an important role in establishing the boundaries of belonging to Britain as a nation. Whereas some elite critics claimed that the Highlanders were peculiarly attached to 'native land', others blamed their emigration – and the subsequent loss of a resource for national defence – on an inherent wanderlust that rendered their loyalty to Britain spurious. The question of whether or not Scottish Highlanders were capable of 'civilization' rested, in part, on their ability to feel a sense of belonging to home and, by extension, to the nation. The contradictions within the debate, which are examined through the Earl of Selkirk's emigration scheme, illustrate the way the discourse of 'home' and 'exile' was harnessed to imperialist and nationalist agendas. 'Exile' reinforced the assumption that North American lands, long inhabited by indigenous American peoples, was effectively empty wildernesses. At the same time, the idea that the Highlands themselves were becoming empty of people justified Lowland Scottish and English colonization into a region that had long been marked by the English state as troublesome and 'barbaric'.

Representations of Highland emigrants as 'exiles' enabled them to be symbolically included as part of the British nation at the very moment that they were physically excluded from living within its boundaries. In India, British literary elites applied a similar use of 'exile' to a very different imperial context. As the East India Company expanded its dominance over large parts of India, debates over company servants' activities in India employed the discourse of belonging in order to disassociate the British nation state from plunder, violence and abuse. In the same manner that Adam Smith refused European enslavers in the Caribbean a position belonging to Europe, Edmund Burke represented East India Company servants as 'wanderers' whose lack of any sympathetic attachment to 'home' served as an explanation for their immorality. That lack of belonging was accompanied by a fear of India as a site of 'moral contagion', in which a culture of 'effeminacy', 'passions' and 'despotism' threatened to undermine the 'rational', 'manly' and inherently freedom-loving English character. As Chapter 5 argues, Sir James Mackintosh's attempts to bring reform to Bombay's governance employed a discourse of 'English' superiority and 'European' civilization. Through his founding of the Bombay Literary Society, he encouraged Bombay's more elite, 'Anglo-Indian' men to identify with Britain as 'home' and to consider themselves as mere sojourners in India. His own rejection of Indian history and culture and his use of 'exile' to describe his and his family's situation enabled him to assure his friends 'back home' that he remained British, despite his distance from metropolitan Britain. Chapter 6 focuses on the Mackintosh parents' attempts to separate their daughters from Bombay's Anglo-Indian society as a site of 'corruption' to young, white girls' morals. This attempted separation reinforced the notion of India as a space of degeneracy and lack. The idea that Indian households were 'messy' and 'divisive' and that Indians lacked 'sympathy' with each other drew on the philosophical arguments that constructed white, Europeans as more civilized and thereby capable of progress. In this context, the image of the orderly and harmonious patriarchal family home played a critical role in constructing notions of white, 'English' respectability as a model for 'civilization' as a whole.

1

The racialization of belonging in Adam Smith's *The Theory of Moral Sentiments*

Fortune never exerted more cruelly her empire over mankind, than when she subjected those nations of heroes to the refuse of the jails of Europe, to wretches who possess the virtues neither of the countries which they come from, nor of those which they go to, and whose levity, brutality and baseness, so justly expose them to the contempt of the vanquished.

Adam Smith, *The Theory of Moral Sentiments* (1759)

In *The Theory of Moral Sentiments,* Adam Smith accused European colonists who owned African slaves in America and the Caribbean of 'brutality and baseness'. Reversing the common, European stereotype of Africans as 'barbaric', Smith represented the enslavers themselves as 'brutes' and 'barbarians' who had reduced a 'nation of heroes' to the most vicious form of slavery.[1] Smith's critique of the European enslavers' brutality connected to his wider argument about the role of 'sympathy' in human society. 'Sympathy', which Smith defined as the 'calling home to oneself' the experience of another person, was what enabled society to function as a whole.[2] 'Sympathy' provided an explanation as to why humans cooperated with others, shared each others' pleasure and pain, and engaged in acts of selflessness. Indeed, for Smith, no individual could survive without the fellow-feeling that enabled them to belong as part of society. Without 'sympathy' society would inevitably descend into the forms of 'brutality' and 'baseness' witnessed on the British-owned plantations in America and the Caribbean. The enslavers' lack of sympathy for the sufferings of the enslaved was proof of the dangers of unchecked power to the progress of society and civilization. By approving of, and sharing, the enslaved Africans' contempt for their captors, Smith extended his own sympathy to the sufferings of the enslaved and refused any identification with the slave-owners. His moral indignation against European enslavers thus took the form of rejection. Refusing them any place of belonging, whether in Europe, America or the Caribbean, Smith cast European enslavers out of society and into exile.

Smith's condemnation of European enslavers played an important role in the emergent debates over the rights and wrongs of slavery and the trans-Atlantic slave trade. In his two-volume *History of the Abolition of the African Slave Trade* (1808), Thomas Clarkson placed Adam Smith at the beginning of a long discussion of 'men of great talents and learning' who had 'promoted the cause of the injured Africans'.[3] Yet whilst Smith's analysis of the unprofitability of slavery as a form of labour in his *Inquiry into the Nature and Causes of the Wealth of Nations* (1776) certainly provided a persuasive socio-economic critique of slavery, his representation of Africans as 'savages' to whose feelings and experiences he paid little attention raises questions about the extent and nature of his abolitionism.[4] By expressing his own moral outrage, Smith was modelling the very 'sympathy' and mode of feeling that he argued represented a higher stage of civilization and virtue; a performance of sentiment that reinforced the superiority of white Europeans over the 'injur'd African'.[5] This chapter explores the relationship between sympathy, stadial theory and racial difference in Smith's *The Theory of Moral Sentiments,* and its implications for ideas of white masculinity and belonging in the later eighteenth and early nineteenth centuries. The chapter begins by situating Smith in the context of imperial expansion, before turning to his definition of 'sympathy' and its relationship to stadial theory as a paradigm of progress and civilization. The next section looks at the ambivalence of Smith's idea of 'sympathy' as a universal concept applicable to all humans and its role in constructing ideas of human difference. As feminist and postcolonial historians have long argued, Enlightenment philosophy posited a universal theory of human progress, which was based on the knowledge, worldview and experience of a very small minority of educated, metropolitan European men.[6] The final section discusses Smith's representation of women, and particularly non-European men, as the counter-points to his argument about 'sympathy', 'virtue' and 'civilization' and the impact that this had on ideas of belonging.

Adam Smith, moral philosophy and imperial expansion

Adam Smith's name and his most substantial work *The Wealth of Nations* (1776) are synonymous with the Scottish Enlightenment. His most recent biographer, Nicholas Phillipson, described him as 'the most celebrated of Scotland's enlightened literati, a man to be visited by cultural tourists on pilgrimage to Edinburgh, a man whose table-talk and eccentricities were to be cherished by locals'.[7] Today, his name lends respectability to neoliberal organizations intent on restoring the 'great nineteenth-century era of free trade and economic expansion'.[8] The influence of *The Wealth of Nations* on thinkers across the world, including on the Bengali philosopher, political and religious thinker, Raja Rammohan Roy, has been well documented.[9] In contrast to the wide geographical reach and impact of his works and ideas, Smith himself barely travelled beyond the British Isles, and never beyond Western Europe. Between 1764 and 1766, he accompanied the Duke of Buccleugh, heir to vast estates in England and Scotland, on a tour of France and Switzerland.[10] Beyond that year acting as tutor to the young heir, and a year spent studying in Oxford, Smith spent most of his life in Glasgow and Edinburgh. He grew up in, and in later life returned to, his family home in Kirkcaldy, where he lived with his mother, Margaret (née Douglas) until they both moved to Edinburgh in 1778, and a cousin, Janet Douglas who acted as their house keeper.[11] Smith's social world was dominated by his attendance at male-only social and debating societies primarily in Edinburgh and Glasgow, including the Edinburgh Select Society, the Oyster Club, the Poker Club, as well as small gatherings in the homes of colleagues and fellow scholars, including that of Lord Kames.[12]

If Smith's life was relatively parochial, his friendship with David Hume, Adam Ferguson and Lord Kames, as well as his subsequent position at the Board of Trade, would have introduced him to imperial administrators and colonists, including Benjamin Franklin.[13] His reading of the reports of colonial travel writers from the Americas, the Pacific and coastal West Africa also informed his thinking. Listed in the catalogue of his library were at least forty-five books of travel writings, including Francois Bernier's *Voyages* (1699) and Anthony Benezet's *Some Historical Account of Guinea* (1771). He also possessed the Quran, translated into French, and Sir William Jones's translations of Persian and Sanskrit poetry.[14] Smith's library, as well as his own published works, is a testimony to the growing awareness of non-European peoples and the emerging hegemony of British imperial rule during the second half of the eighteenth century. The early books on travel writing largely written by French travellers and colonists had, by the 1770s, been eclipsed by the names of British-imperial travel writers, including Cook's voyages to the Pacific and part of Australia. There is a noticeable transition, too, in the knowledge that Smith had of non-European peoples between the 1750s, when he was writing *The Theory of Moral Sentiments*, and *The Wealth of Nations,* which was published in 1776. As Mary Louise Pratt has argued, their representations of non-European peoples played a fundamental role in shaping Enlightenment ideas of the human and non-human world.[15]

Despite Smith's increasing awareness of non-European societies as they were represented through the words of European-imperial male travellers, and his use of them for his theories of development, his own intellectual and social world remained narrowly focused on men from the elite and middling ranks of society. His lecture theatres at the University of Edinburgh, where he taught Rhetoric and Jurisprudence, and at the University of Glasgow where he held the Chair of Logic and was subsequently Professor of Moral Philosophy, were barred to women. So, too, were the clubs and societies where he discussed and developed his ideas. In his writing, Smith excluded women from his imagined audience, referring to women as 'them', and men as 'us' or, in one instance, 'us males'. He also embedded this gendered separation of social and intellectual spheres into his *The Theory of Moral Sentiments,* stating that 'to talk to a woman as we should to a man is improper: it is expected that their company should inspire us with more gaiety, more pleasantry, and more attention'.[16] As feminist historians have long argued, although the discourse of sympathy and sentiment nominally elevated women's status by purporting to honour women's 'natural' sensibility and their 'civilizing' influence upon men, in practice it placed further restrictions on their agency beyond the home.[17] Indeed, Lucinda Cole has argued that Smith's particular definition of sympathy dismissed 'feminine' sensibility as 'weak' and denied women any ability to access a higher, more rational form of sympathy that he associated with virtue.[18] Smith routinely ignored or belittled women's labour, dismissing, for example, the significance of Native American women's agriculture in order to represent the society as belonging to the stage of 'hunters'.[19] Smith was more extreme in his misogyny than either Hutcheson or Hume, but his exclusion of women from his imagined audience was common to all branches of European philosophy. In his lectures, Smith's teacher, Francis Hutcheson, made the gender of his readership explicit when he stated that the aim of Moral Philosophy was to 'direct men to that course of action which tends most effectually to promote their greatest happiness and perfection'.[20]

Moral Philosophy was directed explicitly and exclusively at men, and was centred and narrowly circumscribed around a Europe that was imagined as white. Although there were certainly Black and Asian people living and working in Scotland during Smith's lifetime, the first recorded Black student, William Ferguson, did not matriculate from Edinburgh until 1809.[21] Whether Smith encountered and engaged with any non-white people is a matter of conjecture;

he may have met Samuel Johnson's black servant, Frank Barber, when they visited Edinburgh in the 1770s.[22] In his published work, however, Smith's reference to black people was restricted to enslaved Africans in the Caribbean. Smith's assumption that his audience was located in, or originated from, Europe is evident from his representation of China as a distant civilization, with which only European merchants would have an interest.[23] He wrote of different European nations with a sense of familiarity, proximity and equivalency that is lacking in his discussion of peoples in Asia, Africa or North America, who he tended to refer to homogenously as 'savage nations'. David Hume, to whom Smith was both intellectually and socially close, did acknowledge the existence of people of African descent in Europe, but only to place a complete separation between Africans and white Europeans, and to identify himself and his audience explicitly with white, elite, Europeans. This is most evident in his infamous footnote in his essay, 'Of National Character', in which he claimed that 'there are Negroe [sic] slaves dispersed over Europe, of whom none ever discovered any symptoms of ingenuity though low people, without education, *will start up amongst us*, and distinguish themselves in every profession.'[24]

Despite these prejudices, and their exclusion from lecture theatres, it is clear that women and non-white men did engage with Scottish Enlightenment thought. As Laurent DuBois has shown, ideas and books circulated on the ships bound for colonial ports, informing the thinking of the enslaved and colonized.[25] Both Ignatius Sancho and Olaudah Equiano were familiar with, and employed, Enlightenment thought in their published work against the slave trade.[26] As subsequent chapters show, relatively high-status women, including Elizabeth Hamilton, Maria Edgeworth and Maria Graham, had access to the published works of Scottish Enlightenment in the libraries of their families and friends. They also gained insights into the debates that took place in the lecture theatres and men-only societies through dinner-table conversation and discussions in parlours.[27] Yet regardless of this partial and mediated access, women and non-European people of all genders remained the Others against which Smith formulated his ideas of 'civilization' and societal advance. As the rest of this chapter argues, Smith's idea of 'sympathy', and its relationship to 'progress' and 'civilization' not only excluded those who did not fit his vision of the white, elite and male bodied subject, but it actively employed gendered and racialized tropes in order to illustrate what 'virtue' and 'civilization' was not. In this respect, Smith's idea of 'sympathy' as a form of emotional engagement intersected with his more materialist understanding of societal development that is encapsulated in stadial theory.

Sympathy and stadial theory

Adam Smith began his academic life at the University of Edinburgh in 1748, before moving to the University of Glasgow in 1751. In addition to his lectures on Logic and Metaphysics, he lectured on Natural Jurisprudence and Moral Philosophy, and was appointed Professor of Moral Philosophy in 1752. Only parts of his lectures on Jurisprudence survive from notes taken by his students during the academic sessions of 1762–3 and 1763–4, his own lecture notes were destroyed at his request on his death.[28] However, those few surviving lecture notes, published in 1896 as *Lectures on Jurisprudence,* provide the most comprehensive account of the four-stage theory of societal development, known as 'stadial theory', which would play a fundamental role in shaping and justifying British imperial thought and practice. Stadial theory mapped the progress of human societies according to their modes of acquiring and using property.[29] Smith identified four stages – hunting, pasturage, agricultural and commercial – according to which all human societies could be classified, and through which some societies would pass, or in the case of Europe had passed, sequentially. In the first stage, in which humans subsisted on hunting wild animals and eating wild fruits, the ownership of property was confined to what an individual could physically, and thereby momentarily, lay claim to. Beyond that, there was no sense of long-term ownership and therefore no need for laws of property. In the second stage, as numbers grew, human societies developed the ability to tame animals and to lay claim to those animals that they had reared. Smith identified all 'savage nations', including the 'Tartars' and 'Arabs' who 'subsist by flocks have no notion of cultivating the ground', as living in this stage of 'pasturage'. The cultivation of land in order to grow food, and therefore a much more extensive idea of property in land, developed when a society grew too large to support itself by animals alone. This stage, Smith associated with the 'feudal' period in Europe when a few 'great men' held all the resources and power.[30] The development and improvement of agricultural techniques gradually enabled people to specialize and to exchange their produce, leading, ultimately to the commercial stage. During the agricultural and commercial stages, increasingly complex laws developed in order to regulate and protect an individual's claim to property; Smith's *Lectures* primarily focused on the development of these laws and regulations under different types of government.

In his *Lectures,* as in all of his published works, Smith concentrated on Western Europe, and primarily relied on Greek and Roman Laws to explain the origins and transformation of legal structures as they related to England, Scotland and

France. Where he speculated on the two earlier stages of society, however, he looked to accounts from colonial adventurers and missionaries to North America and Western Africa, including Charlevoix's *Histoire et Description Générale de la Nouvelle-France* (1744), of so-called 'savage' peoples. 'Native American Indians', for example, who Smith defined as 'hunters' offered an insight into the humans living at the earliest stage of society. Smith was not the first to suggest that non-European peoples could provide insights into Europe's past. Lafitau's book, *Moeurs de Sauvage Américains, comparés aux moeurs de premier temps* (1724), based on his observations as a missionary in North America, understood Native American society as a mirror onto Europe's Antiquity.[31] Yet whereas Lafitau situated his study in relationship to biblical questions about the Flood and the origins of man, Smith's more secular approach focused on transition across time. This relied on a method, which Dugald Stewart, Professor of Moral Philosophy at the University of Edinburgh, named 'conjectural history', in which philosophers imagined a European past prior to the existence of written records by observing more 'primitive' or 'savage' non-European societies.[32] In 1799, when James Mackintosh lectured on 'The Law of Nature and Nations' he could state, following the principles of stadial and conjectural theory, that 'history ... is now a vast museum, in which specimens of every variety of human nature may be studied'.[33] Together, stadial theory and conjectural history offered a paradigm for understanding human difference, and plotted a road-map for human development, which placed European societies at the furthest reach of material and social advance.

Stadial theory was primarily a materialist paradigm of human societal development. However, 'sympathy' and emotional attachment also played a role in Smith's argument about the relationship between societal change and land ownership. In *Lectures on Jurisprudence*, Smith assumed that his students were already familiar, whether through his own lectures or their reading, with the idea of 'sympathy' that formed the basis of his *The Theory of Moral Sentiments*.[34] 'Sympathy', which Smith referred to as the 'calling home to ourselves' the experiences of another, referred to the act of forging a connection with other human beings and was fundamental to the progress of society, as well as to virtue.[35] Smith's argument built on Hume's *A Treatise of Human Nature* (1739), which had put forward, but had not substantially developed, the idea of 'sympathy'. Hume's definition of 'sympathy' is clearest in his discussion, 'Of the Love of Fame', which takes place in Book II of *A Treatise on Human Nature*. Here, he reiterated the claim that emotional responses, what he called 'the passions', develop through a relationship to the self and the individual's desire to receive the approval of others. Hume argued that this desire for others to sympathize with our own feelings takes precedence over reason, and is evident even in 'men of the greatest judgment and understanding who find it very difficult to follow their own reason or inclination, in opposition to that of their friends and daily companions'.[36] It was this need for sympathy between people living in close proximity to each other that explained why people of one nation shared a similar character, a theory that Hume would develop in his later essay, 'Of National Character'. Yet beyond this brief explanation, Hume did not really expand upon his notion of 'sympathy' in his *Treatise*. His later revision and abridgement of the *Treatise*, published in 1748 as *An Inquiry Concerning Human Understanding*, excluded 'sympathy' entirely. It was therefore left for Adam Smith to really develop the idea of 'sympathy' into a theory of human society and progress.

Smith's theory of 'sympathy' was part of a wider discussion of sensibility, or 'feeling', that had occupied philosophers, theologians, scientists, novelists and medical practitioners (the distinction was often blurry) since the seventeenth century. This wide-ranging debate was configured around the question of how human beings mediate their own, individual 'passions' – including hunger, pain and sexual desire – in order to live as part of society. As Markman Ellis has argued, both 'sympathy' and 'sensibility' did not derive from Moral Philosophy, rather philosophers were responding to a social and religious climate in which virtue and benevolence, as well as the feeling for others' suffering, was becoming more pronounced.[37] Nonetheless, 'sympathy' became a central preoccupation of philosophers as they sought to explain the relationship between individual feeling, material self-interest and societal progress.[38] Smith explained 'sympathy' as the imaginative leap that a person makes in order to relate to the experiences and feelings of others. For Smith, 'sympathy' is not the actual experience of another person's suffering, but the imaginative leap that we make when we position ourselves in relationship to another person's suffering: 'His agonies, when they are thus brought home to ourselves, when we have thus adapted and made them our own, begin at last to affect us, and we then tremble and shudder at the thought of what he feels.'[39] Although Smith began his explanation of 'sympathy' using the example of the body (a man being beaten on the leg), he argues that we sympathize more with the 'passions', including pride, humanity, love and hate, than with bodily pain. This is because we have no access to the experience of bodily pain except through the passions, so that the bystander's sympathy for the man being beaten extends only to his identification with the *fear* of bodily pain.[40] Furthermore, Smith argues that we sympathize more readily with emotions that we approve of and which resonate with a greater number of people, rather than just an individual. A son who has lost his 'indulgent and respectable' father, for example, will receive sympathy for his grief because his sadness pertains not only to himself for his loss, but for the death of a man who we also approved of in life.[41] In contrast, 'frivolous' complaints (Smith gives the example of bad weather, an uncomfortable journey, a poorly cooked dinner) gain little sympathy from others because they relate only to the self.[42]

For Smith, sympathy with another person's joy or misery is at its strongest when it relates to the wider good of society, not to the individual. A person who indulges in their own, individual misfortune and misery will not inspire others to bring that misfortune 'home to themselves'. Instead, other people will identify with the effect of their behaviour on the people around them and will feel the shame and embarrassment that the person is bringing – whether consciously or not – upon themselves. Smith argues that because we desire sympathy from others, we moderate our expression of feeling so that it is acceptable to the people around us. This process of internalization, in which an individual mediates their own self-interest and controls their passions so as to deserve the approval of society, partly explains why people act in accordance with what society understands to be honourable.[43] Yet Smith was emphatic that people did not act with virtue only to receive the approbation of others, rather virtue meant acting according to the dictates of the 'sacred laws of justice'.[44] The 'impartial spectator', which Smith elsewhere referred to as 'inhabitant of the breast, the man within, the great judge and arbiter of our conduct', mediated the relationship between self-love, other people's feelings and the Divine.[45] Impartial spectatorship, Smith argued, would lead us to 'pursue the most effectual means for promoting the happiness of mankind, and may therefore be said, in some sense, to co-operate with the Deity, and to advance as far as in our power the plan of Providence'.[46] Acting in accordance with the impartial spectator was not the same as following a Divine plan, which, Smith argued, was beyond the human capacity to know.[47] This ambiguous place that Smith afforded to God goes part of the way towards explaining why Smith's *Theory* gained more acceptance than Hume's *Treatise*, with its explicit denial of the soul.

Sympathy and the 'impartial spectator' played a role in Smith's discussion of the development of law, government and property as society progressed from hunting to commerce. As Knud Haakonsen notes, Smith employed the concept of sympathy and impartial spectatorship in order to think about the relationship to morality and law (and their connection to each other).[48] In the case of a violent robbery, for example, where the sympathy lay easily with the person who had been robbed, the 'spectator would justify the first possessor in defending and even in avenging himself when injured, in the manner we mentioned'.[49] In this context, the spectator 'calls home to himself' the feelings of the aggrieved and approves any action he takes to defend himself and reclaim his property. In more complex cases, too, such as claims to a property through prescription, the spectator judged the extent and duration of the claimant's attachment to the property: 'The right of prescription is derived from the opinion of the spectator that the possessor of a long standing has a just expectation that he may use what has been thus possessed.'[50] This conclusion rested on the spectator's sympathy for the feeling of attachment and of the sense of entitlement that the claimant had to the property. A similar formulation is evident in relationship to a woman who commits adultery, where the 'spectator' becomes synonymous with 'the public'. In this case, Smith noted, 'The indignation of the public against the wife arises from their sympathy with the jealousy of the husband.'[51] That jealousy, Smith continued, did not arise from the fear of her bearing another man's child (as Hume had suggested), but from the 'alienation' of her preference, her unique attachment to him as her husband. As Lucinda Cole and Jane Rendall have argued, Smith's 'impartial spectator' was aligned with a 'public' that was assumed to be exclusively male.[52]

Sympathy, belonging and 'the savage'

Although Smith represented 'sympathy', as well as 'impartial spectatorship', as a universal phenomenon, he was ambivalent about whether all peoples, at all stages, felt sympathy. On the one hand, Smith represented 'sympathy' as essential to all humans living in society, regardless of its socio-economic stage. Following Francis Hutcheson, as well as David Hume, Smith regarded the need to live as part of society as constitutive of humanity itself. The idea that humans were formed in relationship to each other as part of society provided one of the foundational premises that characterized the Scottish Enlightenment's approach to the philosophy and history of humankind. In *Treatise of Human Nature*, Hume had stated that ''tis utterly impossible for man to remain in that savage condition, which precedes society; but that his very first state and situation may be justly esteem'd social.'[53] In An Essay on the History of Civil Society (1776), Adam Ferguson concurred: 'Mankind are to be taken in groups, as they have always subsisted.' 'A wild man caught in the woods' was, according to Ferguson, a unique specimen and did not provide any clues from which to draw conclusions about 'man' in general.[54] This conceptualization of 'man' as inherently social, and the role of 'sympathy' in constructing the social, was in part a response to, and rejection of, Thomas Hobbes's theory of natural law and society in the *Leviathan* (1651) which understood 'natural' man to be inherently individualistic and incredibly violent.[55] 'Sympathy' represented part of the opposition to this bleak image of humankind, it rested on the idea that individuals desire society and that they conform not only for material survival, but out of fear of ignominy and exile. In this respect, Smith and subsequent Scottish Enlightenment philosophers understood the desire to belong and the affective forms that humans developed in order to remain as part of society, as central to humanity and human progress.

On the other hand, however, Smith's explanation of 'sympathy' suggested that only those in the more 'refined' stages of society possessed the capacity to sympathize with others. In both *The Theory of Moral Sentiments* and *Lectures on Jurisprudence*, Smith suggested that it was only as society advanced materially that individuals developed their capacity to feel and express sympathy for others. For example, Smith claimed that in the early stages of society the family was joined only through material need rather than by any ties of affection. Their lack of emotional attachment explained why, upon the death of the father, all property was shared equally between the surviving members of the family, rather than being divided up according to the affection that the father had for individual members of his family.[56] Similarly, in the earlier stages of society, where women were regarded merely as possessions, there was no place for jealousy because the man had no ties of affection to the woman. 'The foundation of jealousy is that delicacy which attends the sentiment of love, and it is more or less in different countries in proportion to the rudeness of their manners.'[57] The same was true of relationships between parents and children. In the earliest stages of society, Smith argued, men owned their children and wives had no sense of obligation or necessarily desire to protect or provide for them: 'All kindness betwixt them were reckon'd as acts of benevolence and not as what they were bound in justice to perform.'[58] Amongst 'savages', Smith argued that hardships and constant insecurity of life meant that there was no value placed on sentiment and little sympathy with others. 'Before we can feel much for others, we must in some measure be at ease ourselves,' Smith argued. 'If our own misery pinches us very severely, we have no leisure to attend to that of our neighbour: And all savages are too much occupied with their own wants and necessities, to give much attention to those of another person.'[59]

The ambivalence over whether sympathy was inherent to humans or developed in relationship to societal progress is an irresolvable tension that runs through Smith's work. In his critique of the 'brutality and baseness' of European slave-owners in the Caribbean, Smith referred to enslaved Africans as 'a nation of heroes', explicitly praising their 'heroic and unconquerable firmness'.[60] Yet it was this very 'firmness' that defined the 'savage' and placed 'him' outside of the realms of emotional engagement and thereby of sympathy. Indeed, this lack of sympathy was what explained the brutal regimes of torture that 'savages' inflicted upon their prisoners of war, as well as the ability of the 'savage' to face and witness such torture with apparent indifference and contempt: 'The spectators express the same insensibility; the sight of so horrible an object seems to make no impression on them.'[61] The question of whether the stoicism of the 'savage' was inherent or a learnt response to hardship was irrelevant to Smith, although it did have important implications for the relationship between individual agency and progress, which are discussed in the next chapter. Instead, Smith used the image of the 'savage' as unimpressionable as a contrast to the heightened sensibility of 'civilized' society. The 'general security and happiness which prevails in ages of civility and politeness' meant that passions and pleasures could be more freely expressed. 'A humane and polished people, who have more sensibility to the passions of others, can more readily enter into an animated and passionate behaviour, and can more easily pardon some little excess.'[62]

Smith made frequent use of 'effeminacy' and 'manly' in order to construct the absolute differences between the extremes of 'savage' and 'civilized'. As Silvia Sebastiani has shown, Smith's colleagues, including Hume and John Gregory, promoted the idea that women possessed a 'natural' sensibility and humanity that could act as a 'civilizing' force upon men.[63] Women's private conversation, and particularly their role as mothers, was vital to the construction of a more refined and virtuous society that remained, nonetheless, defined and dominated by men. At the same time, a society that promoted women's 'virtue' by affording them status, but not power, became a critical marker of 'civilization'.[64] Amongst his colleagues, Smith was notably less positive about the role of women and femininity in constructing a virtuous society.[65] In *The Theory of Moral Sentiments*, 'effeminacy' signified a lack of self-control, an excess of emotion, 'the rash, the indolent, the slothful' and 'the voluptuous', all of which would lead to 'ruin' and 'misfortune'.[66] To be 'effeminate' or 'unmanly' was to express too much sensibility and emotion. Crying out in pain, for example, meant one risked being perceived as 'unmanly', whilst the attempt to endure bodily pain without complaint provoked the kind of admiration that Smith held for enslaved

Africans.⁶⁷ Indeed, he argued that the heightened sensibility of the 'ages of humanity and politeness' would appear as the most 'unpardonable effeminacy' to 'savage' nations.⁶⁸ Yet whilst 'civilized' society risked collapse through an excess of sympathy and sensibility, the emotional hardness of earlier stages lacked the sympathy necessary for virtue and progress. What was necessary, Smith argued, was a balance between excessive sensibility, which he associated primarily with women and femininity, and the cold, hyper-masculine stoicism of the 'savage'.

In *The Theory of Moral Sentiments,* Smith placed the 'savage' and the 'civilized' at the two opposite ends of the material, gendered and emotional spectrum. In *Lectures on Jurisprudence* he developed this interrelationship, albeit not explicitly, so that different stages of society had different affective relationship to material, as well as human, property. In the hunting stage, where there was little sense of property ownership, there could be no attachment to material things, including the soil, and therefore idea of theft as a wrong.⁶⁹ Indeed, Smith imagined 'savages', whether living in geographically or historically distant places, as expressing, and possibly also having, few emotional relationships to people or material things. When 'savages' did express their emotions, however, their lack of reason led to irrational and uncontrolled release of passion, resulting in acts of 'furious' violence.⁷⁰ As subsequent chapters show, this idea of 'uncontrolled passion' was used as a frequent marker of inferiority. In the early stages of agricultural societies, where power was concentrated in the hands of a very small number of men, the dominant emotion was one of vanity. The agricultural societies of Western Europe in the aftermath of the fall of Rome were maintained and dependent on the lord whose provision of hospitality forged the bonds of dependency, as well as flattering the vanity of the great man.⁷¹ Smith reiterated this in *The Wealth of Nations,* stating that 'childish vanity' was the main motive upon which the great lords provided hospitality to their dependents.⁷² He paid little attention to the emotional attachment between the lord and his retainer, but his damning critique of the motivations of lords suggest that he saw nothing in that relationship beyond the material. Indeed, he argued that it was vanity and greed that ultimately eroded the power of the lord. Foreign commerce offered the 'great lords' the opportunity to spend their surplus wealth on 'frivolous and useless' material objects rather than on the maintenance of their tenants and retainers. Their materiality and greed, Smith argued, was their downfall: 'and thus for the gratification of the most childish, the meanest, and the most sordid of all vanities, they gradually bartered their whole power and authority'.⁷³

In the commercial age, where even a day labourer earned enough to feed and clothe his family and provide a roof over their heads, sympathy played a much more overt role in society. The apparent misery of the 'poor man' derived, Smith argued, from the lack of remark that he is afforded by society: 'The poor man goes out and comes in unheeded, and when in the midst of a croud is in the same obscurity as if shut up in his own hovel.'[74] In contrast, the 'man of rank' receives praise and recognition for even the most mundane tasks, whilst he barely acknowledged the humanity of those around him.[75] It was the loss of this sympathy, and the great man's 'easy empire over the affections of mankind', rather than the loss of material riches, that rendered the fall from greatness 'insupportable'.[76] Between the two extremes – the 'meanest labourer' and the 'man of rank' – of the commercial stage, Smith positioned the 'middling' ranks of society. They were no less driven by material and emotional desire. Indeed, they aspired to achieve that 'perfect state of happiness' that appeared (however 'delusively') to accrue to the man of rank, and struggled to avoid falling to the obscurity of the 'meanest labourer'.[77] Yet their means of achieving status, and therefore their character, differed dramatically from the 'man of rank'. For them, recognition and power accrued not through inherited wealth and status, but through the 'labour of his body, and the activity of his mind'. Unlike the 'man of rank', who 'shudders with horror at the thought of any situation demanding the continual and long exertion of patience, industry, fortitude, and application of thought', the middling ranks of men worked steadily for recognition, wealth and power.[78]

In *The Theory of Moral Sentiments*, Smith represented men of middling ranks in the commercial stage of society as most likely to possess the emotional attributes necessary for virtue and progress. Because he restricted his idea and examples of 'commercial' societies to European states, and his examples of 'savage' societies to Native American and Africans, he also implied that those men were exclusively of European heritage. That 'European' heritage also meant 'white' is also probable given the slippages between 'white' and 'European' in other Scottish Enlightenment philosophers' writings. Hume's infamous footnote, referred to above, explicitly claimed that 'white' people, even 'the most rude and barbarous … such as the ancient Germans, the present Tartars have still something eminent about them, in their valour, form of government or some other particular'.[79] Whether Smith agreed with this is difficult to say, he made no explicit reference to Hume's footnote, which garnered indignation and dissent from later Scottish Enlightenment philosophers, notably James Beattie and Dugald Stewart. Although he was active in philosophical clubs and societies in Glasgow and Edinburgh during a period in which ideas of racial difference and human origins were being debated, his lectures and published works did not engage directly with either of these issues. He owned both Buffon's *Historie Naturelle* (1752) and Linneaus's *Systema Naturae* (1768), and was friends with scholars, including Lord Kames, who engaged explicitly with questions of human variety.[80] Smith, however, made no explicit reference, for example, to polygenetic theories of human origins, nor did he discuss the 'reasons' for black skin. His claim in *The Wealth of Nations*, that whereas greyhounds, spaniels and mastiffs could be considered to be fundamentally different members of the same species, such differences did not exist between humans, suggests that he believed that all humans shared a single origin.[81]

Despite the lack of clarity on racial difference in Smith's writing, sympathy and stadial theory had important implications for subsequent understandings of racial difference and the construction of white identity. Sympathy was, in effect, a fundamental constituent of both individual and group identity, and of individual identity in relationship to community. Sameness played an important role in this configuration. In his *Treatise of Human Nature*, Hume stated that all 'human creatures' shared a resemblance: 'However the parts may differ in shape and size,' Hume continued, 'their structure and composition are in general the same.'[82] It was because of that resemblance that humans were able to 'enter into the sentiments of others'. Yet, Hume argued, where there are additional aspects of similarity we feel a greater sense of familiarity, and therefore greater sympathy, with people who more closely approximate ourselves. This sense of similarity could derive either from blood relations, or from shared 'custom', for example the same educational background, or through close proximity in space: 'any peculiar similarity in our manners, or character, or country, or language, it facilitates sympathy'.[83] Smith's own representation of human connection suggests a similar understanding. Certainly, he agreed with Hume that sympathetic identification led those who interacted regularly with each other to develop similar habits, passions and manners.[84] Although the impartial spectator mediated this 'natural' identification and sympathy and encouraged men to think beyond their immediate connections and interests, such mediation was always partial. Ultimately, Smith argued that complete and perfect selflessness was impossible, rather 'man' acts in ways that society and the 'spectator' deem moral out of a desire to receive the approbation of other men.

Yet the role of what Hume called 'proximity and likeness' placed supposedly 'natural' limits on the construction of a sympathetic community, which informed the possibilities for recognition and inclusion. In his configuration of sympathy and virtue, Smith placed women and particularly non-European people of all genders outside of his imagined community of sympathy and approbation.

Smith's exclusion of women and non-European 'savages' was based on the idea that for the majority of humankind, the capacity for virtue was circumscribed by a lack of reason, which played a fundamental role in mitigating 'excessive' and self-absorbed passions. For European women, Smith argued that they possessed an excess of sympathy whilst they lacked the reason that enabled them to fully align themselves with the view of the impartial spectator. Smith excluded non-European people from virtue and progress for the same, but opposite, reasons – their extreme lack of emotional expression and lack of reason rendered them unable to identify with others.[85] By representing 'the savage' as unable to 'bring home' to 'himself' the experiences of another, Smith constructed a non-European world in which people were strangers to each other: 'The rules of decorum among civilized nations, admit of a more animated behavior, than is approved of among barbarians. The first converse together with the openness of friends; the second with the reserve of strangers.'[86] Even in marriage, Smith claimed, 'savages' did not express any emotion for their partner, nor did the couple live together in the same house.[87] Without 'sympathy' a person was isolated and alone, a situation that was akin to 'exile', and which, Smith had noted previously, was intolerable for any considerable length of time. Whereas European women had an 'excess' of sympathy, the 'savage's' apparent inability to 'bring home to oneself' the feelings of another suggested that 'savages' did not have the capacity to feel any sense of belonging or community at all.

Conclusion

Smith has long been hailed by historians as a champion of abolition and an outspoken critic of imperialism. Unlike Hume, whose statement of white superiority and questioning of whether Africans could be considered human has been rightly the subject of considerable critique, Smith has largely been lauded for his arguments against both the slave trade and imperial monopolies.[88] Yet his characterization of the 'savage', under which rubric Smith included Africans, both free and enslaved, sits uncomfortably with the celebration of Smith as an abolitionist who championed the cause of the 'injur'd African'. The contradictions of Smith's position, and of British abolitionism in general, are made evident by a pamphlet published anonymously by Arthur Lee, of Westmoreland County, Virginia, in 1764, which defended American slave-owners against Smith's accusations of 'brutality' and 'baseness'. In 'An Essay in Vindication of the Continental Colonies from a Censure of Mr Adam Smith, in His *Theory of Moral*

Sentiments', Lee acknowledged that slaves undergo a 'very severe labour' on the Caribbean plantations, but argued that their living conditions were considerably better than those of the rural peasantry in Ireland or Scotland.[89] The main body of his argument focused on disputing Smith's characterization of African slaves as 'magnanimous' and of the American settlers as 'monsters'. The Africans who worked on the plantations of America and the Caribbean were, Lee argued, 'cruel, vindictive, stubborn, base and wicked'.[90] They paraded their many wives and concubines with no shame or respect for the sanctity of marriage; indeed they held no contract sacred.[91] In contrast, the American settlers hailed from respectable families, 'distinguished, even in Britain, for rank, for fortune, and for abilities'.[92] By leaving Britain to 'extend the dominion of their country', these men 'braved the dangers of an unknown sea and savage land' for the benefit of the commerce and wealth of the mother country, as well as for themselves. Yet rather than gain the approbation of their fellow British subjects, they are treated as 'the servants of Britain' and the 'hardest discipline is used to check their growth and alienate their affections from Britain'.[93] Summarizing his argument, Lee reiterated the comparison between Africans – 'a race the most detestable and vile that ever the earth produced' – and the settlers, 'descended from worthy ancestors …. A humane, hospitable, and polished people'.[94] How, he asked, could such an esteemed philosopher, 'a man of sense', have succumbed to such misguided prejudice?

Ultimately, however, Lee agreed with Smith in his general sentiment against the slave trade, stating that 'the bondage we have imposed on the Africans, is absolutely repugnant to justice' and that slavery and the slave trade should be repressed. Quoting Montesquieu, Lee argued that the barbarous nature of African slaves in the Caribbean posed a physical and moral threat to the 'American islands' and their 'civilized' inhabitants. 'Dastardly as they are', Lee stated, 'under an able leader, they may do much mischief; and as cowards are invariably cruel, should they ever be superior, not a shadow of mercy could be expected.' To live, outnumbered, amongst such a race of 'rogues' risked depraving 'the minds of freemen; steeling their hearts against the laudable feelings of virtue and humanity'.[95] Lee quoted a series of scholarly authorities, including Aristotle, Burke, Hutcheson and Shaftesbury, in order to support his argument for the horrors of the African character. Yet, in fact, he need not have gone beyond Smith's own text to find the same portrayal of Africans, under the rubric of 'savages', as cruel, impulsively violent, prone to falsehood and vengeful. Smith's discussion of enslaved African as 'magnanimous' did not contradict this general characterization. For Smith, 'magnanimity' referred to the Stoic ideal, which renounced all self-interest and concern for the future, and refused to submit to any form of passion. However noble such an endeavour may be, Smith argued that its denial of any relationship between self and society rendered it a state of impossibility, 'beyond the reach of human nature'.[96] The contempt of death and torture that Africans, like all 'savage nations', displayed was what qualified them for this dubious accolade. By labelling enslaved Africans as 'magnanimous', Smith implicitly denied their ability to make the imaginative leap between self and other that was essential for recognition as part of society and humanity. Regardless of whether 'the African' could be considered 'magnanimous' or 'cruel', the lack of ability to 'call home to themselves' the experiences of others placed the African, like all 'savage' nations, outside of society, and thereby also humanity.

Smith's *Theory* constructed an absolute binary between 'civilized' and 'savage' societies that was characterized by the ability or inability to sympathize with others. By using 'civilized nations' and 'Europeans' interchangeably, Smith configured this binary geographically, dividing the world into two, distinct spheres. On one side were the 'civilized' 'European nations', who had the capacity to balance their emotional responses with a 'rational' consideration, enabling virtue and progress. On the other side were the 'savage' nations of Asia, Africa and America, who combined an absolute denial of self with violent and irrational acts based on unregulated passion. Although Smith allowed for the fact that 'virtue' was defined differently by different nations, overall his universalist theory of 'sympathy' and 'reason' as the necessary constituents for virtue, and thereby the progress of society, made it impossible for the 'savage' to progress through 'his' own agency. In Smith's schema, material conditions would generally, although not certainly, change and enable the 'savage' to advance to a state of reason, sympathy and virtue. Yet as far as Smith's theory of 'sympathy' went, the ability to progress through the combination of sensibility, rationality and virtue was proscribed for those in the lower stages of society. In this respect, Smith's philosophy of sympathy and virtue differed very little from Hume's 'philosophical racism': both understood the 'savage' in general, and Africans in particular, as lacking the capacity for selfhood.[97]

2

Dugald Stewart and the colour of progress

> *The influence of the appropriation of land on the moral character ... is firmly illustrated by the contrast which [Mungo] Park has drawn between the Moors who wander and the Negroes who cultivate the earth. The former is rapacious, cruel and bigoted, the latter kind, gently and virtuous.*[1]

By the late eighteenth century, stadial theory had become one of the cornerstones of Scottish Enlightenment thought.[2] Even where philosophers disagreed with Adam Smith's materialist analysis, the idea that societies advanced from savagery to civilization through four stages – hunting, pasturage, agricultural and commercial – comprised the general common-sense of Scottish philosophy. Yet whereas Smith had represented all 'savages' as lacking emotional capacity and thereby a sense of belonging, subsequent philosophers suggested that the instinct to belong was a near-universal human attribute and a sign of moral virtue. 'Man', they argued, shared a common desire to remain at home and, especially in the lower stages of societal development, held a particular attachment to native land. As the quote above from Dugald Stewart's lectures on Moral Philosophy demonstrates, societies that lacked a fixed sense of 'home' were increasingly understood to be morally repugnant. 'Wandering', which was often also associated with polygamy and infanticide, became a sign of immorality and vice. At the same time, those societies that did exhibit a sense of belonging to native land were lauded as examples of 'virtue'. Drawing on the reports of the colonial explorer, Mungo Park, Stewart continued his lecture on the influence of the division and appropriation of land on moral character, by stating that the 'Hottentot' had a longing for 'his native hut' and land: 'To him no water is sweet but that which is drawn from his own well; and no shade refreshing but that of his own Tabba tree.'[3] The image of the home-loving Khoisan in contrast to the 'wandering' Arab affirmed Stewart's belief in interconnection between 'home', 'morality' and 'progress'.

Although the idea of 'home' did not entirely replace 'sympathy' as the glue that held societies together, it played an increasingly important role in configuring a racialized moral discourse that would be harnessed for (and against) imperial rule. This chapter focuses on Dugald Stewart's Lectures on Moral Philosophy, given at the University of Edinburgh between 1785 and 1810. It begins by situating Stewart's life and thought in the context of imperialism and white supremacy, showing how Stewart disseminated ideas of eighteenth-century racial difference through his lectures. Like Smith, Stewart opposed the slave trade, and drew on many of the same arguments against slavery. Yet whilst Stewart's representation of human difference was similar, his understanding of 'progress' was markedly different from Smith's. Turning to Stewart's configuration of 'progress', the chapter then discusses the ways in which Stewart represented white, patriarchal supremacy as part of a divinely ordained, 'natural' law. The chapter then turns to discuss the implications of Stewart's racial thought for the idea of belonging, situating his understanding of belonging in the context of his partial rejection of Adam Smith and John Millar's materialist philosophies, and his partial embrace of Reid's 'Common Sense' philosophy.

Intellectual and imperial networks

Dugald Stewart was born in Edinburgh in 1753, a period of intense intellectual activity which was converging to form what Stewart himself would define as a distinctly 'Scottish school' of Enlightenment philosophy.[4] Stewart was the son of Marjory and Matthew Stewart, both of whom had established roots amongst the upper ranks of Edinburgh's society. As the son of a University of Edinburgh professor, Stewart grew up in the 'Athens of the North' in a world of philosophical societies and 'polite', scholarly conversation. He was a member of the Speculative Society, Newtonian Club and the Royal Society of Edinburgh (formerly the Philosophical Society) and was acquainted with Adam Smith and William Robertson. Stewart was taught Moral Philosophy by Adam Ferguson, who passed his lectures to his student when he left the university to negotiate a peace treaty with the American revolutionaries in 1778.[5] Beyond the male-only boundaries of 'public' institutional life, Stewart interacted with a number of women intellectuals. His second wife, Helen D'Arcy (née Cranstoun, 1765–1838), was a well-respected poet, who played an important role in cultivating her husband's social connections, hosting a literary salon in Edinburgh and writing to Stewart's friends with news on his behalf. Although Helen D'Arcy Stewart was prohibited from attending her husband's lectures, she played an active, though undocumented, role in supporting his philosophical thought and social connections.[6] Writing to William Dunnan, D'Arcy Stewart apologised for her husband's silence and stated that 'during the first weeks of his college labours he has literally not a moment to himself'.[7] The couple were closely connected to other 'bluestocking' women, including Maria Edgeworth, Anna Letitia Barbauld, Maria Graham and Elizabeth Hamilton, who developed and disseminated Stewart's thought in their poetry, travel writing and popular fiction.[8]

Stewart published extensively, including *Elements of the Philosophy of the Human Mind* (1792) and *Dissertation Exhibiting the Progress of Metaphysical, Ethical and Political Philosophy* (1821), but his influence was less directly on the discipline of Moral Philosophy than on the broader intellectual, social and political culture of early-nineteenth-century British liberal imperialism. The circle of men who established the *Edinburgh Review,* including Francis Jeffrey, Henry Brougham, Thomas Carlyle and Francis Horner, were all Stewart's students.[9] As one of the leading quarterlies of its day, the *Edinburgh Review* set the boundaries and the standards not only for literary culture, but also for political critique and public political culture.[10] This coming-together of the intellectual and the political was embodied in the lives of many of Stewart's students. Henry Brougham, for example, was an active Whig politician, as well as a member of the *Edinburgh Review* and a political philosopher. Perhaps the most influential of Stewart's students, James Mill, credited his teacher with 'the taste for the studies which have formed my favourite pursuits and which will be so till the end of my life'.[11] Mill's *The History of British India* (1818) played an exceptionally important role in configuring British ideas about Indian society and culture, and in justifying British rule in India.[12] *The History of British India* earned Mill the position of Chief Examiner of Indian dispatches in the East India Company offices in London; he was just one amongst many of Stewart's students and friends to play a role in British imperial administration in India.[13] In 1805 another of Stewart's friends, Sir James Mackintosh, wrote to Stewart from Bombay, stating that 'your young friends I have frequently seen and when they again visit the Presidency (so we call the capital of an Indian government), I shall not forget that you have an interest in them'.[14] The orientalist, William Erskine, who served as Mackintosh's secretary in Bombay and married his daughter, was also one of Stewart's students.[15]

Although Stewart himself did not travel beyond Western Europe, he was closely connected to, and therefore deeply interested in, the fortunes of the expanding British Empire. During his twenty-five-year tenure as Professor of Moral Philosophy at the University of Edinburgh, he taught three generations of young men who would go on to occupy positions in the upper echelons of British metropolitan and colonial administration. Stewart's eldest son, Matthew, accompanied the earl of Minto to India in 1808, a position that afforded his father much relief compared to the prospect of him going to the Caribbean.[16] Stewart was also well-acquainted with a number of American settler colonists, including

Thomas Jefferson and Benjamin Franklin with whom he corresponded.[17] His friendship with the Douglas family, and particularly Thomas Douglas, fifth earl of Selkirk, who studied under him between 1785 and 1786, brought him into close contact with settler colonists in British North America. Like many of his friends and students, these correspondents all gained, directly or indirectly, from the profits and labour of enslaved Africans both in America and on the Caribbean plantations.[18] Despite his own opposition to slavery, Stewart's godson, Archibald Alison (junior), who attended his lectures on Political Economy between 1808 and 1809, had close familial connections to slave plantations on St Vincent through his wife, for which he received compensation in 1833.[19] Likewise, John William Ward, Earl of Dudley, who lived with the Stewarts in Edinburgh, and kept up a lifetime correspondence with Helen d'Arcy Stewart, owned slave plantations in Jamaica.[20] As subsequent chapters will illustrate, Stewart's social embedding in imperial networks meant that his intellectual thought was disseminated across the British Empire.

Racial difference and slavery

Like many of his colleagues, Stewart's connection with imperial explorers and settler colonists intersected with his philosophical interest in questions of human difference. Stewart was well-acquainted with the explorer, Mungo Park, who relayed his impression of the peoples and places he encountered during his tour along the Niger River in 1796.[21] He sent *Elements of the Philosophy of the Human Mind* to Thomas Jefferson and used Jefferson's *Notes on the State of Virginia* (1785) to furnish his own lectures with examples of 'Negro' character.[22] In neither *Outlines of Moral Philosophy* nor *Elements of the Philosophy of the Human Mind*, however, did Stewart expand upon the debates over racial difference and human origins that were taking place in debating societies as well as in published works of natural history. It is only through his students' lecture notes that his interest in those debates becomes evident. In his lecture of 1793–4, Stewart drew on James Gregory's *Conspectus Medicinae Theoreticae* (1788) to classify humans into six different regional variations (European, Samoite, Tartar, Hindoo, Negro and American) and four different temperaments (melancholic, bilious, sanguine and phlegmatic). He supported Buffon in advocating the original unity of mankind, and refuted Monboddo's argument, stating that the orangutan should be 'ranked among the brutes'.[23] Familiarizing his students with the variety of explanations for human variation, Stewart drew on Montesquieu, Hume and Adam Ferguson. In all his lectures he reiterated the theory that black skin derived from the 'reticular membrane' under the skin. He also attributed some credibility to the idea that climate plays an important role in human intellectual, moral and physical difference, stating that in the temperate zone, 'man arrives at the greatest excellence, both in mind and body'. Conversely, in the extremes of heat and cold, 'the heart is selfish and mercenary, and the spirit grovelling and slavish'.[24] In his lectures of 1801, Stewart justified his discussion of all the various theories in order to show that scholarship on human variation was ultimately inconclusive. Climate, locality and moral causes all influenced the intellectual diversity of man, and, despite his call to optimism elsewhere, in his lecture he stated that there was no certainty that a nation at the highest pitch of civilization would remain so: 'Nations have risen from barbarism to civilization and sunk into rudeness again.' Concluding his section, 'Of man considered as the member of a political body', he stated that 'human genius and character [is] influenced by a great variety of courses, both physical and moral' and that the relationship between the two was yet to be fully understood.[25]

In his discussions of human variation, Stewart cited Kames and Jefferson extensively, but does not appear to have ascribed to their polygenetic theory of human origins in which there were multiple races of humans whose differences were innate.[26] Instead, Stewart leant more towards monogenesis, stating that 'ingenuity, sensibility and enterprise may be displayed by the savage as well as the polished citizen. In their different situations, indeed, these qualities appear in very different lights; but still they are the same'.[27] Overall, Stewart's representation of racial difference did not conform to one or other perspective, and he warned against becoming 'misled by the spirit of system in our speculations concerning what is commonly called the natural progress of society'.[28] Yet he was emphatic about the co-relationship between an individual's physiognomy, moral and intellectual attributes. The relationship between bodily health and moral health was a relatively constant theme in Scottish Enlightenment thought, evident, for example, in John Gregory's statement that the relationship between the human mind and body is 'so intimately connected and have such mutual influence on one another, that the constitution of either examined apart can never be thoroughly understood'.[29] Stewart, however, argued that stature, facial expressions and anatomy, and even hair type, underwent considerable change as society itself progressed. Citing Samuel Stanhope Smith's *Essay on the Causes of the Variety of Complexion and Figure in the Human Species* (1787), Stewart stated that where enslaved Africans on American plantations were 'ill-fed, ill-clothed, ill-lodged' and associated only with their own kind, they had a 'heavy, stupid appearance; their noses are flat, lips thick, hair woolly'. In contrast, the house slaves as a result of living amongst their more 'civilized' masters 'have caught much liveliness and vivacity of expression. Their noses are frequently raised, lips moderately thick, and hair from six to eight inches long (which arises much from their dressing and taking care of it) and their whole appearance extremely agreeable'.[30] As John Greene has illustrated, the aim of Smith's book was to argue for the unity of the human species against Kames's polygenetic argument in *Sketches of the History of Man* (1774). Like Stewart, he primarily understood human difference to be the combined result of climate and stage of society.[31]

At the time that Stewart was writing, the relationship between climate, societal stage and inherited biological markers of human difference was undergoing debate and contestation. Stewart's argument for a co-relationship between bodily attributes, and the moral and intellectual improvement of society was one among a number of Enlightenment theories of human variation, which Stewart himself used and embraced in conjunction with each other.[32] Whereas later-nineteenth-century scientific racists understood anatomy as a fixed sign of moral and/or intellectual status, Stewart understood the body itself as malleable in relationship to moral improvement. 'The bodily constitution of a savage hinders him from refined speculation,' Stewart stated in his lecture of 1778–9, 'but in time Negroes may be as refined as we are.'[33] This argument formed the basis of his critique of slavery. Like many, but by no means all, of his friends and colleagues, Stewart was a strong critic of slavery in general, and Britain's involvement in the trafficking of Africans across the Atlantic and their enslavement in the Americas in particular. Arguing against what he perceived to be Hume's 'inhuman' support for the enslavement of Africans on the grounds of white superiority, Stewart put forward the claim that all human societies could advance to, or fall from, a state of civilization, freedom and refinement. The Greeks, he noted as an example, had once considered other European nations to be 'savages' and 'barbarians'. Yet now the Greeks themselves were in a state of 'abject slavery', whilst those they had once enslaved on the grounds of their inferiority were refined and civilized.[34] With the exception of the years 1793–4, when political turmoil made any critique of the state dangerous and subsequently illegal, Stewart lectured his students on the wrongs of slavery. It was, Stewart claimed, a 'reproach to those enlightened times that after slavery had been banished from Europe, it should be again revived in the European colonies'.[35]

In every lecture Stewart argued that the cruelty of slavery in the Caribbean far exceeded that in Africa from which the slaves were transported, whilst the trade itself fomented wars in Guinea. Even in ancient times, manumission of slaves was common on the deathbed of their masters, and under the emperors the treatment of slaves was mitigated by dictate of the emperors. In the colonies, however, both the transportation and the condition of the enslaved were 'inhumane'. They suffered under the most arbitrary power of their masters, whose defence of slavery and the trade, Stewart rebutted point for point in his lectures of 1778/9 and 1789/90. Slavery, Stewart argued was justifiable only where a man had forfeited his natural right to freedom by breaking society's rules. There could be no grounds for indefinite forfeiture of one's freedom, or unlimited command over another. Being born into slavery went against man's natural freedom. The argument that slavery saved Africans from massacre in Guinea was ridiculous: 'Even supposing the situation worse in Guinea than when reduced to slavery in the West Indies, still we cannot force men to be happy and such kindness would be ridiculous.'[36] Nor was it likely that enslaved Africans were better off than the poor in Britain. These arguments, Stewart argued, were spurious attempts by the pro-slavery lobby to continue an immoral trade that benefitted them: 'It is quite enough to go with the advocates for slavery when they pleaded the expedience of slavery, but we must laugh when they defend it upon humanity.'[37] Following Adam Smith, Stewart argued that slavery was anyway the most unproductive form of labour. Even in the West Indies, where it was understood that only Africans could endure the severity of the labour, slavery could not be justified on moral or economic grounds. Without that labour, planters would have had to use their ingenuity to develop machines that would facilitate labour, rather than trafficking and rendering expendable thousands of men and women. But even if the arguments for slavery had credence, Stewart asked, 'Is it lawful that we should reduce such numbers of our fellow creatures to a state infinitely worse than that of the brutes, merely because we must have sugar and tobacco?'[38]

Yet despite his critique of slavery, Stewart, like the majority of Scottish Enlightenment thinkers, understood Africans to occupy the most extreme end of the spectrum of human diversity, and used 'the Negro' as a symbol of ultimate alterity compared to the white European man. In his lecture series of 1793–4, Stewart stated that 'the intellectual faculties' of Africans were 'very low' and cited Jefferson's doubt, similar to Hume's, that 'any of them could be made to understand a proposition of Euclid. No composition on any subject, whether in verse or prose, has been made by them.'[39] By the early nineteenth century, Stewart had changed his position slightly and placed more emphasis on that 'unfortunate situation in which we see them' than on any 'natural' intellectual inferiority. Citing Jefferson, Stewart argued that slavery placed 'man' in so debased a condition that it was impossible to judge their intellectual or moral powers, or capacity for progress.[40] Yet Stewart's brief consideration of the reasons and causes of the supposed intellectual inferiority of Africans did not undermine his certainty in the fact of their inferiority. 'Negroes', he argued, were 'totally occupied by their present sensations'.[41] This depiction shared many similarities with Adam Smith's representation of 'savages' in general, and Africans in particular, in *The Theory of Moral Sentiments*. Despite their different accounts of the driving force of progress, both Smith and Stewart understood the intellectual, moral and material limitations of 'savages' as preventing them from advancing through their own agency. Like Smith, Stewart represented 'savages' in general and Africans in particular, as responding to their most immediate needs and present circumstances. Acting on instinct and 'present sensations', 'savages' were closer to 'brutes' than they were to 'refined' European men. Yet whereas Smith represented 'savages' as incapable of 'sympathy' and therefore of virtue, Stewart argued that it was a lack of, or an unregulated imagination, that prevented 'savages', as well as the lower orders of his own society, from recognizing the 'benevolent principles of our nature' that encouraged men to act with virtue (Stewart, p. 271).

Stewart defined 'imagination' as a 'complex power', which relied on the coming-together of conception, perception, judgement and the association of ideas in order to create something new.[42] Whilst all human, and many non-human, animals employed a very basic form of abstract reasoning in order to get a task done, to learn from experience, or overcome an obstacle, only humans possessed imagination. The imagination – 'the great spring of human activity, and the principal source of human improvement' – was therefore key to progress and improvement, which was a specifically human trait, without it, Stewart argued, humans 'will become as stationary as that of the brutes'.[43] Citing the examples of the poems of Ossian and Arabian Nights, Stewart argued that imagination inspired the passions and could lead, ultimately, to a refined sensibility and to a civilized and 'cultivated' society. Yet, not all individual humans, or societies, possessed imagination in the same degree. A limited imagination resulted in less sensibility and fellow-feeling, which undermined the bonds of society. On the other hand, too much imagination led to a disordered mind and an excess of 'sensibility and genius approaching insanity'.[44] To develop 'habits of virtue', it was necessary, Stewart argued, to ensure a balance between the two and to develop the ability to control and direct the imagination towards moral improvement. Amongst 'savages' and the 'lower orders', however, the imagination was both limited and easily over-excited. Occupied with 'present sensations and perceptions', the 'savage' had little opportunity to develop the imagination. At the same time, however, amongst those who had few opportunities to exercise their imagination, anything that stimulated the imagination tended to produce a 'violence of enthusiasm' and an 'ungovernable' imagination, rather than moral virtue.[45] According to Stewart, even the apparent eloquence of 'savages' was less a sign of a refined imagination than it was the 'offspring of an impassioned mind striving to compensate for a scanty vocabulary by a variety in the modes of expression'.[46]

Stewart's representation of Africans as incapable of sustained reflection, as preoccupied by their present circumstances and as lacking the ability to compose in verse or prose effectively denied them any imagination at all. This lack ultimately rendered them incapable of the attributes necessary to advance through their own initiative and agency. As subsequent chapters show, this representation played out in different ways in relationship to Indians, women of all societies, and the 'lower' and peripheralized ranks in British society, too. In relationship to enslaved Africans in particular, their apparent inability to direct their thoughts and to look to the future played an important role in Scottish Enlightenment ideas about the future of Africans living in slavery in the Americas. For Stewart, slavery should be abolished gradually, beginning with a 'plan of emancipation' for the children of enslaved Africans, whilst their parents remained enslaved. This was for their own benefit. Not being accustomed to freedom, any 'sudden emancipation' would, Stewart argued, leave them 'ignorant [of] how to conduct themselves'.[47] The 'plan of emancipation' would, presumably, be designed by European men, whose superior wisdom enabled them to guide their moral and material progress. Patience, however, was necessary to ensure that mankind as a species developed at a pace suited to the 'situations and character of nations'.[48] Quoting Condorcet, who within a year of the publication of *Elements* would take his own life rather than face the guillotine, Stewart impressed upon his readers the importance of gradual change: 'If we wish to secure the perfection, and the permanence of freedom, we must patiently wait the period when men, emancipated from their prejudices, and guided by philosophy, shall be rendered worthy of liberty, by comprehending its claims.'[49] Stewart made no mention of the contemporaneous revolution in Haiti, which had overthrown the French colonial government and led to the first declaration of independence of a former slave colony. Yet the philosophy of progress that informed, and was informed by, his experience of the French Revolution, combined with his perception of the intellectual limitations of Africans, influenced his views on the abolition of slavery.

Reason, race and progress

Like his colleagues, including his friend James Burnett, Lord Monboddo, Stewart was interested in understanding physical difference, including sensory impairment, and the implications of physical differences on the boundaries of the human.[50] For Stewart, the unique capacity of the human mind to reason was due to 'man's' ability to recollect and associate impressions in order to make generalizations, what Stewart, following Reid, called 'arbitrary signs'. It was this ability to classify and generalize, and to use language to communicate general laws, that distinguished the human from the animal mind: 'We must allow the brutes sensation, conception, and memory, and perhaps some degree of art. The brutes can indeed use some natural signs, but they never form any arbitrary signs.'[51] By 'natural signs' Stewart meant extra-linguistic forms of communication – grunts and gestures, for example – that he perceived to come prior to the use of language. 'Arbitrary signs', by which he meant language, relied on the ability to use reason and to learn from experience as well as from others and derived from human intellect, not anatomy. Following Erasmus Darwin and John Locke, Stewart understood 'reason' as limited to humans. Whereas 'brutes' lacked the capacity to reason and were guided by instinct and nature, man 'is left in a great measure to regulate his own destiny, by the exercise of reason'.[52] This meant that only humans had the capacity to progress through their own agency.

Yet across his lectures and publications, Stewart defined 'reason' in slightly different ways, which necessarily informed his representation of the human–animal boundary and of the peculiar capacity of humans to progress. In some parts of his work, 'reason' referred to the ability to 'employ a long train of means for accomplishing a particular purpose', and could be witnessed to a limited degree, in animals as well as in humans and was separate from their ability to communicate.[53] In other parts, however, Stewart's use of 'reason' combined the thought process along with the use of language to convey that process into one, inseparable union, which he referred to as 'the power of abstraction'. It was the 'power of abstraction' – the ability to make meaning, to generalize and to classify objects based on individual qualities – not reason alone, that was unique to humans. Without this ability, it was impossible to develop knowledge, to discern universal truths, and to progress. Stewart stated:

> The foundation of all human knowledge must be laid in the examination of particular objects and particular facts; and that it is only as far as our general principles are resolvable into these primary elements, that they possess either truth or utility ... The progress of human reason, which necessarily accompanies the progress of society, is owing to the introduction of general terms, and to the use of general propositions.[54]

An important part of Stewart's understanding of 'the human' thus revolved around the, nominally uniquely human, ability to direct a train of thought towards a particular end – what Stewart, following Hume, called the 'association of ideas' – and to record the thought processes so as to pass on their learning to the next generation. It was this process that enabled humans to progress.

Stewart's understanding of human development through the increasingly complex classification of ideas relied heavily on Smith's essay, 'On the Origins of Language'. Yet whereas Smith had understood this process primarily in relationship to the greater complexity of human material relationships, Stewart was interested in the way that classification on the basis of reason could reveal general, 'natural' laws. Stewart replaced Smith's notion of man's economic self-interest as the 'invisible hand' that drove societal progress, with a more nebulous and more Divinely inspired 'invisible hand' in which even the 'blind' passions and instincts of 'savages' were part of a Divine plan that would lead, ultimately, to progress. Imploring his readers not to despair of the 'fortunes of the human race', he argued that everything in both the moral and material world was part of a 'benevolent design': 'Even in those rude periods of society, when, like the lower animals, he follows blindly his instinctive principles of action, he is led by an invisible hand, and contributes his share to the execution of a plan, or the nature and advantages of which he has no conception.'[55] It was through education, Stewart argued, that this plan would unfold. The aim of philosophers was thereby to study and identify those principles and to educate 'the bulk of a people to possess all the intellectual and moral improvement of which their nature is susceptible.'[56] This raised some difficult questions, however, about who was more or less 'susceptible' to 'intellectual and moral improvement', and what role 'their nature' had upon the types of improvement they could attain. Although in theory Stewart understood every human to have the capacity to progress, he did not perceive everybody to have the same capacity to use reason to direct their own thoughts. 'The bulk of mankind', Stewart wrote, 'condemned as they are to laborious occupations, which are incompatible with intellectual improvement, are perfectly incapable of forming their own opinions on some of the most important subjects that can employ the human mind.'[57] The intellectual limitations of the majority of humankind had important implications for Stewart's imagining of who could act as agents of progress.

In his published work of the 1790s, which drew on and reflected his lectures, Stewart was emphatic about the inevitability of progress and the certainty of an eventual future state of 'moral liberty'. Whereas his predecessors and more senior colleagues, including Adam Smith, Lord Kames, John Millar and Adam Ferguson, warned of the dangers of material luxury in 'effeminising', corrupting and stalling the progress of European societies, Stewart largely believed in the permanence and inevitability of the progress and improvement of the human race.[58] In his belief that every human was capable of reason and virtue, and thereby of progress, Stewart concurred with Reid's argument in *An Inquiry into the Human Mind,* in which he stated:

> The two legged animal that eats of nature's dainties, what his taste or appetite craves, and satisfies his thirst at the crystal fountain, who propagates his kind as occasion and lust prompt, repels injuries, and takes alternate labour and repose, is, like a tree in the forest purely of nature's growth. But this same savage hath within him the seeds of the logician, the man of taste and breeding, the orator, the statesman, the man of virtue, and the saint; which seeds, though planted in his mind by nature, yet through want of culture and exercise, must lie for ever buried, and be hardly perceivable by himself or by others.[59]

Not every human being would necessarily 'thrive and grow up to great perfection', Reid continued, some would take a 'perverted' course, others would stall on the route to perfection, and still others would die-out completely.[60] Yet theoretically all humans had the potential for reason, virtue, and thereby perfection. As with Stewart's universalist framework of belonging, Reid assumed that his own society represented the path that other societies would and should, inevitably, follow. This idea that it was God's plan that some would die-out completely would subsequently provide one of the key excuses for European acts of genocide.

For Stewart, the workings of the mind and the practice of reason were fundamental to the realization of human perfectibility and a more moral future. Following both Hume and Reid's philosophies of the human mind, Stewart understood the mind to be subject to a 'constant current' of ideas (what Hume called 'impressions') running through it, which are directed and re-directed by encounters with other people, places or events. The superior power of the human mind, Stewart argued, lay in its ability to make connections between different ideas and to control and direct the train of ideas towards a specific object. It was through this process that the inventor or philosopher was able to relate general rules to specific ideas, and channel them to discover new ideas and truths.[61] The more active the habits of reflection, the more control a person had over their thoughts, and thereby the more able they were to direct their thoughts towards the discovery of abstract principles and general laws. This ability, Stewart imagined to be confined to a very small number of humanity who would effect this progress for the rest of humankind. For each age, he claimed, there would be one great philosopher who would bring together the 'scattered materials' of the works of many 'men' and harness it to progress. Improvement would not, he argued, come about as the result of any 'original genius', but through the coming-together of 'the intellectual power' of the age in the workings of one mind.[62] Yet within the same passage Stewart also implied that the belief in a single great man was itself a delusion. Ultimately, it was the hands of 'the multitude' – 'such men as ourselves' – who, by working together, contributed towards improvement.[63]

'Such men' as Stewart and his colleagues hardly constituted the 'multitude'. Rather, this statement reveals the very narrow way in which Stewart imagined the agents of progress. The relationship between a Divine plan, human agency and the role of education in effecting progress is somewhat opaque in Stewart's thought. What is clear, however, is that when he imagined the agents of progress, he imagined men like himself. As the previous chapter argued, the men who have largely been credited with founding and developing the fundamental tenets of the 'Scottish Enlightenment' shared a common assumption that women and non-European peoples were, at least in their own times, inferior in both body and mind. Although Stewart was less overtly misogynist than Adam Smith, he nonetheless retained a vision of progress that largely excluded women as agents. In his discussion of 'the female sex' in his early lectures on Moral Philosophy, Stewart argued against the idea that women and men were originally 'of the same nature, abilities, dispositions'. The differences between men and women were, he argued, 'so strong and so general that it seems original':

> Women having in general less philosophical curiosity than men, although there are exceptions to this, and take less pleasure in tracing aspects to their causes, and less able for long and strict reasoning – they certainly however have livelier fancies and are therefore superior to the men in conversation and epistolary correspondence and in the lighter kinds of poetry. The men excel in those kinds which require more depth and strength of mind. They associate ideas quicker and more easily than men, but they have not the power of classifying facts in the same degree.[64]

In his later lecture on Political Economy, Stewart appears to have retained his belief in the absolute differences in the intellectual capacities between men and women. Disregarding the work of Catherine Macaulay, Mary Wollstonecraft, Hannah More and his friends, Maria Edgeworth and Anna Letitia Barbauld, presumably because they did not count as 'systematical writers', Stewart claimed that the question of female education had been 'almost entirely overlooked'. Furthermore, where 'systematical [male] writers' had addressed the issue, he claimed, they tended to either 'undervalue' the 'endowments of women' or put forward the 'visionary and absurd notion' that men and women had equal capacities.[65]

In *The Theory of Moral Sentiments*, Smith had argued that women were unable to engage in higher acts of virtue because they lacked the ability to combine sympathy with the powers of reasoning. Whilst women were able to 'call home to themselves' the experience of another, they rarely exercised the self-command and rationality necessary to sacrifice themselves to the public good.[66] Although Stewart disagreed with the emphasis that Smith placed on sympathy as the explanation for human virtue, his representation of women as less capable of reason than men was similar to Smith's. For Smith, higher levels of virtue were restricted to European men acting in the public sphere, for Stewart virtue and progress would be enabled by the kind of philosophical investigation that was restricted to men and, he implied, impossible for women. The idea that women were naturally less able to engage in 'long and strict reasoning' excluded them from the ability to uncover the 'laws of nature', and thus held significant implications for their ability to act as agents of progress. Stewart did not speculate on the causes of women's 'inferior' minds. However, he was very clear that, despite evidence of exceptions, women's inability to engage in 'long and strict reasoning' was natural and innate. Instead, their 'special accomplishments' included the ability to accommodate themselves to their situation and to 'bear what may be disagreeable' and a taste for those ideas of beauty that derive 'merely from association and fashion' (rather than from nature).[67]

In Stewart's configuration, the majority of labouring men, as well as almost all women and children, in his own society were incapable of sustained reflection. The 'bulk of mankind', he argued, lacked the time and habits to engage in superior intellectual activities: 'Children and persons of little reflection who are chiefly occupied about sensible objects, and whose mental activity is, in a great measure, suspended as soon as their perceptive powers are unemployed, find it extremely difficult to continue awake, when they are deprived of their usual engagements.'[68] He was particularly interested, however, in the differences between men 'like ourselves' and African men as 'savages', whose intellect and virtue he commented upon frequently in his lectures as examples of inferior and different minds. To substantiate his claims about dreaming and the association of ideas, for example, Stewart drew on Thomas Jefferson's *Notes on the State of Virginia*, stating that 'the same thing [the propensity to sleep when not occupied with labour] has been remarked of savages, whose time, like that of the lower animals, is almost completely divided between sleep and their bodily exertions'.[69] Blurring the boundaries between 'man' and 'brute', Stewart effectively understood the majority of humans, to be automatons whose minds responded passively to external stimulus, rather than possessing their own agency and ingenuity. In this respect, Stewart's thought differed little from either Smith or Hume's, discussed in the previous chapter. For all three philosophers, women and non-white people – Africans in particular – lacked the capacity for reason. Yet whereas Smith had attributed the apparent inferiority of non-European men to material hardships – the same hardship that rendered them unable to form emotional attachments through 'sympathy' – Stewart separated intellectual capacity from emotional capacity. As the next section illustrates, this division of intellect and emotion had important implications for his representation of belonging and 'home'.

'Common Sense', sympathy and belonging

As Adam Smith's biographer, Stewart was deeply engaged with and indebted to Smith's thought. Yet he was also closely connected to, if not completely aligned with, the 'Common Sense' school of philosophy, which opposed Smith's materialist analysis. In his lectures on Moral Philosophy, Stewart explicitly disagreed with Smith's argument on sympathy, because it undermined the relationship between 'virtue' and the Divine. According to Stewart's interpretation, which ignored the role of the 'impartial spectator', Smith's definition of 'sympathy' placed too much emphasis on social approval and suggested 'virtue' was dependent on an agreement within any given society, rather than on God-given, natural law. If Smith were correct, Stewart stated in his lecture of 1801, then 'the most selfish would be the most compassionate', and 'sympathy', he concluded, was 'altogether insufficient to account for our ideas of moral distinction; instead, moral qualities were both immutable and existed externally to human perception of them.'[70] Stewart argued that Divinely ordained, universal moral qualities could be discerned from the sense, or feeling, of what was morally right.[71] In his *Outlines of Moral Philosophy* (1793), for example, he stated that 'the emotions excited by the moral conduct of others' provided evidence for whether an action was morally right or wrong, and of the essential nature of moral truths.[72] Stewart's dismissal of sympathy, and his argument for a direct relationship between feeling and moral truth consolidated the relationship between moral superiority and socio-economic progress, which was less explicit and more ambivalent, although certainly latent, in both Smith and Hume's moral philosophy.[73]

Stewart's rejection of Smith's idea of 'sympathy' was part of his adoption and adaption of Thomas Reid's 'Common Sense' philosophy. Reid began his academic tenure at King's College, Aberdeen, before moving to Glasgow University to take up the Chair of Moral Philosophy in 1764, which he gained through the patronage of Lord Kames.[74] A deeply religious man and the son of a minister of the Kirk, Reid was impressed and inspired by Hume's *Treatise on Human Nature* (1739–40), but also concerned about the implications of his conclusions for the belief in God. Along with his colleagues in Aberdeen, who formed a philosophical society referred to as 'the Wise Club', Reid set about a sustained critique of Hume's philosophy, which he published in 1764 as *An*

Inquiry into the Human Mind on the Principles of Common Sense. Drawing on the work of George Turnbull and Francis Hutcheson, Reid opposed Hume's argument that all notions of truth and reality, including moral truths, were the result of impressions on the mind, rather than any natural, immutable Divine law.[75] The question of how humans gained knowledge of the external world was part of a longer philosophical debate that looked back to Descartes and Locke, and intersected with debates over virtue and the nature of truth. Hume's *Treatise* had pushed those philosophical questions to their extreme by arguing that there are no knowable objects external to the human mind and therefore no original principles governing phenomena. Universal, moral truths, Hume argued, were 'chimeras', the result of impressions on the mind, meaning that any certainty of knowledge, or even of the self, was impossible.[76] Reid's response to this was to argue that whilst our knowledge of the world is mediated by our sensations and perceptions of it, the sense we have of the existence of objects, as well as our idea of self and or morality, is enough to constitute a belief in its reality.[77]

Reid's 'Common Sense' philosophy took its name from the position that what would be incomprehensible and absurd to 'a sensible day labourer' was philosophically untenable. Instead, in his very first, opening section of *An Inquiry into the Human Mind,* Reid stated that the mind itself must be attributed to 'the wisdom and skill of the Divine Architect' and argued for a philosophy that limited itself to 'reflection', rather than any attempt to explain the system of the mind.[78] 'Common Sense' philosophy was thus premised on the existence of natural law and a Divinely inspired, universal system of morality, which could be discerned by careful and sustained reflection. Insisting on the existence of Divine truths, 'Common Sense' philosophy argued that what 'every man of sound mind finds himself under the necessity of believing' must be said to exist.[79] By questioning the very foundation of the self – what the 'Common Sense' school referred to as 'scepticism' – Hume was straying outside of the correct limits of philosophy. His argument could have 'no other tendency, than to show the acuteness of the sophist, at the expense of disgracing reason and human nature, making man Yahoos'.[80] This imagery, adopted from Jonathan Swift's *Gulliver's Travels* (1726), referred to the human-like creatures, obsessed with gems and pretty objects, who are ruled by wiser and nobler horse-like creatures. Reid thus combined his objection to 'scepticism' with a critique of materialism, which also targeted, albeit less explicitly, Smith's social and materialist explanation for human progress. Smith's argument, that 'sympathy' with one's fellow humans was the primary motivating factor for virtuous conduct, implied that 'virtue' was dependent on an agreement within society as to what constituted 'virtuous' behaviour, rather than given from God. In his lectures on Moral Philosophy, Stewart followed Reid's critique, placing moral motivations above materialist ones.

Stewart had attended Reid's lectures on Moral Philosophy in Glasgow during the academic year of 1771–2 on the suggestion of his tutor, Adam Ferguson.[81] Although he did not align or affiliate himself directly with the 'Common Sense' school, he shared with it a critique of Hume's 'scepticism' and a rejection of the subjectivist implications of both Hume and Smith's arguments.[82] In *Elements of the Philosophy of the Human Mind*, Stewart argued that materialism was not wrong, but was un-philosophical, proceeding 'on a misapprehension of the proper object of science'. That 'object' was to attempt to understand the 'sensible properties and laws' of the universe and from them to deduct the general laws of nature.[83] He reiterated this approach a year later in *Outlines of Moral Philosophy* when he stated that the role of Moral Philosophy was to 'record the phenomena which it [the universe] exhibits to our observation and to refer them to their general laws'.[84] Continuous observation of natural phenomena would eventually enable philosophers to discover and understand the 'laws of nature' and thereby to better understand what constitutes a 'wise and virtuous conduct in life'.[85] Stewart's belief in the didactic nature of Moral Philosophy provided the grounds for one of his, and his colleagues', key objections to Hume's 'universal scepticism'. Hume's approach to philosophy was not merely false it was, as James Dunbar stated, 'more dangerous than any speculative theory to the morals of the rising generation'.[86] Stewart concurred, arguing that Hume's approach into the 'nature of matter' would lead a reader to a 'complete distrust in his own faculties'.[87] Promoting Reid as the voice of reason against the reckless and dangerous 'empty words' of Humean scepticism, Stewart stated that 'if the moral distinctions be not immutable and external, it is absurd to speak of the goodness or of the justice of God'.[88]

In contrast to Hume's 'talent for plausible disputation', Stewart posited a Moral Philosophy in which the role of the philosopher was less about the 'acquisition of new knowledge, than to unlearn the errors to which he had been taught to give an implicit assent, before the dawn of reason and reflection'.[89] It was this emphasis on the co-relationship between the 'laws of nature' and the 'conduct of life', and the role of reason in discovering a moral path, that guided Stewart's approach to Moral Philosophy. Whilst he argued that education in itself does not 'create our notion of Right and Wrong, or Merit and Demerit', he understood education as fundamental to cultivating virtue according to the principles of natural law.[90] The aim of education, Stewart argued, was 'to cultivate all the various principles of our nature ... in such a manner as to bring them to the greatest perfection of which they are susceptible' and to guide the mind away from 'prevailing errors' and towards 'truth'.[91] Teaching young men to base their actions upon their own reasoning rather than relying on the opinions and authority of others would enable them to act according to the 'great principles of morality'.[92] In his *Dissertation*, written towards the end of his life, Stewart reiterated this perspective. Although he placed less confidence in the 'reasoning powers', he retained a belief throughout his life in the 'gradual effect of good education' in breaking down 'artificial impressions and associations', and ended on a note of optimism that the spread of literature and knowledge would lead ultimately to a future state of 'moral liberty'.[93]

Stewart's belief in the innate virtue of 'man' intersected with his idea of the natural orientation of 'man' towards a fixed and permanent home. This was fundamentally gendered, based on an understanding of fixed property in land and in a woman as wife. Land ownership, Stewart argued, generated 'local attachments' and 'domestic habits', which led to the consolidation of marriage. Marriage, in turn, represented a civilizing force. To illustrate his argument, Stewart cited an example of the 'Indians' in North America who had been introduced to Christianity, but also to a 'settled' life of farming and the 'enjoyments of domestic life', which in turn raised the status of women who 'instead of being considered as the mere objects of sensual indulgence begin to occupy the sphere allotted to them by the author of nature'.[94] This idealization of female 'virtues' and of polygamy as a marker of social corruption was common to the majority of Scottish Enlightenment philosophers.[95] There was little difference, for example, between Stewart's thought and John Millar's. Citing John Hawkesworth's *An Account of the Voyages for Making Discoveries in the Southern Hemisphere* (1773), Millar argued that Tahitians, like all 'savages' living in hot climates, were 'addicted to pleasure' and had no 'reserve or modesty'.[96] In contrast, as societies became 'more civilized' they would begin to value 'female accomplishments and virtues ... In this situation, the women become, neither the slaves, nor the idols of the other sex, but the friends and companions'.[97] Yet whilst Millar, like Smith and Hume, understood sexual mores and personal attachments to be based on historically constituted material conditions, Stewart represented them as universal moral signs.

In *The Origin and Distinction of Ranks*, Millar developed Smith's four-stage theory into a theory of the changing relationship between rights, legal structures and personal relationships. Much like Smith, Millar argued that at the earliest stage there was no explicit structure of government and, because there was no idea of individual property ownership, members of society were equal. Yet even at this early stage, societies often chose one person (Millar assumes that person to be male) as their chief, who commanded their ultimate respect and attachment.[98] In the age of pasturage, that chief gained immense wealth, which he passed on to his sons, so that title and status became hereditary. As property in animals was increasingly accompanied, and in many respects surpassed, by property in land, so the chiefs were able to extend their influence and power.[99] During the age of agriculture, the chief held absolute power over his subordinates who both relied upon and served him, and who gained favour and recognition by going into battle with him. Whereas Smith had implied that this relationship was one of exploitation and servitude, Millar laid emphasis on fealty and bonds of affection between chief and retainer. Millar was also more explicit than Smith about the bonds of attachment between men in the commercial age, when the division of labour, the development of the arts and manufacturers led to an increasing desire for liberty, which contributed to more elaborate government. In more advanced stages of society, however, the 'hardship and dangers of a military life' and the 'ease and pleasure of home' meant that fewer members of a society were willing to leave their homes and go to battle. The attachment to home, to domestic pleasures and the steady industry required for merchants and artisans went alongside an 'independent spirit' that was in contrast to the warlike, but obsequious, character of the later agricultural stage.[100]

Millar's theory of the development of government set-up a contradictory form of attachment in which those at the lower stages of societal development were more attached to 'home' and yet more willing to venture 'abroad' than those in the commercial stage. At the same time, whilst 'men' living in the commercial stage were less willing to leave their homes, their freedom from the bonds of attachment to those in power generated an 'independent spirit' that allowed them greater agency and mobility.[101] Key to Millar's understanding of the development of society was the separation of spheres of power, beginning with the undifferentiated power of the chief in primitive societies, to the atomization of power to the level of the household. He was not entirely sanguine about the development of the 'arts and manufactures' on the moral life of nations. He warned of the dangers of 'luxury' and 'refinement', which had led some 'European countries' towards a 'strong disposition to pleasure' and 'debauchery'.[102] This had a particular effect on the status and treatment of women in society and, related to this, on the forms of attachment that he deemed necessary for virtue and improvement.[103] As far as women's status and position in society was concerned, Stewart's own lectures followed Millar almost to the letter. Like Millar, he argued that in 'savage countries' women were treated as slaves and objects of exchange as a result of their comparative physical weakness. It was only as society advanced and women's 'natural' abilities became useful to men that they gained their affection and status.[104]

As the previous chapter illustrated in relationship to Smith, Enlightenment representations of the position of women in society intersected with their understanding of different modes of belonging and attachment. Yet whereas Millar, building on Smith, understood the status of women in each society in relationship to its own logic of socio-economic production (albeit not without a sense of the moral superiority of commercial society), Stewart was more invested in what the changing status of women said about the 'laws of nature' and 'morality'. In this respect, he dismissed the 'manners of savages and barbarians' claiming that they did not provide any insights into natural law. Stating that 'love can exist in purity only between two', he created a circular argument in which the moral ideals and emotional attachments of his own society became embodiments of 'natural law'.[105] Similarly, whereas Miller's materialist analysis of attachment at different stages of society recognized a multiplicity of different modes and ways of belonging, Stewart represented only one form of belonging – associated with settled status and property – as morally correct. Whilst it is undoubtedly the case that Smith and, in a different way, Miller looked down upon societies at nominally lower stages of development, they did not represent those differences as moral absolutes. Stewart, on the other hand, constructed an absolute moral distinction between attachment to 'native land' as 'home' and wandering; a distinction that mapped on exactly to societies structured around patriarchal property ownership. In doing so, Stewart constructed different ways of relating to land and people not only as inferior, but as universally, morally wrong.

Conclusion

Historians of 'race' and the Scottish Enlightenment have paid close attention to the differences between individual thinkers' representations of 'race', particularly in relationship to their positions on human origins. As they rightly argue, these debates and positions have informed the texture of nineteenth-century racism and its legacy for the present.[106] Yet whilst the differences between Scottish Enlightenment thinkers matter for our understanding of the emergence of 'race science' out of eighteenth-century debates, the commonalities in their discourse of difference and belonging were more powerful in the enactment of white supremacy both in metropolitan Britain and its colonies. Stewart was not alone in constructing wandering as a sign of immorality. In *Sketches of the History of Mankind* (1774), Henry Home, Lord Kames, characterized the Giagas (also referred to as 'Jaga-Casangi'/'Giaga Casingi'[107]) of Western Africa as thoroughly immoral: 'The Giagas, a fierce and wandering nation in the heart of Africa, are in effect land-pirates, at war with all the world. They indulge in polygamy; but bury all their children [at] the moment of birth, and choose in their stead the most promising children taken in war.'[108] Bringing together polygamy, infanticide and wandering, Kames represented the lack of attachment to land as a sign of immorality, much as Stewart did in his lectures. Despite the significant differences between Stewart and Kames's understandings of human origins – Kames maintained a polygenetic understanding of human origins, whilst Stewart concurred with the majority of his colleagues that the human race originated from one source – they shared an understanding of 'wandering' as immoral.[109]

Stewart's idea of 'home' and his construction of wandering as a sign of immorality was part of a wider Scottish Enlightenment discourse of difference and belonging, which consolidated into a binary separation between 'wandering' and 'home' by the early nineteenth century. Although his own philosophical position navigated a somewhat contradictory path between the materialism of Smith and Millar, and the 'Common Sense' philosophy of Reid, his lectures put forward the general tenets of white, European, male superiority that was shared by the majority of his colleagues. Like his colleagues and predecessors, Stewart understood the role of Moral Philosophy both to be an examination of philosophical principles and to provide instruction in moral virtue that would guide the next generation. More than any of his contemporaries, he blended principles and pedagogy to construct what C.B. Bow has called a 'modern programme of moral education'.[110] His lectures therefore offer insight into the ideas of moral virtue, progress and human difference that British imperialists used and adapted in order to configure the meaning of the non-European people who they encountered and over whom they ruled. As the next chapters illustrate, those ideas played a constitutive role in wider debates, policies and representations of colonized peoples and places, as well as to the performance of self amongst colonial elites.

3

The role of 'home' in Edgeworth and Graham's critiques of slavery

Introduction

On 24 September 1821, Maria Graham disembarked from the HMS *Doris*, which had laid anchor eight miles from the port-city of Olinda, the capital of Pernambuco in the northeast of Brazil. The British naval frigate had been sent to Brazil in order to protect British property and interests in the Portuguese colony, which was at that time enmeshed in the revolutionary upheavals that stretched across the Atlantic world. Graham and her party's arrival coincided with the outbreak of a local rebellion against the royalist governor of Pernambuco, General Luiz do Rego; the city was under siege, supplies were low and tensions were running high. Putting curiosity ahead of safety, Graham insisted on visiting Olinda and reported her observations and first impressions of the city in her travel narrative, *Journal of a Voyage to Brazil and Residence There*, which she published in 1824 alongside *Journal of a Residence in Chile*.[1] As with her previous travel writings on India and Italy, Graham discussed the architecture, landscape, modes of transport, and styles of dress and manners of the different groups and classes of people living in the city. Foremost amongst her concerns, however, was the state of enslaved Africans in the Portuguese colony. Graham was emphatic that slavery in any form was morally wrong, economically unproductive and a threat to the progress of society. Her reasons for protesting slavery lay not only on the ground of humanity, but also on what she perceived to be the dangers of racial intermixing. The importation of so many enslaved Africans had resulted in a racially mixed, idle and, Graham implied, morally degenerate society. In an attempt to rectify this 'evil', the 'European Portuguese' were marrying their daughters to 'the meanest clerk of European birth' rather than to 'the richest and most meritorious Brazilian'.[2] Horrified and saddened by the state of the newly arrived slaves at the slave market, she prevailed on their prospective masters 'to think of the evils slavery brings, not only to the negroes but to themselves, not only to themselves but to their family and their posterity'.[3]

Graham's plea to European enslavers drew on four key arguments of the abolition movement.[4] Firstly, she reiterated Adam Smith's argument that slavery as a form of labour was inefficient and economically unproductive, a position that had become widely accepted and well-used in British abolitionist circles. Secondly, she drew on the idea that the absolute power held by the slave-owner was antithetical to British national identity, which embraced liberty and freedom, against corruption and despotism. Intersecting with this, the third argument drew on the idea that living amongst so many 'savages', in the hot climate of the Caribbean and South America, threatened the morals of British men. As the first chapter briefly noted, these three arguments played a significant role in undermining plantation owners' claims to belong to Britain and 'civilization'. Towards the end of the eighteenth century, however, the sin of slave ownership was conceptualized more broadly, to threaten the morality, and ultimately the salvation, of the whole nation.[5] Graham's reference to 'posterity' gestures to this sense of national sin, and the fear that the slave trade was a harbinger of the decline of European civilization. Her fourth, and final, argument focused on the sufferings of the enslaved Africans themselves, the violence and brutality of plantation slavery, as well as the lack of access that enslaved Africans were given to Christian teachings. Amongst the Evangelical Christians who played such a prominent role in the campaign against the slave trade, the failure to spread the word of Christ amongst the colonized and enslaved left them in ignorance: 'While Britain basks in thy full blaze of light/Why lies sad Afric quenched in total night?' asked the abolitionist poet, Hannah More.[6] Associated with this idea that enslaved Africans lacked access to the ultimate spiritual home in heaven was a more secular conceptualization, which Graham employed, of the horror of African enslavement, which dwelled on the African's 'exile' from 'home'.

The previous two chapters traced the changing representations of Africans in Scottish Enlightenment Moral Philosophy, arguing that the ability to feel an emotional connection to place became an increasingly important marker of humanity and virtue. Whereas Adam Smith configured Africans as incapable of sympathy and therefore of 'home', Millar and Stewart argued that Africans, like all 'primitive' peoples, were peculiarly attached to home. This attachment did not in any way disrupt or undermine notions of white, European superiority. Indeed, Stewart's discussion of African minds and their potential for progress consolidated the idea that Africans were incapable of advancing on their own and, by linking inferiority to bodily attributes, planted the seeds for later nineteenth-century 'scientific' racism. In this chapter, I return to the representation of Africans as inherently 'homely' and trace this idea into the more popular published writings of Maria Graham (1785–1848) and Maria Edgeworth (1768–1849). Although excluded from the men-only lecture halls and scholarly societies of eighteenth-century 'polite' society, both Edgeworth and Graham were intellectually engaged with, and their writing informed by, the philosophical debates discussed in the previous two chapters. This chapter considers both Edgeworth and Graham as part of the British-imperial *literati* whose ideas of belonging constituted hegemonic norms. Indeed, if their ideas were taken less seriously by virtue of their status as women, their writings reached a far wider audience than that of their male counterparts. Focusing on their writings on slavery, it argues that the discourse of 'home' and 'exile' played a critical role in both writers' critiques of slavery in the Americas, whilst reassuring white Europeans of their innate superiority over Africans, and enabling white supremacy to remain undisturbed.

For Edgeworth and Graham, as for the majority of their literary friends and colleagues, the wrongs of African slavery did not lie in the restrictions placed upon African's freedom and agency. Although Graham objected to philosophical claims that Africans were intellectually inferior, citing an example of a skilled 'Negro carpenter' whose 'quickness of understanding … gives no countenance to the pretended inferiority of negro intellect', her general representation of the enslaved Africans who she encountered reinforced the image of Africans as abject characters who lacked understanding of their own situation.[7] Similarly, in Edgeworth's narrative, it was not intelligence or ingenuity, but industry and gratitude, that characterized Caesar, the protagonist of her story.[8] This representation of Africans as lacking in the intellectual capacities to effect progress through their own agency echoes Stewart's argument about progress, which was discussed in the previous chapter. Furthermore, the same moral discourse of belonging and attachment that was abstractly related in Stewart's Moral Philosophy is more explicitly represented in both writers' vivid accounts of African enslavement. In both accounts, their critiques of European colonial slavery rested on the sadness of loss and exile that enslavement entailed, and the feelings of the Africans who were separated from family and homeland. This chapter shows how the idea of enslaved Africans as 'exiles' constructed them as abject victims whose plight was made worse by the refusal of enslavers to allow them to form new familial bonds and homes in the Americas. The effect of this discourse of home and exile was twofold. Firstly, it enabled enslaved Africans to appear as familiar, and thereby as sympathetic characters, whose basic desires were familiar to, and approved by, white, middle-class abolitionists. At the same time, the configuration of Africans as homely domesticated the threat that their agency posed to European enslavers. As both narratives suggest, by meeting the homely desires of the enslaved African, social harmony could be restored without undermining white supremacy. The 'grateful' and 'faithful' African enabled white Europeans to imagine a future in which they retained control over the world's resources and over people's labour.

The first section of this chapter situates Graham and Edgeworth in the wider context of resistance to the trafficking and enslavement of Africans in Britain and the Americas. The second section provides a comparative analysis of the use of 'home' and 'exile' in the two texts in which they most closely engaged with the question of African slavery – Edgeworth's short story, 'The Grateful Negro' (1802) set in Jamaica, and Graham's *Journal of a Residence in Brazil* (1824).[9] The two different colonial contexts show how the discourse of 'home' and its intersections with white superiority circulated across different sites of African enslavement and different types of European settler colonialism. The final section examines the role of the discourse of 'home' in consolidating the discursive norms and ideologies of a class-based and racially inscribed patriarchy that justified imperial expansion and white supremacy.

Edgeworth and Graham in context

As women, Maria Edgeworth and Maria Graham (née Dundas) were prohibited from gaining a formal education, and restricted in their intellectual pursuits by gendered norms of propriety. Yet they were deeply engaged with the ideas that were taught and debated in Britain's men-only lecture theatres and societies and played as significant a role as Dugald Stewart in reinterpreting and disseminating Scottish Enlightenment thought.[10] Maria Edgeworth was born and educated in Oxfordshire but spent most of her adult life living on the family's Irish estate, Edgeworthstown. Her mother, Anna Maria Elers (1743–73), died in childbirth when she was only six and it was only from the age of around twelve that she began to develop the intellectual partnership with her father, Richard Lovell Edgeworth (1744–1817), which would establish both father and daughter's literary reputation.[11] Richard Lovell Edgeworth was an elite, 'improving' gentleman who took an interest in agriculture and was a member of the 'Lunar Society', which comprised a number of mid-eighteenth-century gentlemen scholars and entrepreneurs, including Josiah Wedgwood and Erasmus Darwin, whose experiments and theories underpinned the Industrial Revolution.[12] Edgeworth's familiarity with their ideas and works is evident from her own published novels, as well as her letters, which were lightly peppered with references to scientific theories. Writing her brother, Henry, who had attended Stewart's lectures at Edinburgh University, she insisted that she was able to talk and sew at the same time by stating, 'Does not Dr Darwin show that certain habitual motions go on without interrupting trains of thought?'[13]

Nearly twenty years Maria Edgeworth's junior, Maria Graham spent her early years on the Western coasts of Britain where her father worked as a naval officer. Graham also lost her mother, referred to in her autobiography as 'Miss Thompson', at a young age and was sent to a school in Oxfordshire fairly soon after.[14] Like Edgeworth, Graham was exceptionally well read, with a thirst for knowledge that led to her be nicknamed 'metaphysics in muslin' when she visited Edinburgh with her father in 1808.[15] Her diary of 1806 records quotations from Tacitus, Addison and Lord Kames, as well as notes from reading Stewart's *Elements of the Philosophy of the Human Mind*.[16] A generation apart, Graham and Edgeworth appear not to have met in person until 1830, although Edgeworth wrote to Graham prior to her journey to Brazil in 1824, and they had many friends in common, including the Stewarts and Sir James Mackintosh, who she met and stayed with in Bombay in 1809.[17] Edgeworth gained her literary reputation through a series of didactic novels, which, in the words of her father, was aimed to promote 'the progress of education from the cradle to the grave'.[18] These included *Belinda* (1801), which dealt, controversially, with interracial relationships between Africans and British colonists in the Caribbean.[19] Her short stories, gathered together in eighteen volumes under the title *Popular Tales* (1800–4), were intended to reach an audience 'beyond circles which are sometimes exclusively considered as polite'.[20] Graham's literary reputation derived, in her lifetime, from her travel writing, although she is best remembered for her children's history book, *Little Arthur's History of England* (1835). Her first book, *Journal of a Residence in India* (1812), was well received and paved the way for further travel writing on Italy and subsequently South America. Her attempts to publish more academic work, including her *Letters on India* (1813), which drew on Oriental scholarship to explain Indian religion, customs, architecture and society, met with less success and some derision.[21]

Both Edgeworth and Graham turned the academic ideas and philosophical discussion of the Scottish Enlightenment into more tangible forms that could be visualized and understood by people who had not received an education in Logic, Moral Philosophy and Metaphysics. Although in his *Elements of the Philosophy of the Human Mind* (1792) Dugald Stewart warned of the dangers of novels and 'fictitious history', he conceded that in this genre 'displays of character may be most successfully given, and the various weaknesses of the heart exposed'.[22] It was exactly this benefit that Edgeworth sought to engender through her own works of fiction. Edgeworth's novels and *Popular Tales* translated the Political Economy and Moral Philosophy that Stewart was teaching in the university classroom to a much wider audience. Imagining himself into the role of governor of Botany Bay, Sir James Mackintosh wrote that all he would need to bring civilization to an 'unmixed community of ruffians' was a 'penal code from Bentham and Popular Tales from Miss Edgeworth'.[23] Although a more controversial genre for a woman, Graham's travel writing drew on and reconfigured the more acceptable and philosophical writings of scholarly men, including Mackintosh who she first met in Bombay.[24] As Carl Thompson has shown, Graham's discussion of an earthquake that she witnessed in Chile revealed her familiarity with Enlightenment methods of recording and analysing observations of natural phenomena, and her involvement in scholarly debates on natural science; she was the first woman to publish in *Transactions of the Geological Society*.[25] Later in life, Graham played an important role introducing travel writers, particularly women travellers, to her friend and publisher, John Murray, as well as drawing on her extensive imperial networks to source sketches to illustrate his books.[26]

Although Edgeworth and Graham lived very different lives – the former spent almost all of her life on the British Isles, the latter was almost constantly on the move, initially around Britain and then travelling to India, Brazil, Argentina, Chile, and finally Italy – all of their writings addressed aspects of British-imperial expansion. This is hardly surprising, for both women were, in different ways enmeshed in the politics of empire. Edgeworth's family were English Protestants whose inheritance of lands in Ireland derived from the sixteenth century. During the eighteenth century, however, the Edgeworths were largely absentee landlords living in England off of the profits of the estate; Maria Edgeworth used and critiqued their lives and experiences in many of her novels and short stories, including *Castle Rackrent* (1800), *Ennui* (1809) and *The Absentee* (1812). It was only in 1782, the same year that 'Grattan's Parliament' regained some legislative independence from England, that her father moved the family to the Irish estate and began a series of reforms and improvements.[27] Discontent with the restrictions imposed on the Irish Parliament, including the exclusion of 80 per cent of the Catholic population from representation, led to the formation of an armed coalition of Catholic peasants, Presbyterians and Dissenters under the banner of the Society of United Irishmen. In May 1798, resistance reached its peak with the Great Rebellion. Launched with the promise of support from the French Republican army, which was never forthcoming, the Great Rebellion was brutally suppressed by British forces, leading to the Act of Union in 1801.[28] The Edgeworths were largely sympathetic to the cause and were well-acquainted with one of the leaders of the United Irishmen, William Drennan.[29] Yet the family fled their home in Edgeworthstown for their physical safety, an ordeal that Elizabeth Kim has argued informed Maria Edgeworth's writing about rebellion in 'The Grateful Negro'.[30]

Edgeworth's 'The Grateful Negro' and Graham's *Journal of a Residence in Brazil* are two different genres of writing that are situated in two very different socio-economic and political contexts. As a piece of didactic literature, 'The Grateful Negro' is a work of fiction based on a general knowledge of Jamaica that was derived from published reports, rather than the first-hand experience that Graham used in her representation of Brazil. The two regions also had very distinct and separate histories, but shared a common experience of genocide in which the indigenous peoples – the Tupis and Tapuias in Brazil, and the Taínos in Jamaica – were largely exterminated by European colonists in the sixteenth century.[31] Since the mid-sixteenth century, the Portuguese had relied on slave labour, primarily of Africans from Guinea, the Congo and Angola, to cultivate sugar, tobacco and later coffee, to mine for diamonds and gold, and to work in domestic service and agriculture in Brazil.[32] English colonization came comparatively late to Jamaica; the island was seized by Cromwell from the Spanish in 1655 and was officially ceded in 1670, becoming a British colony on the Act of Union in 1707. Although, as Trevor Burnard and John Garrigus point out, the English colonists in Jamaica initially borrowed the methods of sugar manufacturing from the Portuguese in Brazil, by the eighteenth century the process of sugar production was quite different.[33] This, in turn, effected the nature of settler-colonial society, and therefore also social relations between enslaver and enslaved. In eighteenth-century Brazil, a wealthy and consolidated settler society was increasingly patronized by the Portuguese monarchy and integrated into the upper echelons of the imperial administration.[34] Eighteenth-century Jamaica, in contrast, was a plantation colony and frontier society, a place to 'acquire a fortune which could then be spent at home' in Britain.[35]

In the early nineteenth century, the political and economic powers of Portugal and Britain were diametrically opposed. Portugal was a waning imperial power, whose colonial influence in India had long been in decline and whose own, metropolitan, status was precarious. In 1807, when Napoleon invaded Portugal and British naval vessels escorted the Portuguese court from Lisbon to Rio de Janeiro, that subordination was further exposed, whilst the balance between Portuguese colony and metropole was flipped. In the years between 1807 and 1820, Rio de Janeiro represented the seat of Portuguese imperial power; Brazil was afforded the status of a 'kingdom' rather than a 'colony' in 1815.[36] Yet, as Kirsten Schultz argues, the reconfiguration of Brazil as a the 'new Athens' posed considerable challenges for Portuguese claims to a 'European' identity.[37] Whilst Jamaica could be consistently represented as 'Other' to British metropolitan society, the relocation of the Portuguese court and high society to Brazil made that conceptual separation more complex and difficult to sustain. The aim of this chapter is not to offer a comparative view of white society and identity in Jamaica and Brazil, but to show how a British discourse of anti-slavery cut across different imperial geographies of white enslaving societies in the Americas. Although Brazil and Jamaica had different environmental and socio-legal structures they shared a common socio-economic base in African slavery, which had been eschewed as morally repugnant, and criminalized since the mid-eighteenth century, in both metropolitan Britain and Portugal. As Antonio Rocha Penalves has shown, elite Brazilian critics of slavery such as João Severiano Macieal da Costa (1769–1833) and José Bonifácio de Andrada e Silva (1763–1838) were aware of French and British critiques of slavery, including Adam Smith's economic critique.[38] This chapter looks at the how, and to what effect, Edgeworth and Graham mobilized Enlightenment discourses of 'home' and belonging to critique slavery in two different imperial sites.

'The Grateful Negro' and *Journal of a Voyage to Brazil*

Edgeworth's 'The Grateful Negro' was one of a series of short stories published under the title *Popular Tales,* and was set in Jamaica in the midst of a planned uprising of enslaved Africans living and working on British-owned plantations. The main characters of the story were all men. Both Mr Jeffries and Mr Edwards were white, British enslavers who owned neighbouring plantations in Jamaica, but whose politics and practices of slave-ownership were very different. Both Caesar and Hector were enslaved Africans of Koromantyn heritage who were involved in a plot, led by an African woman, Esther, to rise up against their enslavers. The story begins with the prospect of an enslaved African, Caesar, on Jeffries's plantation being sold to pay off his owners' debt, and thereby separated from his Eboe lover, Clara, and the small cottage that he had built and the grounds that he had cultivated. On hearing of his impending sale and separation, Caesar implores Edwards to purchase himself and Clara. Edwards agrees to the purchase and lodges Caesar and Clara in a cottage on his own estate. Caesar is so overcome with gratitude for his benevolent enslaver that he reneges on his commitment to join the rebellion and attempts to dissuade Hector from rebelling too. His loyalty to his enslaver and his treachery towards his enslaved comrades is punished by Esther, an Obeah 'sorceress', who casts a spell over Clara and threatens to kill her if Caesar does not join the rebellion. Caesar, however, persists in his decision and, on the eve of the rebellion, alerts Edwards, who armed himself and 'the negroes on his plantation' and confronted the rebels. Hector attempts, but ultimately fails, to kill Caesar (Edgeworth, p. 236). The rebellion is thwarted, but not before Jeffries's plantation is destroyed, its cruel overseer, Durant 'died in tortures, inflicted by the hands of those who had suffered most by his cruelties'.[39] Edgeworth ends her story with a picture of the Jeffries, who return penniless and in ignominy, railing at the treachery of the whole race of slaves. She concludes, 'Our readers, we hope, will think that at least one exception may be made, in favour of THE GRATEFUL NEGRO.'[40]

Like the majority of her stories, 'The Grateful Negro' taught elite white men the benefits that would accrue if they acted towards their inferiors with a benevolent paternalism, rather than with tyranny. As in Stewart and Smith's Moral Philosophy, Edgeworth understood material wealth and moral virtue to go hand-in-hand; Jeffries's debt was both the result, and overwhelming proof, of his moral shortcomings. Placing the debates over rights and wrongs of the slave trade and slavery in the mouths of Jeffries and Edwards, Edgeworth repeated the arguments of the Scottish Enlightenment abolitionists. As in Stewart's lectures, she argued against the idea that enslavement on a plantation was better than life in Africa, for free labour as a more productive form of labour than slave labour, and implicitly against the idea that of innate African inferiority compared to white men. Yet, as the story continues, it is evident that Edgeworth, like Stewart, cannot conceive of a situation in which Africans are not subservient to white Europeans. Edgeworth's story reflects Stewart's characterization of 'the Negro' (drawn from Jefferson), that, 'they have much humanity and gentleness, natural affection, and gratitude'.[41] She distinguished further between the Koromantyns and the Eboe, the one 'frank, fearless, martial and heroic', the other 'soft, languishing, and timid'.[42] By representing Caesar as Koromantyn and Clara as Eboe, Edgeworth brought together

British understandings of African ethnicity with ideals of masculinity and femininity. Indeed, the women in the majority of Edgeworth's *Popular Tales* act as complements to their husband's or lovers' characters, supporting the main narrative and the moral message. Jeffries's wife is frivolous and materialistic, her vanity leads her to have a female slave – the wife of Hector, who leads the rebellion – severely flogged when she accidentally tears a new dress.⁴³ The loving, gentle, but easily influenced, Clara enables Caesar to perform the role of the strong, virtuous and benevolent patriarch, behaving towards his lover much as his new master, Edwards behaves towards him. Meanwhile, Esther, a character probably based on the Asante Queen, Nana who co-led Tacky's War in Jamaica in 1760, brings racial and gender stereotypes together to signify the superstition and irrationality that Enlightenment thinkers attributed to Africans and women, and particularly African women.⁴⁴

Edgeworth's positive portrayal of Caesar rested on his performance of settled cultivation and heterosexual monogamy, symbolized by his careful attendance to his house and garden, and his kindness towards, and guidance of, his lover, Clara. In his lectures on Political Economy, Stewart had argued that settled cultivation and heterosexual monogamy were inseparable, and both were necessary for the moral and material advance of the human race. 'Marriage', Stewart stated, 'is necessary in the political union, and we shall view it chiefly as resulting from the moral and physical order of nature.' Polygamy, in contrast, was an 'evil' that was destructive to population growth and to morality and was to be found in societies that had been corrupted by luxury, as well as in savage societies, where idleness and the sensual pleasures ruled over industry and virtue.⁴⁵ Focusing on 'savage' societies, however, Stewart argued that the division of land 'produces domestic habits and attachments' and exercises the intellectual and moral faculties of man by forcing 'him' to follow 'some systematic scheme and arrangements in the conduct of life'.⁴⁶ This was particularly the case in relationship to women, who, in 'savage' societies, where strength was the only virtue, were considered mere objects of purchase, rather than of affection, and treated as slaves. Citing Kames's *Sketches on the History of Man* (1778), Stewart stated that women could only be respected 'according as they possess these accomplishments and that turn of mind which naturally engages the men'. Their 'turn of mind' included possessing 'livelier fancies' than men, who have more 'depth and strength of mind', a 'flexibility of temper' and greater ease in 'acquiring habits and accommodating themselves to their situation'. Stewart attributed this final quality to the fact that women, 'as they are not so much arbiters of their own situation as ours, they should more easily bear what may be disagreeable'.⁴⁷

He configured that imbalance as the natural result of the inherent weakness, both physical and mental, of women compared to men. These arguments were represented in Edgeworth's story through the examples of both Mr Edwards and Caesar as manly, rational and industrious.

In 'The Grateful Negro', it was Edwards's benevolence towards his slaves, and his encouragement of their industry and domesticity that led to Caesar's gratitude, and ultimately saved himself and his property from being destroyed in the rebellion. Edgeworth's portrayal of the personalities of Caesar and his friend, and leader of the rebellion, Hector, drew on the two alternating characterizations of Africans in Scottish Enlightenment thought. Both men held a strong desire for revenge against their oppressors, a quality that Edgeworth stated was regarded as a virtue in Koromantyn society, and which sustained the close friendship between them. (This idea that what counted as a virtue differed between societies drew Edgeworth closer to Smith and Hume's 'scepticism' than to Stewart's revision of virtues as Divinely inspired universals.) Yet in Hector, revenge was a 'ruling passion' and a pleasure, whilst Caesar considered revenge to be a duty. This difference meant that whereas Hector, like Adam Smith's 'magnanimous' 'savages', was willing to sacrifice his life for revenge, Caesar's revenge was driven by loyalty and gratitude; he would rather 'devote himself, for the defence of a friend'.[48] This depiction of Caesar echoed Stewart's citation of Jefferson, that 'instances are not rare among them [Africans] of the most scrupulous integrity; of the greatest humanity to the distressed; and of the warmest gratitude to their benefactors'.[49] Indeed, the fictional Caesar's actions in support of his master, and his dedication to a man who he considered his 'friend' acted as an endorsement of this position. Caesar's attachment to domestic habits, and to the white man who had enabled them, led him to betray his friends and his society, and potentially also sacrifice his own and his lover's life, to act instead according to his 'duty' to his benefactor. Overall, whilst Edgeworth was critical of the worst excesses of slavery, her narrative did little to undermine the legitimacy of enslavement or racist representations of Africans. Rather, it envisaged a world in which Africans consented willingly to white supremacy and thereby to their own subjection.

Graham took a more explicit anti-slavery and abolitionist position, using her *Journal of a Voyage to Brazil* to critique slavery in general, and the treatment of enslaved Africans in Brazil in particular. In 1821, the year Graham visited Brazil, an estimated 54,064 enslaved Africans embarked on the voyage from Africa to Brazil. This amounted to 72 per cent of the entire European slave trade for that year.[50] Of the 47,459 enslaved Africans who survived the middle passage in 1821, 10,001 disembarked at Pernambuco.[51] Despite the fact that from 1810 the Portuguese government had signed a number of treaties with the British government agreeing to suppress and gradually abolish the trans-Atlantic slave trade, the importation of enslaved Africans into Brazil had actually increased during the first three decades of the nineteenth century.[52] This expansion was partly the result of the Haitian Revolution, which redirected demand for sugar from Europe and North America to Jamaica, Cuba and Brazil, leading to an increase in the number of plantations, particularly in the northeast of Brazil.[53] The majority of the enslaved worked on plantations and sugar mills, but some worked as farmhands, skilled artisans (masons, tailors, coopers, carpenters) and others, especially women, as domestic help.[54] In her *Journal*, Graham described the variety of living and working conditions of the enslaved Africans who she encountered in Brazil. These ranged from the absolutely desperate circumstances of the newly arrived Africans waiting at the slave market in Pernambuco, who she described as 'the filthiest animals in the streets', to the small communities of enslaved Africans living in the *fazendas* where 'something like the blessings of freedom are enjoyed'.[55] The treatment of the enslaved also varied dramatically, with examples of enslavers manumitting an elderly or sick slave in order to 'turn him out of doors to beg or starve', to those who gave their slaves new clothes, small plots of land and a form of pension upon retirement.[56]

Journal of a Voyage to Brazil begins with a brief narrative of the history of colonial Brazil in order to situate Graham's own observations of the country, including the rebellion in Pernambuco, in the political context of Spanish and Portuguese conquest and colonization of South America. Drawing on Robert Southey's *History of Brazil* (1810), Graham narrated the wars between Portuguese, Dutch, Spanish and French as they vied for control of Brazil's trade and produce; she represented the English as mediators defending Brazil's trade and Portuguese interests from Spanish encroachments. She had very little interest in Brazil's indigenous societies, except as scourges on European colonists' efforts to develop agriculture and trade, or as the beneficiaries of Jesuit attempts at 'civilizations'. Prior to European 'discovery', Brazil, Graham stated, was full of 'hordes of savages' who wandered and had little knowledge of agriculture at all.[57] Comparing Brazil's indigenous peoples to the 'civilized and humane' societies that Europeans encountered in Mexico, Peru and Chile, Graham situated them on the very lowest rungs of the civilizational ladder. Brazil's indigenous peoples were, she stated, 'hunters and cannibals; they wandered, and they made war for food; few of the tribes knew even the cultivation of mandioc, and fewer still had adopted any kind of covering, save paint and feathers for ornament'.[58] As the previous chapter argued, this was not just a socio-economic description, the use of 'wandering' and the reference to nakedness had moral undertones, which enabled Graham to justify European conquest and settlement not as a series of 'splendid and chivalresque pictures that the chronicles of the Corteses, and Pizarros, and Almagros furnish', but of 'plain, and often pathetic scenes of human life'.[59] It is not clear whether her reference to 'wickedness' refers to the deeds of the Portuguese, to the indigenous societies, or to both. Graham acknowledged, with little regret, that the 'wretched Indians' had been largely 'exterminated, or wholly subdued' and the history of the 'present crisis' in Brazil was therefore entirely the history of Portuguese factions.[60]

In her 'Sketch of the History of Brazil', Graham gave very little space to the enslaved Africans who were primarily responsible for clearing and cultivating the lands and working the mines. She made brief mention of the Palmares *qulombo* [maroon state], a self-liberated African society, whose chief 'Zombi' [Zambi] Robert Southey had celebrated as a romantic hero.[61] The Palmares *quilombo* was formed in the seventeenth century and comprised over one thousand formerly enslaved Africans, who had escaped the plantations of Bahia. The population included indigenous and mixed-race people, but was primarily made up of people who themselves, or whose parents, had been trafficked from Angola. Combining Angolan and Brazilian forms of statecraft, the society had a complex political structure and infrastructure, and was necessarily on a constant war-footing against the Portuguese; the Palmares and their resistance to European colonialism retain an important place in the Afro-Brazilian spiritual and historical imagination today.[62] Graham, whose 'History' drew largely on Southey's, downplayed the sophistication of the society, describing the Palmares as having 'some laws, a shadow of the Christian religion, and were agriculturalists. They harassed the Portuguese, and added by their depredations to the general misery'.[63] Although she was deeply critical of Dutch and Portuguese actions towards the indigenous peoples and enslaved Africans in Brazil, Graham represented the final destruction of Palmares in 1694 by the Portuguese colonists as reprisal for Palmarino 'depredations'.[64] Zambi and his followers' refusal to submit in battle and their deaths by suicide instead of capture earned from Graham the same kind of admiration that Smith had professed when he referred to the 'magnanimity' of enslaved Africans. Yet in her own times, the prospect of the rebellion of enslaved Africans, however righteous in principle, filled her with a dread that made it clear exactly where her sympathies lay.

Anti-slavery and the fear of black agency

From Brazil to the Caribbean, Ireland to India, European colonizers lived in constant fear of uprising by the subject populations whose lands, labour and resources they had appropriated for themselves. The fear of the consequences of black agency underlies the narrative plot of Edgeworth's 'The Grateful Negro' and represents a key, preoccupying theme in Graham's *Journal of a Voyage to Brazil*. In this respect, the Haitian Revolution cast a long shadow over both authors' narratives. Edgeworth's narrative relied heavily on Bryan Edwards's account of the Haitian Revolution, in volume three of his *An Historical Survey of the French Colony in the Island of Saint Domingue* (1797). Edwards (1743–1800) was a Wiltshire-born plantation owner, who lived in Jamaica from the age of sixteen where his family owned plantations in St Mary's parish. He was a prominent and politically influential member of the white settler society in Jamaica, a member of Jamaica's assembly and an advocate of the amelioration of the conditions of African slaves on plantations, but an active campaigner for the pro-slavery movement in Parliament.[65] Although Edgeworth may not have met Edwards himself, she did meet a 'great friend' of his whilst on tour in Belgium, and named the planter-hero of her story after him.[66] Edwards was no abolitionist, and like the majority of Scottish Enlightenment thinkers, including Smith, Stewart and Edgeworth herself, he combined critique of slavery with pejorative depictions of Africans as 'savages'. As Paula Dumas notes, his aim in publishing *The History, Civil and Commercial, of the British Colonies in the West Indies* (1793) was to 'prove the abolitionists wrong' about the morality of the planters.[67] To do this, he largely denigrated the character of the enslaved Africans whose labour ensured his vast wealth. In the preface to his volume on Saint Domingo, Edwards prepared his reader for 'scenes of anarchy, desolation, and carnage. We have to contemplate the human mind in its utmost deformity: to behold the savage man, let loose from restraint, exercising cruelties, or which the bare recital makes the heart recoil, and committing crimes which are hitherto unheard of in history'.[68]

For Edwards, the 'barbarities of Africa' could not be expunged even by kindness or blood relationships. He related the history of M. Cardineau, whose sons (the progeny of his rape of an enslaved African woman) murdered him during the Haitian Revolution. He had, Edwards claimed, 'bred them up with great tenderness' and manumitted them in infancy, and in his attempts to save his life had offered them money.[69] The one example of a 'faithful negro' who ensured the safety of his enslavers in the midst of the rule proved the exception to the rule of 'devastation, slaughter, and ruin'.[70] Edwards blamed the 'pestilent reformers' who, through their campaign, had rendered 'the white inhabitants odious and contemptible in the eyes of their own slaves' and led the enslaved to believe in 'such ideas of their natural rights and equality of condition'.[71] Criticizing the 'reformers of the present day', he cautioned against projects that attempted an 'amendment in the condition of human life, faster than nature allows'.[72] His warnings reflected Dugald Stewart's argument, discussed in the previous chapter, that change must be gradual and in keeping with the manners and habits of people, a position that Edgeworth reiterated when she introduced the enslaver, Mr Edwards, the hero of her story: '[Mr Edwards] wished that there was no such thing as slavery in the world; but he was convinced, by the arguments of those who have the best means of obtaining information, that the sudden emancipation of the negroes would rather increase than diminish their miseries.'[73]

Writing seventeen years after the passage of the Act for the Abolition of the Slave Trade, Graham represented 'the English' as morally superior to the Portuguese in Brazil, a fact that she evidenced through their respective treatment of enslaved Africans. In Bahia, she and her 'English' companions passed by a dying African woman and implored their 'Portuguese companions' to take her to hospital. Their dismissal of their request, stating that 'oh, 'tis only a black: let us ride on' and their own assistance to the woman served as evidence of the differences between the two nationalities.[74] She contradicted herself later when she expressed her horror at the cellars in which enslaved Africans who worked for 'English' households lived, yet never did she explicitly critique the English in Brazil for enslaving Africans.[75] Although set in a British colony, Edgeworth's narrative also subtly acquitted British enslavers from the worst brutalities of slavery. In 'The Grateful Negro' it is not Jeffries's actions that lead the enslaved Africans to plot rebellion and revenge, but the acts of his overseer, Durant, whose French name distances him from the English plantation owners. Edgeworth describes Durant as tyrannical, flying into 'violent rage' and 'constantly suspicious', fearful of a rebellion against him.[76] The configuration of the British (or 'English') as less culpable for the horrors of slavery than other Europeans is replicated in other works of abolitionist literature. In *The West Indies*, for example, James Montgomery opened his poem with Britannia's address to Africa, 'thy chains are broken', before immediately situating the origins of slavery in the Americas in Columbus's 'discovery' of America, thus casting the Spanish as 'tyrants' who 'cast away his soul' for gold and riches.[77] As in Edgeworth and Graham's narratives, the atrocities committed by other European nations serve as foils against which British humanitarianism was constructed. Invoking the power of the British-imperial state to address the horrors of the slave market, Graham exclaimed that 'nothing in our power should be considered too little, or too great, that can tend to abolish or to alleviate slavery'.[78]

Yet like many white critics of slavery, Graham's horror at the institution of slavery ran alongside fears about the prospect of the overturning of racial hierarchies. Whilst she had little sympathy for the 'Old Portuguese', she could well imagine their terror of the dangers posed by an 'alarmingly large' 'Negro population' – less than a third of Olinda's population of 70,000 was white.[79] Between 1807 and 1835, Bahia and Pernambuco experienced wave after wave of coordinated armed resistance and rebellion by slaves, which were brutally suppressed by the Portuguese and later, after independence, the Brazilian authorities.[80] The European Portuguese, Graham stated, 'look forward with dread to the event of a revolution, which will free their slaves from their authority, and, by declaring them all men alike, will authorise them to resent the injuries they have so long and patiently born'.[81] Yet whilst in her published writing she offered a more distanced appraisal of the situation, in a letter to her publisher, John Murray, she relayed a sense of her own terror: 'I could tell such stories of Negroes and new slaves – God help us that one half of mankind should be born without hearts'.[82]

It is unclear whether Graham's reference to those 'born without hearts' referred to the old Portuguese regime or to 'Negroes and new slaves'. The ambiguity, however, points to the construction of another binary that ran parallel to, and intersected with, the civilized/savage, black/white binary that dominated Enlightenment philosophy: that of feeling/unfeeling. In this configuration, European enslavers became the 'savages', whose 'brutality and baseness', as Adam Smith had put it, rendered them underserving of sympathy and belonging. As Chapters 1 and 2 argued, whereas Smith had represented Africans as lacking sensibility, by the time Graham was writing, Scottish Enlightenment philosophers configured 'primitive' and 'savage' peoples (the terms were used interchangeably) as having a heightened sense of belonging to 'home'. Imagining the sense of loss of the newly imported enslaved Africans, for example, Graham wrote that they must be 'still smarting under the separation from all that endears the home, *even of a savage*'.[83] The parenthesis points to the universalization of the idea of belonging that is embedded in sentimental discourse; even at the lowest level of civilization and the most 'savage' state, humans possessed an emotional connection to 'home'.[84] This representation of Africans as 'homely' circulated across genres. In her 1806 diary, Graham recorded lines from William Roscoe's poem, 'Mount Pleasant', which included the image of enslaved Africans, ''Torn from each joy that crown'd their native soil/No sweet reflections mitigate their toil'.[85] Similarly, in 'The West Indies', Montgomery described a village scene in an unspecified part of Africa, in which the 'Negro' sits outside his hut, surrounded by his children. His capture and transportation from his home to the Americas leaves him, in Montgomery's words, 'broken hearted' in exile: 'The Negro-exile languish'd in the West/With nothing left of life but hated breath.'[86] Concluding his essay on the wrongs of slavery, the Aberdeen-based philosopher, James Beattie, appealed to Europeans to imagine the terrible sufferings of enslaved Africans who were stolen from their homes and separated from their families: 'What parents and children, and wives and husbands, of great sensibility, may feel on those occasions, I leave it to the good natured reader to imagine. Certain it is, that the spoilers who carry them away never once think of that great matter.'[87]

In both Edgeworth and Graham's writings, 'home' played a constitutive role in humanizing enslaved Africans and critiquing European slavers. Edgeworth's introduction to Caesar as a sympathetic character relied on his pride in his cottage, which he had cultivated 'to a degree of perfection' despite the hard labour that was exacted upon him.[88] The threat of Caesar's separation from his home and from Clara, his wife to be, sets up the narrative for Edwards to take on the role of benefactor and saviour. Whilst Caesar is praised for his industriousness and gratitude, it is Edwards who claims the agency that leads to the defeat of the rebellion, who possesses the power to forgive and thereby to restore an order based on the continuation of more 'benevolent' form of white supremacy. In her *Journal*, Graham relates a dynamic that is remarkable for its similarities to Edgeworth's fictional account. Describing Nossa Senhora da Luz [dos Pinhais de Curitiba], an agricultural and pastoral *fazenda* in Bahia that had been established in 1654, Graham praised their host and superintendent of the plantation, 'Mr Lewis P'.[89] He was, Graham stated, 'one of the few persons whom I have met conversant among slaves, who appears to have made them an object of rational and humane attention'.[90] Like Caesar, the enslaved Africans responded with gratitude and respect, viewing him as a 'king, priest, and prophet'.[91] On this estate, Graham described a 'mulatto boatman' whose industry had enabled him to earn 'a good deal of private property besides doing his duty to his master' and who had bought the freedom of his lover, a 'creole negress'. His intention to buy his own freedom and so to pass on his property to his children provoked Graham's admiration and imagination so much that she wished to turn his story into a novel.[92] Yet the apparently praiseworthy master had refused to allow him his freedom. Graham did not condemn the master (her host), rather it was the romantic spectacle of the desire for family, freedom and home that preoccupied her.

Graham and Edgeworth used the desire for a home that was based on the familiar structures of heterosexuality, patriarchy and property ownership as a way of representing enslaved Africans as capable of virtue and of civilized behaviour. In a similar way, they used 'home' as a means of critiquing the activities and morals of white, European enslavers in Brazil and Jamaica. In Edgeworth's narrative, Jeffries's immorality was signified by his own financial irresponsibility, his frivolous and extravagant house parties, and particularly by his wife's dissolute and idle behaviour. Edgeworth introduces Mrs Jeffries languishing on a sofa, 'fanned by four slaves, two at her head and two at her feet', about to receive a chest of dresses from London. When Hector's wife accidentally tears one of the dresses, Mrs Jeffries is immediately transformed from indolence to an irrational rage and punishes her slave, which serves to heighten Hector's own passion and provoke his desire for 'vengeance' even further.[93] In this domestic scene, the enslaved African and European enslaver are placed on the same emotional footing, both governed by passion rather than by reason, which stirs conflict and undermines what should be the natural hierarchy and order of the household. It is interesting that in the story Edwards does not have a home in Jamaica at all, an absence which suggests that Edgeworth is unable to reconcile her image of a virtuous, white man with the idea of 'home' in the Caribbean.[94] Graham, in contrast, was appreciative of the luxury and taste of the homes of the elite Portuguese in Bahia and commented on the beauty and refinement of the ladies. Yet, according to her narrative, she was quickly disabused of the outward appearance of virtue and purity amongst the European women in Brazil. Raised by 'servants [who] are *slaves*', the European households in Brazil were vulnerable to corruption; a vulnerability that called into question their very status as 'white' and 'European'. The enslaved who worked in them were 'naturally the enemies of their masters, and ready and willing to deceive them, by assisting in the corruption of their families'.[95] The threat the enslaved Africans – 'whose manners were so depraved, and practices so immoral' – posed to the households of Europeans provided Graham with another example of the 'evils of slavery', and she begged the enslavers to think not only for the enslaved but 'to their families and their posterity'.[96]

Conclusion

In Graham and Edgeworth's narratives of enslavement in Brazil and Jamaica, the home and the household were, in different ways, corrupted by slavery. For European enslavers, the threat to the morals and order of their households represented a threat to their own 'posterity'. For the enslaved themselves, it was their inability to form stable, hetero-patriarchal households and to become virtuous through the ownership of the home as property that undermined their humanity. Amongst the critics of slavery in the Caribbean, the fact that Africans could not marry and form stable, patriarchal families was a key argument against slavery. In his 'Essay on the Lawfulness of Slavery', the separation of 'husband from wife, and the child from the parent' provided Beattie with the most compelling evidence for his argument that slavery was 'inconsistent with the dearest and most essential rights of man's nature'.[97] Both Olaudah Equiano and Mary Princes's narratives of their experiences of enslavement place emphasis on the separation from siblings and parents as a symbol of the ultimate barbarity of slavery. In what Vincent Carretta has argued may be a fictionalized part of his narrative, Equiano lays emphasis on his father's status and respectability, the love bestowed upon him by his mother, and the sorrow of being torn from his sister.[98]

As Markman Ellis has argued, it was not necessarily the case that these writers' sentimental cries for the plight of 'exiled' and enslaved Africans were calls for the abolition of slavery.[99] Edgeworth's position was concertedly ameliorist, rather than abolitionist, and whilst Graham was more convinced of the abolitionist cause, she expressed doubts as to whether the best-treated slaves 'might be compared with advantage to that of free servants'.[100] The idea that Africans could be considered the moral and intellectual equals of white Europeans appears to have been an anathema to both women. In her discussion of *Obeah* in 'The Grateful Negro', Edgeworth explicitly compared the 'superstitious credulity of the negroes' to the 'enlightened inhabitants of Europe'.[101] Stewart's formulation of 'savage' minds unregulated was played-out in Edgeworth's narrative of the actions of the 'sorceress' Esther, 'the chief instigator of this intended rebellion', who manipulated the 'ungoverned' imaginations of her fellow enslaved Africans 'to what pitch and purpose she pleased'.[102] Similarly, the idea that enslaved Africans had no conception of the future is suggested in Maria Graham's account of watching a group of slaves singing whilst disembarking from a ship in Cachoeira. 'Poor wretches!' Graham proclaims, 'Could they foresee the slave-market, and the separations of friends and relations that will take place there?'[103] Elsewhere, in an encounter with a group of enslaved Africans at the slave market, she resists the temptation of 'awakening them to a sense of the sad things of slavery'.[104] In both instances, Graham represents herself as able to perceive the wider picture and to imagine the terrible future into which the enslaved were heading, whilst they appear blissfully unaware of their plight. Together, Edgeworth's representation of Africans in the Caribbean as 'superstitious' and 'gullible', and Graham's of newly arrived enslaved Africans in Brazil as naïve, docile and oblivious, reaffirmed the intellectual superiority of themselves as white, educated Europeans.

4

Belonging and exile in the debate over Scottish Highland emigration

Their established character, founded upon the habits which the former state of the country required, do not accord with the condition of the lower classes in an industrious community.
Earl of Selkirk, *Observations on the Present State of the Highlands of Scotland* (1805)
While hopeless through the pathless wilds they roam.
But wherefore exil'd? while afar they rove,
Still glow their filial breasts with patriot love;
The thoughts of home still aching at their heart.
–Anne Grant of Laggan, 'The Highlanders' (1808)

Between 1760 and 1815, over 20,000 Highland Scots emigrated, usually as members of extended families connected through bonds of clanship, to North America.[1] Among them was a group of 800 Highlanders, recruited by Thomas Douglas, fifth earl of Selkirk (1771–1820) from the Isles of Skye and Uist, Ross-shire, Argyllshire and Inverness-shire. In 1803, Douglas transported and settled these Highlanders on what the British had recently renamed 'Prince Edward Island', an island on the Atlantic coast of Canada, long inhabited by the Mi'kmaq people and which they referred to as 'Epekwitk'.[2] Selkirk explained his emigration scheme in a long essay, *Observations on the Present State of the Highlands of Scotland,* published in 1805.[3] In this essay he argued that the emigration and re-settlement of Highlanders would solve the problem of a surplus population whose manners and customs were ill-suited to a 'polite', commercial society, and an industrializing nation. Rather than lose 'the proud spirit that characterised the antient [sic] Highlander', Selkirk argued that the re-settlement of a people accustomed to 'primitive' living in a difficult climate would ensure that they retained their identity, whilst also providing security for the British Empire.⁴ Drawing on Adam Smith and Thomas Malthus's political economic theories, Selkirk argued that the emigration of Highland small-holders and peasantry from the British Isles, and their reinvention as colonial settlers in North America, was an inevitable and necessary concomitant of progress. The initial success of the project proved, in Selkirk's own words, the 'utility that may be derived from a class of people who have hitherto been lost to their native country, and abandoned to their fate in a foreign land. Though little service as manufacturers, it proves that they may be made excellent colonists'.⁵

Selkirk's *Observations* met with praise from a considerable part of the periodical press, including the *Edinburgh Review*, which stated that 'not only will it preserve a better picture, than that has been drawn by any other hand, of a peculiar state of society and manners, highly interesting to the historian; but it forms a large contribution, to the theory of political economy, of most satisfactory deductions and general conclusions'.⁶ Yet if Selkirk's *Observations* was admired for its literary and intellectual skill, his promotion of emigration and settler colonialism contradicted received wisdom regarding the relationship between population expansion and national prosperity. Since the 1770s, elite writers had expressed deep concern about the potential effects of population on the strength and prosperity of the British Isles in general, and the Scottish Highlands in particular.⁷ Critics of his scheme argued that the peasantry formed the bedrock of a nation and that without the peasantry a nation had no way of providing for itself. Quoting lines from Oliver Goldsmith's poem, 'The Deserted Village' (1770) – 'But a bold peasantry, their country's pride/When once destroy'd, can never be supply'd' – they warned about the consequences of losing the nation's manual labour force.⁸ The Scottish Highlands, a 'nursery of soldiers', also provided Britain with the military manpower necessary for the defence of the nation in case of invasion, a particular source of concern during the Revolutionary and Napoleonic wars. Even where elite writers sympathized with the desire of Highlanders to look for alternative livelihoods in North America, they generally agreed with Samuel Johnson that 'some method to stop this epidemic desire of wandering, which spreads its contagion from valley to valley, deserves to be sought with great diligence'.⁹

Political and economic arguments for preventing emigration from the Scottish Highlands were accompanied by appeals to the emotional distress caused by emigration. The idea that emigration represented a form of 'exile' and was attended by an irreparable sadness and loss was reiterated across travel writing, political pamphlets and poetry. In her poem, 'The Highlanders', quoted above, Anne Grant decried the 'exile' of the Highlanders, and imagined their longing to return to their native land, and their pining for 'home'.[10] Writing to John Hatsell in 1806, she criticized her Edinburgh friends who believed that 'the Highlands should be instantly turned into a great sheep-walk and that the sooner its inhabitants leave it, the better for themselves and the community'.[11] From the perspective of critics like Grant, Selkirk's emigration scheme was a callous enterprise that doomed the nation's most vulnerable, but also most valuable, members to a state of 'exile', all for the sake of wealth and profit. Responding to Selkirk's *Observations*, James Gordon of Craig warned that emigration would inevitably lead to misery and distress: 'to the evils of indigence have been superadded the horrors of perpetual banishment'.[12] For Selkirk, however, his emigration project represented the only means of enabling the Scottish Highlanders to remain 'at home' in their culture, language and identity. Far from condemning his Highland recruits to 'exile', he understood their emigration as an escape from the alienation that ran concurrent to the spread of commercial society. In doing so, he offered a very different imagining of belonging in relationship to the boundaries of the British nation.

This chapter situates Selkirk's *Observations* in the context of elite debate about belonging and socio-economic development in relationship to the Highlands of Scotland. It asks what Selkirk's justification for, and his critics condemnation of, emigration can tell us about the discursive role of 'home' and 'exile' in imagining the Highlander's place in Britain's imperial future. The first section locates Selkirk in the intellectual, social and imperial contexts that enabled him to imagine and develop his settler-colonial project. I then turn to Selkirk's argument for emigration in relationship to the wider discussion over population growth and national belonging. The third section examines the idea of Highlanders as simultaneously 'homely' and yet unsuited to modern, British domesticity. The final section discusses the gendering of 'the Highlander' and the complete erasure of Highland women in the debate over Highland belonging to Britain and empire. Overall, the chapter argues that the discourse of 'home' and 'exile' in the debate over Highland emigration reconfigured the meaning of 'the Highlander', from a 'backwards' and 'barbaric' character, to a brave and patriotic, white settler colonist, whilst simultaneously reimagining the affective relationship between metropole and colony.

Thomas Douglas Selkirk: The making of an imperialist

Thomas Douglas was the fifth son of Helen Hamilton (*c.*1738–1802) and Dunbar Douglas (1722–99). He spent his early years on the family's Lowland Scottish estate in Kirkudbright, which his father inherited in 1744. Selkirk's mother spent much of her life pregnant or nursing until the birth of her last child in 1790, when she was fifty-two years old. His father was an 'improving' country gentleman, who used his lands to establish a model farm and develop agricultural techniques. He was also committed to Scottish independence and a supporter of radical Whig causes, including American independence.[13] Selkirk's parents sent him and his brothers to Palgrave Academy, the pedagogically innovative Dissenting school run by Anna Letitia Barbauld and her husband, Rochemont Barbauld. The Barbaulds' school catered for the sons of professionals, merchants and elites. Amongst them was Joseph Priestly's son, Joseph Priestley Jr., who would also grow up to lead a settler-colonial initiative.[14] Barbauld referred to Selkirk's eldest brother, Basil William Douglas, later Lord Daer (1763–94), as 'the finest boy; he is now the finest young man I know', she was similarly fond of, if not as effusive about, the younger brother.[15] After receiving his education at Palgrave, Selkirk went to the University of Edinburgh in 1785, where he studied under Dugald Stewart and became a member of the Speculative Society. He would have been familiar with his lecturer prior to his arrival; Stewart had taught his elder brother and was a regular visitor at the family residence, St Mary's Isle.[16] Although, at the time, Selkirk was fifth in line to inherit his father's title and property, his family was wealthy enough to support him on a tour of Europe in the early 1790s. This gave him an insight into the socio-economic situation in France in the midst of the French Revolution, as well as acquainting him with a number of French *philosophes,* including the Marquis of Condorcet (1743–94).

In 1799, Selkirk's own socio-economic situation changed radically and unexpectedly. Between 1794 and 1799, Selkirk's four older brothers, and his father, died in rapid succession, leaving him the heir to his father's estate. It was this inheritance that enabled him to purchase lands and embark on his project of settling Scottish Highlanders in Eastern Canada in 1803. The tragic, but financially fortuitous, deaths of Selkirk's older brothers were themselves tied-up with British imperialism. In 1794, in the midst of the French Revolutionary wars, Pitt's government sent military reinforcements to put down a series of rebellions launched by a coalition of enslaved Africans, 'free-coloureds', and French republicans in the Caribbean.[17] Amongst the 45,000 British soldiers who died from disease or fighting during that campaign were Alexander Douglas, who died in Guadeloupe in 1794, and Dunbar Douglas junior, who died off St Kitts in 1796.[18] A further Caribbean connection would later consolidate Selkirk's relationship, and his reputation, as a pioneer of settler colonialism in Western Canada. His marriage to Jean Wedderburn-Colville in 1807 connected him to a network of families whose fortunes derived from the ownership of estates and enslaved Africans in Jamaica.[19] In 1802, Selkirk's brother-in-law, Andrew Wedderburn, had inherited properties and land in Britain, and two estates in Jamaica along with their 'negro and other slaves, cattle and stock'.[20] He invested part of his inheritance in Hudson's Bay Company's stocks, and teamed-up with his new brother-in-law in a project to colonize the lands inhabited by Cree- and Athapaskan-speaking people in Western Canada.[21] Between his brothers' deaths in the Caribbean, and his brother-in-law's inheritance from the Caribbean, Selkirk's settler-colonial ambitions were enabled and consolidated.

Selkirk began his settler-colonial project in the early 1800s, setting his sights on a number of potential regions within the United States, including the disputed territory of Louisiana. In 1800, he purchased a tract of land at the mouth of the Great Salmon River in New York State with the intention of colonization.[22] What became of this piece of land is unknown, but it demonstrates Selkirk's involvement in land speculation almost immediately upon assuming his title and inheritance. His initial plans for a settler-colonial project, however, were not focused on Highland Scots, but on Irish Catholics. Selkirk had made a tour of Ireland between 1800 and 1801, when the country was recovering from a series of armed risings by a coalition of Catholic peasants, United Irishmen and French republicans that had begun in 1796, and reached its peak in 1798.[23] Pockets of resistance continued even after the Act of Union of 1800, which dissolved the Irish Parliament and merged it with Westminster. Selkirk would have been familiar with the events in Ireland through his brother, who was friends with one the leaders of the United Irishmen, William Drennan.[24] His plan to emigrate Irish Catholics to Louisiana was directly related to the events of the previous five years. In his proposal to the government requesting help with the costs of passage and settlement, he argued that by emigrating Irish Catholics he would be ridding Ireland of its 'most dangerous subjects'.[25] His proposal was turned down, and what little encouragement he received from Lord Pelham directed him to Scottish Highlanders, and to Epekwitk/Prince Edward Island instead.[26]

Nestled between what is today New Brunswick and Nova Scotia, Epekwitk was one of seven administrative districts that formed the Mi'kmaq's homeland of Mi'kma'ki.[27] In the 1600s, the Mi'kmaw began trading in furs with the French.

By the seventeenth century, French traders and missionaries had settled on Epekwitk and claimed it as part of the colony of Arcadia. The French relinquished official territorial claims as part of the Treaty of Utrecht in 1713, and in 1769 the British claimed dominion over the territory, naming it St John's Island, and subsequently Prince Edward Island. Throughout the period, the Mi'kmaq were involved in territorial and trading disputes with Britain and France. Yet, as in other parts of North America, Australia and the Pacific, the arrival of Europeans meant new diseases, the intensification of conflict, and the introduction of guns and alcohol, all of which radically changed, and in many cases destroyed, the lives of indigenous people. By the time Selkirk purchased land on the island, Mi'kmaw livelihoods and numbers had been much diminished.[28] In his diary of the first few months of the settlement, Selkirk noted that there were very few 'Indians' on the Island, and that those who did inhabit the island survived by hunting and fishing, selling their wares at the Charlotte Town market. These 'Indians', Selkirk claimed, were 'peaceable and harmless' and submitted to 'the authorities in the Island'.[29] Beyond this, his *Observations* made little mention of the indigenous Mi'kmaq or any other indigenous people. A brief claim that his own 'European settlement' had been established without the help of 'native American' people probably referred to white American settler colonists rather than to indigenous Americans.[30] Like the majority of his colleagues, Selkirk dismissed the significance, and all but erased the existence, of indigenous Americans.

Enlightenment, 'improvement' and population management

Selkirk was a young, white man at home in the world. Like the majority of his elite, male contemporaries, he believed in his ability to understand the world, and in his right to impose his own definition of 'progress' upon it. He inherited from his father a fascination with social engineering in the name of 'improvement'. Dunbar Douglas was well acknowledged for his ideas for exploiting Galloway's natural resources, including draining lakes to make use of the clay, the enclosure of land, and the use of marl and sea-shells as a fertilizer for grass.[31] His son, however, was more interested in improving and controlling people. Bumsted notes that at the age of only sixteen Selkirk had constructed a cottage and planned a plantation on his father's estates.[32] Ten years later, he helped to provide famine relief in Kirkudbright, by raising a subscription, assessing the needs, and subsequently distributing meal, to the poor. In his essay documenting the method and process of providing relief by means testing and rationing, Selkirk argued that the poor could be encouraged to change their consumption habits and behaviours, including their diet and modes of cooking, to accommodate the vagaries of the environment and economy.[33] The benefits of his system, he claimed, were not only material. Charitable contributions, rather than a tax, encouraged social harmony by fostering gratitude amongst the poor, and good will amongst the donors: 'The whole formed a chain of good offices, calculated to conciliate the affections of the lower classes of society, draw closer those bonds of union between the different classes of society, on which the stability of social order so essentially depends.'[34] A similar idea of encouraging social hierarchy and harmony would later underpin his settler-colonial plans. In *Observations* he argued against providing settlers with 'gratuitous rations' from the government, which he claimed discouraged labour and self betterment.[35]

Selkirk's interest in population management is also evident in his later critique of the slave trade. In 1807 he made a speech in the House of Lords in support of the Act for the Abolition of the Slave Trade. Refuting the argument that the importation of slaves was necessary because the Caribbean could not support population growth, he argued that the slave trade must be abolished in order to force planters to treat their slaves well. If planters were not able to work their slaves to death, then their numbers would increase according to the capacity of the land to support them.[36] Like Dugald Stewart, Maria Graham and Maria Edgeworth, Selkirk was less interested in the wrongs of chattel slavery as an economic system, and more invested in amelioration of enslaved Africans' conditions. Beyond this brief intervention into the debate over the trans-Atlantic slave trade, however, Selkirk said nothing about Africans at all. In his *Observations*, he made a brief reference to the Maroon settlement in Halifax, but did not comment on the presence of enslaved Africans on Prince Edward Island.[37] In both his discussion of poor relief and his speech supporting the abolition of the slave trade, Selkirk's focus was less on the welfare and well-being of either the enslaved or the poor, than it was on the 'problems' that they posed to the social and economic privileges of the ruling classes in, or from, Britain. Like Dugald Stewart, Maria Graham and Maria Edgeworth, he largely assumed that these privileges naturally accrued to the white, propertied classes of Britain and Europe as a result of their, presumably 'innate', superiority.

Selkirk's arguments about population management were grounded in Enlightenment theories of societal and economic development.[38] Population growth and its relationship to national wealth was a subject on which David Hume, Adam Smith and Adam Ferguson had written at length.[39] All three largely assumed that population growth was a sign of progress and improvement. In his essay, 'Of the Populousness of Ancient Nations', David Hume had stated that 'wherever there are most happiness and virtue, and the wisest institutions, there will also be most people'.⁴⁰ Adam Smith's *Wealth of Nations* developed this discussion to consider the relationship between food supply and population growth. In Smith's thesis, the cultivation and improvement of lands was the starting-point for exchange and transactions; the division of labour and the accumulation of surplus wealth were contingent upon the land yielding enough to feed a larger number of people than those who worked it.⁴¹ Drawing extensively on Smith, Dugald Stewart offered the first systematic course of lectures on Political Economy during the academic year of 1800–1801, which were published posthumously in 1855 as *Lectures on Political Economy*.⁴² His *Lectures* defined 'political economy' as encompassing not just wealth and population, but 'all those speculations which have as their object the great and ultimate end of all regulations, namely the happiness in improvement of political society'.⁴³ The study of Political Economy must, he argued, include the habits and customs of a society in order to ensure that they cooperated 'harmoniously' with legislation and promoted 'social order and happiness'.⁴⁴

Like the majority of Enlightenment philosophers, the boundaries of Stewart's definition of 'society' and 'nation' were ill-defined. As in his Moral Philosophy, he used non-European societies as a comparative back-drop against which to define the manners and customs of European societies. Thus, he contrasted the polygamous practices of 'negroes' and Pacific Islanders, with the monogamous nations of Christian Europe in general, and of Britain in particular. In Smith's thesis, the cultivation and improvement of lands was the starting-point for exchange and transactions; the division of labour and the accumulation of surplus wealth were contingent upon the land yielding enough to feed a larger number of people than those who worked it.⁴⁵ Despite their critiques of the actions of European colonizers, Scottish Enlightenment theories of population growth as a marker of happiness and 'human improvement' implicitly justified white settler colonialism. The ability of European settlers in North America to double their numbers every twenty-five years, especially in contrast to Native American numbers, was a sign of progress. This statistic originated from Benjamin Franklin's 'Observations Concerning the Increase of Mankind' (1754), in which Franklin argued that the growth in numbers of 'purely white' 'English' people was a sign of progress that should be encouraged by the metropolitan government.⁴⁶ This, Smith argued, was evident in the radically different pace of population growth in Britain, and especially the Scottish Highlands, and in North America. In the Highlands, despite high human fertility rates, the population remained low, and infant mortality high, because of the inability of the land to sustain greater numbers.[47] In North America, on the contrary, the white settler population was doubling every fifteen years due to the abundance of land.[48]

By the time Selkirk was writing, Malthus's *An Essay on the Principle of Population* (1798) had consolidated the idea that the availability of food necessarily checked population growth.[49] Like Smith, Malthus used the Highlands as an example of this 'natural' correlation between population density and resources: 'There is reason to believe that the poor and thinly inhabited tracts of the Scottish Highlands, are much distressed by an overcharged population as the rich and populous province of Flanders.'[50] Yet Malthus fundamentally changed the tone of the debate by calling into question the correlation between population growth, prosperity, 'progress' and 'happiness' that had been an underlying assumption in earlier scholarly works. As part of his critique of William Godwin's *Political Justice*, he offered a pessimistic account of the possibilities of either limitless agricultural improvement or any decrease in heterosexual desire that would check reproduction. In Malthus's account there would be no future utopia. Rather, periods of dearth, starvation and misery were inevitable, with the only silver lining being that hardship contributed to 'generate talents' and 'soften and humanize the heart'.[51] 'Evil exists in the world', Malthus concluded, 'not to create despair, but activity'.[52] In the first edition of his *Essay*, Malthus paid little attention to emigration; it was, he argued, an option that even the most desperate would take with the utmost reluctance.[53] As Alison Bashford has noted, his subsequent editions paid much closer attention to the implications of settler colonialism, and warned that 'driving into a corner where they must starve, even the inhabitants of these thinly-people regions, will be questioned in a moral view'.[54] Yet if Selkirk read Malthus's later, heavily revised, editions, he did not pay heed to Malthus's moral qualms about setter colonialism. Rather, he cited the 1798 edition of *An Essay on the Principle of Population,* referring to it as a 'valuable work' and invoking it to support his argument for the managed and voluntary emigration of Highland Scots.[55]

Selkirk's *Observations* drew on the general theory that population growth would constantly outstrip food supply, even where there was considerable agricultural improvement, in order to refute fears that emigration would depopulate the Highlands. At the same time, however, he argued that some element of depopulation was necessary for the Highlands to become economically profitable.[56] This question of how best to 'improve' the Highlands in order to align them with the socio-economic structures of the rest of the British Isles had a long history. Since 1745, when the Hanoverian state comprehensively defeated the second Jacobite rising that had begun from the outer Hebrides, the Highlands had been the target of aggressive state intervention in the name of 'improvement'.[57] Thirteen Jacobite estates in the Highlands were forfeited and placed in the hands of the Commission for Annexed Estates, who managed them on behalf of the Crown for 'the preservation of the publick [sic] peace and the further civilizing of the inhabitants of the Highlands of Scotland'.[58] The Commissioners, including Henry Home, Lord Kames, set about 'improving' the land and society through changes to rent structure and initiatives to claim peat bogs through drainage; their measures were largely unsuccessful. Amongst those landlords who retained their estates, incentives to improvement, including wool manufacturing and the spinning of linen, were provided through government-sponsored institutions, such as the Board of Agriculture.[59] From the 1780s, 'improving' landlords relocated peasants to coastal regions to make room for cattle rearing, to provide labour for newly established fisheries and to help develop the kelp industry.[60] Such measures had been recommended to the government by James Anderson in *Observations on the Means of Exciting a Spirit of National Industry* (1777), who argued that investing in sheep-farming and the wool industry inland, and fisheries in the coastal regions were the best means of developing the Highlands and Hebrides.[61]

Recommendations for investment in agriculture and manufacturing in the Highlands were given widespread support by elite travel writers, who argued that new opportunities would alleviate poverty and thereby also stem the tide of emigrants. Yet looking back on thirty years of investment to 'improve' the Highlands, Selkirk argued that none of these measures had been successful in bringing 'progress' to the region or meeting the needs of its growing population. The lack of markets, and the habits of the people, mitigated against any effort to establish industry. Until there was a considerable change in both, he argued, a rising population would be checked only by emigration, or else by starvation. This, Selkirk wrote, was a truth based upon the 'uncontrovertible general principles' that Malthus had established in his *Essay*.[62] At the same time, Selkirk argued against the idea that emigration would depopulate the Highlands. Responding to Alexander Irvine's *An Inquiry into the Causes and Effects of Emigration*, published in 1802, Selkirk claimed that if emigration were to be encouraged, those who remained behind in the Highlands, 'will find it so much easier to procure employment and subsistence', would be able to marry at a younger age, and so 'the natural increase of population will proceed with more rapidity, till every blank is filled up'.[63] He used statistical records compiled by Alexander Webster and Sir John Sinclair, to show that despite emigration levels, the population of the Highlands had, in fact, increased.[64] Amongst those who had emigrated to the colonies, too, population would increase at an even greater pace because of the abundance of fertile land. Overall, Selkirk argued, it was the *prevention* of managed emigration, rather than its encouragement, that would diminish the population of the Highlands.

In *Observations*, Selkirk challenged the received wisdom that emigration from the Highlands would have negative consequences both for emigrants and for the country they left behind. Based on an 'extensive' tour of the Highlands that he undertook in 1792, Selkirk determined that a key reason for the poverty and under-development of the Highlands was overpopulation. This, he explained using the well-established idea that Highland society occupied an earlier 'stage' in civilizational development, which was referred to by scholars, administrators and travel writers as both 'savage' and 'feudal'. Selkirk argued that whereas a 'superabundant population' had been integral to the structures of power during 'feudal times', the great numbers of people in the Highlands were a burden to economic progress, 'improvement' and the Highlands' integration as part of commercial society. A scheme of managed emigration was therefore necessary for the Highlanders and to the overall 'tranquility and permanent welfare of the kingdom'.[65] Ridding the Highlands of its surplus population would, Selkirk argued, encourage those who stayed behind to 'improve' their lands and align their manners with commercial society. Quoting Adam Smith, he stated that 'the diminution of cottagers, and other small occupiers of land, has in every part of Europe been the immediate forerunner of improvement and better cultivation'.[66] Neither was it just the Highland emigrants' absence that would prove useful to the prosperity of the British nation; by relocating to the precarious peripheries of the British Empire, the Highland emigrants would be transformed from an 'indolent' people to pioneer settler colonists who would ensure that 'our North American possessions may be peopled and brought into cultivation'.[67]

Highland emigration, exile and belonging

Selkirk's argument for managed emigration drew on a scholarly debate over population expansion, national prosperity and emigration that intersected with questions over who belonged to, and in, the nation. In the nascent field of Political Economics, scholars tended to define 'the nation' as coterminous with the political boundaries of the state. Yet disciplinary boundaries were fluid in this period; in other areas of enquiry the same scholars debated the evolution of national identity – referred to as 'character' – and its relationship to manners, custom and morals.[68] Thus, Hume's 'On the Populousness of Ancient Nations' (1742) assumed the coherence of national boundaries, which he later complicated in his essay 'Of National Character' (1748).[69] Similarly, but in reverse chronological order, in *The Wealth of Nations* (1776) Smith assumed a correlation between national and state boundaries for the purposes of focusing on economic wealth, whereas in his earlier *The Theory of Moral Sentiments* (1759), he had paid close attention to the ways in which sympathetic identification informed national character.[70] By the time Selkirk was writing, the role of 'sympathy' in national identity formation had been somewhat eclipsed by a focus on cultural homogeneity, and the idea of distinct 'races' that had roots in the distant past. As Chapter 2 argued, this idea of 'race' and the debate over 'racial' difference was fluid and often ambivalent. Scottish Enlightenment thinkers understood human societies to be inherently distinct – defined by their specific 'manners and customs' and anatomical markers of difference – and, at the same time, destined to follow the same path of socio-economic development, from 'savage' to 'civilized'. These various configurations of national belonging came together in the debate over Highland emigration, and in the question of where the Highlanders, with their distinct language and socio-economic structure, should be positioned vis-à-vis the broader British nation.

For English and Lowland commentators, the Highlands had long been considered a 'backwards' and 'barbaric' periphery. The Society in Scotland for Propagating Christian Knowledge (SSPCK), established in 1709, represented the Highlanders as 'rude, ignorant, and disaffected', enslaved by the 'feudal system', and guided by 'superstition' and 'popery'; it promoted investment in schools and churches in order to acquaint the Highlanders with the 'blessing of the late Glorious revolution'.[71] The SSPCK's model of intervention was given official sanction by the Commissioners for the Annexed Estates, who planned to use the revenues from forfeited Jacobite estates to fund schools, churches and prisons. These practical policies were underpinned by the idea that the Highlanders had failed to develop beyond the shepherding stage. After meeting a landlord in Glenmoriston, John Knox stated that 'his life seemed to be merely pastoral, except that he differed from some of the ancient Nomades [*sic*] in having a settled dwelling'.[72] By the 1780s, there was a general call for state intervention in order to enable the Highlanders to 'catch up' with the rest of the country. Dr James Anderson ended his letter to the government with an entreaty to 'add wealth and population to that district, and to furnish the means of rendering the poor inhabitants of those too long abandoned regions the most active, industrious, and productive citizens of the state'.[73] In *Observations upon Scotch Fisheries, Emigrations, and the Means of Improving the Highlands and Isles* (1794), Hugh Bell, an Edinburgh-based brewer and member of the merchants guild, argued that the state should provide special measures and investment 'for the weak and infirm part of the national family'.[74] Like many other critics of emigration, Bell's call for state intervention represented the Highlanders as the poor cousins whose belonging to the 'national family' entitled them to assistance.

At the same time, another discourse of difference created a more absolute distinction between the Highlanders and their Lowland and English neighbours. In 1765, James Macpherson published *The Works of Ossian*, ostensibly based on the discovery of the prose–poetry of a third-century bard, Ossian. Macpherson's *Ossian* provided 'proof' that the Highlanders were a 'race' separate from the Lowlanders and English, with an ancient, martial tradition and a refined sense of imagination. From the basis of his 'findings', Macpherson argued that the Gaelic-speaking Highlanders were the original 'race' of the British Isles.[75] This argument was disputed by Pinkerton who claimed that it was the English-speaking, Lowland Scots who represented the first significant presence in Scotland. The Highlanders, Pinkerton argued, were relative newcomers who had migrated across to the mainland from Ireland; their arrested development and poverty was a sign of the racial superiority of the 'Gothic', English-speaking Lowlanders.[76] *Ossian* was ultimately revealed to be a fabrication, a pastiche of poetry and myth that Macpherson had compiled, rather than a singular and original epic narrative. Yet the idea that the Highlanders were defined by masculine and heroic virtues continued to inform Scottish identity and, subsequently Romantic literature. Sir Walter Scott referred to Ossian in *Waverley* when he evoked the homo-social camaraderie of the hunt, whilst Anne Grant referenced the debate over racial origins when she claimed that the Highlanders were 'the most ancient, the most unmingled, and original people in Europe'.[77]

These contradictory discourses of difference informed Selkirk's rationale for recruiting Highlanders to act as settler colonists in North America, as well as the wider debate over the Highlanders, the meaning of their emigration and their place in Britain's future. Selkirk himself made no mention of Ossian, but his understanding of the Highlanders, and his justification for emigration, used a combination of stadial theory, which defined Highlanders as 'backward' and 'feudal', and Romantic nationalism, which idealized the Highlanders as an 'ancient' and 'noble' race. In *Observations*, Selkirk argued that 'little more than half a century has passed, since that part of the kingdom was in a state similar to that of England before the Norman conquest'.[78] Although this 'system' had now been abolished, he claimed that 'the customs that arose out of it are not forgotten' and could still be seen in the 'striking peculiarities' of the Highlanders in his own time.[79] Yet whereas the majority of critics of emigration argued that investment in the Highlands would help to consolidate the transition from feudalism to capitalism, Selkirk's proposal sought to arrest that transition:

> Admiring many generous and manly features in their character, I could not observe without regret that rapid decline in their genuine manners, to which the circumstances of the country seemed inevitably to lead. I thought, however, that a portion of the antient [sic] spirit might be preserved among the Highlanders of the New World – that the emigrants might be brought together in some part of our own colonies, where they would be of national utility, and where no motives of general policy would militate (as they certainly may at home) against the preservation of all those peculiarities of customs and language, which they are so reluctant to give up, and which are perhaps intimately connected with many of their most striking and characteristic virtues.[80]

Selkirk envisaged the relocation of the Highlanders as a way of ensuring the preservation of their 'antient [sic] spirit'. Unlike the majority of commentators, who advocated investment in the Highlands in order to help them to assimilate as part of the modern nation, his solution was to remove them from the British Isles, in order to ensure that they retained their distinctiveness. Only by emigrating, he argued, would the Highlanders be able to continue to practise their 'genuine manners'.

Selkirk's critics referred to his emigration scheme as 'unpatriotic', and likened him to the 'unscrupulous' recruiters who were intent on draining the British Isles of its peasantry and manpower.[81] The fear of losing Highland men, who were deemed valuable for their skills as soldiers, was particularly strong. Since the fourteenth century, Highlanders had served as mercenaries in Scandinavia, France, Ireland and the Low Countries; they had a well-established reputation for being fierce and brave fighters. By the 1760s, the Highlands had become a key recruiting ground – a 'nursery of soldiers' – for Britain's wars in Europe, America and Asia.[82] As Stana Nenadic has shown, Highland chiefs gained considerable status and financial rewards for recruiting soldiers from their estates.[83] The Jacobite, Simon Fraser of Lovat, for example, had his forfeited estates returned to him in 1770, after he raised a regiment of clansmen to fight in the French and Indian wars in North America in the 1750s.[84] Both 'at home' and in the British Empire, Highlanders were deemed indispensable to the defence of national interest. The heightened awareness of the threat of invasion during the French Revolutionary and Napoleonic wars raised concerns over the consequences of their mass emigration for the nation's security. In this vein, Alexander Irvine wrote, 'There is more patriotism in contributing to keep the people in their own country, to fight our battles in the time of need and defend every thing that is dear to Britons than in chafing away at the natural guardians of our privileges and independence, to seek an asylum on a foreign shore.'[85]

In *Observations*, Selkirk addressed the anti-emigration argument that a well-populated Highlands provided Britain with a 'nursery of soldiers'. He claimed that the peculiar martial strength of Highland men derived directly from their 'manners and customs'; their bravery was the characteristic 'virtue' of 'feudal times'. The Highlander's lifestyle was 'irregular', 'he' was accustomed either to extreme exertion, 'traversing the wildest mountains amidst the storms of winter', or to extreme idleness.[86] He held 'habits of regular and steady industry' in contempt. It was these character attributes that made the Highland man an excellent warrior, but a poor agriculturalist and contributor to commercial society.[87] As commercial society spread throughout the Highlands, Selkirk argued, so the 'established principles of loyalty', manners and customs of the feudal age would inevitably also decline.[88] The Highlander would be forced to adapt and change his manners, which would in turn undermine his military prowess. As they adapted to the 'coldness' of commercial society, so their 'manly and generous features' would be lost. 'Independently, therefore, of depopulation, that nursery of soldiers which has hitherto been found in the Highlands cannot continue.'[89] By emigrating to North America, however, the Highlander would be able to live according to 'his' own values, 'he' could retain the camaraderie of clanship, and aspire to the pride of property ownership. Whereas critics of emigration understood the Highland emigrant as 'lost' to Britain, Selkirk argued that by retaining 'his' ancient system and martial spirit, the Highlander would remain an attribute to the British Empire.

The loss of 'the Highlander' to the nation's defence was not just a question of military prowess. If the 'martial' spirit of 'the Highlander' would be lost as 'his' manners adapted to the luxury and greater 'effeminacy' of commercial society, so too would 'his' sense of loyalty to the nation. In *Observations*, Selkirk understood the 'improvement' of the land tenure system, and the development of industry and commerce in the Highlands to be critical to the future prosperity of the whole, British nation. This would inevitably entail stripping the Highlanders of their possessions and disabusing them of the sense of hereditary entitlement to lands that they had assumed under clanship. Not only would this transform their character, but it would also harbour a discontent that would be passed down across generations. To illustrate his point, Selkirk cited the historic grievances of Ireland, and noted that where 'irritation' was 'transmitted from generation to generation' it produced dangerous and lasting consequences.[90] As with his earlier proposal to emigrate Irish Catholic rebels to North America, Selkirk understood his Highland settler-colonial project as a means of 'ridding' Britain of potentially dangerous malcontents. The emigration of people who anyway had no sense of belonging and affection for Britain as a commercial society was, therefore, a means of ensuring the nation's future peace and prosperity. For the Highlanders to feel a sense of belonging, Selkirk argued that they required the permanent possession of paternal farms, which they deemed to be 'their just right'.[91] Despite their criticism of emigration, few commentators would have disagreed with the logic of Selkirk's claim; Pennant, Johnson and Irvine all argued that the Highlanders were emigrating partly out of resentment for their lost sense of status and entitlement to land.[92]

Elite representations of the Highlanders' ability to belong, and their particular forms of belonging, played an integral part in what was often an emotionally charged and deeply ambivalent debate over Highland emigration. Samuel Johnson expressed no surprise that, given the 'primitive' situation of the Highlanders and the poverty of 'pastoral life', the Highlander felt no 'strong adherence to his native soil'.[93] Yet he was in the minority; for the majority of writers on the Highland 'problem', including Selkirk, the Highlanders were understood to be particularly attached to native land because of their 'pastoral life'. 'No nation', wrote Alexander Irvine, 'has manifested a stronger attachment to their country, than the Highlanders have shown to their rude mountains, mossy wilds, and deep extending valleys.'[94] Representations of Highlanders as having a peculiarly intense sense of belonging drew on the Scottish Enlightenment stadial theory that was discussed in earlier chapters. In *The Origin and Distinction of Ranks* (1779) John Millar argued that in small, isolated, and 'primitive' communities, such as in the Highlands of Scotland, emotional ties were confined entirely to the clan and their own customs, 'their affections are raised to a greater height, in proportion to the narrowness of that circle to which they are confined.'[95] A 'savage', wrote Millar, 'is never without difficulty prevailed upon to abandon his family and friends, and to relinquish the sight of those objects to which he has been long familiar.'[96] In his lectures Political Economy, Dugald Stewart reiterated this point, using the Scottish Highlanders as an example of the intense attachment to native land and 'that particular spot where we are born' amongst more 'primitive' peoples.[97]

Homely Highlanders? Gender, whiteness and settler colonialism

The belief that 'the Highlander' was particularly attached to 'home' reinforced the idea that emigration was a tragedy for the Highlander, as well as for the Highlands. James Gordon addressed Selkirk directly when he stated that 'happiness, Sir, does [not] often follow in the paths of emigration'.[98] Anne Grant's poem, 'The Highlanders', portrayed Highland emigrants as consumed by the sadness of the loss of homeland:

> Come, trace with curious search what secret cause
> Each native's heart with strong attraction draws,
> Though wealth in happier lands her stores unlock,
> To cling with fervour to his native rock.[99]

Representations of emigration as a form of 'banishment', the ultimate tragedy that could lead only to sadness and despair, were not confined to the debate over Highland emigration. Both Oliver Goldsmith's 'The Deserted Village' and James Graham's 'The Sabbath' represented emigration in general as source of sorrow.[100] Popular political pamphlets, such as that written by Josiah Wedgwood in 1783 to his workers in Staffordshire, discouraged emigration on the grounds that it would lead to 'sickness and despair' borne of an 'unspeakable longing' for one's native country.[101] Like Wedgwood, Grant and Gordon defined emigration as an abject state of loss. James Grahame's poem 'The Sabbath' imagined the Scottish 'exiles' in 'desart [sic] land', whilst Irvine condemned those landlords who were 'driving' their tenants from 'home', 'to wander they know not where.'[102] In doing so, they configured the nation as the only space that could provide 'happiness', meaning and the possibility of a future.

Selkirk offered a different perspective on emigration, settler colonialism and the possibilities of belonging. Whilst he acknowledged that 'to emigrate implies a degree of violence to the strongest feelings of human nature', like Samuel Johnson he argued that when emigration was undertaken with people 'connected by the ties of blood and friendship' it was not an 'exile': 'The number of their friends or relations who have all gone to the same quarter, give it the attraction almost of another home.'[103] His own emigration initiative, he claimed, provided the evidence that emigration need not be a tragedy filled with loss and despair. Selkirk's first three ships, the *Dykes,* the *Polly* and the *Oughton,* set sail from the Western Isles in 1804, and arrived on Prince Edward Island between August and October, carrying 800 passengers predominantly from the Isle of Skye and Ross-shire. After a night spent at the Governor's House, he travelled to Belfast – 'an old French village' – and met his settlers 'scattered along about a mile of Shore' living in barns, 'hovels' and 'whigwams'. The 'picturesque appearance' of the encampment at night, and the zeal and warmth with which the settlers greeted Selkirk the next morning convinced him that his project of preserving the 'antient [sic] spirit' of the Highlanders would be a success: 'They came in general round me with a keenness & warmth that perhaps had a little resemblance to the old feudal times.'[104]

Whereas Selkirk's detractors understood him to be leading the Highlanders into a state of desperation and loss, Selkirk represented himself as rescuing the Highlanders, and their 'authentic' culture, from oblivion in the wake of the poverty and resentment over land expropriation that accompanied the arrival of commercial society in the Highlands. In fact, Selkirk's settlers joined a society that was as fraught with disputes over land tenure and power relations as the one that they had left behind. Since assuming control of the Island from the French, the British government had parcelled-out land to speculators on a relatively ad hoc basis with the criteria being the payment of a quit-rent to the local government. By the 1790s, the majority of landowners were absent from the Island and had failed to cultivate their lands and left their tenants without the means to do so. Critics of the system likened absentee landlords, who looked to their settler-tenants to pay rent without supporting them to improve the lands, to the oppression enacted by Highland chiefs.[105] (As Whitfield and Cahill note, those critics had little to say about the enslavement of Africans on the Island.[106]) The problems of land ownership surface at points in Selkirk's diary, which record brief snippets of negotiations with squatters, usually Loyalists, on land that had subsequently been purchased from the government, and references to the escheating of land. Selkirk also had some trouble convincing his settlers to stay; a group of emigrants from Ross-shire left to join relatives on other parts of the island, or took lands that they perceived to be better quality under different proprietors.[107] Furthermore, the settlers' own, self-styled 'chief' would fairly rapidly lose interest in the day-to-day lives of his followers; Selkirk spent less than two months on Prince Edward Island before travelling to Boston and then back to Britain to oversee the plans for his subsequent settler colonies in Baldoon and Red River. Much like the absentee chiefs of the Highlands, after his initial enthusiasm, he left the majority of the affairs to his agents.[108]

Despite the initial setbacks, Selkirk was optimistic about the future of his settlement. Whilst he did not deny that life in the immediate aftermath of arrival was difficult, he believed that his own method of settling the emigrants and allotting them plots of land would ultimately ensure that they felt a sense of belonging to it. Ensuring that the plots were laid out so that they formed small 'hamlets', each within a mile of each other, Selkirk attempted to alleviate the bewilderment and 'childlike' state that accompanied emigration. Their proximity to each other and their ability to work collectively, he argued, would prevent them from 'sinking under the gloomy impressions of the wilderness', and to develop a sense of belonging and investment in the land: 'As soon too as each has a little done on his own land & has got a little into the custom of looking on it as his own, attachment to spot will arise, & the satisfaction of looking on an independent & permanent property – the pride of being Lairds will keep them firm.'[109] This pride in property and the feeling of belonging that accompanied it was, Selkirk claimed in *Observations,* 'natural to the human breast, and particularly consonant to the antient [sic] habits of the Highlanders'.[110] By 'cultivating' and 'cherishing' this spirit, much as one would tender to saplings newly planted in the ground, the Highlanders would soon get over their loss and develop roots and attachments to their new environment. To illustrate his point, he used the example of a settler of 'very moderate property' from the Isle of Skye, who had named his new property after 'the antient [sic] seat of his family' and was working hard to ensure that 'the House of Auchtertyre' lived up to its once-noble name.[111] The attachment of the Highlanders to their new location proved, in Selkirk's interpretation, that it was not place of birth and environment that informed emotional attachment. Rather, a man's ability to establish himself and his family on land, and to own and improve that land, was key to configuring a sense of belonging. In this respect, the settler colony was not a space devoid of meaning and emotional ties, but a holding space for those members of 'British' society whose future did not accord the nation's 'progress'.

Selkirk's vision for Highland settler colonists rested on the establishment of families on land and their joint efforts to develop, and take pride in, their property for future generations. Yet he made absolutely no mention of Highland women or children in his *Observations* and in his unpublished diary. In his diary, Selkirk noted that the *Polly* had '280 full passengers & nearly 400 souls', where 'full passengers' may refer here to adult males, meaning that at least 120 passengers were women and children.[112] This would accord with the passenger list for the *Oughton,* which sailed to Selkirk's second settlement to Baldoon in 1804 with forty-four female passengers, just under half the total number of passengers on board the ship.[113] Selkirk was not alone in excluding women and girls from his discussion of Highland emigration. Critics of emigration, including Irvine, Gordon and Brown, all assumed 'the Highlander' to be male:

'Every one flatters himself, that if *he* could get once more abroad, *he* would have all *his* wants supplied, and *his* wishes gratified in a moment.'[114] Similarly, when Romantic writers lamented the 'plight' of the Highlander, 'exiled' from native land and doomed to wander alone through the wilderness, they imagined a nominally male figure. Even Anne Grant, who used her position as a woman living in the Highlands to give legitimacy to her observations on Highland culture, referred to 'the Highlander' as 'he'.[115] The absence of women in the debate over Highland emigration had important implications for representations of Highland belonging to Britain, and the Highlanders' future as settler colonists in the British Empire in general, and British North America in particular.

As contemporary travel writers noted, women played an important, and in some cases dominant, role in Highland society in the eighteenth century. In her autobiography, Elizabeth Grant (1797–1885) recalled the grandmothers, aunts and maids who looked after her and her brother during their childhood in the Highlands on the family estate of Rothiemurchus, Strathspey.[116] As Stana Nenadic has discussed, many wealthy widows and spinsters provided the funds for younger male relatives to purchase commissions in the army; the 'nursery of soldiers' was reared and supported by women.[117] At lower socio-economic levels, women played an active role in the household and village economy. During his travels in the Hebrides, Thomas Pennant observed men and women working alongside each other to break up sods, and made frequent mention of women's work growing potatoes, making butter and cheese, manufacturing wool, spinning flax, salting herrings, cutting and grinding corn, and distilling whisky.[118] In his *Tour through the Highlands,* John Knox noted that women from the Isle of Mull would travel to the Lowlands to shear during the harvest, and that even in the winter both women and men ventured down to Inverness or the Coast from Ross-shire, Caithness and Sutherlandshire to purchase provisions.[119]

The absence of women and girls in the discussion over Highland emigration, and the contrast with their presence in Highland travel writing, informed the discursive configuration of difference, belonging and British nationhood. By absenting Highland women and girls from the discussions of emigration and colonial settlement, Selkirk and other writers on Highland emigration imagined the settler colony as a male-dominated, 'masculine' space, whilst the Highlands themselves, once 'manly' and 'martial', became marked as feminine. This feminization is most evident in Wordsworth's 'To a Highland Girl', which explicitly situates the female Highlander in a landscape uninhabited by men: 'Remote from men, thou dost not need/Th' embarrass'd look of shy distress.'[120] On one hand, Wordsworth's expression of admiration for the 'Highland Girl's' 'homely' 'innocence' represents this solitary landscape as a utopia, where the girl is unencumbered by the artificial social graces of commercial society. On the other hand, the absence of men makes 'natural' reproduction impossible, signified in Wordsworth's other poem by the solitary girl's never-ending and thus unresolved song of 'sorrow, loss, or pain'. Ultimately, although Wordsworth expresses his desire to linger with the Highland girl, whether as lover, brother, father or simply spectator, he makes it clear that the 'Sweet Highland Girl' and the 'lonely place' she inhabits have no future in his own world.

If, in Wordsworth's poetry, the Highland girl stood in for a Highlands left behind by progress, other poetry and print-media employed the figure of the lone female in order to lay emphasis on the sadness of emigration. In 'The Deserted Village', Oliver Goldsmith lamented the 'poor houseless shivering female' who had left behind a life lived modestly in a rural 'cottage' to sell sex in the town: 'Now lost to all; her friends, her virtue fled/Near her betrayer's door she lays her head.'[121] William Cobbett's newspaper *The Porcupine* reported stories of 'young, handsome girls' sold into slavery upon their arrival in America, and of an Irish weaver, who arrived 'without a farthing' in America, forced to sell his daughters.[122] In these brief mentions, women were represented as the passive and pitiful victims of sexual exploitation. Their loss of virtue was symbolic of the loss of the simple, innocence of rural life as Britain's peripheries became absorbed into commercial society, and its people evicted from the land, and lost to the nation's future. Their plight was in contrast to the simple, 'homely' warmth of the rural village, whether in Ireland or the Highlands of Scotland. This 'homeliness' reinforced an idea of an idyllic countryside, untainted and uncorrupted by commercial society. References to the 'white slave trade' in Cobbett's newspaper consolidated the idea that emigration was a state of complete abjection.[123] The idea of the 'white slave trade' looked back to an earlier period when European travellers were considerably more vulnerable to captivity, but also created a sense of scandal by placing white people in closer proximity to blackness. Ironically, then, it was the emigration of the Highlanders that brought them into the fold of whiteness.

That the Highlanders became 'white' through their emigration and physical exclusion from British society is clear from the very tone of commentators writing on the socio-economic situation of Highlanders living in the Highlands. Unlike the idealized image of homely Highlanders that was painted in the literature on emigration, travel writers remarked on the lack of comfortable homes and used that lack to demarcate the Highlands from the wealthier, more 'civilized' Lowland regions of Scotland. In her travel narrative, for example,

Dorothy Wordsworth remarked on the transformation of the quality of the houses compared to the Lowlands: 'Here we first saw houses without windows, the smoke coming out of the open window-places.'[124] Her brother, despite his romantic portrayal of the Highland wilderness, referred to Highland houses as 'Hottentotish', thus associating them more with Africans than with white, British 'civilization'.[125] Indeed, by the time the Wordsworths were writing, the material differences between Lowland and English, and Highland, houses had become a generic marker of Highland poverty and difference. Edward Burt, and James Boswell (with Samuel Johnson) all insisted on their right to enter, uninvited, into the homes that they referred to as 'huts' or 'hovels' in order to witness their 'misery' in close quarters.[126] Selkirk himself made little comment on the dwelling-places in the Highlands themselves, but paid close attention in his diary on the types of accommodation used by settlers and the indigenous Mi'kmaq on Prince Edward Island. The whigwam was, he wrote, made of 'large pieces of birch bark', supported by poles and 'set conically and a hole left at the top for the smoke'.[127]

In Selkirk's narrative of the progress of his settlers, the transformation from 'whigwam' and 'huts' to houses served as a signifier for the transition from a 'savage' to a 'settled' and 'civilized' existence. The settlers' initial encampment comprised 'hovels or whigwams, built oblong like the roof of one of our European Cottages, and thatched in general with spruce boughs'.[128] Once they had established themselves on plots of land, they relied on the insights and experiences of earlier immigrants to the Island. Selkirk recorded the advice of Father McEachern, the Catholic priest on the Island, who recommended that houses be initially built small ('12 feet square'), quickly, and with basic materials of wood and stone.[129] More substantial structures with chimneys and stoves could be built later, when the settlers had decided on the best location for their dwelling. In *Observations*, Selkirk wrote that the lots were laid out in small groups of 'four or five families, and sometimes more, who built their houses in a little knot together' where 'the distance between the adjacent hamlets seldom exceeded a mile'.[130] Selkirk's description of small, close-knit settlements comprising homes inhabited by kin 'who sometimes carried on their work in common or, at least, were always at hand to come to each others' assistance' represented a romantic vision of rural, peasant life.[131] Much of this reconstruction of a rural was, in fact, of Selkirk's own imagining, which reflected more on his desire to represent his settlement as reinventing of a rural fantasy than the messy realities of both colonial land settlement, and the complex social lives and material conditions that the Highlanders had left behind them.

Conclusion

For elite writers, the Highlander's incorporation into whiteness came at the point at which 'he' could be recuperated into the project of imperial expansion and no longer represented a threat to Britain's path of 'progress'. The discourse of 'exile' enabled this transition by denying the Highlander any alternative form of belonging beyond the nation, whilst simultaneously refusing 'him' a place in Britain's imperial future. Selkirk, like other Romantic writers, represented the Highlands as a region trapped in a past time, which could not progress except through the penetration of a 'foreign' influence, which would then destroy its authenticity. The Highland present thus became defined only by the echoes and ghosts of what it had once been, whilst 'the Highlander' 'himself' gained his belonging to Britain through the sacrifice of both land and life in the service of imperial expansion.[132] The use of 'exile' in the poetry and critical writing on Highland emigration had a similar effect of reducing the 'authentic' Highlander to a past that cannot be retrieved, whilst simultaneously denying 'him' any possibility of future attachments. In her poem, 'The Highlanders', Anne Grant bitterly lamented the 'banishment' of 'the Highlander', but represented the Highlander's 'exile' from Britain's social landscape as conclusive: 'No tie to love the alter'd land remain'd/Where beasts were free, and free-born men restrained ... Unus'd to imposts new, or customs strange/ Now through the mourning island all is change.'[133] Whilst Grant insisted that the Highlander would not renew 'his' affections for the 'alter'd land', she did not offer any sense of possibility for the cultivation of alternative forms of emotional attachment. Rather, she portrayed the emigrant Highlanders as fixatedly looking backwards to 'his' lost, native land, and emotionally clinging 'with fervor to his native rock'.[134] Grant's answer to the apparent inevitability of 'progress' was simply to immortalize the spectre of loss, whilst denying the Highlanders any alternative form of belonging.[135]

In contrast, Selkirk's solution was to remove the Highlanders from out of the path of progress and thus preserve 'his' 'manly virtues' that signified an earlier, less 'civilized' age. The failures of his project reveal some of the ways in which affective forms and socio-economic structures combined to construct the meaning and boundaries of white British-ness. Towards the end of his *Observations*, Selkirk noted with disappointment that 'after two or three years' the Highlanders appeared to return to 'their old habits of indolence' rather than accumulating more property 'by a continuance of active industry'.[136] This outcome threatened to undermine his argument earlier in *Observations*, that life as a settler colonist would enable the Highlander to feel the 'pride' of property and thus lift 'him' out of the habit of 'extreme indolence'. Instead of revising his hope that the Highlanders could be made 'useful' to an industrializing, imperial nation and commercial society, however, Selkirk attributed this apparent lack of 'ambition' to a problem with the structure of tenure, rather than 'of any inherent disposition'.[137] If the tenures could be re-negotiated, Selkirk implied that the Highland settlers would act with renewed vigour to ensure their future prosperity and that of the nascent settler colony. In many respects, however, the Highlanders' apparent refusal to conform to the 'progress' was exactly what Selkirk had used to justify their emigration and to preserve their 'manliness' and 'gallantry'. These tensions in Selkirk's representation of his emigration scheme encapsulate the wider contradictions of belonging to both Britishness and whiteness. For the Highlanders to belong to both the nation state and the wider 'race' was possible only if they were to conform to the socio-economic norms of 'commercial' society. Difference, in this context, was acceptable only to the extent that it could be harnessed to the interests of capitalist imperialism.

5

Colonial knowledge and the making of white masculinity in Bombay

At 10 'o clock on 20 July 1811, an East India Company sepoy, James Estelow, was hung on the gallows outside the Common Prison in Bombay for what the sentencing judge, Sir James Mackintosh, described as the 'wonton murder of a poor native at Goa'.[1] Estelow's execution, which was witnessed by 'fifty thousand natives' and 'most of the European inhabitants', was the first, and only, case of capital punishment in Bombay under Mackintosh's judicial authority.[2] He had begun his tenure as Recorder of the Court of Bombay with the intention of avoiding the use of capital punishment and of focusing his energies on reform of the police and the jail instead. Yet Estelow's crime, and his failure to show any remorse or to profess any religious beliefs, reassured Mackintosh that 'a more worthless life could not have been sacrificed to the interest of society'. With 'a calm and steady regard to the interest of society', he signed his death warrant.[3] In his journal, the judge made no comment on Estelow's victim, referring to him simply as a 'mean Hindoo', yet he lingered on the identity of the man who, he wrote, had 'died by my doom': 'His name was James Estelow. He was born at a place called Herington in Warwickshire. This place I cannot find in any map or account of the country in my possession.'[4] Mackintosh's inability to locate Estelow on his map of England encapsulates a wider anxiety amongst elite, British commentators about the identities of those who circulated around Britain's imperial sites. As with Scottish Highland emigrants, the status of British men (and some women) who spent most of their lives in India as soldiers, merchants and clerks to the East India Company was a subject of debate. To what extent were these men and women living on the peripheries of empire really be considered British, and how could they be encouraged to act and identify with Britain and whiteness?

For British imperialists, India presented a very different socio-economic and political context compared to North America or the Caribbean. In the latter, widespread massacre of indigenous peoples by Europeans in the sixteenth and seventeenth centuries, as well as their very different relationship to property, left land and resources open to occupation and exploitation. In India, the Mughal Empire's system of governance and resource extraction represented a much more familiar and identifiable political structure for Europeans trying to understand the operations of power. The Mughal emperors had a structure of land ownership, taxation, law and allegiance that looked broadly similar to those that operated in Europe; by the early nineteenth century East India Company officials perceived them to be similar in form to 'feudal' Europe.[5] It was largely this distinct system of governance that prevented European powers from engaging in the kind of settler-colonial practices that defined the Americas. Although in both continents Europeans began the process of colonization by embedding themselves in local trade networks, the kind of inter-marriage between Europeans and indigenous peoples that was present in early colonial America was extremely rare in India.[6] This did not mean that Europeans, including the British, in India did not engage with local peoples or customs – as the next chapter illustrates, the adoption of Indian cultures proved increasingly controversial. Yet the combination of inter-marriage and outright massacre followed by land-grabbing was less a feature of European imperialism in India. Instead, the British East India Company relied on establishing trade agreements with local rulers, pushing the boundaries of those agreements, whilst fortifying, and finally asserting dominance through war, or the threat of war.

By the late eighteenth century, the British East India Company had established control over much of north-eastern India, including Bengal, Bihar and Orissa after the defeat of Siraj-ud-Daula and the granting of the *diwani* by the Mughal Emperor, Shah Alam, in 1765. The right to tax the lands of the extremely fertile Bengal Delta provided the foundation of the Company's rise to prominence in India, with disastrous consequences for the Indian peasantry.[7] It was partly the horrific death toll during the famine of 1770 that led to calls in metropolitan Britain to call company servants' actions to account. In *Wealth of Nations* (1776), Adam Smith noted the devastating impact of European trade and colonization on the indigenous peoples of both the East and West Indies. The 'discovery' of America and of the route to the East by the Cape of Good Hope represented, Smith stated, 'the two greatest and most important events recorded in the history of mankind'.[8] Yet for the 'natives' of each region, the benefits of commerce that should have accrued to all parties had been 'sunk and lost in the misfortunes which they have occasioned'.[9] In India, he argued, these 'misfortunes' derived from monopoly and from the fact that the rulers had no interest in the welfare of the ruled:

> It is a very singular government in which every member of the administration wishes to get out of the country, and consequently to have done with the government as soon as he can, and to whose interest, the day after he has left it and carried his whole fortune with him, it is perfectly indifferent though the whole country was swallowed up by an earthquake.[10]

Yet for the metropolitan government and for the East India Company, British settlement appeared more risky than mis-government and oppression. Discussions over the possibility of promoting British settlement, and thereby a sense of identity with the region and society itself, were foreclosed out of fear of the possibility of a repeat of the American situation.[11]

Whereas elite commentators on the Scottish Highlands worried about the implications of permanent emigration for a people deemed peculiarly attached to 'home', for East India Company servants it was their lack of belonging to anywhere that posed a problem in elite imaginaries. In his 'Speech on Mr Fox's East India Bill' (1783), Edmund Burke had denounced Company servants as young men, 'boys almost', who had left home too early to imbibe 'English' principles and morality. Drawing on Adam Smith's notion of sympathy, Burke represented Company servants as 'birds of prey and passage' whose rootlessness meant that they had no emotional connection with, and therefore concern for, the plight of those whose lands they 'plundered'.[12] Like Smith in his critique of European enslavers in the Caribbean, Burke placed East India Company servants outside of the boundaries of belonging to Britain and Europe. Yet whereas Smith contrasted 'brutality and baseness' of the enslavers with the 'magnanimity' of the enslaved, Burke used the discourse of wandering to create a moral distinction between oppressor and oppressed. The victims of East India Company servants' tyranny were not, Burke claimed, 'gangs of savages, like the Guaranies and Chiquitos who *wander* on the waste borders of the river Amazons, of the Plate'. Rather, the people who they displaced and dispossessed through their plunder were 'for ages cultivated and civilized', comprising men of ancient pedigree, including 'princes once of great dignity authority, and opulence' and a 'nobility of great antiquity and renown'.[13] Using the same moral discourse of 'wandering' that served to undermine, or assert, the humanity and the rights of indigenous Americans, enslaved Africans and emigrant-colonists from the Scottish Highlands, Burke reiterated a moral binary around the idea of a settled and permanent sense of 'home'.

This chapter examines changing representations of India in relationship to changing ideas of racial difference and national belonging in the eighteenth and early nineteenth centuries. Drawing on Mackintosh's letters to friends and patrons from Bombay, his journals documenting his day-to-day activities, and his official reports and addresses to Bombay's imperial class, this chapter examines the ambivalences of race, nationhood and belonging in early nineteenth-century colonial India. It focuses on Sir James Mackintosh's attempt to promote a sense of shared belonging to Britain as 'home' and instil amongst his colleagues in Bombay a particular set of values that he associated with being simultaneously white, European and British. The first section situates Mackintosh in the context of changing ideas of India borne, in part, of Scottish Enlightenment understandings of racial difference, as well as its critiques of imperial monopoly. It then turns to examine the ways that these intellectual debates informed Mackintosh's representation of Bombay's colonial society and his discourse of reform. Finally, the chapter considers Mackintosh's attempt to encourage his 'European' colleagues in Bombay to identify with whiteness and to disseminate a sense of belonging to Britain as 'home' through the establishment of a white, male-only Literary Society, which would, seventeen years after his departure from Bombay, become the Asiatic Society of Bombay. As in the philosophical works discussed in previous chapters, 'white', 'European' and 'British' – or, more commonly, even amongst Scots in India, 'English' – were often used interchangeably to denote belonging to a higher level of civilization. This chapter discusses the slippages between these identities and the role that their conflation played in constructing a racialized form of belonging that could be harnessed to imperial rule in India.

India in the Scottish Enlightenment imagination

Sir James Mackintosh hailed from the Highlands of Scotland, where he was born in 1765 and brought up by his mother, Marjory (née Fraser, d.1778) and aunts in a small village called Clune on the family's estate of Kyllachy.[14] His wider family, part of the wider Clan Chattan, were no strangers to both the perils and the opportunities of British-imperial expansion. Like many Highland Scots, part of the Mackintosh clan had joined the Jacobite cause in 1745; their property was forfeited by the state when the Hanoverian state claimed control over the Highlands in the aftermath of Culloden. In this context of political instability, the Clan Chattan drew on already-established connections to empire.

Mackintosh's maternal relatives, the MacGillivrays, had long-standing links to South Carolina, where they forged trading connections and intermarried with the Muscogee people of that region.[15] His paternal relatives had economic ties and business links to India, in part through a cousin, L. Mackintosh, who had settled in Calcutta after years on board the East India Company's China ships and with whom James Mackintosh briefly corresponded whilst living in Bombay.[16] Like many Highland Scots, therefore, Mackintosh was aware of Britain's imperial exploits and colonial conquests overseas from a very young age. His father, as well as many of his uncles, spent the majority of their lives away from the Highlands, serving in Germany in the Seven Years' war, in Gibraltar (where his mother accompanied her husband and where she died) and in Antigua and Dublin. As noted in the previous chapter, the collapse of the Scottish Highlands as a discreet site of socio-economic power transformed this generation of elite Highland men from chieftains to the military officers in the service of British-imperial expansion.

Born twenty years after the 'Forty-five, James Mackintosh knew little of the world prior to English dominance over, and erasure of, Highland socio-economic structures and culture. Marked out for his academic potential from a young age, he attended King's College, Aberdeen and Edinburgh University, where he studied medicine. Although in his autobiography, written from Bombay in 1804, he suggests that he had arrived independently at his Whig sentiments, it is likely that James Dunbar, who taught him in Aberdeen, and the wide circle of Scottish Enlightenment Whigs who he encountered in Edinburgh, informed his political views and identity.[17] He was, he claimed, an ardent supporter of American independence, despite the fact that his uncles, including Brigadier General Fraser, fought for the Loyalists. A member of the Speculative Society in Edinburgh, Mackintosh occupied the same social and intellectual circles as Dugald Stewart, the Earl of Selkirk, and Maria Edgeworth, and was well-read in Scottish Enlightenment philosophy. By the time he graduated from Edinburgh and left Scotland for London, he was fully immersed in the Anglo-Scottish Whig network that spanned the British Empire.[18]

Mackintosh first came to political and intellectual prominence with the publication of *Vindiciae Gallicae* (1791), a defence of the early French Revolutionaries against Edmund Burke's *Reflections of the Revolution in France* (1790). His intervention used Scottish Enlightenment Moral Philosophy to argue for the need for the reform of British, as well as French, political institutions. Drawing on Hume, Mackintosh argued that the aristocratic rulers in France lacked any sympathetic identification with the nation and had therefore lost the ability and legitimacy to rule.[19] His attribution of political change to 'general causes', rather than to individual actions, and the importance he placed on commerce in driving change, reflected his Scottish education.[20] Like the majority of his friends, Mackintosh subsequently retracted his support for the Revolution as it turned increasingly radical, and deferred to Burke's more conservative position. His philosophical thought is therefore better encapsulated in his 1797 lectures, 'On the Law of Nature and Nations' in which he put forward an argument for the existence of a universal moral framework:

> It shall be my object, in this preliminary, but most important part of the course, to lay the foundations of morality so deeply in human nature, as to satisfy the coldest inquirer; and, at the same time, to vindicate the paramount authority of the rules of our duty, at all times, and in all places, over all opinions of interest and speculations of benefit, so extensively, so universally, and so inviolably, as may well justify the grandest and the most apparently extravagant effusions of moral enthusiasm.[21]

In his belief in man's ability to discover moral laws through sustained observation and study, Mackintosh's general philosophical approach almost exactly followed Dugald Stewart's, discussed in Chapter 2.[22] It was this belief in a universal moral framework that he took with him to Bombay, and which would inform his perspective on Britain's role in India.

Prior to his departure for Bombay in 1804, Mackintosh's understanding of India reflected wider Enlightenment representations of 'the East' as an ancient and unchanging civilization, which was ruled according to a specific type of 'Oriental' despotism. This representation owed much to Montesquieu's *Spirit of the Law* (1748), which cited Pliny to argue that commerce – 'the communication of people' – had never, even in Antiquity, taken place between Europe and the Indies: 'The Indies have ever been the same Indies they are at present; and in every period of time, those who traded to that country must carry specie thither, and brought none in return.'[23] Montesquieu's work laid the foundations for the idea of 'Oriental despotism', characterized by a lack of progress and change, and of passivity and effeminacy, that he attributed to India's heat.[24] For Montesquieu, 'Oriental despotism' was a specifically 'Eastern' form of rule, which applied to the whole of Asia with little distinction between the different types of society that existed across the continent and in contrast to the 'enlightened', progressive despotisms of Europe. The concept played an important role in Scottish Enlightenment characterizations of India. In *An Essay on the History of Civil Society* (1767), for example, Adam Ferguson stated that 'it is in India, and in the regions of this hemisphere, which are visited by the vertical sun, that the arts of manufacture, and the practice of commerce, are of the greatest antiquity, and have survived, with the smallest diminution, the ruins of time, and the revolutions of empire'.[25] Alexander Dow, who published the highly influential 'Dissertation on the Origin and Nature of Despotism in Hindostan', an appendix to his translation of Firishtah's *History of Hindostan* (1768–72), also drew heavily on Montesquieu to argue for the connection between climate and despotism.[26]

Despite Hume's critique of climate theory, and emphasis on 'sympathy' over climate in determining national character, Montesquieu's general argument remained highly influential as an explanation for Indian character and society well into the nineteenth century. For India in particular, the political discourse of 'Oriental despotism' intersected with a racialized and gendered discourse that constructed a homogenous 'Hindu' race, as feminine and weak. In 'A General Idea of the Government and People of Indostan' (1753), Robert Orme drew on Montesquieu to argue that it was the peculiar 'weakness' and 'effeminacy' of the 'original people' of India that enabled them to be ruled by the Mughals, who he defined as 'the descendants of those Moors or Tartars, who under the command of Tamerlane conquered Indostan'.[27] In his 'Dissertation', Dow attributed the heat of the climate to the 'phlegmatic sentiments' of the people of India, which led them to prefer a life of 'indolence' under the 'evils of despotism' than to work for their own freedom. It was the 'indolence' and 'effeminacy' of this 'race of men', Dow argued, that enabled rulers such as Shah Jahan to govern through the fear, rather than through the respect and love of his subjects.[28] These works informed the better-known Scottish Enlightenment representations of India and Indian society. In *An Historical Disquisition Concerning the Knowledge Which the Ancients Had of India* (1791), William Robertson attributed Europeans' sense of superiority to the 'effeminate appearance' and 'unwarlike spirit' of the 'natives of India'.[29] Mackintosh adopted the same characterization of 'Hindus', referring to them as the 'meek and servile natives of Hindostan, who preserve their ingenuity, their skill, and their science, through a long series of ages, under the yoke of foreign tyrants'.[30]

Like Robertson, Mackintosh's early mentions of India represented the 'Hindoo race' as one of the highest and earliest forms of civilization in the world. The opening up of scholarship on India represented, he argued, a 'vast addition' to 'the stock of our knowledge of human nature': 'The records have been partly opened to us of those mighty empires of Asia where the beginnings of civilization are lost in the darkness of an unfathomable antiquity'.[31] Although early travel writers had expressed fascination for, and opinions about, the multifarious religious practices and beliefs in India, it was not until the late eighteenth century that Europeans began learning and engaging with Sanskrit texts. Increasing European-colonial knowledge of India – from Dow's 'Dissertation', to H.B Haldhed's *A Code of Gentoo Laws* (1776), to James Rennell's 'Memoir of a Map of Hindostan' (1782) – provided further examples for theories of human development, as well as complicating and developing those theories.[32] In his 'Discourse on the Law of Nature and Nations' Mackintosh credited the work of the philologist and lawyer, Sir William Jones, 'who has laboured so successfully in Oriental literature'.[33] President and founder of the Asiatic Society of Bengal and judge in the Supreme Court in Calcutta, Jones promoted the study of Indian history, culture and languages, praising Sanskrit as a language that he claimed was 'more perfect than the Greek, more copious than the Latin, and more exquisitely refined than either, yet bearing to both of them a stronger affinity, both in the roots of verbs and in the forms of grammar, than could possibly have been produced by accident'.[34] As Colin Kidd has argued, this was as much a theological as it was a philological argument: Jones's argument for the shared linguistic roots of Sanskrit, Persian, Greek and Latin supported his monogenetic argument for the shared foundations of Hindu, Christian and Jewish origin stories.[35]

The study of Indian languages linked questions of human difference to questions of the nature and extent of East India Company rule in India. In his essay, '*On the Origins of Language* (1767), Adam Smith had argued that language provided an insight into the development of social structures and ideas, which gained in complexity as society itself advanced. It was from the development of language that it was possible to conjecture the development of ideas, and of human societies and institutions.[36] The 'exquisitely refined' languages of India were, therefore, a sign of a highly 'cultivated' society, in which the 'state of things', in Stewart's words, were 'so wonderfully artificial and complicated'.[37] In his lectures on Moral Philosophy in 1801–2, Stewart praised the advanced state of Indian civilization, stating that 'the Hindoo is but a discoloured European'.[38] The choice of 'discoloured' points to the fact that, regardless of their admiration for India's ancient culture, neither Stewart nor any of his colleagues viewed the two 'races' as equal in their own times. Despite his high praise of Indian culture, Jones maintained Europe's superiority and talent, stating that 'the Athenian poet seems perfectly in the right, when he represents Europe as a sovereign princess and Asia as her handmaid ... reason and taste are the grand prerogatives of European minds, the Asiaticks have soard [sic] to loftier heights in the sphere of the imagination'.[39] As Chapter 2 argued, thisdivision between reason and imagination played a constitutive role in justifying the supremacy of white Europeans as the only 'race' capable of progress.

The contrast between the 'rational' 'English' (or 'European') and the 'irrational' unstable 'Oriental' enabled the construction of the emotional and intellectual boundaries of whiteness and belonging to European 'civilization' both within and outside the geo-political boundaries of Europe. Within British political discourse, references to generalized 'Oriental' or 'Asiatic' manners and modes of rule connoted a lack of progress and freedom that, in the European Enlightenment imagination, operated in contrast to 'European' character. Commentators on the socio-economic differences in the Scottish Highlands, for example, likened the Highland peasantry to 'Turkish vassals' who were, wrote John Knox, 'thoughtless of futurity' and 'oppressed in proportion to their improvements'.[40] In *Vindiciae Gallicae* Mackintosh critiqued Louis XVI's attitude to the States General, stating that he spoke to them, 'not as the Chief of a free nation to its sovereign Legislature, but as a Sultan to his Divan'.[41] Similarly, in her critique of Burke's *Reflections on the Revolution,* Mary Wollstonecraft likened Burke's argument for hereditary titles to a brahmin's justification for the maintenance of the caste system.[42] Her better-known *Vindication of the Rights of Woman* (1792) referred to the treatment of women in England as 'Mahometan'.[43] All of these arguments rested on the assumption that readers would automatically associate the 'East' with backwardness and tyranny. This was also Maria Edgeworth's assumption in her story, 'Lame Gervas', in which she characterized Tipu Sultan, ruler of Mysore, as childish and prone to a 'violence of temper, and its sudden changes from joy to rage'.[44] The aim of Edgeworth's story was to show that 'an obscure individual, in a country like England, where arts, sciences, and literature, are open to all ranks, may obtain a degree of knowledge which an eastern despot, in all his pride, would gladly purchase with ingots of his purest gold'.[45]

The discourse of 'Oriental' difference directly informed debates over the character and extent of East India Company's power and rule in India, and the nature of East India Company servants' belonging to Britain. These debates, which reached their height in the impeachment trial of Warren Hastings in 1788, saw the discourse of Eastern 'despotism' and 'tyranny' brought 'home' to metropolitan Britain. Hastings's impeachment trial was based on twenty articles condemning him for bribery, receiving gifts, breaking agreements with Indian princes and forcibly insisting on treaties. Overall, Burke and Richard Sheridan accused Hastings of violating the principles of both British and Mughal (widely referred to as 'Mahometan') law and of ruling despotically and arbitrarily.⁴⁶ In his defence, Hastings claimed that he was governing according to the character and tenets of the Mughal constitution, and in accordance with indigenous custom.⁴⁷ At stake here were less the fortunes of people in India, and more the implications that East India Company misrule held for the idea of Britain. For Mackintosh, who was present at the opening of the trial, the trial itself illustrated the illustriousness of the British nation and particularly of that 'most enlightened audience' who crowded into Westminster to watch its opening proceedings. 'The most enlightened nation on earth', Mackintosh wrote, was called upon to witness and bring to justice the wrongs that oppressed millions of people on the other side of the world.⁴⁸ The violations and excesses of colonial rule were thus embodied and quarantined in the single character of Warren Hastings, who Mackintosh referred to as 'the most powerful and execrable despots that ever insulted heaven with his crimes'.⁴⁹

Like the majority of Scottish Enlightenment thinkers, Mackintosh was critical of aspects of the European-imperial project. His earliest statements on imperialism in India drew heavily on Smith's *The Wealth of Nations*, which critiqued the atrocities committed by Europeans against the 'natives' of both the East and West Indies. Company monopolies, Smith argued, actively prohibited progress by restraining or destroying the production of goods – including spices and opium – in order to prevent competition, and by preventing European settlement and thereby the spread of 'progress'.⁵⁰ In the *Vindiciae Gallicae,* Mackintosh reiterated Smith's argument when he applauded the National Assembly's renunciation of foreign conquest, stating that colonial possessions had been 'unanswerably demonstrated to be commercially useless, and politically ruinous'.⁵¹ Writing to John Whishaw from Bombay in 1808, Mackintosh argued that the Company was complicit in the corruption of its employees:

> The general policy of the Company and its government is to bury such enquiries in obscure committees, and in the few cases where enquiry is made to do no more than send the most flagrant offender home to enjoy his fortune with credit. Indeed, one of these persons suspended here for peculation after one of the private enquiries has been sent back by the Court of Directors and recommended for promotion!⁵²

The fault, he concluded, lay in 'the darkness of monopoly' that obscured every act from judgement by the public.⁵³

Yet whilst Mackintosh's critique of monopoly and of the need to reform the Company remained constant before and after his residence in Bombay, his experiences of living in India, including his tour of the Deccan plateau in the aftermath of the Second Anglo-Maratha wars (1803–5), made him rethink his broader condemnation of European-imperial expansion. Writing to John Moore only a few months after his arrival in Bombay, he stated:

> English power really seems to me to be a blessing to the inhabitants of India. Yet the English government, without a community of interest or of feelings with the governed, is undoubtedly very bad, if it be compared with the second-rate governments of Europe. But, compared with an Indian government, it is angelic; and I conscientiously affirm, that the most impartial philanthropist ought to desire its preservation.[54]

Two years later, he wrote to the Gilbert Elliot, who would soon be appointed governor general, stating that whilst he disapproved of the 'means by which this vast empire has been acquired' he nonetheless believed that 'this Revolution has been every where beneficial to the body of the people and has bestowed on them a degree of security to which they and their ancestors in their most boasted days were strangers'.[55] In Mackintosh's mind, English governance, however, 'corrupted' by Asiatic despotism remained far superior and preferable to any other form of rule. His role as Recorder of the Court of Bombay was, therefore, to further extend English forms of governance and law, and in doing so to bring 'civilization' to the 'most obscure outpost' of the British Empire. Reorienting East India Company servants' sense of belonging and identification away from India and towards 'England' as 'home' played a fundamental role in this project of imperial reform.

The transformation of Bombay

Mackintosh's foremost aim during his seven-year residence as Recorder of the Court was to get rich. Neither the inheritance, and subsequent sale, of his father's estate in Inverness-shire, nor his second wife, Catherine's (née Allen) dowry, had provided him with enough capital to afford the lifestyle of a metropolitan intellectual. A short residence in India would, he hoped, enable him to make enough money to pay off his debts and to save for his family's future back 'home' in Britain. The position provided a salary of £5,000 per year, and the promise of a pension at the end of five years' service, enough, he believed to secure a 'farm to furnish bread for my family in the event of political convulsions'.[56] In this respect, Mackintosh was little different from the majority of his countrymen who went to India in the service of the East India Company. As Margot Finn has illustrated, many Scots from landed and merchant families looked to India as a means of retaining or regaining family fortunes during a period in which the demographic boom, material growth and social aspirations placed considerable economic strain on families.[57] At the very pinnacle of this hierarchy were men such as Lord William Cavendish Bentinck, Governor of Madras and subsequently Governor General of Bengal, who hoped to return 'home' with a fortune of £200,000, which would enable him to return to England assured in his position amongst the landed aristocracy.[58] At the other end of the scale were those who had been impressed into the East India Company army and served as sepoys in its wars; men such as James Estelow, along with the Indian sepoys alongside whom he served, have left barely a trace in the historical record. Yet despite the radical socio-economic differences between them, Bentinck, Mackintosh and Estelow were all positioned in the same web of exploitation of Indian peoples and resources that was fundamentally changing the socio-economic and political landscape of the Indian subcontinent.

Unlike the majority of men of Scottish, Irish, English and Welsh heritage living in India, Mackintosh's position was not sponsored by, or part of, the East India Company. Rather his role was to represent the Crown and hold the Company accountable for its actions in Bombay. From the 1770s, the state's support for the renewal of the East India Company's charter was conditional upon a series of reforms designed to exert greater control and regulation over the Company's military, financial, judicial and trading activities. Parliamentary acts, beginning with the Regulating Act, endeavoured to define the limits of the Company's jurisdictional power vis-à-vis the Crown, as well as Mughal-imperial authority. The former was the immediate result of a credit crisis that had left the East India Company unable to pay its shareholders and offered the government the opportunity to assert greater control in the Company's affairs in India.[59] It asserted the state's rights over all territorial acquisitions overseas and recognized Parliament's right to control Indian affairs. The governor of Bengal became the governor general with power over the Bombay and Madras presidencies in relationship to war and peace with Indian states. A decade later, in 1784, Pitt's India Act established a Board of Control above the Court of Directors, which controlled the military and civil governance and revenues of British territories in the East Indies.[60]

Mackintosh's arrival to take up the position of the Recorder of the Court was one significant symptom of regulatory changes. The Recorder's Court had been established by charter in 1798, with only one judge, Sir William Syer, having served before Mackintosh. The court replaced the Governor's Court, which dealt with criminal matters, and a Court of Requests, which looked at small cases. Fraught with difficulties and dissension, these institutions had been replaced in 1798 by one Recorder's Court, led by a barrister of five years' standing who was to be the head of the Court, responsible for criminal and civil cases in the Recorder's Court, judging ecclesiastic and admiralty cases.[61] The Recorder's Court was under the superintendence of the Supreme Court at Calcutta and itself superintended over the smaller civil courts, the courts of Adawlut, at the district level. Criminal and civil jurisdiction applied to all inhabitants within the Town and Presidency limits and all British subjects in factories or employed by the Company. Questions concerning land, rents, goods and contracts between parties were to be dealt with according to the party's caste and religion, preserving the authority of the heads of families amongst the natives. This final clause meant that 'native' households were dealt with as single units with their heads, in effect, having jurisdiction and free reign over their families.[62] The court therefore employed British law for European subjects, Parsis and Christians, and Hindu and Muslim law depending on the religion of the defendant and the nature of the offence.[63] Meeting quarterly for civil and criminal business, each term comprising twenty days, totalling 110 days per year, Mackintosh worked with a jury of 'European' men and a number of 'native' servants who determined and translated the laws of their respective religions.[64] As a court of oyer and terminer, it covered treasons (except high treason), misdemeanours and felonies, as well as dealing with cases of contract, succession and inheritance.[65] Its establishment marked the increasing centralization of control from Calcutta and ultimately London, and the standardization, codification and Europeanization of legal procedures across India.

Although Bombay had acted as the Company's headquarters in Western India since 1687, regulation and centralization came later to Bombay than to the Madras and Bengal Presidencies.[66] At the beginning of the nineteenth century, Bombay's position as part of the British Empire was in the process of consolidation and its economic viability was in doubt until after 1820, when the East India Company conquered and ceded Gujarat and exploited cotton and opium production.[67] The small governing community of 'English' merchants was more closely allied with, and reliant on, indigenous trade networks than in either Calcutta or Madras. In their private capacity, Company servants acted as agents, borrowing from Indian financiers, lending to Indian merchants, trading in cotton, piece-goods, precious stones, spices and currency.[68] Business connections depended on Indian banking networks and other 'English' agency houses across India. A large number of Hindu merchants alongside a minority of Jews, Muslims, Armenians and Parsis lent money to the Bombay government. These 'shroffs' were essential to the smooth running of trade between Calcutta, Bombay and China. Throughout the eighteenth century, their trade in silk, piece goods and bullion had connected Surat to Calcutta, Bombay and the Middle East.[69] In 1804, however, a decree from the Court of Directors stated that Bombay's civil servants give up their private commercial pursuits or resign their Company positions. The decree saw the transformation of Bombay's government from one dominated by the concerns of private merchants to an administrative government more closely aligned with the British Empire in India as a whole.[70] As Robert Travers has argued, this meant transforming 'suspect mercantile frontiersmen' into 'respectable pillars of empire'.[71] Mackintosh himself played a fundamental role in the attempts to effect that transformation by promoting a vision of white 'British' identity amongst his colleagues in Bombay through two, key channels: police reform and the Bombay Literary Society.

Upon his arrival in Bombay in 1804, Mackintosh had ambitions of bringing 'civilization' to a far corner of the British Empire, whilst also gaining enough wealth to ensure his return 'home'. His plans for this project revolved primarily around the 'European' community, whose manners and morals he attempted to improve in the hopes that they would set a better example to the 'natives' over whom they wielded political power. The idea that India contaminated 'British' or 'English' (he used the terms interchangeably) principles pervaded Mackintosh's personal and official correspondence. Writing to George Moore within a few months of his arrival in Bombay in August 1804, Mackintosh stated that 'the mind seems very materially changed by crossing the sea' and proceeded to describe the 'debility in understanding' that afflicted the 'Anglo-Indians' in Bombay.[72] In a letter to Sharp, he reiterated this point, stating that 'the English of this settlement are not improved like maderia by their voyage'.[73] It was less the voyage itself, however, than the length of time that a person had spent in India that Mackintosh held responsible for their 'degeneracy'. Mackintosh met the 'degeneracy' of English character armed with a belief in the existence of a universal moral which was best demonstrated, and had been best preserved, in 'the constitution of England'.[74] By consolidating English law and structures of governance in Bombay, Mackintosh perceived himself to be bringing universal morality and thereby progress to an 'obscure corner' of empire. At the same time, he used the opportunity to experiment with new ideas of governance drawn partly from the utilitarian ideas of Bentham and Dumont.[75]

Over the seven years during which he resided in Bombay, Mackintosh attempted a number of reforms that he hoped would prove beneficial to Bombay's society.[76] Amongst them was the reform of Bombay's police and prison system. On his arrival in 1804, he set up an enquiry into the structure and function of the police in relationship to law and order on the island and then wrote a report based upon his findings. In this 1811 report, Mackintosh stated that Bombay was governed by 'power without law', 'the greatest inconvenience that can befall any community'.[77] 'A Superintendent of Police may arrest forty men in the morning; he may try, convict and condemn them in the forenoon; and he may close the day by exercising the Royal prerogative of pardon towards them all.'[78] Ultimately, he concluded, 'the whole of what is called the Police has been a course of illegality'.[79] Tracing this 'course of illegality', Mackintosh looked comparatively at English imperial expansion in America and the 'East'.[80] In the case of the former, legislation was vested in a colonial Assembly 'on the same principles with the Parliament of England'.[81] In the 'Eastern dominions of Great Britain', where 'obscure factories' had suddenly turned into a 'great empire', legislation had been slow, ad hoc, and out of character with 'English' principles.[82]

By referring constantly to the virtues of English principles of justice and liberty and contrasting English 'liberty' with 'despotism' in general, Mackintosh made it clear that the current, 'corrupt' regime of policing in Bombay was the antithesis of 'Englishness'. Indeed, he even pointed to England's 'superior regard for the principles of law and liberty' to explain the length of time it had taken for the abuses of the police system to be corrected.[83] At the same time, however, it was this reluctance to impose 'law and liberty' and to base the police on 'British' principles that had led to the problems in Bombay's police system. That reluctance, Mackintosh stated, was understandable. Legislation in Bombay had been established under the shadow of the disputes with the American colonists over the imposition of laws and taxes that led to American independence, 'which naturally created a dread of colonial legislation'.[84] Reiterating Smith and Burke's critique of East India Company servants, Mackintosh also noted that a colony of 'mere sojourners' could not rule with any 'steadiness' or consistency. Ultimately, it was due to Providence and to English strength of mind that the abuses of power had not, in fact, been much worse: 'The numerous and wholesome restraints of laws, of juries, or a vigilant Bar and an enlightened public, with which the wisdom of our ancestors has surrounded an English Judge' had, he claimed, disarmed 'the most depraved disposition of the power to do much evil'.

A much worse abuse of power would have taken place, Mackintosh suggested, amongst the 'native community where the rich are unscrupulous and the poor are unresisting'.[85]

Although the most grievous acts of corruption within the police force had been enacted by British men, Mackintosh blamed the overall problems with Bombay's police system on 'Eastern' influence. His recommendations for reform constructed an absolute difference between men he referred to as 'Europeans' and 'natives'. Emphasizing the need to ensure the police system's 'Europeanisation', Mackintosh demanded that the police force gain legality by following the proper procedures that would lodge Bombay firmly in the web of empire, connecting it to empire through Calcutta to London.[86] His main recommendation, however, was the continuous presence of 'one of the principal English gentlemen of the community', who would act as a public magistrate, which he claimed 'will always be a sufficient security against oppression'.[87] The position of high constable should be bestowed on a 'European of tried integrity' and a 'considerable number of Europeans' sworn in as constables.[88] The power of convicting on small offences would lie with the Justices of the Peace of the petty session, otherwise they would be referred to the Grand Jury.[89] Mackintosh's recommendations placed emphasis less on the constant watch by a police force that had been made-up predominantly of native 'peons', and more on the moral character of upper-middle-class 'Englishmen' to act as an example. Side-lining the fact that it was the 'English' rulers in Bombay who had established the system of policing that was discovered to have been so corrupt and illegal, he ultimately placed the blame on the 'natives'.[90] Indeed, Mackintosh argued, the abuse of power was itself made possible by the fact that there were only a 'handful of timid natives' rather than an 'enlightened public'.[91]

Mackintosh's representation of Indian people as 'timid' drew on, and furthered, Enlightenment stereotypes of 'the East' as irrational and unmanly. His court-room speeches, published in the *Bombay Courier*, contrasted the 'natives of India' with other nations to create a hierarchy of emotional and intellectual character:

> The natives of India, though incapable of the crimes which arise from the violent passions, are beyond every other people of the earth addicted to those vices which proceed from the weakness of natural feeling and the almost total absence of moral restraint ... They are not actively cruel, but they are utterly insensible. They have less ferocity perhaps than most other nations, but they have still less compassion.[92]

Using the court as a platform, trials constructed 'native' character and mores that were implicitly – and sometimes explicitly – contrasted to 'British' or 'European' characteristics. Honesty, integrity, a masculine fortitude and courage were articulated through claims that Indians were inherently dishonest, weak, and lacking in both self-restraint and compassion. Addressing the Jury in October 1806, Mr Thriepland, a barrister in the Recorder's Court, reiterated Mackintosh's representation of 'native' character when he discussed the rarity of highway robbery in India to 'native' character. Lacking the 'daring and determined spirit of villany', the 'boldness as well as depravity' that existed amongst the 'lower classes of Europeans', the 'natives' of India were, Thriepland implied, too cowardly to risk such an offence.[93] In doing so, Thriepland reinforced an increasingly prevalent notion of the weak, mean and timid 'native' in contrast to the manly and determined 'European'.[94] For Mackintosh, these typecasts informed and justified policies that placed 'English' law, and nominally 'English values' at the centre of colonial governance.

Mackintosh's critique of 'native character' was not new, but his insistence on bringing the character and structures of English law to colonial India marked a turn in imperial policy towards what has been referred to as 'Anglicisation'. By the early nineteenth century, the idea that East India Company governance should follow Indian – both Hindu and Muslim – law and custom was eclipsed by the promotion of governance that was more aligned with nominally 'English' and Christian 'values'. These views were most explicitly promoted by Charles Grant, a Highland Scot and subsequently Chairman of the East India Company, who had made his fortune from the silk trade in Bengal.[95] His *Observations on the State of Society among the Asiatic Subjects of Great Britain* (1792) was written from the basis of over twenty years' residence in India and reprinted by the House of Commons in 1813, when the Company's charter was up for renewal. *Observations* documented what Grant believed to be the 'depraved' character and morals of Hindus in general, and Bengalis in particular. A Christian Britain, he argued, had an obligation to deliver the Indian people from 'oppression and injustice', 'on account of the benefits we draw from them, the disadvantages they have suffered, and must still in certain ways suffer from their connection with and the relation in which they stand to us as our subjects'.[96] His solution was to bring morality, respect for law, and thereby 'happiness' to the people of India through instruction, in English, in the 'useful arts' (agriculture, mechanics, etc.) and especially in Christianity. Concluding, Grant stated that 'we cannot renounce them without guilt, though we may also contract great guilt in the government of them'.[97]

Mackintosh disagreed with Grant's views on any official sanction for Christian missionary involvement in India, writing to the earl of Minto that any attempt to promote the Christian religion would lead to the 'destruction of our reputation for good faith (and probably our power) in India'. Yet he concurred with the broader tenets of Grant's argument, especially the idea of promoting instruction 'through colleges and other seminaries of instruction' so that 'their minds should be gradually enlightened'.[98] Without this initial step, Mackintosh argued, it would not be possible for Indians to 'understand the sacred truths we taught them'.[99] In the meantime, it was also necessary for the 'English' themselves to set an example of English and Christian 'virtues' for Indians to follow, an example that was rarely to be found amongst Bombay's 'European' community. Continuing his letter to Minto, Mackintosh stated that 'a sufficient information should be made in the principles and demeanour of the English in India to lead them to think we were serious in our belief of those truths which we endeavour to inculcate, and that we were sincere in our adoration of that God whom we invited them to worship'.[100] His own experience suggested that the 'principles and demeanour' of the 'English' or 'European' community in Bombay were far from offering models of Christian virtue. Writing in his journal about a number of criminal cases over which he had presided as judge – the conviction of two men for offences 'which it is not common to name' and another two cases of cruelty by husbands towards wives – Mackintosh referred to the 'monstrous depravity' of Bombay's small colonial community.[101] The fault, he stated, lay 'in the contempt of all order and authority which the mean character of the government has inspired'.[102] Elsewhere, however, he blamed the Indian climate and culture for the un-English character of the 'English' living in Bombay: 'Every Englishman who resides here very long has I fear his mind either emasculated by submission or corrupted by despotic power. Mr Duncan [Governor of Bombay, dates] may represent one genus, the brahminised Englishman. Lord Wellesley [Governor-General of Bengal, dates] is indisputably at the head of the other, the sultanised Englishman.'[103]

Mackintosh's critique of these two high-ranking administrators of the East India Company, as well as his dismissal of the 'Anglo-Indian' community in Bombay, drew on wider popular discourse of the 'nabob' (a vulgarization of the Persian word for 'ruler' – 'nawab') that had circulated in the British press since the mid-eighteenth century. Plays such as Samuel Foote's *The Nabob* (1772) firmly established East India Company merchants as uncouth 'upstarts', corrupted and 'orientalised' by their exposure to India and Indians.[104] Mackintosh's critique of his colleagues in Bombay did little to undermine that image. At the same time, in his attempts to bring 'English' principles to Bombay's Anglo-Indian community, he set himself up as a harbinger of both 'civilization' and 'Englishness'. In 1805, he wrote to Dugald Stewart, stating that 'I have attempted to do something here by going very much out of my own province. I have tried a Literary Society – but I fear it is only "singing the Lord's song in a strange land"'.[105] His use of a biblical metaphor for a literary and intellectual endeavour is illustrative of the intersections between Christianity, whiteness and notions of 'civilization' that pervaded liberal imperial agendas. No less zealous than the missionaries of whose incursions into India he disapproved, Mackintosh spoke to the Literary Society of the 'victories over barbarism' that their quest for knowledge would effect.[106] For Mackintosh, the Literary Society would not simply be a forum for reporting a wide range of knowledge of India, it would also represent an attempt to 'illuminate and *humanise* the whole race of man'.[107] Stating that the society must be founded upon 'principles of equality' within it, he nonetheless made it abundantly clear that Europeans, 'as detachments of the main body of civilised men' occupied a superior position amongst 'the whole race of man'.[108]

The men that Mackintosh gathered together in 1804 comprised the upper echelons of Bombay's 'European society', occupying the higher positions of the East India Company.[109] In his 'Opening Discourse', Mackintosh acknowledged the influence of the Asiatic Society of Bengal and praised its founder, Sir William Jones, who had 'surpassed all his contemporaries and perhaps even the most laborious scholars of the two former centuries, in extent and variety of attainment'.[110] Yet he lamented the fact that Jones 'seldom directed his mind to those subjects the successful investigation of which confers the name of a "philosopher"'.[111] Dismissive of the interest and value of Jones's orientalism, Mackintosh regretted that he had focused exclusively on 'antiquities'.[112] His muted critique of Jones's intellectual approach in the 'Discourse' was amplified in his private correspondence to friends in Britain. Like Grant, Mackintosh doubted the extent to which India could ever have been considered to have attained a high level of civilization. In his letter to Dugald Stewart, he expressed his disbelief that India could ever have achieved the philosophical and literary sophistication that Jones had accorded it: 'I am not altogether without apprehension that we may all the while be mistaking the hyperbolical effusions of mystical piety for the technical language of a philosophical system.'[113] Unlike scholars, such as William Hodges, who praised the high level of skill in India's ancient architecture, Mackintosh described the temples of Aurangabad, Dowluttabad and Ellora, as 'fantastic, massy and monstrous'. Rather than revealing a once-great culture, they merely bore 'the general character of Eastern art' in which 'the object is to display power'.[114] Writing to Sharp, he dismissed the 'antiquities and mythologies' of India as 'Eastern trash', and assured his friend that he had no intention of 'dabbling' in Orientalism.[115]

Whereas William Jones had encouraged his Asiatic Society to investigate, 'whatever is rare in the stupendous fabric of nature', Mackintosh laid out a research path for his own Literary Society that was based upon 'utility' – the investigation into the 'physical' and 'moral' sciences.[116] Rather than engage in the study of Indian antiquities, Mackintosh guided the members of the Literary Society to pursue mineralogy, botany, to record the 'variations of temperature' and its impact upon health. He urged them to 'transmit, through their immediate superiors, to the scientific depositories of Great Britain, specimens of every mineral, vegetable, or animal production which they conceive to be singular, or with respect to which they suppose themselves to have observed any new and important facts'.[117] In what he termed the 'moral' sciences, Mackintosh outlined a programme of research based upon 'the science of Political Economy'.[118] Above all, Mackintosh promoted the collection of statistical information – 'the numbers of the people; the numbers of births, marriages, and deaths; the proportion of children reared to maturity' (etc.).[119] Encouraging the members of the Society to draw up statistical surveys, Mackintosh promoted such investigations as potentially offering up a fascinating study into the ways in which the 'principles of political economy' might be applied beyond Europe.[120] The aim was to promote that 'useful knowledge' that would have the 'tendency to promote quiet and safe improvement in the general condition of mankind'.[121] Thus, in an unpublished paper entitled 'Observations relating to the population of India', Mackintosh outlined the questions that needed to be researched in order to understand the happiness of the 'natives' in Salsette. Such an understanding could then be used to consider the best methods of taxation on the population.[122] Writing to Sharp, Mackintosh stated that if nothing else, he hoped 'to seek out of it [the Literary Society] at least a good statistical account of Bombay which being the only one ever given of a tropical country will be a novelty very acceptable to political economists'.[123]

The research agenda that Mackintosh set for himself and for the members of the Literary Society is illustrative of the wider relationship between knowledge, imperial expansion and colonial governance. This relationship is made evident in an 1815 review article of Elphinstone's *An Account of the Kingdom of Caubul* alongside Claudius James Rich's *Memoir on the Ruins of Babylon,* was published in the *Edinburgh Review,* almost certainly authored by Mackintosh. The review concluded by praising these publications, as much for their insights into regions that had been previously little known to Europeans, as for what they suggested about the nature of British-imperial rule. 'Meritorious publications by servants of the East India Company have, in our opinion, peculiar claims to liberal commendation' for they symbolized the superiority of the men who governed; men who were more 'sensible and honest' than any who 'could fall to their lot under the government of their own or of any other nation'.[124] Like Mackintosh's address to the Bombay Literary Society, the review suggested that colonial knowledge formed an integral part of the performance of British superiority over Indians, and thereby their right to govern in India. The project of colonial knowledge formation was thus an intrinsic part of the wider project of 'civilizing' the manners and habits of his colleagues in Bombay.

Yet Mackintosh's aim for the Literary Society was not solely about gathering the knowledge necessary for British-imperial governance and the exploitation of resources. Rather, it was as much a means of forging the identities of those in the upper echelons of Bombay's 'European' society. Replicating the clubs and societies to which Mackintosh had belonged in Scotland and England, the Bombay Literary Society functioned as a way of promoting the performance of belonging to 'European civilization'. Thus, Mackintosh began his 'Discourse' on the opening of the Literary Society by constructing his audience as a community of 'Europeans' and as 'civilized men', who shared a common relationship to geographical space and to civilizational stage:

> I hope that we agree in considering all Europeans who visit remote countries, whatever their separate pursuits may be, as detachments of the main body of civilised men, sent out to levy contributions of knowledge, as well as to gain victories over barbarism.[125]

Imagining 'Europe' to be the epicentre of 'civilisation', he conceptualized 'civilisation' geographically in a hierarchy that spanned space as well as time. This conceptualization is further illustrated in numerous disparate comments that fill Mackintosh's diaries and writings from Bombay. Reading about the history of Corsica, for example, Mackintosh was astonished to learn that 'a race so barbarous existed in western Europe' and attributed this barbarity in such close proximity to the epicentre of civilization to its position on 'the frontier between Christendom and Barbary ... most exposed to the Mahometan pirates'.[126]

In his 'Opening Discourse' to the Literary Society Mackintosh promoted a sense of belonging to 'European civilization' amongst its white, male membership, including at various points the Scottish historians of India John Malcolm, William

Erskine and Mountstuart Elphinstone. For Mackintosh himself, however, the Literary Society offered an opportunity to performatively enact his own, superior belonging to metropolitan Britain as 'home'. Encouraged by friends who claimed to be speculating on the 'moral and literary improvement' that would result from his residence in Bombay, Mackintosh represented himself as the harbinger of 'civilisation' to those 'European' men who could spread its efforts further into India itself.[127] In doing so, Mackintosh imagined himself as the bridge between 'Europe' and 'India', informing the members of the Literary Society what it was that 'Europe' wanted to know.[128] Writing to Sharp, he stated that 'I have been obliged [by whom he does not say] to allow Gentz and Camille Jourdan to insert a notice in the German and French Journals announcing that I am here ready to help the literati of the Continent in their enquiries concerning India.'[129] Positioning himself as the 'mouthpiece of Europe', Mackintosh constructed a distance, as well as a hierarchical relationship, between himself and the other members of the Literary Society.

Even as Mackintosh admitted to friends that there were some 'ingenious men' amongst his society, he nonetheless constantly emphasized the inferiority of his 'European' contemporaries in Bombay in relationship to himself and his friends 'back home' in metropolitan Britain. Writing to his wife, Catherine Mackintosh, in 1810, he spoke of his 'unavailing efforts' to establish a 'circle of followers' who might promote 'civilization', and imagined himself as the father of a future community of scholars: 'You will not suppose me mad enough to compare myself with Swift,' he wrote, 'but in considering the small set of friends whom he made after his return to Ireland it is curious that the grandsons of two of them should in forty years become so conspicuous as Sheridan and Grattan.'[130] At the same time, however, he complained of the lack of sophistication amongst the men who surrounded him. Reading Mountstuart Elphinstone's manuscript on the history and geography of the Afghan kingdoms, he again commented that 'the more I read the writings of the ablest men in distant dependencies the more I see how inevitable the language is lost in a colony'.[131] Seeing language as a mirror of the world around him, Mackintosh saw the loss of the English language as the loss of refinement that was a significant part of a 'civilised' character. It was inevitable, therefore, with 'Hindoostani' spoken with inferiors and by children with their *ayahs* that an aspect of 'civilisation' should degenerate with distance from 'civilised' Europe.[132] Thus, Mackintosh concluded, 'It is upon this [the English language] and similar shades that all elegance depends. It is therefore no wonder that taste and elegance are lost in the colonies.'[133]

Conclusion

The late eighteenth century saw a transition in the nature of colonial rule in India, characterized by what Sudipta Sen has called a decline of 'intimacy' and more rigid drawing of the racial colour line in imperial policy, law and practice.[134] This hardening of a racial divide was both reflected in, and constituted through, imperial knowledge of India, which saw a turn away from an appreciation of India's 'ancient' civilization to a blanket dismissal of all Indian 'antiquities' as worthless. Mackintosh epitomized that transition. On visiting the temples of Aurangabad and Ellora, he claimed that 'to pierce a country in all directions with canals is in truth a greater work than any of them' – 'them' being not only the cave temples but all 'the boasted works of Asia from the wall of China to the Pyramids'.[135] In a similar vein, Mackintosh declared on visiting the cave temples on the island of Elephanta that one day, 'Twenty or thirty centuries hence, some nation, whose name is now unknown, may compare these works of barbaric toil with the finished productions of the genius and taste of an English artist'.[136] Whereas Sir William Jones and William Robertson had focused on common mythology and language, placing 'Europe' and 'India' in the same epistemological field, Mackintosh constructed 'India' in opposition to England, whose culture and society he understood to be the pinnacle of 'civilization' that humanity had reached. His representation of India as 'backwards' intersected with his understanding of white men in general, and white 'English' men in particular, as morally superior. As his report on the state of the police illustrates, his characterization of Indians as 'meek', 'timid' and 'corrupt' was in contrast to the assumption that a white 'Englishman' would be more morally, as well as physically robust.

This representation of India as 'backwards' and 'degenerate' and of Indians as 'effeminate' was not new, but Mackintosh's idea of India as simply negative – what Sara Suleri calls 'colonial blankness' – would become increasingly prevalent amongst the metropolitan liberal elite whose writings on India dominated the Victorian imagination.[137] As an epistemological space, India was to be plundered for information that could serve a European project of knowledge formation. Yet, as Mackintosh's attitude to his colleagues' research suggests, to actually engage with that space, to belong to it, was to lose the very element of 'European' civilization that constructed knowledge, which projected itself outwards to discover 'universal' truths. By critiquing his colleagues in Bombay, and by attempting to 'civilize' their manners, Mackintosh positioned himself in closer proximity to a white, European, and specifically English, identity that he understood to be coterminous with 'civilization'. His representation of the Anglo-English community in Bombay as degenerate, rather than different allowed him to position himself as more 'English' than his colleagues in Bombay. Constantly referring back to England, Mackintosh made England the central referent through which he filtered his observations and experiences of India. In doing so, he reiterated his own sense of belonging to 'England' as both 'civilization' and as 'home'.

6

'A hothouse of weeds': reproducing white womanhood in colonial India

In January 1811, Catherine Mackintosh, the sixteen-year-old daughter of Sir James Mackintosh, known to her family as 'Kitty', embarked on a journey from Bombay [Mumbai] to Bushire [Bushehr] on board the ship HMS Lion. As a young person on the cusp of womanhood, Kitty was placed in the care of Lady Ouseley, who was accompanying her husband, Sir Gore Ouseley, and the Persian ambassador, Mirz Abu'l Hasan Khan, to Baghdad. During the voyage, Sir William Wiseman, a twenty-seven-year-old lieutenant on board the *Lion*, 'made love to' Kitty, but did not propose marriage until the ship had docked at Bushehr and her chaperone had left for Tehran.[1] News of Wiseman's professions of love, and his subsequent marriage proposal, reached Kitty's father in Bombay, in May 1811. It generated a flurry of activity and a chain of letters between elite, British-imperial men who expressed their anxiety to act according to propriety. Writing en route to Baghdad, a flustered Sir Gore Ouseley stated that 'I certainly had no conception that a question would arise of so delicate a description' and advocated for Wiseman's character and status, referring to him as 'a young man whom I know to be of the most excellent and honourable disposition'. He believed that Kitty's 'innocent young heart is ... deeply in his favour', and recommended that she marry Wiseman as soon as possible.[2] The reverend on board the *Lion*, however, refused to perform the ceremony without her father's consent, and so Kitty was left unmarried in Bushire in the care of Mrs Bruce, the wife of the Resident, until her elder sister, Mary Rich, arrived to take charge of the 'giddy girl'.[3] Whilst Kitty travelled onward with her sister to Baghdad, Wiseman returned to Bombay to seek permission from James Mackintosh to take his daughter's hand in marriage.

The minor scandal that ensued around Kitty and Wiseman's relationship on board the *Lion* was relatively quickly turned into a 'respectable' arrangement. Although James Mackintosh believed his daughter to be too young to 'bind herself by any declaration', he stated that 'if after a fair time for reflection she persisted in her preferences ... I had no right to object to her choice'.[4] Kitty and William Wiseman were married in Baghdad in January 1812. Fourteen years later they divorced, after Kitty entered into an adulterous relationship with a Mr Turnbull whilst living in Jamaica, a scandal that was kept out of the newspapers by the manoeuvring of Lord Brougham.[5] Kitty's sexual indiscretions embarrassed, but may not have surprised, her immediate family; since her arrival in Bombay at the age of nine, she had been a source of concern to her parents. In their letters and diaries her father and step-mother, Lady Catherine Mackintosh (née Allen, 1765–1830), lamented her 'forwardness'.[6] Despite the 'system of exclusion' that her step-mother had attempted to impose upon her, Kitty had, according to her father, become 'irreclaimably womanised'.[7] Both parents agreed that this outcome was almost entirely attributable to 'the hothouse of an Indian society', where there were few white women who could set an example of feminine virtue. Instead, white girls entered into a society dominated by East India Company men, and were treated as women long before they were mature enough to handle the responsibilities of womanhood. Despite their best efforts, Catherine Mackintosh (senior) concluded that 'the establishments of character must not be hoped for in such a place' as Bombay.[8]

This chapter examines the challenge that white women and girls' presence in colonial India posed to the maintenance and reproduction of white womanhood, and its relationship to the idea of 'home' in the British-imperial imagination. Over the last twenty years, cultural historians have argued that empire was fundamental to the imagining of Britain as a cohesive, racially homogenous, as well as racially superior, nation.[9] As earlier chapters have argued, this racist envisaging of the nation intersected with the concretization of the ideology of 'home', as material and social structure, and a form of emotional identification. In this configuration, the colonies represented a space 'over there', where white men went to act out their ambitions and secure their wealth, returning 'home' to Britain to marry and raise children; white women not only belonged in the metropole, their symbolic association with metropolitan Britain was what gave it the emotional pull of 'home'. The promise of return was thus a promise of: the continuation of patriarchal lineage, of cultural heritage and of national progress. As Chapter 4 argued, the erasure of white women amongst the Highland emigrants was partly what enabled British North America to be emotionally associated with 'exile' even as the region was being developed as a white settler colony. Turning to colonial India, this chapter argues that the Mackintosh family's representation of Bombay as a site of the corruption and crisis of white womanhood enabled British-imperial elites to construct India as inherently 'unhomely'.

Whereas previous chapters used published works of philosophy, pamphlet debates and travel writing to show how elite, British-imperialist writers constructed the ideological norms of 'home', this chapter uses the unpublished writing of the Mackintosh family living in colonial Bombay to show how those same elites internalized and enacted that ideology. The Mackintosh family were members of the extended network of literary and cultural elites in Britain whose writing and thought is the subject of this book. Catherine Mackintosh was a Welsh gentry woman who was closely connected through the marriage of her two sisters, to the Wedgwood family and their literary circle, which included the poet Coleridge, William and Dorothy Wordsworth, Maria Edgeworth and Dugald Stewart.[10] Her husband, Sir James Mackintosh, was a well-known Whig thinker, originally from the Highlands of Scotland, who had made his name as a Scottish philosopher during the debate over the French Revolution.[11] The same year that he and Catherine married, Mackintosh and his new brother-in-law, John Allen, founded 'The King of Clubs', which included many of the prominent socio-economic thinkers of the period, including Malthus, Ricardo and Selkirk, as well as political figures such as Lord Holland and the Marquis of Lansdowne.[12] In 1804, the family travelled to Bombay to take up James Mackintosh's position as Recorder of the Court of Bombay.[13] The Mackintosh children comprised – Mary, Maitland and Kitty – from James Mackintosh's first marriage to Catherine Stuart, and two daughters – Frances and Elizabeth – from his second marriage. Their youngest son, Robert, and the only male heir, was born in Bombay in 1805. Their letters and diaries, written for friends and family 'back home', as well as to each other when apart, are held in the British Library, the National Library of Scotland and the Wedgwood Archive. A great 'journaliser', the majority of these letters and diaries were written by James Mackintosh, but a few were written by the children, and a significant number by Catherine Mackintosh, including an epistolary poem – 'A Political Epistle to Sir J on his return to Bombay from Point de Gaulle' – that is the focus of the final section of this chapter.

The letters and diaries of the Mackintosh family offer an insight into white, family formation in early-nineteenth-century colonial India, and the role of femininity in configuring the meaning of British identity and its relationship to whiteness. This chapter begins by situating the Mackintosh family and household in the wider social and cultural context of early-nineteenth-century colonial India, focusing on the family's daily interactions with Bombay's heterogeneous population. The second section turns to their representations of people in India, and their use of womanhood and the household to portray India as a 'backward' and 'degenerate' society. These representations intersected with wider, Enlightenment ideas of civilization, which posited Indian domesticity and marriage in contrast to an idealized vision of British domestic life and gender relations. As the final section shows, British-imperial elites' fears over the moral 'degeneracy' of Indian domesticity extended to the nominally 'European' society living in colonial India, and informed their representation of white womanhood in colonial India. The Mackintosh parents' concerns over their daughters' moral development in Bombay thus offer insight into the process, as well as the ambivalences, of womanhood, and its intersections with whiteness and belonging.

Gender and whiteness in early-nineteenth-century British India

During the eighteenth and early nineteenth centuries, British migration to India took place almost solely through the channels of East India Company patronage networks and the licensing system that secured the Company the right to control the entry of, as well as to deport, British subjects.[14] By far the majority of people permitted to go to India were young, single men entering the ranks of the East India Company, as merchants, soldiers or administrators. Like the women and girls of the Mackintosh family, the majority of British women who went to India in the late eighteenth and early nineteenth centuries did so as the wives, sisters or servants of elite British-imperial officials.[15] When they arrived in Bombay, they joined a small and very male-dominated society of people – referred to interchangeably as 'Europeans', 'English' and 'Anglo-Indians', but rarely as 'British' – whose lives and livelihoods revolved around Company activities. As a tiny minority, young white women found themselves to be in high demand from East India Company soldiers and officers. In a letter dated 1780 from Bombay, the East India Company cadet, William Lambert, wrote of the dearth of 'ladies' who, he claimed, 'fetch the highest prizes of any one article'.[16] This scenario would have been familiar in Britain through the portrait painted of Anglo-Indian life by Phebe Gibbes in *Hartly House, Calcutta* (1789).[17] Beyond contemporary literature, however, there has been little research into white family formation in colonial India, and the relationship of white women – as sisters, daughters, wives and mothers – to East India Company administration and imperial rule.[18] Until relatively recently, the historiography of white social life in colonial India relied on misogynist stereotypes of the *memsahib* as a dominating and divisive character, whose presence in India undermined collegiality as well as inter-racial harmony. Percival Spear's classic account of Anglo-Indian social life, *The Nabobs*, blamed the 'widening racial gulf' in the nineteenth century on 'the increasing number of [white] women in the settlements … As women went out in large numbers, they brought with them their insular whims and prejudices, which no official contact with Indians or iron compulsion of loneliness ever tempted them to abandon'.[19]

As Ann Stoler has argued for British Malaya and the Dutch East Indies, rather than being the 'fault' of white women, imperial policy allowing white women to marry and live in the colonies was enacted as a means of consolidating the colour line.[20] Until the late eighteenth century, the East India Company encouraged its employees to forge relationships with local Indian women.[21] This was not a new or unique phenomenon in the British Empire. As previous chapters have noted, in the Caribbean and in North America, settler colonists used sex to coerce, terrify and control, as well as to forge lasting relationships with indigenous and non-European people. In the 1730s, for example, James Mackintosh's maternal ancestor, Lachlan MacGillivray, married a Muscogee woman, Sehoy Marchand. Their son, Hobi-Hili-Miko's dual heritage enabled him to consolidate relationships between British colonial trade and the Wind tribe.[22] In India, instances of marriage between British Company servants and Indian women were rare; William Dalrymple's account of the marriage between James Achilles Kirkpatrick and Khair un-Nissa is as unusual as it is fascinating.[23] More commonly, East India Company servants used Indian women to provide domestic and sexual services, whilst Indian women themselves fashioned new lives and identities out of a range of encounters and circumstances.[24] Thomas Williamson's *East India Company Vade Mecum* (1810) devoted considerable space to explaining the manners, beliefs, dress and expectations of different groups of women in India, both as servants and as 'companions' in order to prepare East India Company servants for life in India.[25] Yet, as Durba Ghosh has argued, although some of these relationships may have been loving and committed, evidenced by wills leaving bequests to lovers and children, they were structurally deeply unequal. The informality of these arrangements enabled East India Company men to have all the benefits of a wife whilst in India, and then to return to Britain to make a 'respectable', formal marriage.[26] Their mixed-race children were either removed from their mothers and sent to Britain, or left behind in India, sometimes with provision made for their education, other times in poverty and destitution.[27]

By the end of the century, fears that East India Company servants would comprise a settler society that would demand autonomous rights, and that mixed-race sons climbing the ranks of the Company would undermine the racial hierarchy of rule, led to a shift in official policy on mixed-race relationships. From 1786, in an attempt to deter East India Company servants from recognizing their mixed-race, 'Eurasian' sons, Cornwallis decreed that mixed-race sons would no longer be eligible to serve in the civil or military service of the Company.[28] Despite this legal discrimination against mixed-race relationships, practices of co-habitation clearly continued long after the initial decrees. Williamson noted that 'many European gentlemen' were deeply attached to their Indian lovers. He insisted that 'British damsels' were 'conspicuously preeminent' to the 'Asiatic *chére amie*', but acknowledged the expense of a European wife, and stated that some 'native women' did 'conduct themselves in the most decorous manner, and evinced the utmost fidelity, in every particular, to their keepers'.[29] As the use of 'keepers' would suggest, many of these women were slave-concubines who, along with other servants, were purchased by East India Company servants.[30] Fifteen years later, the advice was more perfunctory and unambiguously against Company servants having relationships with Indian women. In *The General East India Guide and Vade Mecum* (1825), John Borthwick Gilchrist wrote, 'Let me earnestly recommend to you never to form a permanent connection, that is to say to bring under the same roof or tent with yourself a native woman.'[31]

Official discrimination against mixed-race relationships, which Gilchrist referred to as 'wise regulations', did not preclude East India Company servants from engaging in casual sexual relations with Indian women, nor were they intended to.[32] Yet they did give legal credence to the idea that the only legitimate and respectable family was the racially homogenous, heterosexual unit. As Indrani Chatterjee has argued, this policy, as well as practices of abducting mixed-race children from their Indian mothers and placing them in Orphan Schools, intersected with other legislation that enabled the consolidation of British-imperial norms of governance. These norms were based increasingly on white supremacy, defined by sanguinary inheritance rather than through intersecting ideas of kinship, loyalty and affiliation that characterized the Mughal regime.[33] In this respect, the family, and the legitimation of certain familial and affective relationships, lay at the centre of the transition from 'Orientalist' to 'Anglicist' rule in India.[34] As the previous chapter illustrated, Sir James Mackintosh's appointment as Recorder of the Court of Bombay was itself a symptom of this transition. The Recorder's Court over which he presided as judge was a new institution established in 1798 to replace the Mayor's Court and reassert British legal authority criminal and civil cases in the Bombay Presidency. Paid for by the Crown, rather than by the Company, the Recorder's role was to ensure jurisdiction over Company activities and call Company actions to account.[35] For James Mackintosh, this meant bringing 'English' principles of justice, 'morality and independence' to a 'backward' and 'obscure outpost' of the British Empire.[36] Whilst his formal reform initiatives were central to that agenda, his family life, and his relationship to his wife and daughters, also played a significant part in configuring norms associated with whiteness and the assertion of 'British' cultural norms and mores as superior.

Sir James Mackintosh's arrival in Bombay with his British wife and five daughters was itself a symbol of whiteness, in which the heterosexual, racially homogenous, and patriarchal, nuclear family represented the morally superior social unit. As previous chapters have argued, the ideal of the patriarchal nuclear family, gathered together around the hearth and united through bonds of affection, played a significant role in drawing the boundaries of civilization and humanity. In their letters and diaries, the Mackintosh family used the image of the harmonious family to retain this marker of respectability. Writing to his brother-in-law, James Mackintosh described the house in which they resided, situated 'about five miles of excellent road over a flat from our little capital' in the middle of grounds with 'much the character of a fine English Park'.[37] The family subsequently moved further north in Mazagaon, where they rented a neo-Classical house, Tarala, built and owned by the Wadia family, key members of the wealthy Parsi community in Bombay.[38] Describing the family's day-to-day activities in and around the house, James Mackintosh wrote that 'we drink tea and from tea to bed read to our whole family part to the amusement I hope of Kitty and to the instruction of my three elder children'.[39] Their reading comprised a very English canon of Milton, Cowper and Shakespeare. Yet despite this portrait of family intimacy, social interactions and connections went far beyond the nuclear family and the vast walls of their home. As in Britain, Parel and later Tarala were rarely occupied by the family alone. As in other colonial societies, including in Jamaica and in Calcutta, the lack of hotels or 'public accommodation' meant that hospitality towards other white colonists was expected and more extensive than in metropolitan Britain.[40] In 1808, Maria Graham (then Dundas), her brother, sister and father stayed with the Mackintosh family upon their arrival in Bombay, and in 1811, James Mackintosh wrote that 'we are seven in the house: three Nats, Sir William Wiseman, Canning, Daw and I'.[41]

At the same time, the individual members of the Mackintosh family were often relatively dispersed. The youngest member of the family, Robert, was primarily cared for by his two *ayahs*, Louis and Louise, who Mackintosh referred to as 'black Christians called Portuguese'.[42] This rather pejorative description of these servants reflected the disdain in which the Portuguese settlers were held by British colonists. Williamson stated that they 'compose the most contemptible race to be found on earth', and recommended hiring 'Hindoostani' (either Muslim or Hindu) ayahs instead.[43] Despite these racist remarks, Robert's earliest attachments may have been directed more to his *ayahs* than to his birth parents or elder siblings. His elder sisters, Fanny and Bessy, appear to have been educated at home by a governess and, when she proved to be 'worse than useless', by their mother. Based on James Mackintosh's requests to his friends to find a replacement governess, they were taught English literature, modern languages, drawing and music. More importantly, their father emphasized, the governess must have the 'indispensable qualities of morality and temper'.[44] Girls, he believed, should be taught these virtues above all else. Writing to his younger daughters upon their return to England in 1811, he stated, 'No reading is so good as behaving well … I should much, much desire you to be very clever but oh how much more to be very good!'[45] Unlike their younger step-sisters, the three girls from James Mackintosh's first marriage attended a small school for girls run by Mrs Baxter. There is no surviving evidence of Mrs Baxter's school, but it was probably modelled on its counterparts in Calcutta, where a 'proprietress' instructed her pupils in 'reading, spelling, grammar, letter-writing, geography, history, arithmetic, and sewing'.[46] Catherine Mackintosh's brief and derisive reference to Mrs Baxter's school suggests that it was not an ideal institution for raising young, 'respectable' white women; indeed she partly blamed Kitty's 'forwardness' on Mrs Baxter's instruction. Both parents were happier when Kitty was placed with Mrs Ashburner, who offered her an example of 'quiet and useful and uninterrupted employment'.[47]

As in Britain, the Mackintosh household also extended to servants, many of whom lived in quarters in the main house's extensive grounds. Whereas the family's establishment in Britain would have been relatively small, likely to have comprised a cook, a lady's maid and a principal servant, their Bombay establishment was vast. James Mackintosh described his household, which comprised his principal servant named Cowasjee, Catherine's servant, Fudgelo, an assistant named Bala, a coach driver, three or four house keepers, two *chobdars* [attendants], six sepoys who acted as guards, as well as a *havildar* [soldier], and two light bearers.[48] He calculated the annual expense for this retinue of servants, some of whom were paid for by the Company, as 14,000 rupees, leaving him 'only' £3,250 across the year in savings from his annual salary of £5,000.⁴⁹ Despite the fact that there was a constant traffic of Indian servants going back and forth between India and Britain accompanying East India Company servants and their children, it seems that all of the Mackintosh family's servants were local to Bombay.⁵⁰ When Catherine Mackintosh and her younger children returned to England in 1810, however, they brought with them their Indian servant, Osman, who, Fanny Mackintosh wrote, 'liked England very well but felt it very cold'.⁵¹

The Mackintosh family were a minority in a society that was primarily comprised of Indian people from a wide range of religions and heritages. According to James Douglas, the population of Bombay, in 1805, was 150,000, with less than 10 per cent of that population comprising 'European' residents, the majority of whom were men working as merchants, Company servants or military officers.⁵² The main focus of Bombay was the Fort area, in front of which was the Esplanade where visitors to Bombay including itinerant merchants from across Asia would stay in temporary, bamboo houses.⁵³ The Fort area itself was divided into the 'white' and 'black' town: the former the administrative centre of the East India Company, and the latter the residential and bazaar area of Parsi, Armenian, Jewish, Hindu and Muslim traders upon whom the town and Company was heavily, financially reliant. The 'white town' included a Protestant and a Catholic church, a town hall, a theatre, and the 'dingy old' court house, and a hospital.⁵⁴ Maria Graham described the black town as full of narrow lanes, 'dirty, hot and disagreeable', made worse by the fact that much of it was in ruins following a fire in 1802.⁵⁵ To the south of the Fort on the tip of Bombay was Colaba, where East India Company soldiers, primarily young, British men from the lower orders of society, were garrisoned. Beyond the walls of the Fort were the suburbs of Mazagong and Mahim, where Portuguese, Hindu and Muslim communities lived scattered in villages. The Parsis, who owned many of Bombay's buildings, banks and the ship-building industry, rented out houses to elite British imperialists in Parel and Malabar Hill.⁵⁶

For the British in Bombay, social and economic life was less racially segregated and more cosmopolitan than in Calcutta, where wealthy British merchants built 'private mansions' in the 'white town' and largely socialized amongst themselves.⁵⁷ Politically, although the East India Company officially ruled Bombay, governance remained de facto a mixed enterprise, heavily reliant on the support and cooperation of local Indian traders. During the eighteenth century, British merchants had worked closely with, and relied on, Parsi and Hindu bankers, social segregation was therefore defined primarily according to socio-economic status, rather than religion or heritage.⁵⁸ In 1802, for example, the Wadia family had rescued the Bombay government from the brink of financial crisis, and joint initiatives between Parsi and English merchants led to banking and business partnerships.⁵⁹ This close alliance is evident in Mackintosh's report of the alarm felt amongst the 'European community' for the security of 'Daddy's' family [Cursetlee Ardaseer Dady] upon his death and the community's endeavours to come to their aid.⁶⁰ Socially, the large parties and balls that were held with relative frequency included members of the Parsi community. In August 1810, a masked ball was given for the 'whole settlement' at Hormusjee Bomanjee's house, one of the leading Parsi bankers in conjunction with a number of British men.⁶¹ These events included the small number of elite 'European' women who lived in the settlement; indeed, the wives of British-imperial administrators were often expected to organize and host these gatherings. Although Parsi women did not attend public entertainment until the 1840s, it is clear from Mary's letters, as well as Maria Graham's *Journal of a Residence in India* (1812) that elite British, Parsi, Hindu and Muslim women made formal, social visits in private settings.⁶² Writing to her sister from Bushire, Kitty Mackintosh described a visit to the Governor of Bushire's house to visit his wives and compared their dress to that of Parsi women in Bombay, suggesting that she had some acquaintance with them too.⁶³

Like the majority of the 'English' colonists in India in this period, the Mackintosh family would have spoken some Hindustani. In the introduction to his *Hindoostanee Philology: Comprising a Dictionary, English and Hindoostanee* (1790), which was listed as a necessary purchase for East India Company cadets, Dr John Gilchrist noted that learning the language was 'an object of vital importance'.⁶⁴ That many Company servants did not, is suggested by the dire warnings issued by Williamson in his *Vade Mecum* (1810), who reiterated the 'absolute necessity of immediately studying the language' in order not to be over-reliant on Indian servants, or deceived by them. He advised that spending three hours a day studying the language with the help of an 'intelligent linguist' would enable a cadet to become competent enough to transact business after a year.⁶⁵ James Mackintosh himself used Hindustani to communicate with local people and to gain local knowledge whilst on a tour of the Deccan, from Pune to Hyderabad.⁶⁶ However, his skills in South Asian languages would have been vastly inferior to those of his colleagues who had lived in India since their youth. Reflecting on his colleagues' language, he stated, 'we in India are so much accustomed to speak Hindustanee to inferiors that we learn to consider English as too superior and dignified a language to have any familiar phrases'.⁶⁷ Like many Anglo-Indian children, the youngest Mackintosh child, Robert, spoke Hindustani with his *ayahs*; his elder sisters would also have picked up Hindustani through their servants. At their house, Maria Graham noted that six languages were spoken at the breakfast table between guests, the family and the servants: Arabic, Persian, Hindustani, Italian, French and English.[68]

As one of the key nodes in a sea-trade network that linked Persia to the Arab Gulf, to India and China, Bombay provided the Mackintosh family with numerous opportunities to engage with people from different regions across Asia and the Middle East.[69] In an undated letter, probably written in 1809, Fanny Mackintosh reported a conversation with the 'living God', a reincarnation of Morya Gosavi, in Chincore [Chinchwad], who mistook Maria Graham and the Resident of Pune, Mr Russell, for her parents.[70] The nine-year-old reported this in a matter-of-fact way, with no sense that there was very much exceptional about her encounter. Her elder sister, Mary, appeared equally unperturbed by her meeting with wives of the Pasha of Bushehr. She described the Pasha's second, and favourite, wife, as 'a remarkably fine woman of about 30 in every respects preferable to the other, and received me in the politest manner'.[71] With a greater sense of the exceptional nature of his encounters, James Mackintosh wrote of his everyday interactions in Bombay with a wide variety of people who were embedded in networks across and beyond South Asia:

> I have in the same morning received a visit from a Roman Catholic Bishop of the name of Ramazzine from Modena and a descendent of the celebrated physician Ramazzine, a relative of Muraton who wondered that an Englishman should be learned enough to quote Virgil. Of an Armenian archbishop from Mount Ararat[,] of a shroff (money dealer from Benares who came hither by the way of Sychagur [Saugor, now Sagar] and who can draw bills on his correspondents at Cabul) and of the Dustor or chief priest of the Parsees [*sic*] at Surat who is copying out for me the genuine works of Zoroaster.

Yet, Mackintosh declared, 'all this jumble of nations and sages and opinions … is not all worth one afternoon of free and rational conversation at the King of Clubs' and reiterated his longing to return to the familiar and more 'civilized' social life of London. 'I should rather travel to Temple to keep Parson quiet for a week and make a voyage down the Thames to force my way into Jeremy Bentham in Queen Square Place – these are monsters enough for me and fierce as one of them is they suit me much better than Mullas or Pundits.'[72] In her own letters to her husband and her family, Catherine Mackintosh, too, expressed her wish to return to England.[73]

Race and sexuality in British representations of Indian homes

Despite their wide-ranging interactions with the many different people who lived and worked in South Asia, the Mackintosh family dismissed the value of almost everything and everyone living on the Indian subcontinent. James Mackintosh frequently referred to Indian people as 'barbarians' and 'savages'. His daughters picked up on and replicated their father's prejudices, using words associated with animals to describe the people they encountered and, in many respects, relied upon for their day-to-day needs. Kitty referred to the Governor's wives who she visited in Bushire as 'a set of frights … the most mean looking creatures I ever saw'.[74] Her father referred to Mrs Bruce, the woman who looked after her in Bushire, as 'the only semi-European animal in a female form who could assist in transferring Kitty from Lady Ouseley to Mary'; she was of Armenian and European heritage.[75] These pejorative descriptions cannot be read as merely personal prejudices or dismissed as private utterances. Rather, the Mackintosh family's attitudes were part of, and informed by, the long history of European literary representations of non-European people, and women in particular, as inferior to white Europeans, or as less than human. As previous chapters have noted, Scottish Enlightenment scholarship portrayed the whole continent of Asia as a 'stagnant' civilization that had suffered a steep decline since the days of Antiquity.[76] This characterization portrayed India not only as less advanced than Europe, but also as a morally degenerate society. In his *Essay on the History of Civil Society* (1767), Adam Ferguson argued that climate informed the manners and morals of the 'Asiatic' people of India who were, he wrote, 'addicted to pleasure' and 'sunk in effeminacy'.[77] Even William Robertson, whose *Historical Disquisition Concerning the Knowledge Which the Ancients Had of India* (1791) was intended to encourage Europeans to respect India's 'ancient' civilization, represented Indian people as 'effeminate' and weaker than their European counterparts.[78] James Mackintosh continued those theories and stereotypes in his direct observations of Indian society. His diary of 14 November 1808, written from Poonah [Pune], for example, referred to the Peshwa Baji Rao II as 'distinguished by a mixture of superstition and dissolute manners … It does not appear that this sort of profligacy is conceived at all to affect his moral character. Indeed the Hindoos [sic] appear to have expunged purity of manners from their catalogue of virtues'.[79]

As these examples suggest, Scottish Enlightenment ideas of 'Asiatic' culture relied heavily on intersecting concepts of 'natural' and 'moral' sexual practices, gendered embodiments and gender relations. The presumed position of women in society, and their treatment by men, played a critical role in this construction racial and cultural difference. In *Sketches of the History of Man* (1774), Lord Kames related polygamy, which he considered an 'unnatural' vice, specifically to Asia and the 'opulence in a hot climate': 'In the hot climate of Hindostan [*sic*] polygamy is universal, and men buy their wives. The same obtains in China.' It was for this reason, he continued, that 'in hot climates, women remain in the same humble and dependent state, in which all women were originally, when all men were savages'.[80] In his *Lectures on Political Economy*, Dugald Stewart represented monogamous, heterosexual marriage as key to human improvement.[81] Polygamy which he associated with 'negroes, whether Mahometan or Pagan', Pacific Islanders, and all 'climates which exalt the imagination and inflame the passions' was morally wrong.[82] In contrast, Stewart argued that monogamous, heterosexual marriage was everywhere connected to 'the happiness of human life, with the preservation of morals, and the progressive improvement of the species'.[83] Ultimately, Stewart concluded, monogamous marriage was in accordance with the 'law of nature', 'one of the most striking provisions which the economy of nature has made, for those moral and political arrangements which are subservient to the happiness of the individual and the multiplication of the race'.[84]

Popular English literature had long indulged in titillation from the image of Indian women confined to the harems of polygamous Indian princes, representing them as alternately sexually lascivious or the tragic victims of Indian male tyranny.[85] Kames continued his diatribe against sexual practices in Asia by stating that 'where polygamy is indulged, and wives are purchased for gratifying the carnal appetite merely, it is in vain to think of restraining them otherwise than by locks and bars, after having once tasted enjoyment'.[86] The idea that women suffered the most abject oppression under both Muslim and Hindu rulers in India was reiterated in James Mackintosh's observation of the chambers of the Nizam of Hyderabad's *zenana*, which he claimed were 'about ten feet square', dark and dingy.[87] Comparing these to a German account of the seraglio of Constantinople, he represented all *zenanas* as designed for the same and sole purpose of oppressing women:

> The number of women enslaved, and condemned to perpetual imprisonment in such loathsome dungeons – without occupation or amusement, without knowledge or accomplishment, without the possibility of a good quality which could rise so high as to deserve the name of a virtue – is perhaps the strongest instance of low and depraved tyranny that the world exhibits.[88]

James Mackintosh concluded his discussion of the Nizam's *zenana* by contrasting his own understanding of 'the excellence women are capable of' to Indian men's 'tyranny' over their wives.[89]

As scholars writing in the wake of Said have long argued, in eighteenth- and nineteenth-century European texts, 'the harem' served as a marker of 'Eastern' otherness that was mobilized and served imperialist agendas.[90] James Mackintosh's borrowing from a German account of a seraglio in Constantinople illustrates the way in which the *zenana*, removed from the specificities of time and place, circulated as a highly politicized trope. His representation of the Nizam's harem, to which he had no physical access, as a sign of the 'tyranny' under which women lived was corroborated by Maria Graham's account of her visit to her 'friend', Shabab o'dien Mahayr's harem in Bombay. Despite the vast differences in social and political status, and material wealth, between the Nizam of Hyderabad and the Shabab o'dien Mahayr, Maria Graham and James Mackintosh's accounts share the same sentiments and conclusions. Like James Mackintosh, who wrote of the women's quarters that 'light and air seem to be considered as impertinent strangers', Maria Graham laid emphasis on the 'close and disagreeable' nature of the rooms she visited, which she portrayed in implicit contrast to her own light and airy house.[91] Both accounts used the closeness and stuffiness of the rooms of Indian houses as a metaphor for the stagnation of Indian society as a whole, and the oppression of women in particular. Discussing her interactions with the Shabab o'dien Mahayr's female relatives, she found them 'totally devoid of cultivation' and characterized their lives as cycle of 'monotony' interrupted only by births, marriages and deaths.[92] As Indira Ghosh has argued, Graham's account, like those of other nineteenth-century white women, enabled her to construct herself as a free and mobile agent.[93]

Maria Graham and James Mackintosh's representations of Indian women reflect changing British-imperial attitudes towards Indian culture and society more generally. Although European sexualization and exoticization of 'Oriental' women long preceded eighteenth-century literature, until the end of the century British women's reports of their encounters with Asian women were generally respectful. An account by an anonymous British woman, dated 1742, describing her visit to the wives of 'a great man call'd y nabob who is the next person in dignity to the Great Mogull' in Madras suggests mutual respect. After exchanging gifts, the women admired each others' jewellery, and expressed curiosity about their respective dress. The sense of mutual interest is evident in the author's conclusion that 'we was [Sic] the first English women they had ever seen, and I doubt not but we appear'd as Odd to them as they did to us'.[94] In contrast,

Kitty Mackintosh's derisive description of her visit to the wives of the governor of Bushire, much like Maria Graham's depiction, suggests that by the early nineteenth century, that fascination went only one way. British women writers met the apparent excitement and interest that their visit engendered amongst 'native' ladies with contempt and derision. As Indrani Chatterjee notes, British women's dismissal of their Indian counterparts, and their expressions of pity for their subordinate status and lack of mobility, actually shut down the possibility for women's agency in political affairs. Despite their seclusion, women, and particularly mothers, in Mughal India, played an important role in orchestrating the ruling family's future through their filial loyalties and marriage.[95] Women's management of extended kinship networks and their relationships to power would have been familiar to James Mackintosh, as well as to the director of the East India Company, Charles Grant, both of whom grew up in the Highlands of Scotland.

Critiques of the Indian household provided a means of justifying British-imperial rule. In *Observations on the State of Society among the Asiatic Subjects of Great Britain* (1792), for example, Charles Grant advocated the teaching of English and conversion to Christianity in order to change the morals of a people who he regarded as 'exceedingly depraved'. His main examples of that 'depravity' were drawn from his characterization of the 'Hindoo' household as messy, dysfunction and divisive, and familial relationships as devoid of 'natural affection': 'Seldom is a household without its internal divisions, and lasting enmities … the women partake of this spirit of discord. Held in slavish subjection by the men, they rise in furious passions against each other, which vent themselves in such loud, virulent, and indecent railings, as are hardly to be heard in any other part of the world.'[96] Like Adam Smith's characterization of Africans and Native Americans in *The Theory of Moral Sentiments*, Grant connected 'a want of sensibility for others' with a lower stage of civilization.[97] This 'want of sensibility' was, in Grant's representation, evident through the lack of 'filial and paternal affection' as well as in their indifference to the 'conjugal relation'.[98] The idea that Indian people were 'utterly insensible' and lacked compassion even for the most vulnerable in their own society was reiterated in English pamphlets, histories and newspapers. Reporting the Recorder's speech on a child murder case at the session of Oyer and Terminer in 1806, the *Bombay Courier* stated that 'the natives of India, though incapable of the crimes which arise from the violent passions, are beyond every other people of the earth addicted to these vices which proceed from the weakness of natural feeling and the almost total absence of moral restraints'.[99] James Mackintosh, too, understood Indian people of all religions to lack sympathy and thereby moral virtue. This was not only the result of his dealings with criminal prosecutions. In his travel journal he attributed the Nizam of Hyderabad's refusal to inflict capital punishment – a policy that Mackintosh himself attempted in Bombay – not to any genuine feeling for the convicted, but because 'he cares too little for the innocent person who is injured'.[100]

The relationship between Indian people's apparent lack of sensibility and the dysfunctional nature of the household came together in Maria Graham's critique of Indian hospitality upon her visit to meet Shahab o'dien Mahary's wife, Fatima, and female relatives. Her description of Fatima's manner, whilst appreciative of her beauty, was critical of her subservience towards her husband and the 'indolence' and ignorance of the women of the family. The 'monotony' of the women's lives, their 'muttering' of their prayers without understanding them, all constructed Indian women as automatons without any control or agency over their lives. Graham concluded her description with the claim that 'visits in the East are matters of ceremony, not of kindness'.[101] By representing the hospitality she received as a ritual, she reinforced the idea that the Indian household, whether Hindu or Muslim, was itself devoid of feeling and connection: 'She justified her own flippant disregard for her hosts by stating that hospitality was, in fact, considered to be a burden on the visitor, from which the person visited relieves him, as soon as he is satisfied with his company'.[102] Mackintosh remarked similarly when he wrote that 'among the Asiatics, where visit are merely complimentary, the master of the house may, when he pleases … put an end to a ceremony of which the object is purely to honour himself'.[103] These representations supported the idea, discussed in Chapter 1, that only Europeans had the capacity for genuine sensibility and virtue.

The claim that Indians lacked sensibility was reiterated across British travel writings on India, and particularly in discussions of *sati* – the ritual burning of a widow on her husband's funeral pyre, which took place largely amongst Hindus in Northern India. In his *Travels in India during the years 1780, 1781, 1782 and 1783*, William Hodges remarked on the apparent 'apathy and indifference' of the audience who had gathered to witness a funeral in which a young widow had determined to perform *sati*. The audience, he wrote, 'appeared destitute of feeling at the catastrophe that was to take place'. Contrasting his own 'melancholy' at the sight of her death to the 'shouts of the multitude' who appeared to him 'a mass of confused rejoicing', Hodges made a distinction between his own sensibility and virtue and the uncontrolled passions of the Indian crowd.[104] Writing in 1839, Marianne Postans reported on a ceremony in Cutch, expressing her admiration for the courage of the woman who had determined to die on her husband's funeral pyre. Like Hodges, she contrasted the 'fiendish shout of exultation' from the Indian crowd to the 'deep compassion' of the 'English spectators'. They left, she claimed, with a sense of 'a custom so fraught with horror, so incompatible with reason, and so revolting to human sympathy'.[105] This characterization of Indians as lacking in what Smith (as discussed in Chapter 1) had called 'sympathy' served as a justification for British dominance. By the time James Mill published his immensely influential *History of British India* in 1817, the dominant British-imperial discourse on the 'Hindoo' character was one of 'timidity', 'effeminacy' and 'insensibility to the suffering of others'.[106] 'To bring a timid submissive people … up to the manliness of the European character', wrote Grant, 'seems something beyond what has yet been seen, or is reasonably to be expected from the effects of institutions, civil or religious, upon nations.'[107] As the previous chapter discussed, James Mackintosh believed that regardless of the 'evils' of the East India Company's 'commercial and political monopoly', the 'superior morality of the European race' rendered British rule in India, a 'blessing' to its inhabitants.[108]

Bombay and the boundaries of white womanhood

Across their letters and diaries, the Mackintosh family illustrated a firm belief in the 'superior morality of the European race'. Yet they were all deeply critical of Anglo-Indians in Bombay, regarding them as inferior and 'degenerate' versions of metropolitan Europeans – among whom they included themselves – and particularly the English. In 1811, Mary complained to her sister about the 'European' society in Bombay, referring to them as 'gossiping and idle', and similarly blamed their character on the Indian climate.[109] In their letters and diaries, the Mackintosh family reiterated this idea of the unfeeling and unsympathetic 'European' in the colonies. In her poem, written in 1810 as she sailed back 'home' to England with her three children on board the *Cumbrian*, Catherine Mackintosh represented the 'Europeans' living in Bombay as lacking either sentiment or rational thought, the two attributes that defined humanity. Catherine Mackintosh's 'Political Epistle' expressed her relief to be rid of Bombay's society, and wished that her husband, too, could escape from 'those who neither love, nor feel, nor think/But hate, calumniate, dress, and dance, and drink'.[110] The poem begins by pitying her husband's return to Bombay – 'thy loath'd prison' – and compares James Mackintosh to the enslaved 'Negro' who has lost his wife and children, as well as his own freedom, to slavery. In fact, she argues, her husband suffers a worse fate, for 'where thou'art gone there is none to thee a kin', whereas at least the enslaved African has his 'brethren'.[111] This absurd comparison can be seen as a spurious performance of sympathy that reaches out beyond the boundaries of race; an expression of the universality of longing and loss. At the same time, by claiming that James Mackintosh has no 'brethren' left in Bombay – 'no heart responsive to thine own shall beat/No sympathetic glance thine eye shall meet' – Catherine Mackintosh closes down any possibility of Bombay as a 'home'.[112] Indeed, she even erases her step-daughters, two of whom remained with their father in Bombay and represented England as the only possible place of belonging for her husband. Having spilt much ink bemoaning his 'exile' in Bombay and imploring his friends to secure his pension and his 'release', James Mackintosh himself concurred with his wife's assessment of Bombay. Writing in his journal in order to while away his days in 'exile' in Bombay, he relayed the 'monstrous tales of Bombay matrimony', gossip that he derived from the dinner table and the court room.[113] He was particularly outraged by the failure of Mrs Inveraity, niece of the governor, Jonathan Duncan, to visit her uncle as he lay dying. Mrs Inveraity's lack of sympathy and sensibility appeared to Mackintosh to be a sign of the inferiority of 'Europeans' in general, and the 'English' in particular, living in India. He concluded that 'India seems to affect the heart as much as the liver, though the disease is not so often spoken of.'[114]

This idea that India itself undermined the sensibility and virtue of the 'Europeans' living in India played a significant role in constructing the meaning of the 'European' in general, and the 'English' in particular, as inherently and innately moral. James Mackintosh reinforced this idea when he claimed that merely the presence of 'one of the principal English gentlemen' as a Justice of the Peace would be 'sufficient security against oppression'.[115] Yet for those who left Europe too early, there was a risk that the 'bold character and robust constitution' of the European would be undermined by the India's climate of immorality and effeminacy.[116] This was a key concern of the Mackintosh parents. Writing to her husband two years before their departure for Bombay, Catherine Mackintosh stated that 'Mrs Cecil Smith called here and seemed to say that much more was to be feared for the morals of children in the East than for their health or their want of some kind of education'. She continued by disclosing that 'by the time children were ten or twelve years old whatever care mothers could take of them, they become acquainted with every vice and this she meant of females as well I believe as males'.[117] Eight years later, reflecting on her own experience of living in Bombay, Catherine Mackintosh reinforced this message:

> Oh well escap'd that pernicious Isle
> Where vice and folly soon the mind defile
> Where children throw aside their dolls and toys
> For balls, flirtations, less appropriate joys[118]

Mourning the rapid decline of white girls' youthful beauty, Catherine Mackintosh blamed the climate and the sexual mores of Anglo-Indian society for the corruption of virtue. Young white men and women, she argued, became yoked in marriage too early, before they were mature enough to bear its responsibilities. In her poetical narrative, the Company servant casts aside 'his black and stupid temporary mate' for a 'giddy' white girl, 'fresh from Europe of a better cast'.[119] Caring only that his wife is young and white, the Company servant soon discovers that his new wife – 'a mistress in a wife's disguise/empowered to vex ye with domestic strife' – is no less 'stupid' than his 'sable mate'. 'If this be marriage, oh ye saints above ... How much your virtues modern matrons shame', she concluded.[120]

Catherine Mackintosh's critique of Bombay's Anglo-Indian marriages was partly directed at the Company servants who valued only the whiteness, youth and beauty of their future wives. They proposed marriage before they knew anything about the girl's 'principles', 'habits' or 'brains':

> Ye no more want them to think or speak
> Than wish your children or your pigs to squeak
> Enough for you that they are young and gay
> To dance and caper on a gala day[121]

She expressed her horror of the marriage market, where women were picked for show rather than for their virtues. In this respect, Catherine Mackintosh's critique was part of a wider metropolitan discussion taking place around the need for both 'companionate' marriage, and of the importance of motherhood. As Mary Wollstonecraft argued in *A Vindication of the Rights of Woman* (1792), for women to raise healthy and moral children they must themselves be more than 'alluring objects' and capable of rational thought.[122] Although his tone and approach was remarkably different to Wollstonecraft's, the Evangelic writer, John Moir, agreed with the general sentiment: 'All admit the influence of the [female] sex on the present state of the moral world,' he wrote in *Female Education*, 'and yet the [female] sex are but too commonly brought up, as if it were meant they should be of no other use than to vitiate and debase it.'[123] Moir recommended that girls be educated at home rather than at boarding schools, and kept away from all forms of entertainment, especially the theatre. His views were somewhat extreme, yet the majority of commentators, including those, such as Anna Letitia Barbauld, who worked and published, believed that women's work was in the home, raising children: 'If the happiest destination of a woman be fulfilled,' wrote Barbauld, 'they become early engaged in domestic cares and duties.'[124] The 'giddy' white girl whose youth and beauty were the only consideration for her suitor would not, Catherine Mackintosh warned, provide companionship or produce healthy and morally upstanding children.

Catherine Mackintosh's 'A Political Epistle' was not sympathetic to, or particularly interested in, Indian women's relationships to Company servants. Her reference to 'black and stupid temporary mate' reiterated the crude racism of the majority of her British-imperialist friends, in which 'black' represented the lowest levels of humanity. Contrasting the Indian women who were discarded by Company servants in favour of a 'respectable' marriage with a 'giddy' white girl, Catherine Mackintosh wrote:

> Much whiter than thy former one her skin
> But what oh what the difference within!
> One concubine at will and one for life
> Empowered to vex thee with domestic strife[125]

The lack of distinction between these two relationships in the poem is not suggestive of any equality between white and black, rather that the two could be compared lays emphasis on the horrors of Anglo-Indian marriages. Ultimately, 'A Political Epistle' is a warning that superficial and rapid marriages would not lead to domestic happiness and harmony. Marriage and family, with its heavy burdens and responsibilities, should not be entered into at too young an age. Contrasting the youth and lithe beauty of women of England ('the daughters of our land') who spurned 'all but pleasures wild command', with the 'shapelss swol'n squalid figure' of their Anglo-Indian counterparts, Catherine Mackintosh argued for cherishing the fleeting days of carefree and 'youthful joy'.[126] Such, she hoped, would be the destiny of her own three children, and eventually also that of her husband, whose 'return home' to England, 'to range at large thy England's flow'ry fields' would, she implies ensure the family's 'freedom'.[127]

Catherine Mackintosh's critique of Anglo-Indian marriages and domestic relations reinforced the distinction between metropole and colony, underscoring the social and moral inferiority of the latter. Although her insights owed much to her stay with the Mackintosh family in Bombay, Maria Graham's published and well-circulated *Journal of a Residence in India*, offered a slightly different configuration. Beginning her discussion of Anglo-Indian women in Bombay with the statement that 'I found our fair companions like the ladies of all the country towns I know, under-bred and over-dressed, and with the exception of one or two, very ignorant and very grossiere', Maria Graham flattens-out any distinction between the provinces within Britain and those in the colonies.[128] Her only praise was reserved for Mrs Ashburner, who engaged in charitable activities in and around her home in Salsette:

> Mrs As [*sic*] accomplishments are above those of most women. Her drawing is that of an artist ... Her judgment in music is exquisite ... Her language is pure and elegant ... Would that there were a few more such European women in the East, to redeem the character of our country women; and so shew the Hindoo what English Christian women are.[129]

The contrast between the 'idleness' and vanity of the majority of Anglo-Indian women, as well as of their Indian counterparts, and Mrs Ashburner's English Christian womanhood, reinforced the connection between Englishness and virtue. In a letter to her sister, Maitland, Mary Rich made this connection even more explicit. Encouraging her sister to visit her in Bushire, she argued that the more favourable climate would allow Maitland to keep her children with her in the East for a little longer. Unlike most white women in India, her sister was, Mary claimed:

> Capable of educating your daughter, as few mothers are in India. I think it is almost a fortunate circumstance the climate obliges them to send their children to England, as in my opinion education cannot be begun too early and nothing is so destructive of a child's morals and abilities as being neglected till five or six years old, when she has acquired such a habit of idleness which always bring on ill temper that she takes the greatest disgust to those employments she ought to look upon with delight.[130]

Like Mrs Ashburner, Maitland was the exception to the rule of Anglo-Indian ignorance and idleness. Despite their differences in emphasis, all three of these women's critiques of Anglo-Indian society represented India and Anglo-Indian women as inferior versions of metropolitan England. In doing so, they configured the metropole as the ultimate site of both female virtue and of 'home'.

Conclusion

In 1814, the *Christian Observer* published an anonymous article signed by 'a country reader', which objected to Maria Graham's portrayal of 'British ladies in India' and sought to vindicate their reputation. Maria Graham had, the writer claimed, been 'dazzled' by high society, where it was inevitable that she would only meet the more 'frivolous' female members of Anglo-Indian society. Those who embodied the 'highest species of female character' would not 'abandon' their children 'to mercenary protection and unprincipled influence' in order to go to balls and parties.[131] Instead they remained 'quietly at home' engaging in activities that ranged from needlework and reading, to supervising their brothers' studies in Latin, to supporting their husbands' learned pursuits, tending to the sick and educating the poor.[132] The contrast between these English ladies, always productively engaged in activities to support their families, and Indian wives, 'shut up amid a crowd of sycophant dependants, to plot for or against her husband' was evident even to Indian people themselves: 'The native knows the Christian mother is occupied with her children, her patience with them, her watchfulness to restrain from evil, and to stimulate to good.' Ultimately, she was 'not a slave to her husband, but his best friend'.[133] Certainly, there were some white women in India who met Maria Graham's description of idleness and selfishness, but they were not, the author argued, the majority, and their characters were not produced by India but were 'transplanted thither equally with their persons'. To suggest otherwise risked discouraging 'the worthy of her sex' from venturing to India, whilst encouraging those 'of a contrary stamp' to believe that India would make a good home for them.[134]

Although both Mackintosh parents would have agreed with the anonymous 'country reader' of the need for respectable British ladies to live in India, they did not believe that the colony was a suitable place for their own daughters. Their constant reiteration of England as 'home' reveals a wider ambivalence around about the position of white women and girls in the colonies, and their role in British-imperial expansion. On the one hand, white women enabled British-imperialist men to enact the norms of 'respectable', white society and to model the idealized, patriarchal home. On the other hand, white women's presence in the colonies disrupted the conceptual distinction between metropolitan Britain as 'home' and the colonies as 'away' – a separation that endured long after the consolidation of white settler colonies.[135] In India, this conceptual separation was all the more important because of the radical difference that 'the East' represented in the European-imperial imaginary. The idea of India as an 'unhomely' space intersected with the racialized imagery of 'the East' as luxurious, effeminate and despotic, as well as backwards and barbaric. By teaching their daughters to dismiss Indian peoples as inferior, and to reject India as 'home', the Mackintosh family configured metropolitan Britain – a place that their youngest children had never really known – as the only possible space of belonging and progress.

Conclusion

> There was no noise, nothing on the coffin lid but I felt that you were in it as if my heart went out of my body as it were into the coffin as it disappeared. I shed no tears, felt no horror but a quiet consciousness that everything was finished that the whole of my existence was conveyed away in this coffin with a kind of strange identity with the coffin itself.[1]

This book has traced the discourse of 'home' and 'exile' in the philosophical, political, literary and epistolary work of a network of British-imperial literary elite, whose writings fundamentally informed the affective structures of belonging in the Anglo-imperial world of the nineteenth century. Whether they travelled far from their places of birth or not, their lives and their ideas were fundamentally shaped by British-imperial expansion. Through their writings, they shaped the ways in which British imperialists understood imperial space and colonized subjects, as well as how they justified imperial dominance. The quote above, however, comes from a letter written by Lady Catherine Mackintosh (née Allen) who, unlike the majority of people discussed, did not write for a wider public. Indeed, compared to the volumes of words produced and published by her friends and contemporaries, she barely wrote at all. When she did, her handwriting was frequently small, cross-hatched and almost illegible. Catherine Mackintosh was an educated Welsh woman, born in 1765, the daughter of a landowner who owned and managed many of the coal mines in South Wales. One of nine sisters, two of whom married into the Wedgwood family, she was part of an elite, often radical, and literary world long before she married James Mackintosh in 1797.[2] The quote that begins this conclusion forms part of a letter, written in 1808, when she was living in Bombay with her children. In it, she briefly described a fragment of a dream she had whilst her husband was away touring the Deccan in the aftermath of the Second Anglo-Maratha war. She provided little context for the dream itself, it comes after reports of gossip about a sexual liaison and brief mention of the death of an acquaintance, MrStrachey: 'These things are not pleasant to us even when they happed to people whom we are little interested.'[3] Perhaps it was her very lack of sentiment over this particular death that provoked her dream.

In many ways, Catherine Mackintosh's dream was the starting-point for my research into ideas of belonging in the British Empire; this book is the product of my attempt to think through its implications. It remains for me a source of disquiet. In Catherine Mackintosh's dream, the disappearance of an unmarked coffin can be read as the complete loss of self, an unbecoming, an emptiness. That the loss of self takes place in and through the loss of her husband speaks to the position of subjection in which British women were placed, legally and often socially, upon marriage. Yet in the context of this book, and of the collection of letters of which this fragment is a part, it is the colonial framework that determines my reading. The disappearance of the unmarked coffin evokes the many millions of African bodies dumped without ceremony in the Atlantic Ocean; or, the thousands of famine victims thrown in the Ganges or left to rot on the streets of Calcutta in 1770. It speaks to what Orlando Patterson, in the context of slavery, called 'social death' and what Saidiya Hartman defines as the process of being 'obliterated in the making of human commodities'.[4] To talk of social death in the context of the colonizer, however, seems a perverse reversal of a relationship of domination that has profoundly shaped the inequalities of the modern world. To give credence to the fears of the colonizer risks re-centring the feelings of the oppressor whilst minimizing the radical inequities and violence that structured the relations between colonizer and colonized. And yet there can be no surprise that the subconscious fears of the colonizer should resonate with the horror of colonization and enslavement. If, as Fanon argued, the denial of subject-hood formed the cornerstone of European colonial power, then that same denial haunted imperialists whose sense of self was contingent upon it.[5] Colonizer–colonized is, after all, a two-sided formation.

This book has traced the discursive process through which the denial of colonized selfhood took place, a process that went hand-in-hand with the construction of whiteness. Focusing on Adam Smith's *The Theory of Moral Sentiments*, it began with the Enlightenment idea and ideal of selfhood, showing how the very notion of an individual and autonomous 'self' was already defined by race and gender. If this period saw the 'making' of modern notions of an individual self, then enslaved Africans were present, and their selfhood denied, at the very outset of that making.[6] The self, in other words, was always already marked as white. By focusing on 'home' – a structure that combines the social, spatial, material and emotional forms – rather than 'self', I hope to have shown how this whiteness became the silent referent, the normative ideal through which the self was configured. As the first two chapters illustrated, ideas of belonging intersected with notions of the self and the development of society; these ideas underwent subtle changes during the period. Whereas Smith denied that any human society in the early stages of development had the capacity for selfhood and belonging, Dugald Stewart's reconfiguration of Smith's materialist philosophy of progress put forward a vision of 'home' that brought the moral and material together. In his lectures, belonging to 'home' became a sign of both moral virtue and material stage, whilst 'wandering' stood in as a marker of both 'savagery' and immorality.

By the early nineteenth century, the ideology of 'home' structured the emotional landscape of the Anglo-imperial world. Based on a vision of patriarchal order, settlement, property ownership and a racialized nativism, 'home' represented a fantasy of wholeness in a world increasingly fractured by difference and dispersal. In many respects, the project of empire was a project of moving and placing bodies in space to serve the material needs of the metropole and the abstract needs of capital. Through their many different forms of writing, the literary elite who have been the subject of this book contributed to giving meaning to those bodies, mobilities and spaces. Chapters 1 and 2 showed how Scottish Enlightenment philosophers constructed black bodies as lacking in emotional and intellectual capacity, denying their ability (as well as that of all women) to act as agents of their own vision of 'progress'. Despite Smith and Stewart's critiques of slavery, the philosophy of white, male superiority gave strength and legitimacy to white supremacy. As Chapters 3 to 6 illustrated through different case studies, this configuration of bodily difference mapped-on to configurations of space and belonging. Chapter 3 showed how the humanity of enslaved Africans was contingent upon them conforming to a narrow vision of 'home' that re-inscribed patriarchal master–slave relations and shored-up white supremacy. In contrast, for elite commentators on the Highlands of Scotland, discussed in Chapter 4, the meaning of their emigration to America rested on the question of the nature of their belonging. Could their apparent attachment to 'native land' really be understood in terms of national bonds, or was it borne of an identification with structures and loyalties that were incompatible with modern nationhood and a commercial society? Were Highlanders 'homely' or inherently prone to wandering? Similarly, in India, questions about East India Company servants' belonging were the subject of debate and distrust. In this context, colonial knowledge formation and racial hierarchy were harnessed to the project of promoting an identification with 'civilization', whiteness and

Britain as 'home'. For the Mackintosh family themselves, discussed in Chapter 6, the threat of losing their identity played out in relationship to their daughters' white femininity. 'Home', in this context, is evident as a gendered performance of respectability and whiteness.

The bifurcation of metropolitan and colonial space as 'home' and 'exile' marked the former as emotionally sustaining, and the latter as defined by lack. Like many abolitionists, Graham's plea for pity for enslaved Africans revolved around their status as exiles, although she simultaneously cast doubt on their sense of belonging and attachment at all. The discourse of 'exile' played a greater role in the debate over Highland emigration, where the construction of British North America as 'exile' foreclosed the possibility of a new relationship to 'home', whilst simultaneously representing their loss to the nation as a tragic inevitability. Equally, for the Mackintosh family, their configuration of Bombay as 'exile' served to reiterate their belonging to metropolitan Britain as 'home'. In this context, 'exile' and the lamentation for an ever-deferred future of emotional wholeness as 'home' denied responsibility for a present in which different peoples were reliant on each other in increasingly wide webs of co-production, exploitation and resistance. Ironically, this idea of 'home' as a moral imperative was configured and disseminated by a generation of British men and women whose own lives were defined by wandering. The messy realities of their own home-lives – in which servants were the primary carers for children; aunts, cousins and friends lived as part of the same household; and many uncles and sons spent most of their lives far away from 'home' – did little to undermine the narrow ideology of 'home'. In doing so, they denied the possibilities of multiple and alternative forms of belonging beyond the boundaries of patriarchal land ownership and the nation.

Although the ideas of a network of white, British imperialists writing over two hundred years ago may seem far removed from the problems of today, the discourse of 'home' and 'exile' and its role in racism and white supremacy has left a lasting legacy. The idealization of 'home' as a fixed and settled site of productive and reproductive labour continues to haunt today's representation of mobility and belonging in new contexts of mass mobility, an ongoing refugee crisis and a renewed campaign against Roma travellers in the UK. In each of these politicized discourses, to return 'home' or to settle 'at home' becomes the only legitimate aspiration and state of being. Like the enslaved Africans of the white imagination, today's refugees are deemed worthy of sympathy and charity only if they prove themselves to be abject 'exiles'. It is noticeable that when newspapers seek to stir hatred of difference, they use 'migrant labour' instead of 'refugee'; a sign of the enduring power of 'wandering' to be associated with immorality. The increasing demonization of Roma travellers relies on the same fear and suspicion of mobility that saw native American peoples dismissed as 'barbaric' and, in the mid-nineteenth century, Indian tribes criminalized and forcibly settled on land. As Black feminists and feminists of colour have long argued, 'home' need not be marked by a border or even defined by a feeling of safety and return.[7] Rather, to live 'at home' may be simply to embrace the very sense of uncertainty and inbetween-ness that Enlightenment thinkers marked as aberrant and eschewed as 'wilderness'.

Notes

Introduction

1. M Graham to Mackenzie, undated, NLS, MS 6366: Private letters from Calcutta in case of the death of Gordon Mackenzie, 23.
2. John Howard Payne, *Home, Sweet Home* (Boston, MA: Lee and Shepard, c.1880)
3. 'Homesickness, n.' OED Online, September 2019. Oxford University Press, https://www.-oed-com.ezproxy.nottingham.ac.uk/view/Entry/87934 [accessed 2 December 2019].
4. Josiah Wedgwood, *An Address to the Workmen in the Pottery on the Subject of Entering into the Service of Foreign Manufacturers* (Newcastle: J. Smith, 1783), p.15.
5. 'Homely' in Samuel Johnson, *A Dictionary of the English Language*, 2 vols, vol. 1. (11th edn, London: Johnson, Dilly, Roibinson and Richardson, 1799), n.p.
6. Catherine Hall and Sonya Rose (eds), *At Home with the British Empire: Metropolitan Culture and the Imperial World* (Cambridge: Cambridge University Press, 2006).
7. 'Trans-Atlantic Slave Trade: estimates', https://www.slavevoyages.org/assessment/estimates [accessed 2 December 2019].
8. James Horn, *British Diaspora: Emigration From Britain, 1680–1815* (Oxford: Oxford University Press, 1998), p.50.
9. P.J. Marshall, 'The British in Asia: Trade to Dominion, 1700–1765' in P.J. Marshall and Alaine Low (eds), *The Oxford History of the British Empire: Vol II: The Eighteenth Century* (Oxford: Oxford University Press, 1998), p.495.
10. Subhas Ranjan Chakrabarty, 'Colonialism, Migration and Resource Crisis', *CRG Research Paper Series, Policies and Practices*, vol. 42 (2011), http://www.mcrg.ac.uk/PP42.pdf [accessed 2 December 2019].
11. See Kate Fullagar and Michael A. McDonnell (eds), *Facing Empire: Indigenous Experiences in a Revolutionary Age* (Baltimore, MD: Johns Hopkins University Press, 2018).
12. T.M. Devine, *Scotland's Empire, 1600–1815* (London: Penguin, 2004), ch.1.
13. Dirk Kolff, *Naukar, Rajput and Sepoy: The Ethnohistory of the Military Labour Market in Hindustan, 1450–1850* (Cambridge: Cambridge University Press, 1990), ch. 1.
14. Amalendu Guha, 'Parsi Seths as Entrepreneurs, 1750–1850', *Economic and Political Weekly*, 5, 35 (1970), p.109.

15 The historiography of this transition is vast. See, for example, Maxine Berg, 'In Pursuit of Luxury: Global History and British Consumer Goods in the Eighteenth Century', *Past and Present*, 182 (2004), pp.85–142; Emma Griffin, *A Short History of the British Industrial Revolution* (Basingstoke and New York: Palgrave Macmillan, 2010); Margaret Hunt, *The Middling Sort: Commerce, Gender and the Family in England, 1680–1780* (Berkeley and Los Angeles: University of California Press, 1996); J.G. Barker-Benfield, *The Culture of Sensibility: Sex and Society in Eighteenth-Century Britain* (Chicago, IL: Chicago University Press, 1992).

16 J.G.A Pocock, *Virtue, Commerce and History: Essays on Political Thought and History, Chiefly in the Eighteenth Century* (Cambridge: Cambridge University Press, 1985), ch.11; Gordon Pentland, *Radicalism, Reform and National Identity in Scotland, 1820–1833* (Rochester, NY: Boydell Press, 2008); Catherine Hall, Jane Rendall and Keith McClelland, *Defining the Victorian Nation: Class, Race, Gender and the Reform Act of 1867* (Cambridge: Cambridge University Press, 2000).

17 Joanna Innes and Arthur Burns, 'Introduction' in Joanna Innes and Arthur Burns (eds), *Rethinking the Age of Reform: Britain, 1780–1850* (Cambridge: Cambridge University Press, 2003), p.2.

18 Alan Lester, 'Imperial Circuits and Networks: Geographies of the British Empire', *History Compass*, 4, 1 (2006), pp.124–41; Zoe Laidlaw, *Colonial Connections 1815–45: Patronage, the Information Revolution and Colonial Government* (Manchester and New York: Manchester University Press, 2005), ch.2; Frederick Cooper and Ann Stoler, 'Between Metropole and Colony: Rethinking a Research Agenda' in Frederick Cooper and Ann Stoler (eds), *Tensions of Empire: Colonial Cultures in a Bourgeois World* (Berkeley and Los Angeles: University of California Press, 1997), pp.1–56; Mary Louise Pratt, *Imperial Eyes: Travel Writing and Transculturation* (London: Routledge, 1992), pp.31–5.

19 See Catherine Hall, *Macaulay and Son: Architects of Imperial Britain* (New Haven, CT: Yale University Press, 2014).

20 P.J. Marshall, 'Britain and the World in the Eighteenth Century I: Reshaping the Empire', *Transactions of the Royal Historical Society*, 6, 8 (1998), pp.1–18; P.J. Marshall, 'Britons and the World in the Eighteenth Century: II Britons and Americans', *Transactions of the Royal Historical Society*, 6, 9 (1999), pp.1–15.

21 Michael A. Mcdonnell, 'The Indigenous Architecture of Empire: the Anishinaabe Odawa in North America' in Kate Fullagar and Michael McDonnell (eds), *Facing Empire*, pp.48–71. See Chapter 4.

22 D.C. Geggus, 'The Caribbean in the Age of Revolution' in David Armitage and Sanjay Subrahmanyam (eds), *The Age of Revolutions in Global Context, c.1760–1840* (Basingstoke: Palgrave Macmillan, 2010), pp.83–100. See Chapter 3.

23 C.A. Bayly, *The New Cambridge History of India, Vol II: Indian Society and the making of the British Empire* (Cambridge: Cambridge University Press, 1988), ch.3; Sekar Bandyopadhyay, *From Plassey to Partition* (Hyderabad: Orient Longman, 2004).

24 Susanne Seymour, Stephen Daniels and Charles Watkins, 'Estate and Empire: Sir George Cornewan's Management of Moccas, Herefordshire and La Taste, Grenada, 1771–1819', *Journal of Historical Geography*, 24, 3 (1998), pp.313–51.
25 Margot Finn and Kate Smith (eds), *The East India Company at Home* (London: UCL Press, 2018).
26 Dorinda Outram, *The Enlightenment* (2nd edn, Cambridge: Cambridge University Press, 2005), pp.13–16; Simon Gikandi, *Slavery and the Culture of Taste* (Princeton, NJ and Oxford: Princeton University Press, 2011); Beth Kowaleski-Wallace, 'Women, China and Consumer Culture in Eighteenth-Century England', *Eighteenth-Century Studies*, 29, 2 (1995/6), pp.153–67.
27 Rob Skinner and Alan Lester, 'Humanitarianism and Empire: New Research Agendas', *The Journal of Imperial and Commonwealth History*, 40, 5 (2012), pp.729–47.
28 David Hume, 'Essay XX: Of National Characters' in *Essays and Treatises on Several Subjects*, 4 vols (London and Edinburgh: T. Cadell, 1770), iv, note M, p.259.
29 Silvia Sebastiani, 'Race and National Characters in Eighteenth-Century Scotland: the Polygenetic Discourses of Kames and Pinkerton', *Cromohs*, 8 (2003), pp.1–14; Nicholas Hudson, 'From "Nation" to "Race": The Origin of Racial Classification in Eighteenth-Century Thought', *Eighteenth-Century Studies*, 29, 3 (1996), pp.247–64; Colin Kidd, *The Forging of Races: Race and Scripture in the Protestant Atlantic World, 1600–2000* (Cambridge: Cambridge University Press), ch.5.
30 Emmanuel Eze, 'Hume, Race, and Human Nature', *Journal of the History of Ideas*, 61, 4 (2000), pp.691–8.
31 Stuart Hall, 'Subjects in History: Making Diasporic Identities' in Wahneema Lubiano (ed.), *The House That Race Built* (New York: Vintage Books, 1998), pp.289–91.
32 Andrew Curran, *The Anatomy of Blackness: Science and Slavery in an Age of Enlightenment* (Baltimore, MD: Johns Hopkins University Press, 2011).
33 Jennifer Morgan, 'Male Travellers, Female Bodies, and the Gendering of Racial Ideology' in Antoinette Burton and Tony Ballantyne (eds), *Bodies in Contact: Rethinking Colonial Encounters in World History* (Durham, NC and London: Duke University Press, 2005), p.65.
34 Joan Paul-Rubiés, 'Were Early Modern Europeans Racist?' in Amos Morris-Reich and Dirk Rupnow (eds), *Ideas of 'Race' in the History of the Humanities* (Cham: Palgrave Macmillan, 2017), pp.33–87.
35 Roxann Wheeler, *The Complexion of Race: Categories of Difference in Eighteenth-Century British Culture* (Philadelphia, PA: Philadelphia University Press, 2010).
36 Steve Garner, 'Atlantic Crossing', *Atlantic Studies*, 4, 1 (2007), pp.117–32.
37 Sara Ahmed, 'A Phenomenology of Whiteness', *Feminist Theory*, 8, 2 (2007), pp.149–68.

38 Cheryl Harris, 'Whiteness as Property', *Harvard Law Review*, 106, 8 (1993), p.1721.
39 Dana Rabin, '"In a Country of Liberty?": Slavery, Villeinage and the Making of Whiteness in the Somerset Case (1772)', *History Workshop Journal*, 72 (2011), pp.5–29.
40 Ibid., p.23.
41 Felicity Nussbaum, *The Autobiographical Subject: Gender and Ideology in Eighteenth-Century England* (Baltimore, MD and London: Johns Hopkins University Press, 1989), pp.50–5. Nussbaum's later work deals more centrally with the intersections between racism and sexism, see, for example, Felicity Nussbaum, *The Limits of the Human: Fictions of Anomaly, Race, and Gender in the Long Eighteenth Century* (Cambridge: Cambridge University Press, 2003).
42 Dror Wahrman, *The Making of the Modern Self: Identity and Culture in Eighteenth-Century England* (New Haven, CT: Yale University Press, 2004), p.278.
43 Sarah Knott, *Sensibility and the American Revolution* (Chapel Hill: University of North Carolina Press, 2009), pp.4–15.
44 Davidoff and Hall, *Family Fortunes:*
45 For the legal idea of, and claims to, British subjecthood, see Sudipta Sen, *Distant Sovereignty: National Imperialism and the Origins of British India* (New York: Routledge, 2002); Hannah Weiss Muller, *Subjects and Sovereign, Bonds of Belonging in the Eighteenth-Century British Empire* (New York: Oxford University Press, 2017).
46 Kathleen Wilson, *Island Race: Englishness, Empire and Gender in the Eighteenth Century* (New York: Routledge, 2003).
47 Colin Kidd, 'North Britishness and the Nature of Eighteenth-Century Patriotisms', *The Historical Journal*, 39, 2 (1996), pp.361–82; *Subverting Scotland's Past: Scottish Whig Historians and the Creation of Anglo-British Identity c.1689–1830* (Cambridge: Cambridge University Press, 1993).
48 Saree Makdisi, *Making England Western: Occidentalism, Race and Imperial Culture* (Chicago, IL and London: University of Chicago Press, 2011). See also David Robinson, 'Orientalism or Meridionism? British Identity Formation through Travel Writing on India and Italy, 1760–1860', Unpublished PhD Thesis, University of Nottingham, 2020.
49 Jennifer Pitts, *A Turn to Empire: The Rise of Imperial Liberalism in Britain and France* (Princeton, NJ: Princeton University Press, 2006); Sankar Muthu, *Enlightenment against Empire* (Princeton, NJ: Princeton University Press, 2003).
50 Uday Singh Mehta, *Liberalism and Empire* (Chicago, IL: University of Chicago Press, 1999).
51 See Bruno Latour, *We Have Never Been Modern*, trans. Catherine Porter (Cambridge, MA: Harvard University Press, 1993), pp.1–24; Donna Harraway,

'Situated Knowledges: The Science Question in Feminism and the Privilege of Partial Perspective', *Feminist Studies*, 14, 3 (1988), pp.575–99.

52 David Lambert and Alan Lester, 'Introduction: Imperial Spaces, Imperial Subjects' in David Lambert and Alan Lester (eds), *Colonial Lives across the British Empire: Imperial Careering in the Long 19th Century* (Cambridge: Cambridge University Press, 2006), pp.1–31.

53 Alan Lester, 'British Settler Discourse and the Circuits of Empire', *History Workshop Journal*, 54 (2002), pp.24–48.

54 BL Add MS 78764, Richard Sharp to James Mackintosh, 18 January 1805, London, p.23.

55 David Knapman, *Conversation Sharp: the Biography of a London Gentleman Richard Sharp (1759–1835) in Letters, Prose and Verse* (Dorchester: The Dorset Press, 2003); Onni Gust, 'Remembering and Forgetting the Scottish Highlands: Sir James Mackintosh and the Forging of a British Imperial Identity', *Journal of British Studies*, 52 (2013), pp.1–23.

56 For imperial letters, see Sarah Pearsall, *Atlantic Families: Lives and Letters in the Later Eighteenth Century* (Oxford: Oxford University Press, 2008) and Laura Ishiguro, *Nothing to Write Home About: British Family Correspondence and the Settler-Colonial Everyday* (Vancouver: UBC Press, 2019).

57 BL Add MS 78764, London 18 January 1805 Sharp to Mackintosh, p.23.

58 Sigmund Freud, *The Uncanny*, trans. David Mclintock (London: Penguin, 2003), p.151.

Chapter 1

1 Adam Smith, *The Theory of Moral Sentiments. Or, an Essay towards an Analysis of the Principles by Which Men Naturally Judge Concerning the Conduct and Character, First of Their Neighbours, and Afterwards of Themselves. To Which Is Added, a Dissertation on the Origins of Language* (4th edn, Edinburgh and London, 1774, first published in 1759), p.316.

2 Ibid.

3 Thomas Clarkson, *The History of the Abolition of the African Slave-Trade by the British Parliament*, 2 vols, vol. 1 (London: Longman, Hurst, Reed and Orme, 1808), p.86.

4 Adam Smith, *The Wealth of Nations*, edited with an introduction by Andrew Skinner, Book I (London: Penguin, 1999, first published in 1776), pp.183–4.

5 For a wider analysis of this 'outrage', see Michael E. Woods, 'A Theory of Moral Outrage: Indignation and Eighteenth-Century British Abolitionism', *Slavery and Abolition*, 36, 4 (2015), pp.662–83.

6   Uday Singh Mehta, *Liberalism and Empire: A Study in Nineteenth-Century British Liberal Thought* (Chicago, IL and London: University of Chicago Press, 1999); Felicity Nussbaum, *Torrid Zones: Maternity, Sexuality and Empire in Eighteenth-Century English Narratives* (Baltimore, MD: Johns Hopkins University Press, 1995), pp.192–210; Sylvia Tomaselli, 'The Enlightenment Debate on Women', *History Workshop Journal*, 20 (1985), pp.101–24; Barbara Taylor and Sarah Knott (eds), *Women, Gender and Enlightenment* (Basingstoke: Palgrave Macmillan, 2005); Amit Rai, *Rule of Sympathy: Sentiment, Race, and Power, 1750–1850* (Basingstoke: Palgrave Macmillan, 2002).

7   Nicholas Phillipson, *Adam Smith: An Enlightened Life* (New Haven, CT and London: Yale University Press, 2010), p.1.

8   As well, presumably, as its vast inequalities and oppressions. See, for example, Adam Smith Institute, https://www.adamsmith.org/about-adam-smith [accessed 10 August 2019].

9   J.S. Narayan Rao, 'Adam Smith in India' in Hiroshi Mizuta and Chuhei Sugiyama (eds), *Adam Smith: International Perspectives* (Basingstoke and London: The Macmillan Press, 1993), p.266.

10 Philipson, *Adam Smith*, pp.180–3.

11 Ibid., p.257.

12 Ibid., p.113; R.A. Houston, *Social Change in the Age of Enlightenment: Edinburgh, 1660–1760* (Oxford: Oxford University Press, 1994); Davis D. McElroy, *Scotland's Age of Improvement: A Survey of Eighteenth-Century Literary Clubs and Societies* (Washington, DC: Washington State University Press, 1969).

13 Michael Atiya, 'Benjamin Franklin and the Edinburgh Enlightenment', *Proceedings of the American Philosophical Society*, 150, 4 (December 2006), pp.591–606.

14 James Bonar and John Gray, *A Catalogue of the Library of Adam Smith* (London and New York: Macmillan 1894).

15 Mary Louise Pratt, *Imperial Eyes: Travel Writing and Transculturation* (London and New York, 1992). See also, Alexander Garrett, 'Anthropology: The "Original" of Human Nature' in Alexander Brodie (ed.), *The Cambridge Companion to the Scottish Enlightenment* (Cambridge: Cambridge University Press, 2003), pp.79–93.

16 Smith, *Theory*, p.39. For further discussion of Smith's gendered exclusions, see Lucinda Cole, '(Anti)Feminist Sympathies: The Politics of Relationship in Smith, Wollstonecraft, and More', *ELH*, 58 (1991), pp.107–40; Maureen Harkin, 'Smith's *The Theory of Moral Sentiments:* Sympathy, Women and Emulation', *Studies in Eighteenth-Century Culture*, 24 (1995), pp.175–90; Chris Nyland, 'Adam Smith, Stage Theory and the Status of Women', *History of Political Economy*, 25, 4 (1993), pp.617–40; Jane Rendall, 'Virtue and Commerce: Women in the Making of Adam Smith's Political Economy' in Ellen Kennedy and Susan Mendus (eds), *Women in Western Political Philosophy* (Brighton: Wheatsheaf Press, 1987). In relationship to

Enlightenment thought in general: Barbara Taylor, 'Enlightenment and the Uses of Woman', *History Workshop Journal*, 74, 1 (2012), pp.79–87; Karen O'Brien, *Women and the Enlightenment in Eighteenth-Century Britain* (Cambridge: Cambridge University Press, 2009); G.J. Barker-Benfield, *The Culture of Sensibility: Sex and Society in Eighteenth-Century Britain* (Chicago, IL and London: The University of Chicago Press, 1992), pp.132–41.

17 Rendall, 'Virtue and Commerce'; Jane Rendall, 'Women and the Public Sphere', *Gender and History*, 11, 3 (1999), pp.475–88; Leonore Davidoff and Catherine Hall, *Family Fortunes: Men and Women of the English Middle Class* (Chicago, IL: University of Chicago Press, 1987).

18 Lucinda Cole, '(Anti-)Feminist Sympathies: The Politics of Relationship in Smith, Wollstonecraft, and More', *ELH*, 58, 1 (1991), pp.115–17.

19 Adam Smith, *Lectures on Jurisprudence*, R.L. Meek, D.D. Raphael and P.G. Stein (eds) (Oxford: Oxford University Press, 1978), p.15.

20 Francis Hutcheson, *A System of Moral Philosophy in Three Books to Which Is Prefixed an Account of the Life, Writings and Character of the Author by the Reverend William Leechman*, vol. 1 (London: Millar and Longman, 1755), p.1.

21 UncoverEd: a collaborative decolonial research project, http://uncover-ed.org/1809-william-fergusson/ [accessed 10 August 2019].

22 Frank Barber is mentioned in James Boswell, *The Journal of a Tour to the Hebrides*, edited, with an Introduction and Notes by Peter Levi (London: Penguin Books, 1984, first published in 1786), p.201; See also: Peter Fryer, *Staying Power: The History of Black People in Britain* (London and New York: Pluto Press, 2010, first published in 1984), pp.424–6; David Olusoga, *Black and British: A Forgotten History* (London: Palgrave Macmillan, 2016), pp.99–101.

23 Smith, *Theory*, p.211.

24 David Hume, *Essays and Treatises on Several Subjects in Four Volumes*, vol. 1. Essay XX: Of National Character (London and Edinburgh, 1770), note M, p.259. Italics mine. For discussion of the racism in this essay, see Emmanuel Eze, 'Hume, Race, and Human Nature', *Journal of the History of Ideas*, 61, 4 (2000), pp.691–8; John Immerwahr, 'Hume's Revised Racism', *Journal of the History of Ideas*, 53, 3 (1992), pp.481–86; Sylvia Sebastiani and Aaron Garret, 'David Hume on Race' in Naomi Zack (ed.), *The Oxford Handbook of Philosophy of Race* (Oxford: Oxford University Press, 2017), pp.31–43.

25 Laurent Du Bois, 'An Enslaved Enlightenment: Rethinking the Intellectual History of the French Atlantic', *Social History*, 31, 1 (2006), pp.1–14.

26 Elizabeth Jane Wall Hinds, 'The Spirit of Trade: Olaudah Equiano's Conversion, Legalism, and the Merchants' Life', *African American Review*, 32, 4 (1998), pp.635–47; Vincent Carretta, 'Three West Indian Writers of the 1780s Revisited and Revised', *Research in African Literatures*, 29, 4 (1998), pp.73–87; Lisa Lowe, *The Intimacies of Four Continents* (Durham, NC: Duke University Press, 2015), ch.2.

27 See Introduction, Chapters 3 and 5 in particular. See also, Jane Rendall, 'Bluestockings and Reviewers: Gender, Power and Culture in Britain, c.1800–1830', *Nineteenth-Century Contexts*, 26, 4 (2004), pp.355–74; Jane Rendall, 'Adaptations: History, Gender, and Political Economy in the Work of Dugald Stewart', *History of European Ideas*, 38, 1 (2012), pp.143–61; O'Brien, *Women and Enlightenment*, pp.1–34; Rosalind Carr, *Gender and Enlightenment Culture in Eighteenth-Century Scotland* (Edinburgh: Edinburgh University Press, 2014), ch.2.
28 Phillipson, *Adam Smith*, pp.3–4; Rendall, 'Virtue and Commerce', pp.62–3.
29 Silvia Sebastiani, *Scottish Enlightenment: Race, Gender and the Limits of Progress* (Basingstoke: Palgrave Macmillan, 2013), pp.75–6; Ronald Meek, 'Adam Smith, Turgot and the Four Stages Theory', *Journal of the History of Political Economy*, 3, 1 (1971), pp.9–27.
30 Adam Smith, *Lectures*, pp.14–37.
31 Joseph François Lafitau, *Moeurs des Sauvages Ameriquains Comparées aux moeurs des premiers temps* (Paris, 1724), https://archive.org/details/cihm_01690/page/n5 [accessed 10 August 2019]. For the French Enlightenment see David Harvey, *The French Enlightenment and Its Others: The Mandarin, the Savage and the Invention of the Human Sciences* (Basingstoke: Palgrave Macmillan, 2012), pp.69–95.
32 Dugald Stewart, 'An Account of the Life and Writings of the Author' in Adam Smith (ed.), *Essays on Philosophical Subjects* (Basil: James Dicker, 1799), pp.xliv–xlix; H.M. Hopfl, 'From Savage to Scotsman: Conjectural History in the Scottish Enlightenment', *Journal of British Studies*, 17, 2 (1978), pp.19–40.
33 James Mackintosh, 'Law of Nature and Nations' (1799)', in Donald Winch (ed. and intro.), *Vindiciae Gallicae and Other Writings on the French Revolution* (Indianapolis, IN: Liberty Fund, 2006), p.219.
34 See, for example, the reference to 'sympathy' in Smith, *Lectures*, p.184.
35 Smith, *Theory*.
36 Hume, *A Treatise on Human Nature*, ed. and intro. L.A. Selby-Bigger (Oxford: Clarendon Press, 1894), vol. 2, p.73.
37 Markman Ellis, *The Politics of Sensibility: Race, Gender and Commerce in the Sentimental Novel* (Cambridge: Cambridge University Press, 2004), pp.14–15.
38 See Alexander Brodie, 'Sympathy and the Impartial Spectator' in Knud Haakonssen (ed.), *The Cambridge Companion to Adam Smith* (Cambridge: Cambridge University Press, 2006), pp.158–88.
39 Smith, *Theory*, p.3
40 Ibid., p.43.
41 Ibid., p.82.
42 Ibid., p.68.
43 This is the general argument of Part I, Section I 'Of the Sense of Propriety' and is discussed again throughout, particularly in Part II Section I: 'Of the sense of merit and dismerit.'

44 Smith, *Theory*, p.143
45 Ibid., p.213. See also, Charles Griswold, *Adam Smith and the Virtues of Enlightenment* (Cambridge: Cambridge University Press, 1999), pp.141-2.
46 Ibid., pp.237-8.
47 Griswald, *Adam Smith and the Virtues of Enlightenment*, p.141.
48 Knud Haakonsen, *Natural Law and Moral Philosophy* (Cambridge: Cambridge University Press, 1996), pp.159-60.
49 Smith, *Lectures*, p.17
50 Ibid., p.32.
51 Ibid., pp.438-9.
52 Rendall, 'Virtue and Commerce'; Cole, '(Anti-)Feminist Sympathies'.
53 Hume, *Treatise*, vol. 3, p.64.
54 Adam Ferguson, *An Essay on the History of Civil Society* (5th edn, London and Edinburgh, 1782), pp.5-6.
55 Brodie, 'Sympathy and the Impartial Spectator', p.160; H.M. Hopfl, 'From Savage to Scotsman', 17, 2 (1978), p.26.
56 Smith, *Lectures.*, p.39.
57 Smith, *Theory,* p.439.
58 Ibid., p.172.
59 Smith, *Theory*, p.313.
60 Ibid.
61 Ibid., p.319.
62 Ibid., p.317.
63 Sebatsiani, *Scottish Enlightenment*, ch.5.
64 Jane Rendall, 'Gender, Race and the Progress of Civilization: Introduction' in Barbara Taylor and Sarah Knott (eds), *Women, Gender and Enlightenment* (Basingstoke: Palgrave Macmillan, 2005), pp.70-2; Chris Nyland, 'Adam Smith, Stage Theory and the Status of Women', *History of Political Economy*, 25, 4 (1993), pp.617-40.
65 Rendall, 'Virtue and Commerce'.
66 Smith, *Theory*, p.278.
67 Ibid., p.41
68 Ibid.
69 Smith, *Lectures*, pp.16-18; p.408.
70 Smith, *Theory*, p.278
71 Smith, *Lectures*, pp.48-51.
72 Smith, *Wealth of Nations*, book III, p.515.
73 Ibid., p.512.
74 Smith, *Theory*, p.85.
75 Ibid., pp.87-88 & 94.

76 Ibid., p.94.
77 Smith, *Theory*, p.87.
78 Smith, *Theory*, p.95.
79 Hume, 'On National Character', p.259.
80 *A Catalogue of the Library of Adam Smith*, p.17 & p.59. For Lord Kames's views on racial difference, see Silvia Sebastiani, 'Race and National Characters in Eighteenth-Century Scotland: The Polygenetic Discourses of Kames and Pinkerton', *Cromohs Virtual Seminars*, 8 (2003), pp.1–14. For broader discussion of ideas of race in the Scottish Enlightenment, see Colin Kidd, *The Forging of Races: Race and Scripture in the Protestant Atlantic World* (Cambridge: Cambridge University Press, 2006); Andrew Curran, *The Anatomy of Blackness: Science and Slavery in an Age of Enlightenment* (Baltimore, MD: Johns Hopkins University Press, 2011); Roxann Wheeler, *The Complexion of Race: Categories of Difference in Eighteenth-Century British Culture* (Philadelphia, PA: University of Pennsylvania Press, 2000); Emmanuel Eze, *Race and the Enlightenment: A Reader* (Oxford: Wiley-Blackwell, 1997); Robert Bernasconi and Tommy Lott, *The Idea of Race* (Indianapolis, IN and Cambridge: Hackett, 2000); Brendan O'Flaherty and Jill Shapiro, 'Apes, Essences, and Races: What Natural Scientists Believed about Human Variation, 1700–1900' in David Colander, Robert Prasch, Felhuni Sheth (eds), *Race, Liberalism and Economics* (Ann Arbor: University of Michigan Press, 2004), pp.21–55; Kaija Tiianen-Tiller, *The Problem of Humanity: Blacks in the European Enlightenment* (Helsinki: Suoen Historiallinen Seura, 1994).
81 Smith, *Wealth of Nations*, p.120.
82 Hume, *Treatise*, vol. 2, p.75
83 Ibid., pp.75–6.
84 See, in particular, Smith's discussion of the manners of different professions in *Theory*, p.305.
85 Ibid., pp.285–6.
86 Ibid., p.317.
87 Ibid., p.314.
88 Srividhya Swaminathan, 'Adam Smith's Moral Economy and the Debate to Abolish the Slave Trade', *Rhetoric Society Quarterly*, 37, 4 (2007), pp.481–507; David Brion Davis, *The Problem of Slavery in Western Culture* (Oxford: Oxford University Press, 1966); Brycchan Carey, *British Abolitionism and the Rhetoric of Sensibility* (Basingstoke: Palgrave Macmillan, 2005); Jennifer Pitts, *A Turn to Empire* (Princeton, NJ: Princeton University Press, 2006), ch.2.
89 Arthur Lee, *An Essay in Vindication of the Continental Colonies of America from a Censure of Mr Adam Smith, in His Theory of Moral Sentiments with Some Reflections on Slavery by an American* (London: Beckett and De Hont, 1764), pp.v–vi.
90 Ibid., p.38.

91 Ibid., pp.v–vi.
92 Ibid., p.19.
93 Ibid., pp.18–19.
94 Ibid., pp.30–1.
95 Ibid., p.41.
96 Smith, *Theory*, p.105.
97 See Emmanuel Eze, 'Hume, Race, and Human Nature', *Journal of the History of Ideas*, 61, 4 (2000), pp.691–8. For discussion of Hume's 'racism', see John Immerwahr, 'Hume's Revised Racism', *Journal of the History of Ideas* 53, 3 (1992), pp.481–48; Sylvia Sebastiani and Aaron Garret, 'David Hume on Race' in *The Oxford Handbook of Philosophy of Race,* Naomi Zack (ed.) (Oxford: Oxford University Press, 2017), pp.31–43. For wider discussions of Enlightenment racism, see Tiianen-Tiller, *The Problem of Humanity*; Joan Paul-Rubies, 'Were Early Modern Europeans Racist?' in Amos Morris-Reich and Dirk Rupnow (eds), *Ideas of Race in the History of the Humanities* (Basingstoke: Palgrave Macmillan, 2017).

Chapter 2

1 Archibald Alison, 'Lectures on Moral Philosophy, 1808', EUA, Gen. 1382–5, vol. 4, p.67.
2 See H.M. Hopfl, 'From Savage to Scotsman: Conjectural History in the Scottish Enlightenment', *Journal of British Studies*, 17, 2 (1978), pp.19–40; J.G.A. Pocock, *Barbarism and Religion, v.4 Barbarians, Savages and Empire* (Cambridge: Cambridge University Press, 2005), pp.186–7.
3 Alison, 'Lectures', p.67.
4 Silvia Sebastiani, *The Scottish Enlightenment: Race, Gender and the Limits of Progress* (Basingstoke: Palgrave Macmillan, 2013), pp.1–2;
5 Gordon MacIntyre, *Dugald Stewart: The Pride and Ornament of Scotland* (Brighton: Sussex Academic Press, 2003), pp.30 & p.43. Until recently, Stewart was somewhat overlooked by intellectual historians of the Scottish Enlightenment. A recent special collection provides a re-evaluation of his work. See Knud Haakonssen and Paul Wood, 'Introduction', *History of European Ideas*, 38, 1 (2012), pp.1–4. See also C.B. Bow, 'Dugald Stewart and the Legacy of Common Sense in the Scottish Enlightenment' in C.B. Bow (ed.), *Common Sense in the Scottish Enlightenment* (Oxford: Oxford University Press, 2018), pp.200–17; Prior to this the most extensive intellectual histories of Stewart is Donald Winch, 'The System of the North: Dugald Stewart and His Pupils' in Stefan Collini, Donald Winch and John Burrow (eds), *That Noble Science of Politics: A Study in Nineteenth-Century Intellectual History* (Cambridge: Cambridge University Press, 1983), pp.23–61;

Paul Wood, 'Dugald Stewart and the Invention of 'the Scottish Enlightenment' in Paul Wood (ed.), *The Scottish Enlightenment: Essays in Reinterpretation* (Rochester, NY: University of Rochester Press, 2000), pp.1–35; Knud Haakonssen, *Natural Law and Moral Philosophy: From Grotius to the Scottish Enlightenment* (Cambridge: Cambridge University Press, 1996), ch.7.

6   Pam Perkins, 'Stewart [née Cranstoun], Helen D'Arcy (1765–1838)' in Oxford Dictionary of National Biography, https://doi.org/10.1093/ref:odnb/6618 [accessed 22 August 2019].

7   Helen D'Arcy Stewart to William Drennan, 31 December 1807, EUA Dcc. 1. 100/2 ff1-4, p.3.

8   See Jane Rendall, '"Elementary Principles of Education": Elizabeth Hamilton, Maria Edgeworth and the Uses of Common Sense Philosophy', *History of European Ideas*, 39, 5 (2013), pp.613–30; Richard De Ritter 'Female Philosophers and the Comprehensive View: Elizabeth Hamilton's *Letters on the Elementary Principles of Education*', *European Romantic Review*, 23, 6 (2012), pp.689–705; William McCarthy, *Anna Letitia Barbauld: Voice of the Enlightenment* (Baltimore, MD: Johns Hopkins University Press, 2008). For Graham and Edgeworth, see Chapter 3.

9   Winch, 'The System of the North'; Cristina Paoletti, 'Common Sense in the Public Sphere: Dugald Stewart and the *Edinburgh Review*', *History of European Ideas*, 31, 1 (2012), pp.163–4.

10 William Christie, *The Edinburgh Review in the Literary Culture of Romantic Britain: Mammoth and Maglonyx* (London: Pickering and Chatto, 2009), p.25.

11 Quoted in Donald Winch, 'Introduction' in James Mill (ed.), *Selected Economic Writings* (Edinburgh: Oluiver Boyd for the Scottish Economic Society, 1966), https://oll.libertyfund.org/pages/mill-james-1773-1836 [accessed 22 August 2019].

12 See Javed Majeed, *Ungoverned Imaginings: James Mill's the History of British India and Orientalism* (Oxford: Oxford University Press, 1992); also, Chapter 6 below.

13 Uday Singh Mehta, *Liberalism and Empire: A Study in Nineteenth-Century British Liberal Thought* (Chicago, IL and London: University of Chicago Press, 1999), p.64.

14 Sir James Mackintosh to Dugald Stewart, Bombay, 2 November 1805, BL Add 78764, p.58.

15 See below Chapters 5 and 6. See also Martha McClaren, *British India and British Scotland, 1780–1830: Career Building, Empire Building, and a Scottish School of Thought on Indian Governance* (Akron, OH: The University of Akron Press, 2001) p.65; Jane Rendall, 'Scottish Orientalism: From Robertson to James Mill', *The Historical Journal*, 25, 1 (1982), pp.43–69.

16 Dugald Stewart to William Drennan, Belfast, 20 September 1808, EUA D.12.30, p.5.

17 'Thomas Jefferson to Dugald Stewart, 21st June 1789', https://founders.archives.gov/documents/Jefferson/01-15-02-0207 [accessed 22 August 2019].

18 Lucia Stanton, 'The Other End of the Telescope: Jefferson through the Eyes of His Slaves', *The William and Mary Quarterly*, 57, 1 (2000), pp.151–92.

19 'Sir Archibald Alison 1st Bart', https://www.ucl.ac.uk/lbs/person/view/46692 [accessed 22 August 2019].
20 'John William Ward, Earl of Dudley', https://www.ucl.ac.uk/lbs/person/view/1283343189 [accessed 22 August 2019]; Samuel Henry Romilly (ed.), *Letters to Ivy from the First Earl of Dudley* (1905), pp.321–2.
21 Linda Andersson Burnett and Bruce Buchan, 'The Edinburgh Connection: Linnean Natural History, Scottish Moral Philosophy and the Colonial Implications of Enlightenment Thought' in Hannah Hodacs, Kenneth Nyberg and Stéphane Van Damme (eds), *Linnaeus, Natural History and the Circulation of Knowledge* (Oxford: Voltaire Foundation, 2018), pp.161–82.
22 'Dugald Stewart to Thomas Jefferson, 1st October 1792', https://founders.archives.gov/documents/Jefferson/01-24-02-0395 [accessed 22 August 2019].
23 Bell, 'Lectures', pp.269–70. Strangely, Stewart doesn't explicitly mention Linneaus's *Systema Naturae* (1735), which the majority of his Aberdeen-based colleagues relied on.
24 Ibid., p.284.
25 James Bridges [Dugald Stewart], 'Lectures on Moral Philosophy', 1801–2, EUA, Dc5.88, p.380.
26 For Kames, see Silvia Sebastiani, 'Race and National Characters in Eighteenth-Century Scotland: The Polygenetic Discourses of Kames and Pinkerton', *Cromohs*, 8 (2003), pp.1–14. For Jefferson, see Nicholas E. Magnis, 'Thomas Jefferson and Slavery: An Analysis of His Racist Thinking as Revealed by His Writings and Political Behaviour', *Journal of Black Studies*, 29, 4 (1999), pp.491–509.
27 Bridges, 'Lectures', p.371.
28 Ibid., p.370.
29 Dr Gregory, 'The State of Man Compared with That of the Rest of the Animal Creation', 11 October 1758, AUA, MS 3/07/1/3, p.29.
30 Bell, 'Lectures', p.280. For Samuel Stanhope Smith, see John Greene, 'The American Debate on the Negro's Place in Nature, 1780–1815', *Journal of the History of Ideas*, 15, 3 (1954), pp.384–96; Mathew Mason, *Slavery and Politics in the Early American Republic* (Chapel Hill: University of North Carolina Press, 2006), p.149.
31 Greene, 'The American Debate', pp.384–5.
32 For the Scottish Enlightenment context in particular, see Sebastiani, *Scottish Enlightenment,* Colin Kidd, *The Forging of Races: Race and Scripture in the Protestant Atlantic World, 1600–2000* (Cambridge: Cambridge University Press, 2006). For the wider context of European/Western intellectual thought on race see Andrew Curran, *The Anatomy of Blackness: Science and Slavery in an Age of Enlightenment* (Baltimore, MD: Johns Hopkins University Press, 2011).
33 Walker, 'Lectures', p.364.
34 Ibid., p.364.
35 Ibid., p.364.

36 Anon, 'Lectures', n.p.
37 Ibid., n.p.
38 Walker, 'Lectures', p.369.
39 Bell, 'Lectures', p.270.
40 Bridges, 'Lectures', p.356.
41 Ibid., p.356
42 Stewart, *Elements,* p.253.
43 Ibid., p.279.
44 Ibid., pp.273–4.
45 Ibid., p.272.
46 Ibid., p.66.
47 Anon, 'Lectures', n.p.
48 (Stewart, p. 138).
49 Stewart, *Elements*, p.137.
50 Silvia Sebastiani, 'Challenging Boundaries: Apes and Savages in Enlightenment' in Silvia Sebastiani, Wulf Hund, and Charles Mills (eds), *Simianization: Apes, Gender, Class and Race* (Vienna: LIT, 2015), pp.105–38.
51 J Lee Eden [Dugald Stewart] 'Lectures on Moral Philosophy' 1796, EUA, Dc8.143, p.19.
52 Eden, 'Lectures', p.18.
53 Stewart, *Elements,* p.110.
55 Ibid., pp.144–5.
56 Ibid., p.15.
57 Ibid., p.17.
58 Sebastiani, *The Scottish Enlightenment,* ch.6.
59 Thomas Reid, *An Inquiry into the Human Mind*, ed. and intro. Timothy Duggan (Chicago, IL and London: University of Chicago Press, 1970), p.6.
60 Ibid., p.6.
61 Stewart, *Elements,* pp.67–8.
62 Cristina Paoletti has argued that Stewart modified his optimism in response to critique by his student, Francis Jeffrey. However, the idea of the heroic male embodiment of an age was taken forward by another of his students, Thomas Carlyle. See Paoletti, 'Common Sense'; for Carlyle's 'The Hero as Man of Letters' see Catherine Hall, 'The Economy of Intellectual Prestige: Thomas Carlyle, John Stuart Mill, and the Case of Governor Eyre', *Cultural Critique*, 12 (1989), p.174.
63 Ibid.
64 Anon. [Dugald Stewart], 'Lectures on Moral Philosophy', 1789 & 1790, EUA, Gen 1987-9, n.p.
65 Dow [Dugald Stewart], 'Lectures on Political Economy', 1808–9, EUA, Dc 3105, vol. 1, pp.26–7.
66 See previous chapter.

67 Anon, 'Lectures', n.p.
68 Stewart, *Elements*, p.174.
69 Ibid., p.174.
70 James Bridges, Lectures on Moral Philosophy, 1801–2, EUA, Dc5.88, p.193.
71 Haakonsen, *Natural Law*, pp.228–9.
72 Dugald Stewart, *Outlines of Moral Philosophy. For the Use of Students in the University of Edinburgh* (Edinburgh: William Creech and Thomas Cadell, 1793), pp.113–14.
73 See Chapter 2.
74 Alexander Broadie, 'Reid in Context' in Terence Cuneo and René Van Woudenberg (eds), *The Cambridge Companion to Thomas Reid* (Cambridge: Cambridge University Press, 2004), p.32.
75 Broadie, 'Reid in Context', pp.40–1; See also, Haakonssen, *Natural Law*, ch.6.
76 David Hume, *A Treatise on Human Nature*, vol. 1, ed. and intro. L.A. Selby-Bigger (Oxford: Clarendon Press, 1894), p.95.
77 James Van Cleve, 'Reid's Theory of Perception' in *Cambridge Companion to Thomas Reid*, pp.103–5.
78 Reid, *An Inquiry*, pp.3 & 8.
79 René van Woudenberg, 'Reid and Personal Identity' in *Cambridge Companion to Thomas Reid*, p.216.
80 Reid, *An Inquiry*, p.16.
81 MacIntyre, *Dugald Stewart*, p.21.
82 Haakonssen, *Natural Law*, p.226.
83 Dugald Stewart, *Elements on the Philosophy of the Human Mind* (London: William Tegg, 1853), p.3.
84 Stewart, *Outlines*, p.3.
85 Ibid., pp.5 & 11.
86 James Dunbar, *Essays on the History of Mankind in Rude and Cultivated Ages* (London and Edinburgh: Strahan; Cadell; Balfour, 1780), pp.34–5.
87 Stewart, *Outlines*, p.5; Dugald Stewart, 'Dissertation First: Exhibiting a general view of the progress of metaphysical, ethical and political philosophy since the revival of letters in Europe', part II in *Supplement to the Fourth, Fifth and Sixth Editions of the Encyclopaedia Britannica with Preliminary Dissertations of the History of the Sciences, Volume Fifth* (London: Archibald Constable and Company, Edinburgh and Hurst, Robinson and Company, 1824), p.176.
88 Stewart, *Outlines*, p.135.
89 Stewart, *Elements*, p.18.
90 Ibid., p.116.
91 Ibid., p.11.
92 Ibid., p.17.
93 Stewart, *Dissertation*, pp.210–11.

94 Alison, 'Lectures', p.69.
95 See Pat Moloney, 'Savages in the Scottish Enlightenment's History of Desire', *Journal of the History of Sexuality*, 14, 3 (July 2005), pp.237–65.
96 Millar, *Origins,* pp.28–30.
97 Ibid., p.89.
98 Ibid., pp.146–7.
99 Ibid., p.159.
100 Ibid., pp.222 & 242.
101 Ibid., p.242.
102 Ibid., pp.106–8.
103 Richard Olson, 'Sex and Status in Scottish Enlightenment Social Science: John Millar and the Sociology of Gender Roles', *History of the Human Sciences*, 11, 1 (1998), pp.73–100; Jane Rendall, 'Gender, Race and the Progress of Civilization: Introduction' in Barbara Taylor and Sarah Knott (eds), *Women, Gender and Enlightenment* (Basingstoke: Palgrave Macmillan, 2005), pp.71–4.
104 Anon, 'Lectures on Moral Philosophy Delivered by Professor Dugald Stewart, 1789 & 1790', EUA, Gen 1987–9, n.p.
105 James Bridges, 'Lectures on Moral Philosophy, 1801–2', EUA, Dc5.88, p.314.
106 Kidd, *The Forging of Races*; Sebastiani, *The Scottish Enlightenment*; Curran, *Anatomy of Blackness*; Emmanuel Eze, 'Hume, Race, and Human Nature', *Journal of the History of Ideas*, 61, 4 (2000), pp.691–8; Roxann Wheeler, *The Complexion of Race: Categories of Difference in Eighteenth-Century British Culture* (Philadelphia, PA: University of Pennsylvania Press, 2000).
107 Henry Home, Lord Kames, *Sketches of the History of Man Considerably Enlarged by the Last Additions and Corrections of the Author*, 3 vols, vol. 1, ed. and intro. James Harris (Indianapolis, IN: Liberty Fund, 2007), https://oll.libertyfund.org/titles/2032 [accessed 12 July 2019], p.66.
108 See Júnia Ferreira Furtado, 'Evolving Ideas: J.B. d'Anville's Maps of Southern Africa, 1725-1749', *Imago Mundi*, 69, 2, pp.202–15.
109 For Kames, see Sebastiani, 'Race and National Characters in Eighteenth-Century Scotland', pp.1–14.
110 Bow, *Dugald Stewart and the Legacy of Common Sense,* p.202.

Chapter 3

1 Maria Graham, *Voyage to Brazil and Residence There during Part of the Years 1821, 1822, 1823* (London: Longman, Hurst, Rees, Orme, Brown and Green, and Murray, 1824). For Graham's biography, see Regina Akel, *Maria Graham: A Literary Biography* (Amherst, NY: Cambria Press, 2009), especially ch.5.
2 Graham, *Journal,* p.126.

3 Ibid., p.228.
4 For discussion of the anti-slavery debate, see Thomas Bender (ed.), *The Antislavery Debate: Capitalism and Abolitionism as a Problem in Historical Interpretation* (Berkeley and Los Angeles: University of California Press, 1992); Srividhya Swaminathan, *Debating the Slave Trade: Rhetoric of British National Identity, 1759–1815* (Surrey: Ashgate, 2009); Stephen Ahern (ed.), *Affect and Abolition in the Anglo-Atlantic, 1770–1830* (Surrey: Ashgate, 2013); Brycchan Carey, *British Abolitionism and the Rhetoric of Sensibility: Writing, Sentiment, and Slavery, 1760–1807* (Basingstoke: Palgrave, 2005); Brycchan Carey, Markman Ellis and Sara Salih, *Discourses of Slavery and Abolition: Britain and Its Colonies, 1760–1838* (Basingstoke: Palgrave, 2004); Maurice Jackson, *Let This Voice Be Heard: Anthony Benezet, Father of Atlantic Abolitionism* (Philadelphia, PA: University of Pennsylvania Press, 2009), ch.6.
5 Richard Huzzey, 'The Moral Geography of British Anti-Slavery Responsibilities', *Transactions of the RHS*, 22 (2012), pp.111–39.
6 Hannah More, 'Slavery' (1787), https://www.poetryfoundation.org/poems/51885/slavery [accessed 27 September 2018].
7 Graham, *Journal*, p.198.
8 For a discussion of gratitude, see George Boulukos, *The Grateful Slave: The Emergence of Race in Eighteenth-Century British and American Culture* (Cambridge: Cambridge University Press, 2008), especially, ch.6.
9 Maria Edgeworth, *Popular Tales*, vol. 3 (London: J. Johnson, 1804), pp.193–240.
10 See Introduction. See also, Jane Rendall, '"Elementary Principles of Education": Elizabeth Hamilton, Maria Edgeworth and the Uses of Common Sense Philosophy', *History of European Ideas*, 39, 5 (2013), pp.613–30.
11 Marilyn Butler, *Maria Edgeworth: A Literary Biography* (Oxford: Oxford University Press, 1972), ch.1.
12 Jenny Uglow, *The Lunar Men: The Friends Who Made the Future, 1730–1810* (London: Bloomsbury, 2002).
13 Maria Edgeworth to Henry Edgeworth at Edinburgh, Edgeworthstown, March 1806 in Augustus Hare (ed.), *The Life and Letters of Maria Edgeworth*, vol. 1 (Boston, MA and New York: Houghton, Mifflin and Company, 1895), p.148.
14 See Maria Graham 'Reminiscences' in Rosamund Brunel Gotch (ed.), *Maria, Lady Callcott: The Creator of 'Little Arthur'* (London: John Murray, 1937), pp.24–5. Also, Regina Akel, *Maria Graham: A Literary Biography* (New York: Cambria Press, 2009).
15 Gotch, *Maria*, p.12.
16 'Journal of reflections and extracts made by Lady Callcott in 1806 when she was 21', Bodleian Library, Oxford, Ms. ENg.e.2428, pp.6–44.
17 Edgeworth to Miss Ruxton, 8 December 1830, Life and Letters, vol. 2, p.15; Akel, *Maria*, p.195.

18 Richard Lovell Edgeworth, 'Preface' to Maria Edgeworth *Ennui*, ed. Marilyn Lake (London: Penguin, 1992), p.141.
19 Suvendrini Perera, *Reaches of Empire: The English Novel from Edgeworth to Dickens* (New York: Columbia University Press, 1991), pp.15–34.
20 Richard Lovell Edgeworth, 'Preface' to Maria Edgeworth, *Popular Tales*, vol. 1 in *Tales and Novels by Maria Edgeworth*, vol. 4 of 18 (London: Baldwin and Cradock, 1832), p.1.
21 See Onni Gust, 'Mobility, Gender and Empire in Maria Graham's *Journal of a Residence in India* (1812)', *Gender and History*, 29, 2 (2017), pp.273–91.
22 Dugald Stewart, *Elements on the Philosophy of the Human Mind* (London: William Tegg, 1853), p.279.
23 BL Add MS 52451a, Mackintosh to Sharp, Bombay, 25 July 1807, p.46.
24 Akel says plagiarized. See Akel, *Maria*, pp.61–2.
25 Carl Thompson, 'Earthquakes and Petticoats: Maria Graham, Geology and Early Nineteenth Century "Polite" Science', *Journal of Victorian Culture*, 17, 3 (2012), pp.329–46.
26 NLS MS 40186, Mrs Callcott to John Murray, 5 Albermarle Street, London, 14 November 1829, p.56; Mrs Callcott to John Murray, 1833, p.91.
27 See Marilyn Butler, *Maria Edgeworth*, ch.2. For context, see Christine Kinealy, 'At Home with the Empire: The Example of Ireland' in Hall and Rose, pp.77–100 and Denis O'Hearn, 'Ireland in the Atlantic Economy' in Terence McDonough (ed.), *Was Ireland a Colony? Economics, Politics and Culture in Nineteenth-Century Ireland* (Dublin: Irish Academic Press, 2005), pp.3–26.
28 John Brims, 'Scottish Radicalism and the United Irishmen' in David Dickson, Keogh Daire, and Kevin Whelan (eds), *The United Irishmen: Republicanism, Radicalism and Rebellion* (Dublin: The Lilliput Press, 1993), pp.151–66; Kevin Whelan, 'Ireland, Scotland and Britain in the Long Eighteenth Century' in Terry Brotherstone, A. Clark and K Whelan (eds), *These Fissured Isles: Ireland, Scotland and the Making of Modern Britain, 1798–1848* (Edinburgh: Edinburgh University Press, 2005), pp.43–60.
29 Marilyn Butler, 'Edgeworth, the United Irishmen, and "More Intelligent Treason"' in Heidi Kaufman and Christopher Fauske (eds), *An Uncomfortable Authority: Maria Edgeworth and Her Contexts* (Newark, NJ: University of Delaware Press, 2004), pp.33–61.
30 Elizabeth Kim, 'Maria Edgeworth's *The Grateful Negro*: A Site for Rewriting Rebellion', *Eighteenth-Century Fiction*, 16, 1 (2003), pp.103–26.
31 For Jamaica, see Lesley-Gail Atkinson (ed.), *The Earliest Inhabitants: The Dynamics of the Jamaican Taíno* (Kingston: University of West Indies Press, 2006). For Brazil, see Mark Meuwese, 'The Opportunities and Limits of Ethnic Soldiering: The Tupis and the Dutch-Portuguese Struggle for the Southern Atlantic, 1630–1657' in Wayne E. Lee (ed.), *Empires and Indigenes: Intercultural Alliance, Imperial Expansion and*

Warfare in the Early Modern World (New York and London: New York University Press, 2011), pp.193–221. For genocide, see Patrick Wolfe, 'Settler Colonialism and the Elimination of the Native', *Journal of Genocide Research*, 8, 4 (2006), pp.387–409.
32 Mieko Nishida, *Slavery and Identity: Ethnicity, Gender and Race in Salvador, Brazil, 1808–1888* (Bloomington and Indianapolis, IN: Indiana University Press, 2003), pp.13–15; For overviews of Brazilian slavery in the nineteenth century, see James Rawley with Stephen Behrendt, *The Transatlantic Slave Trade: A History* (Rev. edn, Lincoln and London: University of Nebraska Press, 2005), ch.2; Leslie Bethell, *The Abolition of the Brazilian Slave Trade: Britain, Brazil and the Slave Trade Question, 1807–1869* (Cambridge: Cambridge University Press, 1970), ch.1; Rafael Marquese and Ricardo Salles, 'Slavery in Nineteenth-Century Brazil: History and Historiography' in Dale Tomich (ed.), *Slavery and Historical Capitalism during the Nineteenth Century* (London: Lexington Books, 2017), pp.123–69.
33 Trevor Burnard and John Garrigus, *The Plantation Machine: Atlantic Capitalism in French Saint-Domingue and British Jamaica* (Philadelphia, PA: University of Pennsylvania Press, 2016), p.4.
34 Kirsten Schultz, 'The Crisis of Empire and the Problem of Slavery: Portugal and Brazil, c.1700–1820', *Common Knowledge*, 11, 2 (2005), pp.264–82.
35 Catherine Hall, *Civilizing Subjects: Metropole and Colony in the English Imagination, 1830–1867* (Cambridge: Polity Press, 2002), p.69.
36 Sanjay Subrahmanyam, *The Portuguese Empire in Asia, 1500–1700* (2nd edn, Chichester: John Wiley & Sons, 2012), ch.6.
37 Schultz, 'The Crisis of Empire', pp.254–82.
38 Antonio Penalves Rocha, 'Idiéas antiescravistas da Ilustração na sociedade escravista brasileria', *Revista Brasileira de História*, 20, 39 (2000), pp.37–68. Thanks to Jane-Marie Collins for her help in understanding and contextualizing this article.
39 Edgeworth, 'The Grateful Negro', p.239
40 Ibid., p.240.
41 Archibald Bell, 'Lectures on Moral Philosophy by Dugald Stewart, 1793–4' EUA Dc-4-97, p.136.
42 Edgeworth, 'The Grateful Negro', pp.205–6.
43 Ibid., pp.229–30.
44 Trevor Burnard, *Master, Tyranny and Desire: Thomas Thistlewood and His Slaves in the Anglo-Jamaican World* (Chapel Hill: University of North Carolina Press, 2004), pp.170–4; Diana Paton, 'Obeah Acts: Producing and Policing the Boundaries of Religion in the Caribbean', *Small Axe*, 28 (March, 2009), pp.1–18; Alison Harvey, 'West Indian Obeah and English "Obee": Race, Femininity, and Questions of Colonial Consolidation in Maria Edgeworth's *Belinda*' in Julie Nash (ed.), *New Essays on Maria Edgeworth* (Aldershot: Ashgate, 2006), pp.1–30.
45 Dugald Stewart, *Lectures on Political Economy*, vol. 1, ed. William Hamilton (Edinburgh: Thomas Constable, 1855), p.70. See also Chapter 6 below.

46 Archibald Alison, [Dugald Stewart] 'Lectures on Moral Philosophy', 1809, EUA Gen 1385, vol. IV, p.67.
47 Anon, [Dugald Stewart], 'Lectures on Moral Philosophy' (1789 & 1790), EUA, Gen 1987-9, n.p.
48 Edgeworth, 'The Grateful Negro', p.209.
49 James Bridges, [Dugald Stewart], 'Lectures on Moral Philosophy' (1801-2), EUA, Dc5.88, p.356.
50 http://www.slavevoyages.org/assessment/estimates [accessed 27 September 2018].
51 Ibid.
52 Bethell, *The Abolition of the Brazilian Slave Trade*, pp.12-25; For details of the treaties, see Jane Elizabeth Adams, 'The Abolition of the Brazilian Slave Trade', *The Journal of Negro History*, 10, 4 (1925), pp.607-37.
53 Nishida, *Slavery and Identity*, p.15; Herbert Klein and Ben Vinson III, *African Slavery in Latin America and the Caribbean* (2nd edn, Oxford and New York: Oxford University Press, 2007), p.102.
54 Karia M. de Queirós Mattoso, *To Be a Slave in Brazil, 1550-1888*, trans. Arthur Goldhammer (New Brunswick, NJ: Rutgers University Press, 1996), pp.71-3.
55 Graham, *Journal*, p.105; p.144.
56 Ibid,, p.144; p.196.
57 Ibid., p.2.
58 Ibid., p.1.
59 Ibid., p.2.
60 Ibid., p.3.
61 Robert Southey, *History of Brazil* (London: Longman, Hurst, Rees, and Orme, 1810), pp.24-9.
62 Robert Nelson Anderson, 'The *Quilombo* of Palmares: A New Overview of a Maroon State in Seventeenth-Century Brazil', *Journal of Latin American Studies*, 28 (1996), pp.545-66; Abdias Do Nascimento and Elisa Larkin Nascimento, *Africans in Brazil: A Pan-African Perspective* (Trenton, NJ: African World Press, 1992), p.84.
63 Graham, *Journal*, p.23.
64 Ibid., p.29.
65 Richard B. Sheridan, 'Edwards, Bryan', *ODNB*, https://doi.org/10/1093/ref:odnb/8531 [accessed 7 September 2019]; Paula Dumas, *Proslavery Britain: Fight for Slavery in an Era of Abolition* (Basingstoke: Palgrave Macmillan, 2016), pp.78-9.
66 Edgeworth, *Life and Letters*, vol. 1, p.93.
67 Dumas, *Proslavery*, p.78
68 Bryan Edwards, *The History, Civil and Commercial of the West Indies: An Historical Survey of the French Colony in the Island of Saint Domingo*, 5 vols, vol. 3 (5th edn, London: Whittaker, Reid, Nunn, Richardson etc, 1819), p.xvii.
69 Edwards, *An Historical Survey*, p.79
70 Ibid., p.87.

71 Edwards, *An Historical Survey,* p.90.
72 Ibid., p.xvii.
73 Edgeworth, 'The Grateful Negro', p.195.
74 Graham, *Journal,* p.145.
75 Ibid., p.149.
76 Edgeworth, 'The Grateful Negro', p.213 & p.225.
77 James Montgomery, *The West Indies and Other Poems* (6th edn, London: Longman, Hurst, Rees, Orme and Brown, 1823), p.11.
78 Graham, *Journal,* p.105.
79 Ibid., p.125.
80 de Queirós Mattoso, *To Be a Slave in Brazil,* pp.142–3.
81 Graham, *Journal,* p.126.
82 Maria Graham to John Murray, Pernambuco, 23 September 1821, NLS, Acc.12604/1185, n.p.
83 Graham, *Journal,* p.195.
84 For discussion of sentimental discourse, see Markman Ellis, *The Politics of Sensibility* (Cambridge: Cambridge University Press, 1996).
85 Graham, 'Journal of Reflections', p.63; William Roscoe, *Mount Pleasant: A Descriptive Poem* (Warrington: Jonson, 1777), pp.13–14.
86 Montgomery, *The West Indies,* p.41.
87 James Beattie, 'On the Lawfulness and Expediency of Slavery, Particularly That of the Negroes', AUA, 30/49/1 (1778), p.13.
88 Edgeworth, p. 198.
89 For the wider context of slavery and the plantation economy in Bahia, see Stuart Schwartz, *Slaves, Peasants and Rebels: Reconsidering Brazilian Slavery* (Urbana: University of Illinois Press, 1992), p.143.
90 Graham, *Journal,* p.197.
91 Ibid., p.196.
92 Ibid., p.198.
93 Edgeworth, 'The Grateful Negro', pp.228–9.
94 For British identity and the Caribbean, see Christer Petley, '"Home" and "This Country": Britishness and Creole Identity in the Letters of a Transatlantic Slaveholder', *Atlantic Studies: Global Currents,* 6, 1 (2009), pp.43–61.
95 Graham, *Journal,* p.226.
96 Ibid., p.228.
97 Beattie, 'Essay', pp.4–5.
98 Vincent Caretta, 'Oulaudah Equiano or Gustavas Vassa? New Light on an Eighteenth-Century Question of Identity', *Slavery & Abolition,* 20, 3 (1999), pp.96–105.
99 Ellis, *The Politics of Sensibility,* ch.3. See also, George Boulukos, 'Maria Edgeworth's "Grateful Negro" and the Sentimental Argument for Slavery', *Eighteenth-Century Life,* 23, 1 (1999), pp.12–29.

100 Graham, *Journal*, p.280.
101 Edgeworth, p. 215.
102 Edgeworth, 'The Grateful Negro', pp.218–19.
103 Graham, *Journal*, p.155.
104 Ibid., p.228.

Chapter 4

1 T.M. Devine, *Scotland's Empire, 1600–1815* (London: Penguin, 2004), p.129.
2 Simone Poliandri, *First Nations, Identity, and Reserve Life: The Mi'kmaq of Nova Scotia* (Nebraska: University of Nebraska Press, 2011).
3 Thomas Douglas Selkirk, *Observations on the Present State of the Highlands of Scotland, with a View of the Causes and Probable Consequences of Emigration by the Earl of Selkirk* (London and Edinburgh: Longman, Hurst, Rees, and Orme; Constable & Co, 1805).
4 Ibid., p.205.
5 Ibid., p.231.
6 'Art. XIII Observations on the Present State of the Highlands of Scotland; with a View of the Causes and Probable Consequences of Emigration. By the Earl of Selkirk', *The Edinburgh Review: Or Critical Journal* VII (October 1805), p.187.
7 Eric Richards, *Debating the Highland Clearances* (Edinburgh: Edinburgh University Press, 2007).
8 Oliver Goldsmith, 'The Deserted Village' (1770), https://www.poetryfoundation.org/poems/44292/the-deserted-village [accessed 8 December 2019]; Alexander Irvine, *An Inquiry into the Causes and Effects of Emigration from the Highlands and Western Islands of Scotland with Observations on the Means to Be Employed for Preventing It* (Edinburgh and London: Mundell & Son; Longman and Rees, 1802).
9 Samuel Johnson, *A Journey to the Western Islands of Scotland in 1775*, ed. Peter Levi (London: Penguin, 1984), p.102.
10 Anne Grant of Laggan, 'The Highlanders' in *The Highlanders and Other Poems* (2nd edn, London: Longman, Hurst, Rees, and Orme, 1808), pp.16–101.
11 Anne Grant of Laggan, 'Letter XIII Anne Grant to John Hatsell, London, Stirling 27th November 1806' in J.P. Grant (ed.), *Memoir and Correspondence of Mrs Grant of Laggan Author of 'Letters from the Mountains', 'Memoirs of an American Lady'*, vol. 1 (London, 1844), pp.81–2.
12 James Gordon of Craig, *Eight Letters on the Subject of the Earl of Selkirk's Pamphlet on Highland Emigration as They Latterly Appeared under the Signature of Amicus in One of the Edinburgh Newspapers*, Second Edition with Supplementary Remarks (Edinburgh and London: John Anderson; Longman, Hurst, Rees, and Orme, 1806), pp.46–7.

13 J.M. Bumsted, *Lord Selkirk: A Life* (Winnipeg: University of Manitoba, 2008), p.10.
14 Robert Schofield, 'Priestley, Joseph (1733–1804)' in *Oxford Dictionary of National Biography* (Oxford: Oxford University Press, 2013), https://doi.org/10.1093/ref:odnb/22788 [accessed 8 December 2019].
15 William McCarthy, *Anna Letitia Barbauld: Voice of the Enlightenment* (Baltimore, MD: Johns Hopkins University Press, 2008), p.185.
16 Gordon Macintyre, *Dugald Stewart: The Pride and Ornament of Scotland* (Brighton: Sussex Academic Press, 2003), p.110.
17 Michael Duffy, 'The French Revolution and British Attitudes to the West Indian Colonies' in David Barry Gaspar and David Patrick Geggus (eds), *A Turbulent Time: The French Revolution and the Greater Caribbean* (Bloomington and Indianapolis: Indiana University Press, 1997), pp.78–101.
18 David Dobson, *Scottish Soldiers in Colonial America*, vol. 3 (Baltimore, MD: Genealogical Publishing Co., 2004), p.17; Duffy, 'The French Revolution and British Attitudes to the West Indian Colonies', p.87.
19 Bumsted, *Lord Selkirk: A Life*, 12?
20 'James Wedderburn Colvile, 28th Aug 1739–14th Dec 1807', in Legacies of British Slave-Ownership Database, http://wwwdepts-live.ucl.ac.uk/lbs/person/view/2146643501 [accessed 12 November 2018].
21 J.M. Bumsted, *Fur Trade Wars* (Winnipeg: University of Manitoba, 1999), pp.18–19; 36–9; 42–3.
22 Helen I. Cowan, 'Selkirk's Work in Canada: An Early Chapter', *The Canadian Historical Review*, 9, 4 (1928), pp.299–308.
23 John Brims, 'Scottish Radicalism and the United Irishmen' in David Dickson, Keogh Daire, and Kevin Whelan (eds), *The United Irishmen: Republicanism, Radicalism and Rebellion* (Dublin: The Lilliput Press, 1993), pp.151–66; Kevin Whelan, 'Ireland, Scotland and Britain in the Long Eighteenth Century' in *These Fissured Isles: Ireland, Scotland and the Making of Modern Britain, 1798–1848* (Edinburgh: Edinburgh University Press, 2005), pp.43–60; Bumsted, *Lord Selkirk: A Life*, 12.
24 Brims, 'Scottish Radicalism and the United Irishmen'.
25 J.M. Bumsted, *The People's Clearance: Highland Emigration to British North America* (Edinburgh: Edinburgh University Press, 1982), p.110.
26 Bumsted, ibid., pp.110–11.
27 Poliandri, *First Nations, Identity, and Reserve Life: The Mi'kmaq of Nova Scotia*, p.33.
28 Jennifer Reid, *Myth, Symbol, and Colonial Encounter: British and Mi'kmaq in Acadia, 1700–1867* (Ottawa: University of Ottawa Press, 1995), p.27; Poliandri, *First Nations, Identity, and Reserve Life: The Mi'kmaq of Nova Scotia*, pp.35–8.
29 Selkirk, *Lord Selkirk's Diary, 1803–4: A Journal of His Travels in British North America and the Northeastern United States* (Toronto: Champlain Society, 1958).

30 Selkirk, *Observations*, pp.230–1.
31 James Webster, *General View of the Agriculture of Galloway, Comprehending the Stewartry of Kirkudbright and Shire of Wigton* (Edinburgh: John Paterson, 1794), pp.4, 20, 34.
32 J.M. Bumsted, 'Introduction' in *The Collected Writings of Lord Selkirk, 1799–1809*, vol. I, The Manitoba Record Society Publications, VII (Winnipeg: University of Manitoba, 1984), p.12.
33 Thomas Douglas Selkirk, 'Untitled Pamphlet on Poor Relief in Scotland, c.a. 1799' in J.M. Bumsted (ed.), *The Collected Writings of Lord Selkirk, 1799–1809*, vol. 1 (Manitoba: The Manitoba Record Society, 1984), pp.87–100.
34 Ibid., p.96.
35 Selkirk, *Observations*, p.193.
36 'Parliamentary Debates – Slave Trade Abolition Bill', 5 February 1807, 667–8; Bumsted, *Lord Selkirk: A Life*, 157–8.
37 Harvey Amani Whitfield and Barry Cahill, 'Slave Life and Slave Law in Colonial Prince Edward Island, 1769–1825', *Acadiensis: Journal of the History of the Atlantic Region*, 38, 2 (2009), pp.29–51.
38 E.A. Wrigley, *Poverty, Progress, and Population* (Cambridge: Cambridge University Press, 2004), ch.12.
39 Archibald Bell, 'Lectures on Moral Philosophy by Dugald Stewart Delivered at the University of Edinburgh' (April 1793), pp.146–9, Dc-4-97, Edinburgh University Archive.
40 David Hume, 'Discourse X: Of the Populousness of Antient Nations' in *Essays and Treatises on Several Subjects*, vol. 4 (3rd edn, London and Edinburgh: A. Millar; A. Kincaird and A. Donaldson, 1754), p.140.
41 Adam Smith, *The Wealth of Nations* (1776), ed. Andrew Skinner, vol. 1 (Edinburgh: Penguin, 1999), pp.268–9.
42 Macintyre, *Dugald Stewart: The Pride and Ornament of Scotland*, 109.
43 John Dow, p.1.
44 Ibid., p.27.
45 Smith, *The Wealth of Nations*, 1, pp.268–9.
46 Benjamin Franklin, *Observations Concerning the Increase of Mankind and the Peopling of Countries* (Boston, MA: S. Kneeland, 1755), p.10.
47 Smith, *The Wealth of Nations*, 1, p.182.
48 Ibid., p.173.
49 Eric Richards, 'Malthus and the Uses of British Emigration' in Kent Fedorowich and Andrew Thompson (eds), *Empire, Migration and Identity in the British World* (Manchester: Manchester University Press, 2013), pp.42–59.
50 Thomas Malthus, 'An Essay on the Principle of Population (1798)' in Thomas Mayhew (ed.), *An Essay on the Principle of Population and Other Writings* (London: Penguin Random House, 2015), p.64.

51 Ibid., p.154.
52 Ibid., p.163.
53 Eric Richards, 'Malthus and the Uses of British Emigration', pp.42–59.
54 Alison Bashford, 'Malthus and Colonial History', *Journal of Australian Studies*, 36, 1 (2012), p.104.
55 Selkirk, *Observations*, p.112.
56 Ibid., pp.75–91.
57 Fredrick Jonsson Albritton, *Enlightenment's Frontier: The Scottish Highlands and the Origins of Environmentalism* (New Haven, CT and London: Yale University Press, 2013); C. George Caffentzis, 'Civilizing the Highlands: Hume, Money and the Annexing Act', *Historical Reflections*, 31, 1 (2005), pp.169–94; Peter Womack, *Improvement and Romance: Constructing the Myth of the Highlands* (Basingstoke: The Macmillan Press, 1989); Bumsted, *The People's Clearance*.
58 *A Bill Intitled An Act for Annexing Certain Forfeited Estates in Scotland to the Crown Unalienably* (London, 1752), p.4.
59 Albritton, *Enlightenment's Frontier*, ch.1.
60 T.M. Devine, *The Scottish Clearances: A History of the Dispossessed 1600–1900* (London: Penguin Random House, 2018), p.247.
61 James Anderson, 1777.
62 Selkirk, p. 112.
63 Selkirk, *Observations*, p.112; Irvine, A*n Inquiry into the Causes and Effects of Emigration from the Highlands and Western Islands of Scotland with Observations on the Means to Be Employed for Preventing.*
64 Ibid., p.112.
65 Ibid., p.2.
66 Ibid., p.36.
67 Selkirk, p.222.
68 See Silvia Sebastiani, 'National Character and Race: A Scottish Enlightenment Debate' in Thomas Ahnert and Susan Manning (eds), *Character, Self, and Sociability in the Scottish Enlightenment* (New York: Palgrave Macmillan, 2011), pp.187–205.
69 Hume, 'Discourse X: Of the Populousness of Antient Nations'; David Hume, 'Essay XX: Of National Character' in *Essays and Treatises on Several Subjects*, 4 vols, vol. 1 (London and Edinburgh: T. Cadell; A. Kincaird and A. Donaldson, 1770), pp.247–69.
70 Smith, *The Wealth of Nations* (1776); Adam Smith, *The Theory of Moral Sentiments. Or, an Essay towards an Analysis of the Principles by Which Men Naturally Judge Concerning the Conduct and Character, First of Their Neighbours, and Afterwards of Themselves. To Which Is Added, a Dissertation on the Origins of Language* (1759) (4th edn, Edinburgh and London, 1774).
71 *An Account of the Society in Scotland for Propagating Christian Knowledge.* (Edinburgh: A. Murray and J. Cochran, 1774), pp.1–2.

72 John Knox, *A Tour through the Highlands of Scotland, and the Hebride Isles, in 1786* (London, Edinburgh and Glasgow: J. Walter; R Faulder; W. Richardson; W. Gordon and C. Elliot; Dunlop and Wilson, 1787), p.28.

73 Robert Fraser, *A Letter to the Right Hon. Charles Abbot, Speaker of the House of Commons, Containing an Inquiry into the Most Effectual Means of the Improvement of the Coasts and Western Isles of Scotland and the Extension of the Fisheries, with a Letter from Dr Anderson to the Author of the Same Subject* (London: W. Bulmer and Co. and G. and W. Nicol, 1803), p.96.

74 Hugh Bell, *Observations upon Scotch Fisheries, Emigrations, and the Means of Improving the Highlands and Isles* (Edinburgh: Bell and Bradfute, 1792), p.4.

75 Colin Kidd, 'Gaelic Antiquity and National Identity in Enlightenment Ireland and Scotland', *The English Historical Review*, 109, 434 (November 1994), pp.1197–214; Kenneth McNeil, *Scotland, Britain, Empire: Writing the Highlands* (Columbus: The Ohio State University Press, 2007); Kate Trumpener, *Bardic Nationalism: The Romantic Novel and the British Empire* (Princeton, NJ: Princeton University Press, 1997); Dafydd Moore, 'James Macpherson and "Celtic Whiggism"', *Eighteenth-Century Life*, 30, 1 (2006), pp.1–24.

76 McNeil, *Scotland, Britain, Empire*, 36–9.

77 Walter Scott, *Waverley, or 'Tis Sixty Years Since* (London: Adam and Charles Black, 1892), p.150.

78 Selkirk, *Observations*, 10.

79 Ibid., p.10.

80 Ibid., p. 3.

81 See, for example, Gordon of Craig, *Eight Letters on the Subject of the Earl of Selkirk's Pamphlet on Highland Emigration as They Latterly Appeared under the Signature of Amicus in One of the Edinburgh Newspapers, Second Edition with Supplementary Remarks*.

82 Stana Nenadic, 'Impact of the Military Profession on Highland Gentry Families, c.1730–1830', *The Scottish Historical Review* LXXXV, 1, 219 (April 2006), pp. 75–99; Stana Nenadic, *Lairds and Luxury: The Highland Gentry in Eighteenth-Century Scotland* (Edinburgh: Edinburgh University Press, 2007), p.8; Bruce Lenman, *The Jacobite Clans of the Great Glen, 1650–1784* (2nd edn, Aberdeen: Scottish Cultural Press, 1995), pp. 213–14; Charles W.J. Withers, *Gaelic Scotland: The Transformation of a Culture Region* (London and New York: Routledge, 1988), p.79; Devine, *Scotland's Empire, 1600–1815*, ch.13.

83 Nenadic, 'Impact of the Military Profession on Highland Gentry Families, c.1730–1830'.

84 Robert Clyde, 'Fraser, Archibald Campbell, of Lovat' in *Oxford Dictionary of National Biography*, 2004, https://doi.org/10.1093/ref:odnb/10104

85 Irvine, *An Inquiry into the Causes and Effects of Emigration*, p.157.

86 Selkirk, p. 49.

87 Selkirk, *Observations*, p.49.
88 Ibid., p.161.
89 Ibid., p.67.
90 Ibid., p.121.
91 Ibid., p.120.
92 Irvine, *An Inquiry into the Causes and Effects of Emigration*, 60–1; Johnson, *A Journey to the Western Islands of Scotland in 1775*, p.103; Thomas Pennant, *A Tour in Scotland and Voyage to the Hebrides in 1772*, vol. 1 (Chester: John Monk, 1774), pp.353–4.
93 Johnson, *A Journey to the Western Islands*, p.105.
94 Irvine, *An Inquiry into the Causes and Effects of Emigration*, p.1.
95 John Millar, *The Origin and Distinction of Ranks, or an Inquiry into the Circumstances Which Give Rise to Influence and Authority, in the Different Members of Society* (4th edn, Edinburgh and London: William Blackwood; Longman, Hurst, Ress & Orme, 1806), p.142.
96 Ibid., pp.144–5.
97 Bell, 'Lectures on Moral Philosophy by Dugald Stewart Delivered at the University of Edinburgh', p.65.
98 Gordon of Craig, *Eight Letters on the Subject of the Earl of Selkirk's Pamphlet on Highland Emigration*, p.46.
99 Grant of Laggan, 'The Highlanders', p.25.
100 James Graham, *The Sabbath: A Poem, First American* (New York: Ronalds and Loudon, 1805); Goldsmith, 'The Deserted Village', 1770.
101 Josiah Wedgwood, *An Address to the Workmen in the Pottery on the Subject of Entering into the Service of Foreign Manufacturers* (Newcastle, CT, Staffordshire: J. Smith, 1783), pp.7–8.
102 Graham, *The Sabbath: A Poem*; Irvine, *An Inquiry into the Causes and Effects of Emigration*, p.156.
103 Selkirk, *Observations*, pp.168–70; Johnson, *A Journey to the Western Islands of Scotland in 1775*, p.102.
104 Selkirk, *Observations*, 192.
105 J.M. Bumsted, *Land, Settlement, and Politics on Eighteenth-Century Prince Edward Island* (Montreal and Kingston: McGill-Queen's University Press, 1987), p.182; Bumsted, *Lord Selkirk: A Life*, p.97.
106 Whitfield and Cahill, 'Slave Life and Slave Law in Colonial Prince Edward Island, 1769–1825'.
107 Thomas Douglas Selkirk, *Lord Selkirk's Diary, 1803–4*, p.28.
108 Bumsted, *The People's Clearance*, p.203.
109 Selkirk, *Lord Selkirk's Diary, 1803–4*, p.33.
110 Selkirk, *Observations*, p.209.

111 Ibid., p.210.
112 Selkirk, *Lord Selkirk's Diary, 1803-4*, p.12.
113 Bumsted, *The People's Clearance: Highland Emigration*, p.262.
114 Irvine, *An Inquiry into the Causes and Effects of Emigration*, p.61.
115 Anne Grant, *Essays on the Superstitions of the Highlanders of Scotland*, 2 vols, vol. 1 (London: Longman, Hurst, Rees, Orme and Brown, 1811).
116 Elizabeth Grant, *Memoirs of a Highland Lady: The Autobiography of Elizabeth Grant of Rothiemurchus Afterwards Mrs Smith of Baltiboys, 1797–1830*, ed. Stratchy, Lady (London: John Murray, 1911), pp.7–9.
117 Nenadic, *Lairds and Luxury: The Highland Gentry in Eighteenth-Century Scotland*, pp.27–9.
118 Pennant, *A Tour in Scotland and Voyage to the Hebrides in 1772*, pp.315–31.
119 Knox, *A Tour through the Highlands of Scotland, and the Hebride Isles, in 1786*, p.clxiv.
120 William Wordsworth, 'To a Highland Girl (At Inversneyde, upon Loch Lomond)' in Jared Curtis (ed.), *Poems of William Wordsworth*, vol. 1, Collected Reading Texts from The Cornell Wordsworth (Pentrith: Humanities-Ebooks, LLP, 2009), pp.662–4.
121 Oliver Goldsmith, 'The Deserted Village' in Thomas Janes (ed.), *The Beauties of the Poets. Being a Collection of Moral and Sacred Poetry, from the Most Eminent Authors* (London: Cicero Press, 1788), p.90.
122 William Cobbett, 'White Slave Trade', *The Porcupine*, 11 November 1800, 11th edn.
123 Ibid.
124 Dorothy Wordsworth, *Recollections of a Tour Made in Scotland, A.D. 1803*, ed. J.C. Shairp (New York: G.P. Putnam's Sons, n.d.), p.68.
125 Ibid., p.81.
126 James Boswell and Peter Levi, *Journal of a Tour to the Hebrides with Samuel Johnson*, LLD (1785) (London: Penguin, 1984), p.10;
127 Selkirk, *Lord Selkirk's Diary*, p.15.
128 Ibid., p.12.
129 Ibid., p. 23.
130 Selkirk, *Observations*, p.198.
131 Ibid., p.198.
132 McNeil, *Scotland, Britain, Empire*, ch.4.
133 Grant of Laggan, 'The Highlanders', p.93.
134 Ibid., p.94.
135 Saree Makdisi, *Romantic Imperialism: Universal Empire and the Culture of Modernity* (Cambridge: Cambridge University Press, 1998), ch.4.
136 Selkirk, *Observations*, p.211.
137 Ibid.

Chapter 5

1. Sir James Mackintosh, Journal, 15–20 July 1811, BL Add MS 524538b, p.73.
2. Ibid., p.80.
3. Ibid., p.79.
4. Ibid., p.80.
5. For the nature and variety of power in eighteenth-century India see Seema Alavi, *The Eighteenth Century in India* (New Delhi: Oxford University Press, 2007), pp.1–56; C.A. Bayly, *Indian Society and the Making of the British Empire* (Cambridge: Cambridge University Press, 1988), pp.13–31; Sekar Bandyopadhyay, *From Plassey to Partition* (Hyderabad: Orient Black Swan, 2004); Jon Wilson, *The Domination of Strangers: Modern Governance in Eastern India, 1780–1835* (Basingstoke: Palgrave Macmillan, 2008), ch.2. For the use of 'feudal', see Norbert Peabody, 'Tod's Rajast'han and the Boundaries of Imperial Rule in Nineteenth-Century India', *Modern Asian Studies*, 30, 1 (1996), pp.185–220; Sudipta Sen, *Distant Sovereignty: National Imperialism and the Origins of British India* (New York: Routledge, 2002), ch.2.
6. See Durba Ghosh, *Sex and the Family in Colonial India: The Making of Empire* (Cambridge: Cambridge University Press, 2006), pp.26–31.
7. P.J. Marshall, *Bengal: The British Bridgehead, Eastern India 1740–1828* (Cambridge: Cambridge University Press, 1988). For famine and environmental change, see Vinita Damodaran, 'The East India Company, Famine and Ecological Conditions in Eighteenth-Century Bengal'; Vinita Damodaran, Anna Winterbottom and Alan Lester (eds), *The East India Company and the Natural World* (London: Palgrave Macmillan, 2015), pp.80–101.
8. Adam Smith, *The Wealth of Nations*, ed. and intro. Andrew Skinner, Book IV (London: Penguin, 1999, first published in 1776) p.209.
9. Ibid.
10. Ibid., p.225.
11. P.J. Marshall, 'The Whites of British India, 1780–1830: A Failed Colonial Society?', *The International History Review*, 12, 1 (1990), p.31.
12. Uday Singh Mehta, *Liberalism and Empire: A Study in Nineteenth-Century British Liberal Thought* (Chicago, IL and London: University of Chicago Press, 1999), p.172.
13. Edmund Burke, 'Speech on Fox's East India Bill, December 1 1783' in Edmund Burke (ed.), *Select Works of Edmund Burke*, vol. 4 (Indianapolis, IN: Liberty Fund, 1999), https://oll.libertyfund.org/titles/659 [accessed 1 July 2019], pp.107–8.
14. For Mackintosh's biography, see Patrick O'Leary, *Sir James Mackintosh: The Whig Cicero* (Aberdeen: Aberdeen University Press, 1989). His early years are represented in his unpublished autobiography, written from Bombay on 16 August 1804, BL Add MS 53436b, pp.1–3.

15 See Chapter 4.
16 NLS, MS6360, L Mackintosh, Calcutta to James Mackintosh, Bombay 25 November 1805, p.94.
17 Autobiography, pp.3–5. For Scottish Enlightenment Whiggism, see Colin Kidd, *Subverting Scotland's Past: Scottish Whig Historians and the Creation of an Anglo-British Identity, c.1689–1830* (Cambridge: Cambridge University Press, 1993).
18 Jane Rendall, 'Scottish Citizens of London: Whigs, Radicals, and the French Revolution, 1788–1795' in Stana Nenadic (ed.), *Scots in London in the Eighteenth Century: Patronage, Culture and Identity* (Lewisburg: Buckness University Press, 2010), pp.272–99.
19 James Mackintosh, 'Vindiciae Gallicae: Defence of the French Revolution and its English Admirers against the Accusations of the Right Honourable Edmund Burke' (1791) in Donald Winch (ed. and intro.), *Vindiciae Gallicae and Other Writings on the French Revolution* (Indianapolis, IN: Liberty Fund, 2006), pp.27–32.
20 Knud Haakonsen, *Natural Law and Moral Philosophy: From Grotius to the Scottish Enlightenment* (Cambridge: Cambridge University Press, 1996), pp.268–9.
21 James Mackintosh, 'A Discourse on the Law of Nature and Nations' in Winch (ed.), *Vindicae Gallicae*, p.226.
22 Winch, 'Introduction', *Vindiciae Gallicae*, p.xv.
23 M. de Montesquieu, *The Complete Works of M. Montesquieu*, vol. 1, translated from the French by K. Secondat (Dublin, 1777), p.24.
24 Silvia Sebastiani, *The Scottish Enlightenment: Race, Gender and the Limits of Progress*, trans. Jeremy Carden (New York: Palgrave Macmillan, 2013), p.27.
25 Adam Ferguson, *An Essay on the History of Civil Society* (Edinburgh and London: Millar and Kaddel; Kincaid and Bell, 1767), p.169.
26 Robert Travers, *Ideology and Empire in Eighteenth-Century India* (Cambridge: Cambridge University Press, 2007), p.63.
27 Robert Orme, *Historical Fragments of the Mogul Empire, of the Morattoes, and of the English Concerns in Indostan* (London: F. Wingrave, 1805), p.421; Sinharaja Tammita Delgoda, 'Nabob, Historian and Orientalist.' Robert Orme: the life and career of an East India Company Servant (1728–1801), *JRAS*, 3, 2, 3 (1992), p.365.
28 Alexander Dow, *The History of Hindostan, translated from the Persian*, 3 vols, vol. ii (3rd edn, London: John Murray, 1792), p.279.
29 William Robertson, *An Historical Disquisition Concerning the Knowledge Which the Ancients Had of India* (London and Edinburgh: Strahan and Cadell; Balfour, 1791), p.335.
30 Mackintosh 'Law of Nature and Nations', p.219.
31 Ibid., p.219.
32 For the discussion of 'colonial knowledge' of India, see Bernard Cohn, *Colonialism and Its Forms of Knowledge: The British in India* (Princeton, NJ: Princeton University Press, 1996); Rosanne Rocher, 'British Orientalism in the Eighteenth

Century: the Dialectics of Knowledge and Government' in Carol A. Breckinridge and Peter van der Veer (eds), *Orientalism and the Postcolonial Predicament* (Philadelphia: University of Pennsylvania Press, 1993), pp.215–59.
33 Mackintosh, p. 219.
34 Sir William Jones, 'The Third Anniversary Discourse, delivered 2 February 1786, in *Asiatick Researches*, vol. I (5th edn, London, 1806), pp.422–3. For a full discussion of Jones's argument and its influence, see Thomas Trautmann, *Aryans and British India* (Berkeley: University of California Press, 1997).
35 Colin Kidd, *The Forging of Races: Race and Scripture in the Protestant Atlantic World, 1600–2000* (Cambridge: Cambridge University Press, 2006), pp.116–17.
36 See Dugald Stewart, 'An Account of the Life and Writings of the Author' in Adam Smith (ed.), *Essays on Philosophical Subjects* (Basil: James Dicker, 1799), pp.xliv–xlix; H.M. Hopfl, 'From Savage to Scotsman: Conjectural History in the Scottish Enlightenment', *Journal of British Studies*, 17, 2 (1978), pp.19–40.
37 Ibid.
38 [Dugald Stewart] James Bridges, 'Lectures on Moral Philosophy', 1801–2, Edinburgh University Archives, Dc5.88, p.360.
39 William Jones, 'The 2nd Anniversary Discourse, 24 February 1785 by the President on the Superiority of European Talents' in *Asiatick Researches*, vol. I (5th edn, London, 1806), pp.406–7.
40 John Knox, *A Tour through the Highlands of Scotland, and the Hebride Isles, in 1786* (London, Edinburgh, and Glasgow: Walter; Faulder; Richardson; Gordon and Elliot; Dunlop and Wilson, 1787), p.365.
41 Mackintosh, *Vindiciae Gallicae*, p.24.
42 Mary Wollstonecraft, *A Vindication of the Rights of Men in a Letter to the Right Honourable Edmund Burke Occasioned by His Reflections on the Revolution in France* (2nd edn, London: J. Johnson, 1790), p.130. See also Daniel O'Neill, *The Burke-Wollsotnecraft Debate: Savagery, Civilization, and Democracy* (University Park: University of Pennsylvania State, 2007).
43 Mary Wollstonecraft, *A Vindication of the Rights of Woman*, ed. and intro. Miriam Brody (London, 2004, first published in 1792), p.28. See also Felicity Nussbaum, *Torrid Zones: Maternity, Sexuality, and Empire in Eighteenth-Century English Narratives* (Baltimore, MD and London: The Johns Hopkins University Press, 1995), pp.192–3.
44 Maria Edgeworth, 'Lame Gervas' (1804), *Popular Tales*, vol. IV (London: Baldwin and Chadock, 1832), pp.52–3;
45 Ibid., p.57.
46 Nicholas Dirks, *The Scandal of Empire: India and the Creation of Imperial Britain* (Cambridge, MA and London: Harvard University Press, 2006), pp.100–5; Sara

Suleri, *The Rhetoric of English India* (Chicago, IL and London: University of Chicago Press, 1992).
47 Mithi Mukherjee, 'Justice, War, and the Imperium: India and Britain in Edmund Burke's Prosecutorial Speeches in the Impeachment Trial of Warren Hastings', *Law and History Review*, 23, 3 (2005), p.604.
48 Letter 684: James Mackintosh to John Wilde, Inverness, 26 February 1788, NLS Mss 582: S.N.P.G. Watson Autographs: Literary and Scientific, p.179.
49 Ibid.
50 Ibid., pp.220–1.
51 Mackintosh, *Vindiciae Gallicae*, p.122.
52 Mackintosh to Whishaw, Bombay 20 February 1808, NLS MS 2521, Single Letters, f.135.
53 Ibid.
54 Mackintosh to Moore, Bombay, 6 August 1804, BL Add MS 78763, p.155.
55 Mackintosh to Minto, Bombay 21 February 1806, NLS MS 11732–3, 1st Earl of Minto papers, p.33.
56 Mackintosh to Sharp, 7 July 1808, BL Add MS 52451a, p.48.
57 Margo Finn, 'Anglo-Indian Lives in the Later Eighteenth and Early Nineteenth Centuries', *Journal for Eighteenth-Century Studies*, 33, 1 (2010), pp.49–65.
58 Lord William Bentinck to his brother the Marquis of Litchfield, 6 September 1805, Manuscripts and Special Collections, University of Nottingham, Pw H 249, n.p.
59 P.J. Marshall, *Problems of Empire: Britain and India, 1757–1813* (Historical Problems: Studies and Documents, 3) (London: George Allen and Unwin, Ltd; New York: Barns and Noble, 1968), pp.32–3.
60 Bandyopadhyay, *From Plassey to Partition*, pp.77–8.
61 S.M. Edwardes, *Gazetteer of Bombay City and Island*, 3 vols, vol. ii (Bombay: The Times Press, 1909–10), p.219.
62 Announcement of the new law Bombay Courier, 17 March 1798, no.286.
63 William Morely, *The Administration of Justice in British India; It's Past History And Present State Comprising An Account Of The Laws Peculiar To India* (London: Williams and Norgate, 1858), p.96.
64 Nivedita Vatal, 'Sir James Mackintosh and his contribution to developments in Bombay, 1804–1811', Unpublished MPhil thesis, University of Bombay (1989–1991), pp.102–3.
65 Gazetteer of Bombay City, ii, pp.219–21; M.P. Jain, Outlines of Indian Legal History (3rd edn, Bombay: N.M. Tripathi Private Ltd, 1972), p.139.
66 Meera Kosambi, *Bombay and Poona: A Socio-Ecological Study of Two Indian Cities, 1650–1900* (Stockholm: Universitet Stockholms, 1980), p.36.
67 See Amar Farooqui, *Opium City: The Making of Early Victorian Bombay* (New Delhi: Three Essays Collective, 2006), p.8.

68 Pamela Nightingale, *Trade and Empire in Western India, 1784–1806* (Cambridge South Asian Studies, Number 9) (New York: Cambridge University Press, 1970), pp.20–2.
69 Michelguglielmo Torri, 'Trapped inside the Colonial Order: The Hindu Bankers of Surat and Their Business World during the Second Half of the Eighteenth Century', *Modern Asian Studies*, 25, 2 (1991), pp.54–7; Lakshmi Subramanian, *Indigenous Capital and Imperial Expansion: Bombay, Surat and the West Coast* (New York: Oxford University Press, 1996), pp.1–15.
70 Nightingale, *Trade and Empire*, ch.7; Marshall, *The Making and Unmaking*, p.241.
71 Travers, *Ideology and Empire*, p.231.
72 Mackintosh to Moore, Bombay, 6 August 1804, BL Add MS 78763, p.155.
73 Mackintosh to Moore, Bombay, 6 August 1804, BL Add MS 78763, p.155.
74 Mackintosh, 'A Discourse', pp.226–39.
75 Mackintosh to Sharp, Bombay, 14 August 1804, BL Add MS 52451a, p.8.
76 Mackintosh to Sharp, Bombay, 14 March 1807, BL Add MS 52451a, p.39.
77 *Letter from the Honourable Sir JM, with a Report on the Police of the Island of Bombay, October 1811, Papers on the Police of Bombay in an Analytical Digest of All the Reported Cases Decided in the Supreme Courts of Judicature in India in the Courts of the Hon. East India Company and on Appeal from India by Her Majesty in Council Together with an Introduction, Notes, Illustrative and Explanatory and an Appendix by William H Morley*, ii. (London: Wm H Allen and Co., Leadenhall Street, 1849), p.510.
78 Ibid., p.511.
79 Ibid., p.507.
80 Ibid., pp.503–5.
81 Ibid., p.503.
82 Ibid.
83 Ibid.
84 Ibid., p.504
85 Ibid., p.512.
86 Ibid., p.515.
87 Ibid., p.522.
88 Ibid., p.524.
89 Ibid., p.522.
90 Ibid., p.512.
91 Ibid., p.511.
92 Saturday, 19 April, *Bombay Courier*, 1806, no.709.
93 Saturday 23 October, *Bombay Courier*, 1806, no.736. Such a sentiment would not have been expressed in the early period in Bengal where 'dacoitry' was perceived to be a big problem, sparking fierce debate over how to deal with it. See Radhika

Singha, *A Despotism of Law: Crime and Justice in Early Colonial India* (Delhi: Oxford University Press, 1998), pp.27–32.
94   Bombay Courier, Saturday, 23 October 1806, no.736.
95   Penelope Carson, 'Grant Charles (1746–1823)', *Oxford Dictionary of National Biography*, https://doi.org/10.1093/ref:odnb/11248 [accessed 8 December 2019].
96   Charles Grant, *Observations on the State of Society among the Asiatic Subjects of Great Britain, Particularly with Respect to Morals and on the Means of Improving It – Written Chiefly in the Year 1792* (London: House of Commons, 1813), p.23.
97   Ibid.
98   James Mackintosh to the Earl of Minto, Bombay, 21 February 1806, NLS, MS11732-3, p.62.
99   Ibid., p.59.
100 Ibid., p.59.
101 Journal, 13 February 1811, BL Add MS 52438a, p.58.
102 Ibid.
103 Mackintosh to Sharp, Bombay, 14 August 1804, BL Add MS 52451a, p.7.
104 Christina Smylitopoulos, 'Rewritten and Reused: Imaging the Nabob through "Upstart Iconography"', *Eighteenth-Century Life*, 32, 2 (2008), pp.39–59.
105 Mackintosh to Dugald Stewart, Bombay, 2 November 1805, BL Add MS 78764, p.56.
106 Ibid., p.398.
107 Ibid. Italics added.
108 Ibid.
109 For a list of the members of the Bombay Literary Society see *Transactions of the Literary Society of Bombay* (London: Longman, Hurst, Rees, Orme and Brown; John Murray, 1819), pp. v–vi.
110 Mackintosh, 'Discourse Read at the Opening of the Literary Society of Bombay, 20th November 1804' in Sir James Mackintosh (ed.), *The Miscellaneous Works of the Right Honourable Sir James Mackintosh* (Boston, MA: Philips, Samson and Company, 1857), p.399.
111 Ibid.
112 Ibid.
113 Ibid., p.55.
114 14 December 1810, BL Add MS 52437, p.211.
115 Mackintosh to Sharp, Bombay, 24 February 1806, p.12.
116 Mackintosh, 'Discourse … Literary Society of Bombay', p.400.
117 Ibid.
118 Ibid., p.401.
119 Ibid.
120 Ibid.
121 Ibid., p.403.

122 'Questions relating to the population of India, Salsette on Indian revenue October 1809', BL Add MS 78755, pp.1–17.
123 Mackintosh to Sharp, Bombay, 24 February, 1806, p.12.
124 Anon, 'Art. VII. *An Account of the Kingdom of Caubul and Its Dependencies in Persia, Tartary and India: Comprising a View of the Afghan Nation, and a History of the Dooraunee Monarchy*, By the Hon. Mountstuart Elphinston, Resident at the Court of Poona, and late Envoy to the King of Caubul. 4to. Longman & Co., and Murray, London, 1815. *Memoir on the Ruins of Babylon*. By Claudius James Rich, Esq. Resident at the Court of the Pacha of Bagdad. 8vo. Longman & Co., and Murray, London, 1815. *Description du Pachalie de Bagdad*. 8vo. Paris, 1809', *The Edinburgh Review, or Critical Journal*, vol. XXV (Edinburgh and London: Constable, Longman, Hurst, Rees, Orme and Brown, 1815), p.441.
125 Mackintosh, 'Discourse … Literary Society of Bombay', p.398.
126 16 August 1810, BL Add MS 52437, pp.95–6.
127 Mrs Taylor to Mackintosh, Norwich, 7 November 1805, BL Add MS 52451b, p.117.
128 Mackintosh, 'Discourse … Literary Society of Bombay', p.399.
129 Mackintosh to Sharp, 14 August 1804, BL Add MS 52451a, p.9.
130 17 February, 1811, BL Add MS 52438a, p.90.
131 14 April 1811, p.129.
132 Janet Sorensen, *The Grammar of Empire in Eighteenth-Century British Writing* (Cambridge and New York: Cambridge University Press, 2000), p.12.
133 16 February 1811, BL Add MS 52438a, p.65.
134 Sen, *Distant Sovereignty*, ch.5.
135 14 December 1810, BL Add MS 52437, p.212.
136 *Memoirs of the Life*, pp.265–6.
137 Suleri, *Rhetoric of English India*, p.22.

Chapter 6

1 Sir James Mackintosh to Lady Catherine Mackintosh, Bombay, 3 August 1811, BL Add MS 78769, pp.179–80.
2 G. Ouseley to Sir James Mackintosh, 29 March 1811, BL Add MS 78766, p.121.
3 Mary Rich to Maitland Erskine, Bussorah, 24 April 1811, BL Add MS 80759, p.267.
4 J. Mackintosh to C. Mackintosh, 3 August 1811, p.180.
5 'An Act to dissolve the Marriage of Sir Saltonstall Wiseman, Baronet, with Katherine Wiseman his now Wife, and to enable him to marry again, and for other Purposes therein mentioned', House of Commons Sessional Papers: Private Acts (1815-34), Private Acts, pp.1–4, https://parlipapers.proquest.com/parlipapers/docview/t70.d75.pa-000460?accountid=8018 [accessed 28 June 2019]; 'Minutes of

Evidence taken upon the second reading of the Bill intitled, "An Act to dissolve the Marriage of Sir William Saltonstall Wiseman, Baronet, with Katherine Wiseman'" in The House of Lords Sessional Papers, 1801–33, vol. 173 (1824), pp.4–15.

6   J Mackintosh, Tuesday, 30 May 1810, BL Add MS 78769, p.27.
7   J Mackintosh, Sunday, 22 April 1810, 78769, p.18.
8   C Mackintosh to J Mackintosh, London, 30 October 1810, 78769, p.88.
9   See Catherine Hall, 'Introduction: Thinking the Postcolonial, Thinking Empire' in Catherine Hall, *Cultures of Empire: Colonizers in Britain and the Empire in the 19th and 20th Centuries: A Reader* (New York: Routledge, 2000), pp.1–33.
10 See Emma Darwin, *A Century of Family Letters, 1792–1896*, ed. Henrietta Litchfield (New York: D Appleton and Company, 1915), vol. 1, pp.1–19.
11 See Patrick O'Leary, *Sir James Mackintosh: The Whig Cicero* (Aberdeen: Aberdeen University Press, 1989).
12 'Register of the King of Clubs, 1798–1823', BL Add MS 37337, n.p.
13 Onni Gust, 'Empire, Exile, Identity: Locating Sir James Mackintosh's Histories of England', Unpublished PhD, UCL (2011), ch.3.
14 P.J. Marshall, 'The Whites of British India, 1780–1830: A Failed Colonial Society?' *The International History Review*, 12, 1 (1990), p.28.
15 Joan Mickelson Gaughan, *The 'Incumberances': British Women in India, 1615–1856* (Delhi: Oxford University Press, 2013), pp.104–15; Tillman W. Nechtman, *Nabobs: Empire and Identity in Eighteenth-Century Britain* (Cambridge: Cambridge University Press, 2010), pp.193–5.
16 Margaret Makepeace, 'Cadet William Lambert Writes from Bombay in 1780' https://blogs.bl.uk/untoldlives/2018/11/cadet-william-lambert-writes-from-bombay-in-1780.html [accessed 28 June 2019].
17 Phebe Gibbes, *Hartly House, Calcutta*, ed. Michael J. Franklin (Manchester: Manchester University Press, 2019); Kate Teltscher, *India Inscribed: European and British Writing on India, 1600–1800* (Delhi: Oxford University Press, 1995).
18 Margot Finn, 'The Female World of Love and Empire: Women, Family and East India Company Politics at the End of the Eighteenth Century', *Gender and History*, 31, 1 (2019), p.11.
19 Percival Spear, *The Nabobs: A Study of the Social Life of the English in Eighteenth-Century India* (London and Dublin: Curson Press, 1980, first published in 1932), p.141.
20 Ann Laura Stoler, 'European Communities and the Boundaries of Rule', *Comparative Studies in Society and History*, 31, 1 (1989), p.144.
21 Durba Ghosh, *Sex and the Family in Colonial India: The Making of Empire* (Cambridge: Cambridge University Press, 2006), pp.76–9; William Dalrymple, *White Mughals: Love and Betrayal in Eighteenth-Century India* (London: HarperCollins, 2003), pp.34–9, 50–2. See Sudipta Sen, 'Imperial Subjects of Trial: On the Legal Identity of Britons in Late Eighteenth-Century India', *Journal of British Studies*, 45 (2006), p.541.

22 John Walton Caughey, *MacGillivray of the Creeks* (Norman: Oklahoma University Press, 1938), pp.9–11; Onni Gust, 'Remembering and Forgetting the Scottish Highlands: Sir James Mackintosh and the Forging of a British Imperial Identity', *Journal of British Studies*, 52, 3 (2013), p.628.

23 Dalrymple, *White Mughals*.

24 Durba Ghosh warns historians against constructing Indian women as one-dimensional victims and flattening out the wide range of experiences and practices that they employed in relationship to East India Company men. Ghosh, *Sex and the Family*, pp.24–5.

25 Thomas Williamson, *East India Vade-Mecum, or Complete Guide to Gentlemen Intended for the Civil, Military, or Naval Service of the Hon. East India Company*, 2 vols, vol. 1 (London: Black, Parry, and Kingsbury, 1810), pp.344–83; pp.414–15.

26 Ghosh, *Sex and the Family*, p.29; See also, Margot Finn, 'Anglo-Indian Lives in the Later Eighteenth and Early Nineteenth Centuries', *Journal for Eighteenth-Century Studies*, 33, 1 (2010), pp.49–65.

27 Christopher Hawes, *Poor Relations: The Making of a Eurasian Community in British India, 1773–1833* (Richmond, VI: Curzon, 1996), ch.2.

28 Ghosh, *Sex and the Family*, p.8.

29 Williamson, *Vade Mecum*, p.345.

30 Indrani Chatterjee, 'Colouring Subalterniety: Slaves, Concubines, and Social Orphans in Early Colonial India' in Gautam Bhadra, Gyan Prakash and Susie Tharu (eds), *Subaltern Studies*, vol. X (Oxford: Oxford University Press, 1999), pp.56–7; On slave-ownership by East India Company officers in India, see Margot Finn, 'Slaves out of Context', *Transactions of the Royal Historical Society*, Sixth Series, 19 (2009), pp.181–203.

31 J.R. Gilchrist, *The General East India Guide and Vade Mecum for the Functionary, Government Officer, Private Agent, Trader or Foreign Soujourner in British India* (London: Kingsbury, Parbury & Allen, 1825), p.524.

32 Ibid., p.525.

33 Chatterjee, 'Coloring Subalterniety', pp.71–8.

34 For discussion of the transition from 'Orientalism' to 'Anglicism' see Chapter 5.

35 Announcement of the new law Bombay Courier, 17 March 1798, no.286; William Morely, *The Administration of Justice in British India; it's past history and present state comprising an account of the laws peculiar to India* (London, 1858), p.96; See also Sen, 'Imperial Subjects of Trial', pp.532–55; Lauren Benton, *Law and Colonial Cultures: Legal Regimes in World History, 1400–1900* (Cambridge: Cambridge University Press, 2002), ch.IV.

36 'Letter from the Honourable Sir James Mackintosh, with a report on the police of the Island of Bombay, October 1811' in William Morely, *An Analytical Digest of Tll the Reported Cases Decided in the Supreme Courts of Judicature in India in the Courts of the Honourable East India Company*, vol. 1 (London: Allen and Co., 1849), p.519.

37 J. Mackintosh to John Allen, 22 February 1805, BL Add MS 78768, p.63.
38 James Douglas, *Glimpses of Old Bombay and Western India* (London: S. Low, 1900), p.111. For a history of the leading Parsi families, see Jesse S. Palsetia, *Jamsetjee Jejeebhoy of Bombay: Partnership and Public Culture in Empire* (New Delhi: Oxford University Press, 2015).
39 J. Mackintosh to J. Allen, 22 February 1805, BL Add MS 78768, p.62.
40 Maria Graham, *Journal of a Residence in India* (Edinburgh: Constable and Co., 1812), p.6; Anne Katharine Elwood, *Journey Overland from England by the Continent of Europe, Egypt, and the Red Seat to India* (London: Henry Colburn and Richard Bentley, 1830), 2 vols, vol. 1, pp.365–6.
41 J. Mackintosh, 17 June, BL Add MS 52438b, p.8.
42 Mackintosh to Allen, 22 February 1805, p.64.
43 Williamson, *Vade Mecum*, p.351.
44 J. Mackintosh to R. Sharp, 7 July 1808, BL Add MS 52451a, p.76; J. Mackintosh to R. Sharp, Bombay 16 May 1805, p.25.
45 J. Mackintosh to F. Mackintosh, 10 August 1811, BL Add MS 78769, p.196.
46 William Adams, *Reports on the State of Education in Bengal*, ed. Anakhnath Basu (Calcutta: University of Calcutta, 1941), p.41.
47 C. Mackintosh to J. Mackintosh, 30 October 1810, BL Add MS 78769, p.88.
48 J. Mackintosh to John Allen, 22 February 1805, BL Add MS 78768, p.62.
49 Ibid., p.65.
50 See Williamson, *East India Vade Mecum*, vol. 1, p.336; J. Mackintosh to Basil Montagu, 3 March 1805, BL Add MS 78765, p.37; Rosina Vizram, *Asians in Britain* (London: Pluto Press, 2002), pp.6–8.
51 F. Mackintosh to J. Mackintosh, 1810, BL Add MS 52452, p.44.
52 James Douglas, *Glimpses of Old Bombay and Western India* (London: Sampson Low, Marston and Co., 1900), p.3. See also, Meera Kosambi, 'Bombay and Poona: A Socio-ecological Study of Two Indian Cities, 1650–1900' in M.S.A. Rao, C. Bhat, I.N. Kadejer (eds), *A Reader in Urban Sociology* (Hyderabad: Orient Longman, 1991), pp.58–9.
53 Marianne Postans, *Western India in 1838* (London: Saunders and Otley, 1839), pp.30–8.
54 Douglas, *Glimpses*, p.11.
55 Graham, *Journal*, p.12.
56 Mariam Dossal, *Imperial Designs and Indian Realities: The Planning of Bombay City, 1847–1895* (New York: Oxford University Press, 1991); Amar Farooqui, *Opium City: The Making of Early Victorian Bombay* (New Delhi, 2006); Prashant Kidambi, *The Making of an Indian Metropolis: Colonial Governance and Public Culture in Bombay, 1890–1920* (Aldershot: Ashgate, 2007), ch.2; Swati Chattopadhay, 'Nineteenth-Century British Attitudes towards Calcutta and Bombay' in S.J. Neary, M.S. Symes and F.E. Brown (eds), *The Urban Experience: A People-Environment*

Perspective (London: Taylor and Francis, 1994); Sujata Patel and Alice Thorner (eds), *Bombay: Metaphor for Modern India* (Bombay: Oxford University Press, 1995).

57 P.J. Marshall, 'The White Town of Calcutta under the Rule of the East India Company', *Modern Asian Studies*, 34, 2 (2000), p.314.
58 Pamela Nightingale, *Trade and Empire in Western India, 1784–1806* (Cambridge: Cambridge University Press, 1970); Jesse S. Palsetia, *Jamsetjee Jejeebhoy of Bombay*.
59 James Douglas, *Glimpses*, vol. II, p.111; Maria Graham, *Journal*, p.42.
60 BL Add MS 52437, 29 July 1810, pp.71–2.
61 J. Mackintosh, Monday 6 August 1810, BL Add MS 52437, p.80.
62 Douglas, *Glimpses*, p.24.
63 C. Mackintosh to Maitland Erskine, March 24 1811, BL Add MS 80759, p.253.
64 John Borthwick Gilchrist, *Hindoostanee Philology: Comprising a Dictionary, English and Hindoostanee; with a Grammatical Introduction* (London: Kingsbury, Parbury, and Allen, 1825), p.ii.
65 Williamson, *Vade Mecum*, pp.172–7.
66 *Memoirs of the Life of the Right Honourable Sir James Mackintosh*, ed. Robert Mackintosh (London: Edward Moxon, 1835), p.475.
67 J. Mackintosh, 16 February 1810, BL Add MS 52438a, p.64.
68 J. Mackintosh, 27 August 1808, n.p.
69 Claude Markowitz, 'Bombay as a Business Centre in the Colonial Period: A Comparison with Calcutta' in Patel and Thorner, *Bombay*, pp.26–46.
70 F. Mackintosh to Mary Rich, undated, Wedgwood Archives, 32610-59, n.p.
71 Mary Rich to Maitland Erskine, 23 April, 1810 BL Add MS 80759, p.156.
72 J. Mackintosh to R. Sharp, 14 August 1804, BL Add MS 52451a, pp.7–8.
73 C. Mackintosh to J. Mackintosh, 17 November 1808, BL Add MS 78768, p.84.
74 C. Mackintosh (jnr) to Maitland Erskine, 24 March 1811, p.253.
75 J. Mackintosh to C. Mackintosh, 3 August 1811, BL Add MS 78769, p.179.
76 See Chapter 5.
77 Adam Ferguson, *An Essay on the History of Civil Society* (5th edn, London: T. Cadell, 1782), p.85.
78 William Robertson, *An Historical Disquisition Concerning the Knowledge Which the Ancients Had of India* (London and Edinburgh: T. Cadell and E. Balfour, 1791), p.335.
79 J. Mackintosh, 'Tour of India, 1808', Wedgwood Archives, 32708-59, p.3.
80 Henry Home, Lord Kames, *Sketches of the History of Man*, vol. 1 (1778), pp.52–3, https://oll.libertyfund.org/titles/kames-sketches-of-the-history-of-man-vol-1 [accessed 1 July 2019].
81 Dugald Stewart, *Lectures on Political Economy*, ed. William Hamilton, vol. 1 (Edinburgh: Thomas Constable, 1877), pp.60–83.

82 Stewart, *Lectures*, p.85.
83 Ibid., p.79.
84 Ibid., p.91.
85 Balachandra Rajan, *Under Western Eyes: Indian from Milton to Macaulay* (Durham and London: Duke University Press, 1999).
86 Kames, *Sketches,* p.296.
87 Mackintosh, *Memoirs of the Life*, p.508.
88 Ibid.
89 Ibid.
90 Joanna de Groot, 'Oriental Feminotopias? Montagu's and Montesquieu's "Seraglios" Revisited', *Gender and History*, 18, 1 (2006), pp.66–86.
91 Graham, *Journal,* p.18, Mackintosh, *Memoirs of the Life*, p.508. See also Onni Gust, 'Mobility, Gender and Empire in Maria Graham's Journal of a Residence in India (1812)', *Gender and History*, 29, 2 (2017), pp.275–91.
92 Graham, pp. 18–19.
93 Indira Ghose, *Women Travellers in Colonial India: The Power of the Female Gaze* (New York: Oxford University Press, 1998).
94 'Part of a letter from a Lady at Fort St George' (1742), UoN MS&SC, MeX1/3 n.p.
95 Chatterjee, 'Introduction', *Unfamiliar Relations*, pp.25–7.
96 Charles Grant, *Observations on the State of Society among the Asiatic Subjects of Great Britain* (London 1792 (Ordered, by the House of Commons, to be printed 15 June 1813)), p.28. For further discussion of representations of Indian domesticity, see Sudipta Sen, *Distant Sovereignty: National Imperialism and the Origins of British India* (London and New York: Routledge, 2002), ch.4.
97 Grant, *Observations,* p.29.
98 Ibid.
99 'Session of Oyer and Terminer', *Bombay Courier*, 19 April 1806, no.709.
100 Mackintosh, *Memoirs*, p.500.
101 Graham, *Journal*, p.19.
102 Ibid.
103 Mackintosh, *Memoirs*, p.278.
104 William Hodges, *Travels in India during the years 1780, 1781, 1782 and 1783* (London: J Edwards, 1793), pp.82–3.
105 Marianne Postans, *Cutch, or Random Sketches Taken during a Residence in One of the Northern Provinces of Western India* (London: Stewart and Murray, 1839), pp.68–9.
106 James Mill, *The History of British India*, vol. 1 (3rd edn, London: Baldwin, Cradock and Joy 1826), pp.403–4.
107 Grant, *Observations*, p.198.
108 Mackintosh, *Memoirs*, p.443.

109 M. Rich to M. Erskine, 27 June 1811, BL Add MS 80759, p.294.
110 C. Mackintosh, 'A Political Epistle to Sire J M on his return to Bombay from Point de Galle, with notes. Cumbrian at Sea, 1 May 1810', BL Add MS 78771a, p.140.
111 Ibid., p.141.
112 Ibid., p.139.
113 J. Mackintosh, Saturday 10 August 1811, BL Add MS 52439b, p.97.
114 Ibid.
115 J. Mackintosh 'Report on the Police', p.522.
116 Ibid.
117 C. Mackintosh to J. Mackintosh, March 1802, BL Add MS 78768, p.48.
118 C. Mackintosh, 'Political Epistle', p.144.
119 Ibid., p.142.
120 Ibid., p.143.
121 Ibid.
122 Mary Wollstonecraft, *A Vindication of the Rights Woman (1792)*, ed. and intro. Miriam Brody (London: Penguin, 2004), p.12 and pp.64–5.
123 John Moir, *Female Tuition: An Address to Mothers on the Education of Daughters* (Dublin: W. Sleater, 1787), p.iv.
124 Anna Letitia Barbauld, *The Female Speaker: Or, Miscellaneous Pieces in Prose and Verse* (Boston, MA: Wells and Lily, 1824, first published in 1811), p.iv.
125 C. Mackintosh, 'Political Epistle', p.144.
126 Ibid.
127 Ibid., p.140.
128 Graham, *Journal of a Residence*, p.23.
129 Ibid., p.115.
130 M. Rich to M. Erskine, 29 May 1811, pp.275–6.
131 Anon., 'British Ladies in India Defended Against Maria Graham' in Josiah Pratt and Zacharay Macaulay, *The Christian Observer*, vol. 13 (London: Ellerton and Henderson, 1814), pp.637–42.
132 Ibid., p.638.
133 Ibid., p.639.
134 Ibid.
135 Adele Perry, '"Is Your Garden in England, Sir": James Douglas' Archive and the Politics of Home', *History Workshop Journal*, 70, Autumn, 2010, pp.67–85.

Conclusion

1 Catherine Mackintosh to James Mackintosh, Sunday 4 December, 1808, BL Add MS 78768, p.95.

2 Elisabeth Inglis-Jones, 'A Pembrokeshire County Family in the Eighteenth Century', *National Library of Wales Journal*, XVII, 2 (1971), https://www.genuki.org.uk/big/wal/PEM/Jeffreyston/Allen
3 Ibid., p.95.
4 Orlando Patterson, *Slavery and Social Death: A Comparative Study* (Cambridge, MA: Harvard University Press, 1982). For a critique of the ways in which historians have implemented this concept, see Vincent Brown, 'Social Death and Political Life in the Study of Slavery', *American Historical Review*, 114, 5 (2009), pp.1231–49.
5 Frantz Fanon, *The Wretched of the Earth* (New York: Grove Press, 1968), pp.212–15.
6 See Dror Wahrman, *The Making of the Modern Self: Identity and Culture in Eighteenth-Century England* (New Haven, CT: Yale University Press, 2004).
7 Gloria Anzaldúa, *Borderlands/La Frontera: The New Mestiza* (San Francisco, CA: Aunt Lute Books, 1987); Gloria Anzaldúa and Annalouise Keating (eds), *This Bridge We Call Home* (New York: Routledge, 2002); Barbara Smith (ed.), *Home Girls: A Black Feminist Anthology* (New York: Kitchen Table: Women of Color Press, 1983).

Bibliography

Databases and online archives and dictionaries

Founders Online, https://founders.archives.gov
Legacies of British Slave-Ownership, https://www.ucl.ac.uk/lbs/
Oxford Dictionary of National Biography, https://www.oxforddnb.com
Slave Voyages, https://www.slavevoyages.org

Archival sources

Aberdeen University Archives

MS 30/2/566 Elizabeth Montagu to James Beattie
MS.30/31/335 James Beattie to Elizabeth Montagu
MS 30/49/1 James Beattie, 'On the Lawfulness and expediency of slavery particularly that of the Negroes written in the year 1778'.
MS 3/07/1/3 Dr Gregory, 'The State of Man Compared with that of the Rest of the Animal Creation', 11 October 1758.
NS 145/1 Rules and Minutes of the Philosophical Society in Aberdeen

Bodleian Library, Oxford University

MS Eng.e.2328-9 Callcott Collection

British Library (BL)

Add MS 78763-78817 Mackintosh family correspondence
Add MS 52436-52453 Mackintosh family correspondence

Edinburgh University Archives (EUA)

Gen 2023: Abbreviations from Lectures on Moral Philosophy, Sofias Walker, 1778–9, v.II
Gen 1987–9: Lectures on Moral Philosophy delivered by Prof Dugald Stewart, 1789 & 1790 (anonymous)

Dc-4-97: Archibald Bell, Lectures on Moral Philosophy by Dugald Stewart, delivered at the University of Edinburgh, 1793–4
Dc8.143 Attendance at class, J Lee Eden, 1796, 7-7,8-8,9
Dc5.88, James Bridges, Lectures on Moral Philosophy, 1801–2
Dc 3105, Lectures on Political Economy by Dugald Stewart, John Dow, 1808–9, vol. 1
Dc8.177 Dugald Stewart, Conjectures Concerning the Origin of the Sanskrit
Gen 1382–5 Lectures on Moral Philosophy, Archibald Alison, 1808–9

National Library of Scotland (NLS)

MS 11726-33 1st Earl of Minto Papers
MS 11293 1st Earl of Minto Papers
MS 6366: Private letters from Calcutta in Case of the Death of Gordon Mackenzie
MS 40186 John Murray Papers
MS 673 Letters to Archibald Constable
MSS 581-2: S.N.P.G Watson Autographs: literary and scientific
MS 6360 Correspondence of L Mackintosh, merchant in Calcutta

University of Nottingham Manuscripts and Special Collections

Pw H 249 – Lord William Bentinck to his brother the Marquis of Litchfield, 6 September 1805

Wedgwood Museum Archives

29516-144: Mrs Mackintosh to Messrs Wedgwood
18973-92: J Mackintosh to J Wedgwood
16774-92: J Mackintosh to J Wedgwood
32288-58: R Mackintosh to Mrs Rich
32607-59: F Mackintosh to Mrs Rich
9873-11: J Mackintosh to J Wedgwood
32708-59: J Mackintosh's Tour of India, 1808

Published Primary Sources

Newspaper sources and periodicals

Bombay Courier
Bombay Gazette
The Christian Observer
The Edinburgh Review, Or Critical Journal
The Porcupine

Reports

An Account of the Society in Scotland for Propagating Christian Knowledge. Edinburgh: A. Murray and J. Cochran, 1774.

An Act to dissolve the Marriage of Sir Saltonstall Wiseman, Baronet, with Katherine Wiseman his now Wife, and to enable him to marry again, and for other Purposes therein mentioned, House of Commons Sessional Papers: Private Acts (1815–1834), Private Acts, 1–4.

A Bill Intitled An Act for Annexing Certain Forfeited Estates in Scotland to the Crown Unalienably. London, 1752.

'Letter from the Honourable Sir James Mackintosh, with a report on the police of the Island of Bombay, October 1811', in William Morely, *An Analytical Digest of All the Reported Cases Decided in the Supreme Courts of Judicature in India in the Courts of the Honourable East India Company*, 2 vols. London: Allen and Co., 1849.

'Minutes of Evidence taken upon the second reading of the Bill intitled, "An Act to dissolve the Marriage of Sir William Saltonstall Wiseman, Baronet, with Katherine Wiseman"', in *The House of Lords Sessional Papers*, 1801–1833, vol. 173 (1824), pp.4–15.

Literary sources

Asiatic Society of Bombay, *Transactions of the Literary Society of Bombay*. London: Longman, Hurst, Rees, Orme and Brown; John Murray, 1819.

Barbauld, Anna Letitia, *The Female Speaker: Or, Miscellaneous Pieces in Prose and Verse*. Boston, MA: Wells and Lily, 1824, first published, 1811.

Bell, Hugh, *Observations upon Scotch Fisheries, Emigrations, and the Means of Improving the Highlands and Isles*. Edinburgh: Bell and Bradfute, 1792.

Boswell, James, *Journal of a Tour to the Hebrides with Samuel Johnson, L.LD* (1785). London: Penguin, 1984.

Burke, Edmund, 'Speech on Fox's East India Bill, December 1 1783', in *Select Works of Edmund Burke*, edited by Edmund Burke, vol. 4. A New Imprint of the Payne Edition. Indianapolis, IN: Liberty Fund, 1999, https://oll.libertyfund.org/titles/659

Clarkson, Thomas, *The History of the Abolition of the African Slave-Trade by the British Parliament*, vol. i, 2 vols. London: Longman, Hurst, Reed and Orme, 1808.

de Montesquieu, M., *The Complete Works of M. Montesquieu*, translated from the French by K Secondat, vol. 1. Dublin: Evans and Davies, 1777.

Dow, Alexander, *The History of Hindostan*, translated from the Persian, 3rd edn, 3 vols. London: John Murray, 1792.

Dunbar, James, *Essays on the History of Mankind in Rude and Cultivated Ages*. London and Edinburgh: Strahan; Cadell; Balfour, 1780.

Edgeworth, Maria, *Popular Tales*, vol. iii. London: J. Johnson, 1804.
Edgeworth, Maria, *Ennui*, edited and introduced by Marilyn Lake. London: Penguin, 1992.
Edwards, Bryan, *The History, Civil and Commercial of the West Indies: An Historical Survey of the French Colony in the Island of Saint Domingo*, 5th edn, vol. iii, 5 vols. London: Whittaker, Reid, Nunn, Richardson etc., 1819.
Elwood, Anne Katharine, *Journey Overland from England by the Continent of Europe, Egypt, and the Red Seat to India*, 2 vols. London: Henry Colburn and Richard Bentley, 1830.
Ferguson, Adam, *An Essay on the History of Civil Society*, 5th edn. London and Edinburgh, 1782.
Franklin, Benjamin, *Observations Concerning the Increase of Mankind and the Peopling of Countries*. Boston, MA: S. Kneeland, 1755.
Fraser, Robert, *A Letter to the Right Hon. Charles Abbot, Speaker of the House of Commons, Containing an Inquiry into the Most Effectual Means of the Improvement of the Coasts and Western Isles of Scotland and the Extension of the Fisheries, with a Letter from Dr Anderson to the Author of the Same Subject*. London: W. Bulmer and Co. and G. and W. Nicol, 1803.
Gilchrist, J.R., *The General East India Guide and Vade Mecum for the Functionary, Government Officer, Private Agent, Trader or Foreign Soujourner in British India*. London: Kingsbury, Parbury & Allen, 1825.
Gilchrist, John Borthwick, *Hindoostanee Philology: Comprising a Dictionary, English And Hindoostanee; with a Grammatical Introduction*. London: Kingsbury, Parbury, and Allen, 1825.
Goldsmith, Oliver, 'The Deserted Village', in *The Beauties of the Poets. Being a Collection of Moral and Sacred Poetry, from the Most Eminent Authors*, edited by Thomas Janes, 86–101. London: Cicero Press, 1788.
Gordon of Craig, James, *Eight Letters on the Subject of the Earl of Selkirk's Pamphlet on Highland Emigration as They Latterly Appeared under the Signature of Amicus in One of the Edinburgh Newspapers*, 2nd edn. Edinburgh and London: John Anderson; Longman, Hurst, Rees, and Orme, 1806.
Graham, James, *The Sabbath: A Poem, First American*. New York: Ronalds and Loudon, 1805.
Graham, Maria, *Journal of a Residence in India*. Edinburgh: Constable and Co., 1812.
Graham, Maria, *Voyage to Brazil and Residence There during Part of the Years 1821, 1822, 1823*. London: Longman, Hurst, Rees, Orme, Brown and Green, and Murray, 1824.
Graham, Maria, 'Reminiscences', in *Maria, Lady Callcott: The Creator of 'Little Arthur'*, edited by Rosamund Brunel Gotch, 1–85. London: John Murray, 1937.
Grant, Charles, *Observations on the State of Society among the Asiatic Subjects of Great Britain, Particularly with Respect to Morals and on the Means of Improving It – Written Chiefly in the Year 1792*. London: House of Commons, 1813.

Grant, Elizabeth, *Memoirs of a Highland Lady: The Autobiography of Elizabeth Grant of Rothiemurchus Afterwards Mrs Smith of Baltiboys, 1797–1830*, edited by Lady Stratchy. London: John Murray, 1911.

Grant of Laggan, Anne, 'The Highlanders', in *The Highlanders and Other Poems*, 2nd edn, 16–124. London: Longman, Hurst, Rees, and Orme, 1808.

Grant of Laggan, Anne, *Essays on the Superstitions of the Highlanders of Scotland*, vol. I, 2 vols. London: Longman, Hurst, Rees, Orme and Brown, 1811.

Grant of Laggan, Anne, *Memoir and Correspondence of Mrs Grant of Laggan Author of 'Letters from the Mountains', 'Memoirs of an American Lady'*, edited by J.P. Grant, vol. 1. London: Longman, Brown and Green, 1844.

Hare, Augustus, ed. *The Life and Letters of Maria Edgeworth*, vol. 1. Boston and New York: Houghton, Mifflin and Company, 1895.

Hodges, William, *Travels in India during the Years 1780, 1781, 1782 and 1783*. London: J. Edwards, 1793.

Home, Henry, Lord Kames, *Sketches of the History of Man Considerably Enlarged by the Last Additions and Corrections of the Author*, edited and introduced by James Harris, 3 vols. Indianapolis, IN: Liberty Fund, 2007.

Hume, David, *A Treatise on Human Nature*, edited and introduced by L.A. Selby-Bigger, 2 vols. Oxford: Clarendon Press, 1896.

Hume, David, *Essays and Treatises on Several Subjects*, 4 vols. London and Edinburgh: T. Cadell, 1770.

Hutcheson, Francis, *A System of Moral Philosophy in Three Books to Which Is Prefixed an Account of the Life, Writings and Character of the Author by the Reverend William Leechman*. London: Millar and Longman, 1755.

Irvine, Alexander, *An Inquiry into the Causes and Effects of Emigration from the Highlands and Western Islands of Scotland with Observations on the Means to Be Employed for Preventing It*. Edinburgh and London: Mundell & Son; Longman and Rees, 1802.

Johnson, Samuel, *A Journey to the Western Islands of Scotland in 1775*, edited by Peter Levi. London: Penguin, 1984.

Jones, Sir William, 'The Second Anniversary Discourse, 24th Feb. 1785 by the President on the Superiority of European Talents', in *Asiatick Researches*, 5th edn, vol. I, 406–7. London, 1806.

Jones, Sir William, 'The Third Anniversary Discourse, delivered 2 February 1786', in *Asiatick Researches*, 5th edn, vol. I, 422–3. London, 1806.

Knox, John, *A Tour through the Highlands of Scotland, and the Hebride Isles, in 1786*. London, Edinburgh and Glasgow: J. Walter; R Faulder; W. Richardson; W. Gordon and C Elliot; Dunlop and Wilson, 1787.

Lafitau, Joseph François, *Moeurs des Sauvages Ameriquains Comparées aux moeurs des premiers temps*. Paris: Saugrain; Charles Estienne Hochereau, 1724.

Lee, Arthur, *An Essay in Vindication of the Continental Colonies of America from a Censure of Mr Adam Smith, in His Theory of Moral Sentiments with Some Reflections on Slavery by an American*. London: Beckett and De Hont, 1764.

Mackintosh, James, 'Discourse Read at the Opening of the Literary Society of Bombay, 20th November 1804', in *The Miscellaneous Works of the Right Honourable Sir James Mackintosh*, edited by Sir James Mackintosh. Boston, MA: Philips, Samson and Company, 1857.

Mackintosh, James, 'Law of Nature and Nations (1799)', in *Vindiciae Gallicae and Other Writings on the French Revolution*, edited and introduced by Donald Winch. Indianapolis, IN: Liberty Fund, 2006.

Mackintosh, Rober, *Memoirs of the Life of the Right Honourable Sir James Mackintosh*. London: Edward Moxon, 1835.

Malthus, Thomas, *An Essay on the Principle of Population and Other Writings*, edited by Thomas Mayhew. London: Penguin Random House, 2015.

Mill, James, *The History of British India*, 3rd edn. London: Baldwin, Cradock and Joy, 1826.

Millar, John, *The Origin and Distinction of Ranks, or an Inquiry into the Circumstances Which Give Rise to Influence and Authority, in the Different Members of Society*, 4th edn. Edinburgh and London: William Blackwood; Longman, Hurst, Ress & Orme, 1806.

Moir, John, *Female Tuition: An Address to Mothers on the Education of Daughters*. Dublin: W. Sleater, 1787.

Montgomery, James, *The West Indies and Other Poems*, 6th edn. London: Longman, Hurst, Rees, Orme and Brown, 1823.

Orme, Robert, *Historical Fragments of the Mogul Empire, of the Morattoes, and of the English Concerns in Indostan*. London: F. Wingrave, 1805.

Payne, John Howard, *Home, Sweet Home*. Boston, MA: Lee and Shepard, c.1880.

Pennant, Thomas, *A Tour in Scotland and Voyage to the Hebrides in 1772*, vol. 1. Chester: John Monk, 1774.

Postans, Marianne, *Cutch, or Random Sketches Taken during a Residence in One of the Northern Provinces of Western India*. London: Stewart and Murray, 1839.

Postans, Marianne, *Western India in 1838*. London: Saunders and Otley, 1839.

Reid, Thomas, *An Inquiry into the Human Mind*, edited and introduction by Timothy Duggan. Chicago, IL and London: University of Chicago Press, 1970.

Robertson, William, *An Historical Disquisition Concerning the Knowledge Which the Ancients Had of India*. London and Edinburgh: Strahan and Cadell; Balfour, 1791.

Roscoe, William, *Mount Pleasant: A Descriptive Poem*. Warrington: Jonson, 1777.

Scott, Walter, *Waverley, or 'Tis Sixty Years Since*. London: Adam and Charles Black, 1892.

Selkirk, Thomas Douglas, *Observations on the Present State of the Highlands of Scotland, with a View of the Causes and Probable Consequences of Emigration by the Earl of Selkirk*. London and Edinburgh: Longman, Hurst, Rees, and Orme; Constable & Co., 1805.

Selkirk, Thomas Douglas, *Lord Selkirk's Diary, 1803–4: A Journal of His Travels in British North America and the Northeastern United States*. Toronto: Champlain Society, 1958.
Selkirk, Thomas Douglas, 'Untitled Pamphlet on Poor Relief in Scotland, c.a. 1799', in *The Collected Writings of Lord Selkirk, 1799–1809*, edited by J.M. Bumsted, vol. 1, 87–100. Manitoba: The Manitoba Record Society, 1984.
Smith, Adam, *The Theory of Moral Sentiments. Or, an Essay towards an Analysis of the Principles by Which Men Naturally Judge Concerning the Conduct and Character, First of Their Neighbours, and Afterwards of Themselves. To Which Is Added, a Dissertation on the Origins of Language*. 4th edn. Edinburgh and London, 1774.
Smith, Adam, *The Wealth of Nations*, edited with an introduction by Andrew Skinner, Book I. London: Penguin, 1999, first published, 1776.
Smith, Adam, *Lectures on Jurisprudence*, edited by R.L. Meek, D.D. Raphael and P.G. Stein. Oxford: Oxford University Press, 1978.
Southey, Robert, *History of Brazil*. London: Longman, Hurst, Rees, and Orme, 1810.
Stewart, Dugald, *Outlines of Moral Philosophy. For the Use of Students in the University of Edinburgh*. Edinburgh: William Creech and Thomas Cadell, 1793.
Stewart, Dugald, 'An Account of the Life and Writings of the Author', in *Essays on Philosophical Subjects*, edited by Adam Smith, xliv–xlix. Basil: James Dicker, 1799.
Stewart, Dugald, 'Dissertation First: Exhibiting a General View of the Progress of Metaphysical, Ethical and Political Philosophy since the Revival of Letters in Europe', part II in *Supplement to the Fourth, Fifth and Sixth Editions of the Encyclopaedia Britannica with Preliminary Dissertations of the History of the Sciences, Volume Fifth*. Archibald Constable and Company, Edinburgh and Hurst, Robinson and Company, London, 1824.
Stewart, Dugald, *Elements on the Philosophy of the Human Mind*. London: William Tegg, 1853.
Stewart, Dugald, *Lectures on Political Economy*, edited by William Hamilton, vol. 1. Edinburgh: Thomas Constable, 1877.
Webster, James, *General View of the Agriculture of Galloway, Comprehending the Stewartry of Kirkudbright and Shire of Wigton*. Edinburgh: John Paterson, 1794.
Wedgwood, Josiah, *An Address to the Workmen in the Pottery on the Subject of Entering into the Service of Foreign Manufacturers*. Newcastle: J. Smith, 1783.
Williamson, Thomas, *East India Vade-Mecum, or Complete Guide to Gentlemen Intended for the Civil, Military, or Naval Service of the Hon. East India Company*, 2 vols. London: Black, Parry, and Kingsbury, 1810.
Wollstonecraft, Mary, *A Vindication of the Rights of Men in a Letter to the Right Honourable Edmund Burke Occasioned by His Reflections on the Revolution in France*, 2nd edn. London: J. Johnson, 1790.
Wollstonecraft, Mary, *A Vindication of the Rights of Woman*, edited and introduced by Miriam Brody. London: Penguin Classics, 2004, first published, 1792.
Wordsworth, Dorothy, *Recollections of a Tour Made in Scotland, A.D. 1803*, edited by J.C. Shairp. New York: G.P. Putnam's Sons, n.d.

Wordsworth, William, 'To a Highland Girl (At Inversneyde, upon Loch Lomond)', in *Poems of William Wordsworth*, edited by Jared Curtis, vol. 1, 662–4. Collected Reading Texts from The Cornell Wordsworth. Pentrith: Humanities-Ebooks, LLP, 2009.

Published secondary sources

Adams, Jane Elizabeth, 'The Abolition of the Brazilian Slave Trade', *The Journal of Negro History*, 10, 4 (1925), 607–37.
Adams, William, *Reports on the State of Education in Bengal*, edited by Anakhnath Basu. Calcutta: University of Calcutta, 1941.
Ahern, Stephen, ed., *Affect and Abolition in the Anglo-Atlantic, 1770–1830*. Surrey: Ashgate, 2013.
Ahmed, Sara, 'A Phenomenology of Whiteness', *Feminist Theory*, 8, 2 (2007), 149–68.
Akel, Regina, *Maria Graham: A Literary Biography*. Amherst, NY: Cambria Press, 2009.
Alavi, Seema, *The Eighteenth Century in India*. New Delhi: Oxford University Press, 2007.
Albritton, Fredrick Johnsson, *Enlightenment's Frontier: The Scottish Highlands and the Origins of Environmentalism*. New Haven, CT and London: Yale University Press, 2013.
Amani Whitfield, Harvey and Barry Cahill, 'Slave Life and Slave Law in Colonial Prince Edward Island, 1769–1825', *Acadiensis: Journal of the History of the Atlantic Region* 38, 2 (2009), 29–51.
Anderson, Robert Nelson, 'The *Quilombo* of Palmares: A New Overview of a Maroon State in Seventeenth-Century Brazil', *Journal of Latin American Studies*, 28 (1996), 545–66.
Andersson Burnett, Linda and Bruce Buchan, 'The Edinburgh Connection: Linnean Natural History, Scottish Moral Philosophy and the Colonial Implications of Enlightenment Thought', in *Linnaeus, Natural History and the Circulation of Knowledge*, edited by Hannah Hodacs, Kenneth Nyberg and Stéphane Van Damme, 161–86. Oxford: Voltaire Foundation, 2018.
Anzaldúa, Gloria, *Borderlands/La Frontera: The New Mestiza*. San Francisco, CA: Aunt Lute Books, 1987.
Anzaldúa, Gloria and Analouise Keating, eds, *This Bridge We Call Home*. New York: Routledge, 2002.
Atiya, Michael, 'Benjamin Franklin and the Edinburgh Enlightenment', *Proceedings of the American Philosophical Society*, 150, 4 (December, 2006), 591–606.
Atkinson, Lesley-Gail, ed., *The Earliest Inhabitants: The Dynamics of the Jamaican Taíno*. Kingston: University of West Indies Press, 2006.
Bandyopadhyay, Sekar, *From Plassey to Partition*. Hyderabad: Orient Black Swan, 2004.
Barker-Benfield, J.G., *The Culture of Sensibility: Sex and Society in Eighteenth-Century Britain*. Chicago, IL: Chicago University Press, 1992.

Bashford, Alison, 'Malthus and Colonial History', *Journal of Australian Studies* 36, 1 (2012), 99–110.
Bayly, C.A., *The New Cambridge History of India, Vol II: Indian Society and the Making of the British Empire*. Cambridge: Cambridge University Press, 1988.
Bender, Thomas, ed., *The Antislavery Debate: Capitalism and Abolitionism as a Problem in Historical Interpretation*. Berkeley and Los Angeles: University of California Press, 1992.
Benton, Lauren, *Law and Colonial Cultures: Legal Regimes in World History, 1400–1900*. Cambridge: Cambridge University Press, 2002.
Berg, Maxine, 'In Pursuit of Luxury: Global History and British Consumer Goods in the Eighteenth Century', *Past and Present*, 182 (2004), 85–142.
Bernasconi, Robert and Tommy Lott, *The Idea of Race*. Indianapolis, IN and Cambridge: Hackett Publishing, 2000.
Bethell, Leslie, *The Abolition of the Brazilian Slave Trade: Britain, Brazil and the Slave Trade Question, 1807–1869*. Cambridge: Cambridge University Press, 1970.
Bonar, James and John Gray, *A Catalogue of the Library of Adam Smith*. London and New York: Macmillan, 1894.
Boulukos, George, 'Maria Edgeworth's 'Grateful Negro' and the Sentimental Argument for Slavery', *Eighteenth-Century Life*, 23, 1 (1999), 12–29.
Boulukos, George, *The Grateful Slave: The Emergence of Race in Eighteenth-Century British and American Culture*. Cambridge: Cambridge University Press, 2008.
Bow, C.B., 'Dugald Stewart and the Legacy of Common Sense in the Scottish Enlightenment', in *Common Sense in the Scottish Enlightenment*, edited by C.B. Bow, 200–17. Oxford: Oxford University Press, 2018.
Brims, John, 'Scottish Radicalism and the United Irishmen', in *The United Irishmen: Republicanism, Radicalism and Rebellion*, edited by David Dickson, Keogh Daire, and Kevin Whelan, 43–60. Dublin: The Lilliput Press, 1993.
Brion Davis, David, *The Problem of Slavery in Western Culture*. Oxford: Oxford University Press, 1966.
Broadie, Alexander, 'Reid in Context', in *The Cambridge Companion to Thomas Reid*, edited by Terence Cuneo and René Van Woudenberg, 31–52. Cambridge: Cambridge University Press, 2004.
Brodie, Alexander, 'Sympathy and the Impartial Spectator', in *The Cambridge Companion to Adam Smith*, edited by Knud Haakonssen, 158–88. Cambridge: Cambridge University Press, 2006.
Brown, Vincent, 'Social Death and Political Life in the Study of Slavery', *American Historical Review*, 114, 5 (2009), 1231–49.
Bumsted, J.M., *The People's Clearance: Highland Emigration to British North America*. Edinburgh and Winnipeg: Edinburgh University Press and Winnipeg University Press, 1982.
Bumsted, J.M., *Land, Settlement, and Politics on Eighteenth-Century Prince Edward Island*. Montreal and Kingston: McGill-Queen's University Press, 1987.

Bumsted, J.M., *Fur Trade Wars*. Winnipeg: University of Manitoba, 1999.
Bumsted, J.M., *Lord Selkirk: A Life*. Winnipeg: University of Manitoba, 2008.
Burnard, Trevor, *Master, Tyranny and Desire: Thomas Thistlewood and His Slaves in the Anglo-Jamaican World*. Chapel Hill: University of North Carolina Press, 2004.
Burnard, Trevor and J. Garrigus, *The Plantation Machine: Atlantic Capitalism in French Saint-Domingue and British Jamaica*. Philadelphia: University of Pennsylvania Press, 2016.
Butler, Marilyn, *Maria Edgeworth: A Literary Biography*. Oxford: Oxford University Press, 1972.
Butler, Marilyn, 'Edgeworth, the United Irishmen, and "More Intelligent Treason"', in *An Uncomfortable Authority: Maria Edgeworth and Her Contexts*, edited by Heidi Kaufman and Christopher Fauske, 33–61. Newark: University of Delaware Press, 2004.
Caffentzis, C. George, 'Civilizing the Highlands: Hume, Money and the Annexing Act', *Historical Reflections*, 31, 1 (2005), 169–94.
Caretta, Vincent, 'Oulaudah Equiano or Gustavas Vassa? New Light on an Eighteenth-Century Question of Identity', *Slavery & Abolition*, 20, 3 (1999), 96–105.
Carey, Brycchan, *British Abolitionism and the Rhetoric of Sensibility*. Basingstoke: Palgrave Macmillan, 2005.
Carey, Brycchan, Markman Ellis and Sara Salih, eds, *Discourses of Slavery and Abolition: Britain and Its Colonies, 1760–1838*. Basingstoke: Palgrave, 2004.
Carr, Rosalind, *Gender and Enlightenment Culture in Eighteenth-Century Scotland*. Edinburgh: Edinburgh University Press, 2014.
Carretta, Vincent, 'Three West Indian Writers of the 1780s Revisited and Revised', *Research in African Literatures*, 29, 4 (1998), 73–87.
Caughey, John Walton, *MacGillivray of the Creeks*. Norman: University of Oklahoma Press, 1938.
Chakravarty, Subhas Ranjan, 'Colonialism, Migration and Resource Crisis', *CRG Research Paper Series, Policies and Practices*, vol. 42 (2011), http://www.mcrg.ac.uk/PP42.pdf [accessed 2 December 2019].
Chatterjee, Indrani, 'Colouring Subalterniety: Slaves, Concubines, and Social Orphans in Early Colonial India', *Subaltern Studies*, edited by Gautam Bhadra, Gyan Prakash and Susie Tharu, vol. X, 49–97. Delhi: Oxford University Press, 1999.
Chattopadhay, Swati, 'Nineteenth-Century British Attitudes towards Calcutta and Bombay', in *The Urban Experience: A People-Environment Perspective*, edited by S.J. Neary, M.S. Symes and F.E. Brown, 455–67. London: E&FN SPON, 1994.
Christie, William, *The Edinburgh Review in the Literary Culture of Romantic Britain: Mammoth and Maglonyx*. London: Pickering and Chatto, 2009.
Cohn, Bernard, *Colonialism and Its Forms of Knowledge: The British in India*. Princeton, NJ: Princeton University Press, 1996.
Cole, Lucinda, '(Anti)feminist Sympathies: The Politics of Relationship in Smith, Wollstonecraft, and More', *ELH*, 58 (1991), 107–40.

Cooper, Frederick and Ann Stoler, 'Between Metropole and Colony: Rethinking a Research Agenda', in *Tensions of Empire: Colonial Cultures in a Bourgeois World*, edited by Cooper and Stoler, 1–56. Berkeley and Los Angeles: University of California Press, 1997.

Cowan, Helen I., 'Selkirk's Work in Canada: An Early Chapter', *The Canadian Historical Review*, 9, 4 (1928), 299–308.

Curran, Andrew, *The Anatomy of Blackness: Science and Slavery in an Age of Enlightenment*. Baltimore, MD: Johns Hopkins University Press, 2011.

Dalrymple, William, *White Mughals: Love and Betrayal in Eighteenth-Century India*. London: HarperCollins, 2003.

Damodaran, Vinita, 'The East India Company, Famine and Ecological Conditions in Eighteenth-Century Bengal', in *The East India Company and the Natural World*, edited by Vinita Damodaran, Anna Winterbottom and Alan Lester, 80–101. London: Palgrave Macmillan, 2015.

Daniels, Stephen, Susanne Seymour, and Charles Watkins, 'Estate and Empire: Sir George Cornewan's Management of Moccas, Herefordshire and La Taste, Grenada, 1771–1819', *Journal of Historical Geography*, 24, 3 (1998), 313–51.

Davidoff, Leonore and Catherine Hall, *Family Fortunes: Men and Women of the English Middle Class, 1780–1850*, Rev. edn. London: Routledge, 2002.

De Groot, Joanna, 'Oriental Feminotopias? Montagu's and Montesquieu's "Seraglios" Revisited', *Gender and History*, 18, 1 (2006), 66–86.

De Ritter, Richard, 'Female Philosophers and the Comprehensive View: Elizabeth Hamilton's *Letters on the Elementary Principles of Education*', *European Romantic Review*, 23, 6 (2012), 689–705.

Delgoda, Sinharaja Tammita, '"Nabob, Historian and Orientalist." Robert Orme: The Life and Career of an East India Company Servant (1728–1801)', *JRAS*, 3, 2 (1992), 363–76.

Devine, T.M., *Scotland's Empire, 1600–1815*. London: Penguin, 2004.

Devine, T.M., *The Scottish Clearances: A History of the Dispossessed 1600–1900*. London: Penguin Random House, 2018.

Dirks, Nicholas, *The Scandal of Empire: India and the Creation of Imperial Britain*. Cambridge, MA and London: Harvard University Press, 2006.

Dobson, David, *Scottish Soldiers in Colonial America*, vol. 3. Baltimore, MD: Genealogical Publishing Co., 2004.

Dossal, Mariam, *Imperial Designs and Indian Realities: The Planning of Bombay City, 1847–1895*. New York: Oxford University Press, 1991.

Douglas, James, *Glimpses of Old Bombay and Western India*. London: S. Low, 1900.

Du Bois, Lauren, 'An Enslaved Enlightenment: Rethinking the Intellectual History of the French Atlantic', *Social History*, 31, 1 (2006), 1–14.

Duffy, Michael., 'The French Revolution and British Attitudes to the West Indian Colonies', in *A Turbulent Time: The French Revolution and the Greater Caribbean*, edited by David Barry Gaspar and David Patrick Geggus, 78–101. Bloomington and Indianapolis: Indiana University Press, 1997.

Dumas, Paula, *Proslavery Britain: Fight for Slavery in an Era of Abolition*. Basingstoke: Palgrave Macmillan, 2016.

Edwardes, S.M., *Gazetteer of Bombay City and Island*, 3 vols. Bombay: The Times Press, 1909–10.

Ellis, Markman, *The Politics of Sensibility: Race, Gender and Commerce in the Sentimental Novel*. Cambridge: Cambridge University Press, 2004, 14–15.

Eze, Emmanuel, 'Hume, Race, and Human Nature', *Journal of the History of Ideas*, 61, 4 (2000), 691–8.

Fanon, Franz, *The Wretched of the Earth*. New York: Grove Press, 1968.

Farooqui, Amar, *Opium City: The Making of Early Victorian Bombay*. New Delhi: Three Essays Collective, 2006.

Ferreira Furtado, Júni, 'Evolving Ideas: J.B. d'Anville's Maps of Southern Africa, 1725–1749', *Imago Mundi*, 69, 2 (2017), 202–15.

Finn, Margo, 'Anglo-Indian Lives in the Later Eighteenth and Early Nineteenth Centuries', *Journal for Eighteenth-Century Studies*, 33, 1 (2010), 49–65.

Finn, Margot, 'Slaves Out of Context', *Transactions of the Royal Historical Society*, Sixth Series, 19 (2009), 181–203.

Finn, Margot, 'The Female World of Love and Empire: Women, Family and East India Company Politics at the End of the Eighteenth Century', *Gender and History*, 31, 1 (2019), 7–24.

Fryer, Peter, *Staying Power: The History of Black People in Britain*. London and New York: Pluto Press, 2010 (first published, 1984).

Fullagar, Kate and Michael A. McDonnell, eds, *Facing Empire: Indigenous Experiences in a Revolutionary Age*. Baltimore, MD: Johns Hopkins University Press, 2018.

Garner, Steve, 'Atlantic Crossing', *Atlantic Studies*, 4, 1 (2007), 117–32.

Garrett, Alexander, 'Anthropology: The "Original" of Human Nature', in *The Cambridge Companion to the Scottish Enlightenment*, edited by Alexander Brodie, 79–93. Cambridge: Cambridge University Press, 2003.

Geggus, D.C., 'The Caribbean in the Age of Revolution', in *The Age of Revolutions in Global Context, c.1760–1840*, edited by David Armitage and Sanjay Subrahmanyam, 83–100. Basingstoke: Palgrave Macmillan, 2010.

Ghose, Indira, *Women Travellers in Colonial India: The Power of the Female Gaze*. New York: Oxford University Press, 1998.

Ghosh, Durba, *Sex and the Family in Colonial India: the Making of Empire*. Cambridge: Cambridge University Press, 2006.

Gikandi, Simon, *Slavery and the Culture of Taste*. Princeton, NJ and Oxford: Princeton University Press, 2011.

Greene, John, 'The American Debate on the Negro's Place in Nature, 1780–1815', *Journal of the History of Ideas*, vol. 15, 3 (1954), 384–96.

Griffin, Emma, *A Short History of the British Industrial Revolution.* Basingstoke and New York: Palgrave Macmillan, 2010.
Griswold, Charles, *Adam Smith and the Virtues of Enlightenment.* Cambridge: Cambridge University Press, 1999.
Guha, Amalendu, 'Parsi Seths as Entrepreneurs, 1750–1850', *Economic and Political Weekly*, 5, 35 (1970), M107–15.
Gust, Onni, 'Remembering and Forgetting the Scottish Highlands: Sir James Mackintosh and the Forging of a British Imperial Identity', *Journal of British Studies*, 52 (2013), 1–23.
Gust, Onni, 'Mobility, Gender and Empire in Maria Graham's *Journal of a Residence in India* (1812)', *Gender and History*, 29, 2 (2017), 273–91.
Haakonssen, Knud, *Natural Law and Moral Philosophy: From Grotius to the Scottish Enlightenment.* Cambridge: Cambridge University Press, 1996.
Hall, Catherine, 'The Economy of Intellectual Prestige: Thomas Carlyle, John Stuart Mill, and the Case of Governor Eyre', *Cultural Critique*, 12 (1989), 167–96.
Hall, Catherine, 'Introduction: Thinking the Postcolonial, Thinking Empire', in *Cultures of Empire: Colonizers in Britain and the Empire in the 19th and 20th Centuries: A Reader*, edited by Catherine Hall, 1–33. New York: Routledge, 2000.
Hall, Catherine, *Civilizing Subjects: Metropole and Colony in the English Imagination, 1830–1867.* Cambridge: Polity Press, 2002.
Hall, Catherine, *Macaulay and Son: Architects of Imperial Britain.* New Haven, CT: Yale University Press, 2014.
Hall, Catherine and Sonya Rose, eds, *At Home with the British Empire: Metropolitan Culture and the Imperial World.* Cambridge: Cambridge University Press, 2006.
Hall, Catherine, Jane Rendall and Keith McClelland, *Defining the Victorian Nation: Class, Race, Gender and the Reform Act of 1867.* Cambridge: Cambridge University Press, 2000.
Hall, Stuart, 'Subjects in History: Making Diasporic Identities', in *The House That Race Built*, edited by Wahneema Lubiano, 289–301. New York: Vintage Books, 1998.
Harkin, Maureen, 'Smith's *The Theory of Moral Sentiments*: Sympathy, Women and Emulation', *Studies in Eighteenth-Century Culture*, 24 (1995), 175–90.
Harraway, Donna, 'Situated Knowledges: The Science Question in Feminism and the Privilege of Partial Perspective', *Feminist Studies*, 14, 3 (1988), 575–99.
Harris, Cheryl, 'Whiteness as Property', *Harvard Law Review*, 106, 8 (1993), 1710–91.
Harvey, Alison, 'West Indian Obeah and English "Obee": Race, Femininity, and Questions of Colonial Consolidation in Maria Edgeworth's *Belinda*', in *New Essays on Maria Edgeworth*, edited by Julie Nash, 1–30. Aldershot: Ashgate, 2006.
Harvey, David, *The French Enlightenment and Its Others: The Mandarin, the Savage and the Invention of the Human Sciences.* Basingstoke: Palgrave Macmillan, 2012.
Hawes, Christopher, *Poor Relations: The Making of a Eurasian Community in British India, 1773–1833.* Richmond: Curzon, 1996.

Hopfl, H.M., 'From Savage to Scotsman: Conjectural History in the Scottish Enlightenment', *Journal of British Studies*, 17, 2 (1978), 19–40.

Horn, James, *British Diaspora: Emigration from Britain, 1680–1815*. Oxford: Oxford University Press, 1998.

Houston, R.A., *Social Change in the Age of Enlightenment: Edinburgh, 1660–1760*. Oxford: Oxford University Press, 1994.

Hudson, Nicholas, 'From "Nation" to "Race": The Origin of Racial Classification in Eighteenth-Century Thought', *Eighteenth-Century Studies*, 29, 3 (1996), 247–64.

Hunt, Margaret, *The Middling Sort: Commerce, Gender and the Family in England, 1680–1780*. Berkeley and Los Angeles: University of California Press, 1996.

Huzzey, Richard, 'The Moral Geography of British Anti-Slavery Responsibilities', *Transactions of the RHS*, 22 (2012), 111–39.

Immerwahr, John, 'Hume's Revised Racism', *Journal of the History of Ideas*, 53, 3 (1992), 481–4.

Innes, Joanna and Arthur Burns, eds, *Rethinking the Age of Reform: Britain, 1780–1850*. Cambridge: Cambridge University Press, 2003.

Ishiguro, Laura, *Nothing to Write Home About: British Family Correspondence and the Settler-Colonial Everyday*. Vancouver: UBC Press, 2019.

Jackson, Maurice, *Let This Voice Be Heard: Anthony Benezet, Father of Atlantic Abolitionism*. Philadelphia: University of Pennsylvania Press, 2009.

Kidambi, Prashant, *The Making of an Indian Metropolis: Colonial Governance and Public Culture in Bombay, 1890–1920*. Aldershot: Ashgate, 2007.

Kidd, Colin, *Subverting Scotland's Past: Scottish Whig Historians and the Creation of Anglo-British Identity c.1689–1830*. Cambridge: Cambridge University Press, 1993.

Kidd, Colin, 'Gaelic Antiquity and National Identity in Enlightenment Ireland and Scotland', *The English Historical Review*, 109, 434 (November 1994), 1197–214.

Kidd, Colin, 'North Britishness and the Nature of Eighteenth-Century Patriotisms', *The Historical Journal*, 39, 2 (1996), 361–82.

Kidd, Colin, *The Forging of Races: Race and Scripture in the Protestant Atlantic World, 1600–2000*. Cambridge: Cambridge University Press, 2006.

Kim, Elizabeth, 'Maria Edgeworth's *The Grateful Negro*: A Site for Rewriting Rebellion', *Eighteenth-Century Fiction*, 16, 1 (2003), 103–26.

Kinealy, Christine, 'At Home with the Empire: The Example of Ireland', in *At Home with the British Empire*, edited by Catherine Hall and Sonya Rose, 77–100. Cambridge: Cambridge University Press, 2006.

Klein, Herbert and Ben Vinson III, *African Slavery in Latin America and the Caribbean*, 2nd edn. Oxford and New York: Oxford University Press, 2007.

Knapman, David, *Conversation Sharp: The Biography of a London Gentleman Richard Sharp (1759–1835) in Letters, Prose and Verse*. Dorchester: The Dorset Press, 2003.

Knott, Sarah and Barbara Taylor, eds, *Women, Gender and Enlightenment*. Basingstoke: Palgrave Macmillan, 2005.

Knott, Sarah, *Sensibility and the American Revolution*. Chapel Hill: University of North Carolina Press, 2009.

Kolff, Dirk, *Naukar, Rajput and Sepoy: The Ethnohistory of the Military Labour Market in Hindustan, 1450–1850*. Cambridge: Cambridge University Press, 1990.

Kosambi, Meera, *Bombay and Poona: A Socio-ecological Study of Two Indian Cities, 1650–1900*. Stockholm: Universitet Stockholms, 1980.

Kowaleski-Wallace, Beth, 'Women, China and Consumer Culture in Eighteenth-Century England', *Eighteenth-Century Studies*, 29, 2 (1995/6), 153–67.

Laidlaw, Zoe, *Colonial Connections 1815–45: Patronage, the Information Revolution and Colonial Government*. Manchester and New York: Manchester University Press, 2005.

Lambert, David and Alan Lester, 'Introduction: Imperial Spaces, Imperial Subjects', in *Colonial Lives across the British Empire: Imperial Careering in the Long 19th Century*, edited by David Lambert and Alan Lester, 1–31. Cambridge: Cambridge University Press, 2006.

Latour, Bruno, *We Have Never Been Modern*, trans. Catherine Porter. Cambridge, MA: Harvard University Press, 1993.

Lenman, Bruce, *The Jacobite Clans of the Great Glen, 1650–1784*, 2nd edn. Aberdeen: Scottish Cultural Press, 1995.

Lester, Alan, 'British Settler Discourse and the Circuits of Empire', *History Workshop Journal*, 54 (2002), 24–48.

Lester, Alan, "Imperial Circuits and Networks: Geographies of the British Empire," *History Compass*, 4, 1 (2006), 124–41.

Lester, Alan and Rob Skinner, 'Humanitarianism and Empire: New Research Agendas', *The Journal of Imperial and Commonwealth History*, 40, 5 (2012), 729–47.

Lowe, Lisa, *The Intimacies of Four Continents* (Durham: Duke University Press, 2015).

MacIntyre, Gordon, *Dugald Stewart: The Pride and Ornament of Scotland*. Brighton: Sussex Academic Press, 2003.

Magnis, Nicholas E., 'Thomas Jefferson and Slavery: An Analysis of His Racist Thinking as Revealed by His Writings and Political Behaviour', *Journal of Black Studies*, 29, 4 (1999), 491–509.

Majeed, Javed, *Ungoverned Imaginings: James Mill's The History of British India and Orientalism*. Oxford: Oxford University Press, 1992.

Makdisi, Saree, *Making England Western: Occidentalism, Race and Imperial Culture*. Chicago, IL and London: University of Chicago Press, 2011.

Makepeace, Margaret, 'Cadet William Lambert Writes from Bombay in 1780', https://blogs.bl.uk/untoldlives/2018/11/cadet-william-lambert-writes-from-bombay-in-1780.html [accessed 28 June 2019].

Marquese, Rafael and Ricardo Salles, 'Slavery in Nineteenth-Century Brazil: History and Historiography', in *Slavery and Historical Capitalism during the Nineteenth Century*, edited by Dale Tomich, 123–69. London: Lexington Books, 2017.

Marshall, P.J., *Problems of Empire: Britain and India, 1757–1813*. Historical Problems: Studies and Documents, 3. London: George Allen and Unwin, Ltd; New York: Barns and Noble, 1968.
Marshall, P.J., *Bengal: The British Bridgehead, Eastern India 1740–1828*. Cambridge: Cambridge University Press, 1988.
Marshall, P.J., 'Britain and the World in the Eighteenth Century I: Reshaping the Empire', *Transactions of the Royal Historical Society*, 6, 8 (1998), 1–18.
Marshall, P.J., 'The British in Asia: Trade to Dominion, 1700–1765', edited by P.J. Marshall and Alaine Low, *The Oxford History of the British Empire: Vol II: The Eighteenth Century*, 487–507. Oxford: Oxford University Press, 1998.
Marshall, P.J., 'Britons and the World in the Eighteenth Century: II Britons and Americans', *Transactions of the Royal Historical Society*, 6, 9 (1999), 1–15.
Mason, Mathew, *Slavery and Politics in the Early American Republic*. Chapel Hill: University of North Carolina Press, 2006.
McCarthy, William, *Anna Letitia Barbauld: Voice of the Enlightenment*. Baltimore, MD: Johns Hopkins University Press, 2008.
McClaren, Martha, *British India and British Scotland, 1780–1830: Career Building, Empire Building, and a Scottish School of Thought on Indian Governance*. Akron, OH: The University of Akron Press, 2001.
Mcdonnell, Michael A., 'The Indigenous Architecture of Empire: The Anishinaabe Odawa in North America', in *Facing Empire: Indigenous Experiences in a Revolutionary Age*, edited by Kate Fullagar and McDonnell, 48–71. Baltimore, MD: Johns Hopkins University Press, 2018.
McElroy, Davis D., *Scotland's Age of Improvement: A Survey of Eighteenth-Century Literary Clubs and Societies*. Washington, DC: Washington State University Press, 1969.
McNeil, Kenneth, *Scotland, Britain, Empire: Writing the Highlands*. Columbus: The Ohio State University Press, 2007.
Meek, Ronald, 'Adam Smith, Turgot and the Four Stages Theory', *Journal of the History of Political Economy*, 3, 1 (1971), 9–27.
Mehta, Uday Singh, *Liberalism and Empire*. Chicago, IL: University of Chicago Press, 1999.
Meuwese, Mark, 'The Opportunities and Limits of Ethnic Soldiering: The Tupis and the Dutch-Portuguese Struggle for the Southern Atlantic, 1630–1657', in *Empires and Indigenes: Intercultural Alliance, Imperial Expansion and Warfare in the Early Modern World*, edited by Wayne E. Lee, 193–221. New York and London: New York University Press, 2011.
Mickelson Gaughan, Joan, *The 'Incumberances': British Women in India, 1615–1856*. Delhi: Oxford University Press, 2013.
Moloney, Pat, 'Savages in the Scottish Enlightenment's History of Desire', *Journal of the History of Sexuality*, 14, 3 (July 2005), 237–65.
Moore, Dafydd, 'James Macpherson and "Celtic Whiggism"', *Eighteenth-Century Life*, 30, 1 (2006), 1–24.

Morely, William, *The Administration of Justice in British India; It's Past History and Present State Comprising an Account of the Laws Peculiar to India*. London: Williams and Norgate, 1858.

Morgan, Jennifer, 'Male Travellers, Female Bodies, and the Gendering of Racial Ideology', in *Bodies in Contact: Rethinking Colonial Encounters in World History*, edited by Antoinette Burton and Tony Ballantyne, 54–66. Durham and London: Duke University Press, 2005.

Mukherjee, Mithi, 'Justice, War, and the Imperium: India and Britain in Edmund Burke's Prosecutorial Speeches in the Impeachment Trial of Warren Hastings', *Law and History Review*, 23, 3 (2005), 589–630.

Muthu, Sankar, *Enlightenment against Empire*. Princeton, NJ: Princeton University Press, 2003.

Narayan Rao, J.S., 'Adam Smith in India', in *Adam Smith: International Perspectives*, edited by Hiroshi Mizuta and Chuhei Sugiyama, 261–78. Basingstoke and London: The Macmillan Press, 1993.

Nascimento, Abdias Do and Elisa Larkin Nascimento, *Africans in Brazil: A Pan-African Perspective*. Trenton, NJ: African World Press, 1992.

Nechtman, Tillman W., *Nabobs: Empire and Identity in Eighteenth-Century Britain*. Cambridge: Cambridge University Press, 2010.

Nenadic, Stana, 'Impact of the Military Profession on Highland Gentry Families, c.1730–1830', *The Scottish Historical Review* LXXXV, 1, 219 (April 2006), 75–99.

Nenadic, Stana, *Lairds and Luxury: The Highland Gentry in Eighteenth-Century Scotland*. Edinburgh: Edinburgh University Press, 2007.

Nightingale, Pamela, *Trade and Empire in Western India, 1784–1806*. Cambridge South Asian Studies, Number 9. New York: Cambridge University Press, 1970.

Nishida, Mieko, *Slavery and Identity: Ethnicity, Gender and Race in Salvador, Brazil, 1808–1888*. Bloomington and Indianapolis: Indiana University Press, 2003.

Nussbaum, Felicity, *The Autobiographical Subject: Gender and Ideology in Eighteenth-Century England*. Baltimore, MD and London: Johns Hopkins University Press, 1989.

Nussbaum, Felicity, *Torrid Zones: Maternity, Sexuality and Empire In Eighteenth-Century English Narratives*. Baltimore, MD: Johns Hopkins University Press, 1995.

Nussbaum, Felicity, *The Limits of the Human: Fictions of Anomaly, Race, and Gender in the Long Eighteenth Century*. Cambridge: Cambridge University Press, 2003.

Nyland, Chris, 'Adam Smith, Stage Theory and the Status of Women', *History of Political Economy*, 25, 4 (1993), 617–40.

O'Brien, Karen, *Women and the Enlightenment in Eighteenth-Century Britain*. Cambridge: Cambridge University Press, 2009.

O'Flaherty, Brendan and Jill Shapiro, 'Apes, Essences, and Races: What Natural Scientists Believed about Human Variation, 1700–1900', in *Race, Liberalism and Economics*, edited by David Colander, Robert Prasch, Felhuni Sheth, 21–55. Ann Arbor: University of Michigan Press, 2004.

O'Hearn, Denis, 'Ireland in the Atlantic Economy', in *Was Ireland a Colony? Economics, Politics and Culture in Nineteenth-Century Ireland*, edited by Terence McDonough, 3–26. Dublin: Irish Academic Press, 2005.

O'Leary, Patrick, *Sir James Mackintosh: The Whig Cicero*. Aberdeen: Aberdeen University Press, 1989.

Olson, Richard, 'Sex and Status in Scottish Enlightenment Social Science: John Millar and the Sociology of Gender Roles', *History of the Human Sciences*, 11, 1 (1998), 73–100.

Olusoga, David, *Black and British: A Forgotten History*. London: Palgrave Macmillan, 2016.

O'Neill, Daniel, *The Burke-Wollsotnecraft Debate: Savagery, Civilization, and Democracy*. University Park: University of Pennsylvania State Press, 2007.

Outram, Dorinda, *The Enlightenment*, 2nd edn. Cambridge: Cambridge University Press, 2005.

Palsetia, Jesse S., *Jamsetjee Jejeebhoy of Bombay: Partnership and Public Culture in Empire*. New Delhi: Oxford University Press, 2015.

Paoletti, Cristina, 'Common Sense in the Public Sphere: Dugald Stewart and the *Edinburgh Review*', *History of European Ideas*, 31, 1 (2012), 163–4.

Patel, Sujata and Alice Thorner, eds, *Bombay: Metaphor for Modern India*. Bombay: Oxford University Press, 1995.

Paton, Diana, 'Obeah Acts: Producing and Policing the Boundaries of Religion in the Caribbean', *Small Axe*, 28 (March 2009), 1–18.

Patterson, Orlando, *Slavery and Social Death: A Comparative Study*. Cambridge, MA: Harvard University Press, 1982.

Paul-Rubiés, Joan, 'Were Early Modern Europeans Racist?', in *Ideas of 'Race' in the History of the Humanities*, edited by Amos Morris-Reich and Dirk Rupnow, 33–87. Cham: Palgrave Macmillan, 2017.

Peabody, Norbert, 'Tod's Rajast'han and the Boundaries of Imperial Rule in Nineteenth-Century India', *Modern Asian Studies*, 30, 1 (1996), 185–220.

Pearsall, Sarah, *Atlantic Families: Lives and Letters in the Later Eighteenth Century*. Oxford: Oxford University Press, 2008.

Pentland, Gordon, *Radicalism, Reform and National Identity in Scotland, 1820–1833*. Rochester, NY: Boydell Press, 2008.

Perera, Suvendrina, *Reaches of Empire: The English Novel from Edgeworth to Dickens*. New York: Columbia University Press, 1991.

Perry, Adele, '"Is Your Garden in England, Sir": James Douglas' Archive and the Politics of Home', *History Workshop Journal*, 70 (Autumn 2010), 67–85.

Petley, Christer, '"Home" and "This Country": Britishness and Creole Identity in the Letters of a Transatlantic Slaveholder', *Atlantic Studies: Global Currents*, 6, 1 (2009), 43–61.

Phillipson, Nicholas, *Adam Smith: An Enlightened Life*. New Haven, CT and London: Yale University Press, 2010.

Pitts, Jennifer, *A Turn to Empire: The Rise of Imperial Liberalism in Britain and France*. Princeton, NJ: Princeton University Press, 2006.

Pocock, J.G.A., *Virtue, Commerce and History: Essays on Political Thought and History, Chiefly in the Eighteenth Century*. Cambridge: Cambridge University Press, 1985.

Pocock, J.G.A., *Barbarism and Religion, v.4 Barbarians, Savages and Empire*. Cambridge: Cambridge University Press, 2005.

Poliandri, Simone, *First Nations, Identity, and Reserve Life: The Mi'kmaq of Nova Scotia*. Nebraska: University of Nebraska Press, 2011.

Pratt, Mary Louise, *Imperial Eyes: Travel Writing and Transculturation*. London: Routledge, 1992.

Queirós Mattoso, Karia M de, *To Be a Slave in Brazil, 1550–1888*, trans. Arthur Goldhamme. New Brunswick, NJ: Rutgers University Press, 1996.

Rabin, Dana, '"In a Country of Liberty?": Slavery, Villeinage and the Making of Whiteness in the Somerset Case (1772)', *History Workshop Journal*, 72 (2011), 5–29.

Rai, Amit, *Rule of Sympathy: Sentiment, Race, and Power, 1750–1850*. Basingstoke: Palgrave Macmillan, 2002.

Rajan, Balachandra, *Under Western Eyes: Indian from Milton to Macaulay*. Durham and London: Duke University Press, 1999.

Rawley, James with Stephen Behrendt, *The Transatlantic Slave Trade: A History*, Rev. edn. Lincoln and London: University of Nebraska Press, 2005.

Reid, Jennifer, *Myth, Symbol, and Colonial Encounter: British and Mi'kmaq in Acadia, 1700–1867*. Ottawa: University of Ottawa Press, 1995.

Rendall, Jane, 'Scottish Orientalism: From Robertson to James Mill', *The Historical Journal*, 25, 1 (1982), 43–69.

Rendall, Jane, 'Virtue and Commerce: Women in the Making of Adam Smith's Political Economy', in *Women in Western Political Philosophy*, edited by Ellen Kennedy and Susan Mendus, 53–71. Brighton: Wheatsheaf Press, 1987.

Rendall, Jane, 'Women and the Public Sphere', *Gender and History*, 11, 3 (1999), 475–88.

Rendall, Jane, 'Bluestockings and Reviewers: Gender, Power and Culture in Britain, c.1800–1830', *Nineteenth-Century Contexts*, 26, 4 (2004), 355–74.

Rendall, Jane, 'Gender, Race and the Progress of Civilization: Introduction', in *Women, Gender and Enlightenment*, edited by Barbara Taylor and Sarah Knott, 70–4. Basingstoke: Palgrave Macmillan, 2005.

Rendall, Jane, 'Scottish Citizens of London: Whigs, Radicals, and the French Revolution, 1788–1795', in *Scots in London in the Eighteenth Century: Patronage, Culture and Identity*, edited by Stana Nenadic, 272–99. Lewisburg, PA: Buckness University Press, 2010.

Rendall, Jane, 'Adaptations: History, Gender, and Political Economy in the Work of Dugald Stewart', *History of European Ideas*, 38, 1 (2012), 143–61.

Rendall, Jane, '"Elementary Principles of Education": Elizabeth Hamilton, Maria Edgeworth and the Uses of Common Sense Philosophy', *History of European Ideas*, 39, 5 (2013), 613–30.

Richards, Eric, 'Malthus and the Uses of British Emigration', in *Empire, Migration and Identity in the British World*, edited by Kent Fedorowich and Andrew Thompson, 42–59. Manchester: Manchester University Press, 2013.

Robinson, David, 'Orientalism or Meridionism? British Identity Formation through Travel Writing on India and Italy, 1760–1860', PhD Thesis, University of Nottingham, Nottingham, 2020.

Rocha, Antonio Penalves, 'Idiéas antiescravistas da Ilustração na sociedade escravista brasileira', *Revista Brasileira de História*, 20, 39 (2000), 37–68.

Rocher, Rosanne, 'British Orientalism in the Eighteenth Century: The Dialectics of Knowledge and Government', in *Orientalism and the Postcolonial Predicament*, edited by Carol A. Breckinridge and Peter van der Veer, 215–59. Philadelphia, PA: University of Pennsylvania Press, 1993.

Schultz, Kirsten, 'The Crisis of Empire and the Problem of Slavery: Portugal and Brazil, c.1700–1820', *Common Knowledge*, 11, 2 (2005), 264–82.

Schwartz, Stuart, *Slaves, Peasants and Rebels: Reconsidering Brazilian Slavery*. Urbana: University of Illinois Press, 1992.

Sebastiani, Silvia, 'Race and National Characters in Eighteenth-Century Scotland: The Polygenetic Discourses of Kames and Pinkerton', *Cromohs*, 8 (2003), 1–14.

Sebastiani, Silvia, 'National Character and Race: A Scottish Enlightenment Debate', in *Character, Self, and Sociability in the Scottish Enlightenment*, edited by Thomas Ahnert and Susan Manning, 187–205. New York: Palgrave Macmillan, 2011.

Sebastiani, Silvia, *Scottish Enlightenment: Race, Gender and the Limits of Progress*. Basingstoke: Palgrave Macmillan, 2013.

Sebastiani, Silvia, 'Challenging Boundaries: Apes and Savages in Enlightenment', in *Simianization: Apes, Gender, Class and Race*, edited by Silvia Sebastiani, Wulf Hund, and Charles Mills, 105–38. Vienna: LIT, 2015.

Sebastiani, Sylvia and Aaron Garret, 'David Hume on Race', in *The Oxford Handbook of Philosophy of Race*, edited by Naomi Zack, 31–43. Oxford: Oxford University Press, 2017.

Sen, Sudipta, *Distant Sovereignty: National Imperialism and the Origins of British India*. New York: Routledge, 2002.

Sen, Sudipta, 'Imperial Subjects of Trial: On the Legal Identity of Britons in Late Eighteenth-Century India', *Journal of British Studies*, 45 (2006), 532–55.

Singha, Radhika, *A Despotism of Law: Crime and Justice in Early Colonial India*. Delhi: Oxford University Press, 1998.

Smith, Barbara, ed. *Home Girls: A Black Feminist Anthology*. New York: Kitchen Table: Women of Color Press, 1983.

Smylitopoulos, Christina, 'Rewritten and Reused: Imaging the Nabob through "Upstart Iconography"', *Eighteenth-Century Life*, 32, 2 (2008), 39–59.

Sorensen, Janet, *The Grammar of Empire in Eighteenth-Century British Writing*. Cambridge and New York: Cambridge University Press, 2000.

Spear, Percival, *The Nabobs: A Study of the Social Life of the English in Eighteenth-Century India*. London and Dublin: Curson Press, 1980, first published, 1932.

Stanton, Lucia, 'The Other End of the Telescope: Jefferson through the Eyes of His Slaves', *The William and Mary Quarterly*, 57, 1 (2000), 151-92.

Stoler, Ann Laura, 'European Communities and the Boundaries of Rule', *Comparative Studies in Society and History*, 31, 1 (1989), 134-61.

Subrahmanyam, Sanjay, *The Portuguese Empire in Asia, 1500-1700*, 2nd edn. Chichester: John Wiley & Sons, 2012.

Subramanian, Lakshmi, *Indigenous Capital and Imperial Expansion: Bombay, Surat and the West Coast*. New York: Oxford University Press, 1996.

Suleri, Sara, *The Rhetoric of English India*. Chicago, IL and London: University of Chicago Press, 1992.

Swaminathan, Srividhya, 'Adam Smith's Moral Economy and the Debate to Abolish the Slave Trade', *Rhetoric Society Quarterly*, 37, 4 (2007), 481-507.

Swaminathan, Srividhya, *Debating the Slave Trade: Rhetoric of British National Identity, 1759-1815*. Surrey: Ashgate, 2009.

Taylor, Barbara, 'Enlightenment and the Uses of Woman', *History Workshop Journal*, 74, 1 (2012), 79-87.

Teltscher, Kate, *India Inscribed: European and British Writing on India, 1600-1800*. Delhi: Oxford University Press, 1995.

Theordor Koditschek, *Liberalism, Imperialism, and the Historical Imagination: Nineteenth-Century Visions of a Greater Britain*. New York: Cambridge University Press, 2011.

Thompson, Carl, 'Earthquakes and Petticoats: Maria Graham, Geology and Early Nineteenth Century "Polite" Science', *Journal of Victorian Culture*, 17, 3 (2012), 329-46.

Tiianen-Tiller, Kaija, *The Problem of Humanity: Blacks in the European Enlightenment*. Helsinki: Suoen Historiallinen Seura, 1994.

Tomaselli, Sylvia, 'The Enlightenment Debate on Women', *History Workshop Journal*, 20 (1985), 101-24.

Torri, Michelguglielmo, 'Trapped inside the Colonial Order: The Hindu Bankers of Surat and Their Business World during the Second Half of the Eighteenth Century', *Modern Asian Studies*, 25, 2 (1991), 54-7.

Trautmann, Thomas, *Aryans and British India*. Berkeley: University of California Press, 1997.

Travers, Robert, *Ideology and Empire in Eighteenth-Century India*. Cambridge: Cambridge University Press, 2007.

Trumpener, Kate, *Bardic Nationalism: The Romantic Novel and the British Empire*. Princeton, NJ: Princeton University Press, 1997.

Uglow, Jenny, *The Lunar Men: The Friends Who Made The Future, 1730-1810*. London: Bloomsbury, 2002.

Van Cleve, James, 'Reid's Theory of Perception', in *The Cambridge Companion to Thomas Reid*, edited by Terence Cuneo and René Van Woudenberg, 101–33. Cambridge: Cambridge University Press, 2004.

van Woudenberg, René, 'Reid and Personal Identity', in *Cambridge Companion to Thomas Reid*, edited by Terence Cuneo and René Van Woudenberg, 204–21. Cambridge: Cambridge University Press, 2004.

Vatal, Nivedita, 'Sir James Mackintosh and His Contribution to Developments in Bombay, 1804–1811', Unpublished MPhil thesis, University of Bombay, 1989–1991.

Wahrman, Dror, *The Making of the Modern Self: Identity and Culture in Eighteenth-Century England*. New Haven, CT: Yale University Press, 2004.

Wall Hinds, Elizabeth Jane, 'The Spirit of Trade: Olaudah Equiano's Conversion, Legalism, and the Merchants' Life', *African American Review*, 32, 4 (1998), 635–47.

Weiss Muller, Hannah, *Subjects and Sovereign, Bonds of Belonging in the Eighteenth-Century British Empire*. New York: Oxford University Press, 2017.

Wheeler, Roxann, *The Complexion of Race: Categories of Difference in Eighteenth-Century British Culture*. Philadelphia, PA: Pennsylvania University Press, 2010.

Whelan, Kevin, 'Ireland, Scotland and Britain in the Long Eighteenth Century', in *These Fissured Isles: Ireland, Scotland and the Making of Modern Britain, 1798–1848*, edited by Terry Brotherstone, A. Clark and K. Whelan, 43–60. Edinburgh: Edinburgh University Press, 2005.

Wilson, Jon, *The Domination of Strangers: Modern Governance In Eastern India, 1780–1835*. Basingstoke: Palgrave Macmillan, 2008.

Wilson, Kathleen, *Island Race: Englishness, Empire and Gender in the Eighteenth Century*. New York: Routledge, 2003.

Winch, Donald, 'The System of the North: Dugald Stewart and His Pupils', in *That Noble Science of Politics: A Study in Nineteenth-Century Intellectual History*, edited by Stefan Collini, Donald Winch and John Burrow, 23–61. Cambridge: Cambridge University Press, 1983.

Winch, Donald, *Vindiciae Gallicae and Other Writings on the French Revolution*. Indianapolis, IN: Liberty Fund, 2006.

Withers, Charles W. J., *Gaelic Scotland: The Transformation of a Culture Region*. London and New York: Routledge, 1988.

Wolfe, Patrick, 'Settler Colonialism and the Elimination of the Native', *Journal of Genocide Research*, 8, 4 (2006), 387–409.

Womack, Peter, *Improvement and Romance: Constructing the Myth of the Highlands*. Basingstoke: The Macmillan Press, 1989.

Wood, Paul, 'Dugald Stewart and the Invention of 'The Scottish Enlightenment'', in *The Scottish Enlightenment: Essays in Reinterpretation*, edited by Paul Wood, 1–35. Rochester, NY: University of Rochester Press, 2000.

Woods, Michael E., 'A Theory of Moral Outrage: Indignation and Eighteenth-Century British Abolitionism', *Slavery and Abolition*, 36, 4 (2015), 662–83.

Wrigley, E.A., *Poverty, Progress, and Population*. Cambridge: Cambridge University Press, 2004.

Index

Aberdeen, University of 51, 75, 107, 168n23
abolitionism 17, 20, 23, 34, 38, 40, 42–3, 45, 59–62, 66–7, 69, 72–3, 77, 85, 154, 172n4
Addison, Joseph 63
Afghanistan 124
Africa 4, 6, 13, 21, 23, 25, 36, 42, 57, 66, 69, 73
Africans 4, 6, 8–9, 15–17, 19–20, 23, 30–2, 34–7, 40–5, 50, 57, 59–63, 65–9, 71–7, 82–3, 85, 96, 100, 105, 109, 141, 151–154
   depicted as Hottentots 16, 37, 100
   depicted as Moors 37, 109
   depicted as Negroes 7, 16, 23, 37, 40, 42–3, 60–2, 65, 66–9, 72–5, 77, 83, 86, 139, 143
   women 8, 66, 68, 70–1
Alison, Archibald (junior) 40
Allen, John 129
American colonies 5, 9, 14–15, 17, 19–21, 34–6, 40–2, 61, 66, 75, 99, 117, 128, 153–4
American revolution 38, 82, 105, 107, 117
Americans (colonists) 39–40, 84, 86, 104, 116
Americans (indigenous) 6, 17, 22, 25, 32, 54, 65, 70, 79, 83–4, 86, 98, 103–5, 106, 112, 131, 141, 154
Americas 1, 4–6, 14–15, 17, 19–21, 23, 25, 35–6, 40, 42, 45, 54, 60–3, 66, 70, 73, 75, 79–80, 82, 86–7, 89, 91–4, 99, 103–4, 117, 128, 131, 153–4
Anderson, James 88, 90–1
   Observations on the Means of Exciting a Spirit of National Industry 88
Anglicanism 5
anglophone World 16
Angola 65, 71

Arabian Gulf. *See* Persian Gulf
Arabian Nights 44
Arabic 137
Arabs 24, 37
Arcadia 84
Argentina 64
Argyleshire 79
Aristotle 35
Armenians 116, 135, 137–8
Asia 4, 6, 23, 36, 92, 108–10, 135, 137–8, 142. *See also*, South Asia
Asiatic Society of Bengal 110, 121–2
Asiatic Society of Bombay 106. *See also* Bombay Literary Society
Atlantic Ocean 4, 42, 59, 79, 85, 152
Aurangabad 121, 125
Australia 21, 64, 84

Baghdad 127–8
Bahia 73–6, 176n89
Baldoon 96–7
Barbary 123
Barbauld, Anna Letitia 39, 49, 82, 146
Barbauld, Rochemont 82
Barber, Frank 23, 162n22
Beattie, James 32, 75, 77
   'Essay on the Lawfulness of Slavery' 77
Belfast 96
Belgium 72
Bell, Hugh 91
   Observations upon Scotch Fisheries, Emigrations, and the Means of Improving the Highlands and Isles 91
belonging 3, 7–8, 10–12, 14–18, 20, 28, 38, 50–1, 56, 61, 66, 79, 89, 94–5, 97–8, 102, 105–6, 111, 113, 125–6, 130, 144, 149, 151–4. *See also*, home
Benezet, Anthony 21
   Some Historical Account of Guinea 21
Bengal 1, 4, 104, 114–15, 119

Bengalis 21, 119
Bentham, Jeremy 13, 64, 117, 137
Bernier, Francois 21
    Voyages 21
Bihar 104
Boddington and Co. 14
Bomanjee, Hormusjee 136
Bombay (Mumbai) 13, 18, 39, 63, 103,
    106–8, 112–17, 120–1, 123–30,
    132–7, 140–5, 147, 154
  'Anglo-Indian' elites 18, 106, 116,
    120–1, 126, 129–30, 134–6, 143–5,
    147
  Court of Requests 115
  European community in 106, 116,
    120–1, 123–4, 126, 129, 133–6,
    143–4
  Governor's Court 115
  legal reforms 18, 103, 106, 115–18,
    132–3
  police 117–18
  prisons 117
  Recorder's Court 103, 115, 132–3, 141
Bombay Courier 118, 141
Bombay Literary Society 18, 106, 116,
    121–4, 189n109
Bonaparte, Napoleon 66
Boston 96
Boswell, James 13, 100, 162n22
Botany Bay 64
Brazil 59, 63–6, 69–73, 76–7, 173n31
  critiques of slavery in 66
  Palmares *Quilombo* 71
Brazilians (colonisers) 59, 65–6, 74, 76
Brazilians (indigenous) 65, 70–1
Britain 3–6, 9–13, 15, 17–18, 21, 39,
    42–3, 57, 60, 62–5, 70, 80–1,
    83–6, 88–94, 96, 98–9, 101, 104–8,
    111–13, 121–2, 124, 128–31,
    133–5, 143, 148–9, 153–4. *See
    also*, England, Scotland, Ireland,
    Wales
  abolitionism 17, 20, 23, 34, 38, 40,
    42–3, 45, 60–2, 66–7, 69, 72–3, 77,
    85, 154, 172n4
  Act for the Abolition of the Slave Trade
    (1807) 73, 85
  Act of Union (1707) 65
  Act of Union (1800) 83

Anglo-British identity 11, 106
army 65, 80, 82, 92–3, 98, 103, 135
Board of Agriculture 88
Board of Trade 21
British Crown 88, 114, 133
child labour 7
clubs and societies 12–13, 21–2, 32, 38,
    51, 129, 137
domestic space 10–11, 81, 130
education 5, 62, 64, 82, 108
elites 5–6, 12–13, 14, 17, 62–3, 80,
    84–5, 94, 101, 103, 105, 107, 113,
    123, 129, 148
government 12, 70, 82–3, 85–6, 88, 90,
    96, 105, 113–14
Great Reform Act (1832) 5
Hanoverian state 88, 106
health provision 5
humanitarianism 7, 73
identity overseas 116, 119, 129,
    159n45, 176n94
India Act (1784) 114
industrialisation 5–6, 10, 63, 79, 102
landholding 5, 64, 82, 88, 93, 95–6, 114
law 5, 9, 111, 115, 117
material consumption 6, 7, 85
men 6, 12, 60, 103, 114, 118, 135–6,
    154
middle classes 5, 9–10, 62, 118
morality 7, 60, 105
national identity 3, 5, 10–11, 15, 17–18,
    60, 89, 98, 101–2, 103, 106, 126,
    128–9, 176n94
parliamentary acts 5, 65, 73, 83, 85,
    114
political repression 4
poor of 4, 43–5, 84–5, 87, 91, 99
population growth 5, 86
prisons 5, 90
Regulating Act (1773) 114
Royal Navy 1, 4, 59, 63, 66
Second Anglo-Maratha war 113, 151
social hierarchies 7, 85
subjecthood 11, 159n45
urbanisation 5
women 6, 12, 130, 140–1, 148, 152
Britannia 73
British empire 1–5, 10–15, 19–21, 24, 39–40,
    57, 60–1, 63–4, 73, 79–82, 84, 89,

92–3, 98, 101, 103–4, 106–8, 112–13, 115–16, 123, 125, 127–8, 133, 135–6, 140–1, 143, 146, 148, 151–4
colonised 3, 4, 6, 12, 17, 23, 57, 60, 65, 83–4, 100, 112, 131, 151–2
colonists 16–17, 21, 35, 39–40, 63, 65, 72–3, 80–1, 83–4, 87–9, 91, 94–8, 102, 105, 117, 131–2, 134, 136, 152
elites 3–5, 11–13, 15, 17–18, 21–2, 39, 62, 80–2, 84, 88, 94, 101, 103, 105, 107, 127, 129–30, 135–6, 148, 151, 153–4
expansion of 6, 10, 12, 15, 17, 39, 64–5, 83–4, 101, 104, 118, 122, 161n6
imperial *literati* 12, 21, 61, 129, 151, 153–4
intellectual networks 3, 12–14, 23, 38–40, 61, 63–4, 107–8, 122–3, 137, 151
maps 12
migration 2, 4, 11, 17, 65, 79–81, 87–94, 96, 105, 114, 130, 153
military service 4, 65, 80, 82, 92–3, 98, 103, 114, 132, 134–5
naval service 1, 4, 59, 63, 66
plantations 4, 5, 7, 14, 19, 35, 40, 60, 65–7, 72–3, 84
racial difference (notions of) 3, 5, 11–12, 57, 60
resource extraction 6, 12, 72, 114, 123
settler colonialism 39–40, 62, 65, 80–7, 89, 91, 94–8, 102, 104–5, 128, 131, 148
subalterns (colonial) 3–4, 6, 12, 60, 65, 104, 114
subalterns (metropolitan) 3, 12, 17, 35, 43–5, 79–80, 88, 100
travel within 1, 3–4, 16, 103, 113–14, 130, 153
use of indigenous labour 6, 65, 72
violence 3, 12–13, 17, 104, 152
whiteness (perceived superiority of) 3, 5–7, 9, 11, 17–18, 43, 57, 60–1, 67, 77, 81, 85–6, 99, 106, 113, 117–18, 121, 123, 125–6, 133, 138, 149
British Library 129
British Malaya 131
Brougham, Henry (1st Baron Brougham) 39, 128
Buffon, Comte de 33, 40. *See also* Leclerc, Georges-Louis

Burke, Edmund 12, 18, 35, 105, 107–8, 111, 117
 Reflections on the Revolution in France 107, 111
 'Speech on Mr Fox's East India Bill' 105
Burnett, James (Lord Monboddo) 40, 45
Burns, Arthur 5
Burt, Edward 100
Bushire (Bushehr) 127, 136–8, 141, 147

Cachoeira 77
Caithness 98
Calcutta (Kolkata) 1, 4, 14, 107, 115–16, 118, 133–5, 152
 Adawlut 115
 Supreme Court of 110, 115
Canada 79, 82–3, 98
Canning, George 133
Cape of Good Hope 4, 104
capitalism 4, 10, 14, 92, 102, 153
Caribbean 4, 6, 18–20, 23, 30, 35, 39–40, 42–3, 60, 63, 72, 76–7, 82–3, 103, 105, 131, 176n94
Carlyle, Thomas 39, 169n62
Catholicism 65, 83, 90, 94, 100, 135, 137
Cavendish Bentinck, William (Lord) 114
Charlevoix, Pierre François Xavier de 25
 Histoire et Description Générale de la Nouvelle-France 25
Charlotte Town 84
Chile 64, 70
China 5–6, 23, 107, 116, 125, 137, 139
 Great Wall of 125
Chincore (Chinchwad) 137
Christ 60
Christian Observer 148
Christianity 5, 54, 60, 71, 86, 90, 110, 115, 119–21, 134, 141, 147–8
 Catholicism 65, 83, 90, 94, 100, 135, 137
 Christian world 123
 dissenters 65, 82
 evangelicalism 60, 145–6
 Jesuit order 70
 missionaries 15, 25, 120–1
 presbyterianism 65
 protestantism 5, 64, 135

Clan Chattan 106
Clarkson, Thomas 20
  History of the Abolition of the African Slave Trade 20
class 3, 10–11, 62
climate theory 4–5, 8, 41–2, 54, 60, 79, 109, 120, 122, 138–9, 143, 145, 147
Clune 106
Cobbett, William 99
  The Porcupine 99
Colaba 135
Coleridge, Samuel Taylor 129
'colonial archive' 14
Columbus, Christopher 73
Commission for Annexed Estates 88, 90. See also, Scotland – Jacobite Rising)
Condorcet, Marquis de 45, 82. See de Caritat, Marie Jean Antoine Nicolas
Congo 65
Constantinople 139–40
Cook, James (Captain) 21
Cooper, Anthony Ashley (4th Earl of Shaftesbury) 35
Cornwallis, General Charles (Earl Cornwallis) 132
Corsica 123
Cowper, William 133
Cromwell, Oliver 65
Cuba 70
Culloden, battle of 11
Cursetjee, Ardaseer 136
Cutch 142

D'Arcy Stewart (née Cranstoun), Helen 38, 40
Darwin, Erasmus 46, 63
de Andrada e Silva, José Bonifácio 66
de Caritat, Marie Jean Antoine Nicolas (Marquis de Condorcet) 45, 82
de Stael, Madame 13
Deccan Plateau 113, 136, 151
Defoe, Daniel 2
Delhi 6
Descartes, René 52
diaries 3, 11–12, 14, 63, 74, 96–7, 106, 128–9, 133, 143–4
Diderot, Denis 12
disease 3, 82, 84, 144
do Rego Barreto, General Luis 59

Douglas, Alexander 82–3
Douglas, Basil William (Lord Daer) 82
Douglas, Dunbar (4th Earl of Selkirk) 82–4
Douglas, James 135
Douglas, Janet 21
Douglas, Thomas (5th Earl of Selkirk) 17, 40, 79–80, 87–98, 100–2, 107, 129
  biographical summary 82–5
  emigration schemes 17, 79–81, 83, 87–9, 91–7, 100–2
  Observations on the Present State of the Highlands of Scotland 79–81, 84–5, 87, 89, 91–3, 97, 100–2
  opposition to slavery 85
  views on British poor 84–5
  views on indigenous Americans 85
Dow, Alexander 109–10
  'Dissertation on the Origin and Nature of Despotism in Hindostan' 109–10
Dowluttabad 121
Drennan, William 65, 83
Dublin 107
Dudley, Earl of. See Ward, John William
Dumont, Pierre Étienne Louis 117
Dunbar, James 53, 107
Duncan, Jonathan (Governor of Bombay) 120, 144
Dunnan, William 38
Dutch East Indies 131
Dutch empire 6, 70–1, 131

East (western views of) 11, 107, 108–11, 118, 138, 140, 144, 147–9
East India Company 1, 4–6, 17–18, 39, 103–5, 107, 110–17, 119–21, 123, 128, 130–3, 135–6, 141, 143, 145–6, 153, 192n24, 192n30
  behaviour of company personnel 17–18, 104–5, 111–12, 115–16, 118, 120, 123, 128, 131–2, 136, 145–6
  Board of Control 114
  Court of Directors 112, 114, 116
  India Act (1784) 114
  Regulating Act (1773) 114
East Indies 104, 108, 112, 114
Edgeworth, Henry 63
Edgeworth, Maria 16, 23, 39, 49, 59, 61–9, 72–3, 75–7, 85, 107, 111, 129
  The Absentee 64
  Belinda 63

biographical summary 62–5
Castle Rackrent 64
Ennui 64
'The Grateful Negro' 16, 61–2, 65–7, 69, 72–3, 77
'Lame Gervas' 111
Popular Tales 63–4, 66, 68
views on slavery 61, 66, 69, 77, 85
Edgeworth, Richard Lovell 62
Edgeworthstown 62, 65
Edinburgh 1, 14, 21, 23, 32, 38, 40, 63, 81, 91, 107
 Royal Society of 38, *See also* Philosophical Society
 University of 15, 22, 24–5, 38, 63, 82, 107
Edinburgh Review 39, 80, 122
Edinburgh Select Society 21
Edwards, Bryan 72–3
 An Historical Survey of the French Colony in the Island of Saint Domingue 72
 The History, Civil and Commercial, of the British Colonies in the West Indies 72
effeminacy 18, 30–1, 47, 93, 108–9, 118, 125, 138, 143–4, 149
Egypt 125
 pyramids 125
Elephanta 125
Elers, Anna Maria 62
Elliott, Gilbert 113
Elliot-Murray-Kynynmound, Gilbert (1st Earl of Minto) 39, 120
Ellora 121, 125
Elphinstone, Mountstuart 122, 124
 An Account of the Kingdom of Caubul 122
emotion 2, 5, 10, 14
England 11, 17, 21, 24, 64, 92, 100, 111, 113–4, 123, 125–6, 134, 137, 143–4, 146–7
 Anglo-British identity 11, 106
 colonisation within British Isles 4, 17, 91, 106–7
 Englishness 11, 18, 111, 116, 125–6
 history 11
 law 116–17, 129
 literature 139, 141
 masculinity, notions of 11
 national identity 11
 Norman conquest of 92
 English 64, 73, 90–1, 106, 114, 116, 130, 136, 143–4, 147
 English language 124, 136–7, 141
 exceptionalism 11
 perception of 'Englishness' 10–11, 18, 91, 105, 111, 116–17, 119–21, 125
 whiteness as part of identity 11
Enlightenment 7–10, 12, 15–16, 22–3, 38, 42, 56, 64, 66, 68, 74, 84–6, 108, 111, 118, 130, 152, 154–5. *See also*, Scottish Enlightenment
 biological essentialism 8
 critiques of European imperial practices 12, 15, 86
 debate over human origins 7
 Eurocentrism 7
 notion of civilisation 15
 notion of human difference 7–9, 15
 notion of human nature 15, 25, 28, 33, 36, 51–2, 108, 153
 notion of self 8–10, 25–7, 36, 52, 152–3
 notion of white superiority 7, 9, 12
 racism 7–9, 12, 74, 152–3, 166n97, 168n32
 representations of 'the East' 106, 108–11, 138, 149
 role in European imperialism 12, 15, 47, 57, 119, 143
 theories on human mind 7
 views of non-Europeans 7, 12, 15, 22, 67–8, 106, 108–11, 138, 153
 views on women 7, 22, 56, 68, 152, 161n16
environment 1, 4, 184n7
Equiano, Olaudah 23, 77
Erskine, Maitland (née Mackintosh) 129, 147
Erskine, William 39, 124
Estelow, James 103, 114
Europe 2–6, 13, 18, 20–1, 23–5, 31–2, 39, 42, 47, 55, 60, 70, 84, 86, 89, 92, 100, 104–5, 108, 110–11, 113, 122–5, 138, 144
Europeans 4–8, 12, 16, 18–20, 30, 32, 34, 36, 43–5, 48, 50, 57, 61–2, 72, 74–6, 85–6, 99, 103–5, 110–11, 115–16, 118, 120–1, 123–4, 136, 142–4, 147

perceived difference to non-Europeans 6–8, 12, 15–16, 18, 23, 25, 33–4, 43–4, 49–50, 57, 60–1, 67, 77, 85–6, 110–11, 116, 119, 121, 123, 125–6, 130, 132, 138, 140, 142–4
European imperialism 2–4, 6, 12, 15, 22, 42, 62, 65, 70–1, 73, 86, 103–4, 112–13, 149, 152
  colonised 23, 57, 59, 65, 70–2, 104
  colonists 19, 35, 59, 65, 70, 75–6
  displacement of people 3–4, 71, 104
  elites 20
  expansion 3–4, 6, 20, 62, 70, 72, 113
  genocide 48, 65, 103, 174n31
  intellectual networks 12
exile 2–3, 12, 15–17, 29, 60–2, 75, 79–81, 88, 95, 98, 101, 128, 144, 151, 154–5
expropriation 3, 6, 12, 17, 72, 104. *See also* plunder

family 10, 12, 18, 29, 61, 75, 91, 129–30, 132–4, 139, 141, 146
Fanon, Frantz 152
femininity 22, 30–1, 68, 98, 109, 125, 128–9, 134, 145, 147–8, 154
feminism 20, 22, 155
Ferguson, Adam 28–9, 38, 40, 47, 53, 85, 108–9, 138
  An Essay on the History of Civil Society 28–9, 108–9, 138
fertility 5, 87
Firishtah 145
  History of Hindostan 145
Flanders 89
food 4–5
Foote, Samuel 120
  The Nabob 120
France 6, 21, 25, 65–6, 70, 82, 84, 92, 107
  abolitionism 66
  French Enlightenment 8, 163n31
  philosophy 82, 163n31
  republicans 82–3, 107
Frankfurt School 12
Franklin, Benjamin 21, 40
  'Observations Concerning the Increase of Mankind' 86
Fraser, Simon (General) 107
Fraser, Simon (of Lovat) 92
French 8, 21, 66, 73, 82–4, 96, 124

French empire 6, 45
French language 137
French Revolution 45, 65, 80, 82, 93, 107–8, 112, 129

Gaelic language 91
gender 10–11, 54, 62, 81, 95, 109, 130, 138, 152, 154
genocide 48, 65, 103, 174n31
Germans 32
Germany 107, 124, 139–40
Gibbes, Phebe 130
  Hartley House, Calcutta 130
Gibraltar 107
Gilchrist, John Borthwick 132, 136
  Hindoostanee Philology: Comprising a Dictionary, English and Hindoostanee 136
  The General East India Guide and Vade Mecum 132
Glasgow 21, 32
  University of 22, 24, 51
Glenmoriston 90
Goa 103
God 27, 47–9, 51, 53, 120. *See also* providence
Godwin, William 87
  Political Justice 87
Gohar, Ali (Shah Alam II) 104
Goldsmith, Oliver 16, 80, 95, 99
  'The Deserted Village' 80, 95, 99
Gordon, James (of Craig) 81, 95, 97
Graham, James 95
  'The Sabbath' 95
Graham, Maria 1–2, 10, 16, 23, 39, 59–66, 69–77, 85, 133, 135–7, 139–42, 147–8, 154
  'Atala in the Wilderness' 1–2, 10
  biographical summary 63–5
  Journal of a Residence in Chile 59
  Journal of a Residence in India 63, 136, 147
  Journal of a Voyage to Brazil 16, 59, 62, 65–6, 69–70, 72, 73
  Letters on India 63
  Little Arthur's History of England 63
  opposition to slavery 59–60, 66, 69–70, 76–7, 85
  sentimental discourse 74, 176n84

'Sketch of the History of Brazil' 71
views on non-Europeans 59–60, 70–1, 140, 142
Grant, Anne (of Laggan) 79, 81, 91, 95, 98, 101
'The Highlanders' 79, 81, 95, 101
Grant, Charles 119–21, 141, 143
Observations on the State of Society among the Asiatic Subjects of Great Britain 119, 141
Grant, Elizabeth 98
Great Reform Act (Britain, 1832) 5
Great Salmon River 83
Greece (ancient) 24, 42
Greece (modern) 42
Greek 110
Greene, John 42
Gregory, James 40
Conspectus Medicinae Theoreticae 40
Gregory, John 30, 41
Guadaloupe 83
Guinea 42, 43, 65
Gujarat 115

Haiti 6, 45, 70
Haitian revolution 6, 70, 72
Haldhed, Nathaniel Brassey 110
A Code of Gentoo Laws 110
Halifax (Nova Scotia) 85
Hamilton, Elizabeth 23, 39
Hamilton, Helen 82
Hasan Kahn, Mirz Abu'l 127
Hastings, Warren 111–12
Hatsell, John 81
Hawkesworth, John 54
An Account of the Voyages for Making Discoveries in the Southern Hemisphere 54
Hebrides 88, 98
Herington (Warwickshire) 103
heteronormativity 3, 68, 75–7, 87–8, 132–3, 138–9, 146
Highlanders (Scottish) 4, 17, 79–81, 87, 89–102, 103, 105–7, 111, 119, 128, 141, 153–4
agriculture 4, 88, 93–4
attachment to 'native' land 17, 79, 81, 94–5, 98, 101, 153
emigration 17, 79–81, 87–101, 103, 105, 128, 153–4
itinerancy 17, 80, 95, 98, 153

likened to Africans 100
perceived as 'uncivilised' 17, 81, 89–92, 94, 99–101
perceived unsuitability to industrialising Britain 79–81, 88, 93–4, 96–7, 101–2
positive perceptions of 81, 91–3, 98
service in British forces 80, 92–3, 101, 107
service in overseas armies 4, 92
women 81, 97–9
Highlands (Scottish) 4, 14, 17, 79–82, 86–102, 105, 107, 111, 129, 153–4
Hinduism 103, 109–10, 115, 119, 134–7, 139, 141–3, 147
law 115, 119
Hindustani 146–7
Historiography 9–12
Britain, 4–5, 11
British empire 5–7, 11, 13, 128, 130–1
colonial India 130–1, 192n24
eighteenth century 9
Enlightenment 20, 34, 56–7, 166n5
Europe 9
family 10
feminist 20, 22, 155
material culture 6–7
postcolonial 20, 140
race 9, 56, 128
selfhood 9–10
slavery 34, 197n4
HMS *Doris* 59
HMS *Lion* 127
Hobbes, Thomas 29
Leviathan 29
Hodges, William 121, 142–3
Travels in India during the Years 1780, 1781, 1782 and 1783 142
Holland, Lord. *See* Vassall-Fox, Henry
Holland House 13
home 1–3, 5–7, 9–12, 14–18, 37, 50, 54–7, 59–62, 65–6, 74–5, 81, 92, 95, 105–6, 113, 116, 124–6, 128–9, 144, 146–9, 151–5
belonging 3, 7–8, 10–12, 14–18, 20, 28, 38, 50–1, 56, 61, 66, 79, 88, 94–5, 97–8, 102, 105–6, 111, 113, 125–6, 130, 144, 149, 151–4
racialised 8, 13, 19, 37, 106, 153
Home, Henry (Lord Kames) 21, 33, 41–2, 47, 51, 57, 63, 68, 88, 139

Sketches of the History of Man 42, 57, 68, 139
    views on racial difference 33, 165n80
homely (changing meaning of) 2, 61–2, 74, 81, 95, 99, 153
homesickness 2
Horner, Francis 39
House of Commons 119
House of Lords 85
Hudson's Bay Company 83
humanity (notions of) 3, 7–8
Hume, David 7, 12, 15, 21–3, 25–8, 30, 32–4, 36, 40, 42, 43, 46, 48, 50–4, 69, 85–6, 90, 107, 109
    An Inquiry Concerning Human Understanding 26
    'Of National Character' 7, 23, 26, 90
    notion of human difference 7, 33–4
    notion of sympathy 25–6, 33, 36
    notion of white superiority 7, 23, 32, 34, 36, 42, 50
    'scepticism' school of thought 51–3
    'Of the Populousness of Ancient Nations' 86, 90
    A Treatise on Human Nature 25–8, 33, 52
    views on women 22, 30
Hutcheson, Francis 22, 28, 35, 52
    views on women 22
Hyderabad 136
    Nizam of 139–41

immorality 16–18, 37, 43, 57, 76, 144, 153, 155
India 1, 4–6, 16–18, 39, 59, 63–4, 66, 72, 103–4, 106–16, 118–20, 122–5, 128–32, 135–44, 146–9, 153–4, 184n5
    anglicisation of 119, 132
    Anglo-Indian marriages 131, 145–6
    Anglo-Indian society 18, 104, 116–17, 120–1, 130–1, 134–7, 143, 144–5
    Anglo-Indian sexual relationships 131–2, 145–6
    banditry 119, 189n94
    British migration to 114, 130
    British power expanded in 6, 114, 115–16, 125
    cities and towns 4
    climate 109, 120, 138–9, 147
    colonial society 39, 103–4, 106, 114–16, 120, 124, 128–37, 144, 146–7
    colonial study of 16, 39, 109–10, 124–5, 185n32
    countryside 4
    culture 16, 105, 110, 120–2
    Europeans in 103–6, 109–11, 115–16, 123–4, 130–2, 134–5, 138, 144
    famine 4, 104, 152, 184n7
    history 16, 122
    indigenous power structures 6, 104, 109, 112, 141, 184n5
    languages of 110, 124, 136–7
    law 114–15, 117
    memsahib stereotype 131
    migration 4
    peasants 4
    perceived as civilised 105, 108–9, 125, 138, 140
    perceived as site of immorality 17–18, 116, 120–1, 127–8, 130, 138–9, 141–5, 148
    orphan schools 132
    religious practices 63, 109–10, 135, 142–3
    sati ritual 142–3
    Second Anglo-Maratha war 113, 151
    society 184n5
    Victorian imagination of 125
Indian Ocean 4
Indians 4, 45, 62, 103–4, 109, 114–16, 118–20, 125, 131–2, 135, 138–43, 154
    domesticity 18, 130, 189n96
    financiers 116
    homes 18, 130, 138–42, 189n96
    men 140
    merchants 116
    military service 4, 132
    'nabob' discourse 120, 131
    perceived as effeminate 18, 108–9, 125, 138, 143–4, 149
    perceived as inferior to Europeans 110–11, 116–20, 124–5, 138–43, 147
    perceived as passive 108
    princes 111, 139
    service in British armies 114, 134
    trade 4, 134–7
    women 4, 131–2, 139–43, 146–8, 191n24
industrial revolution 5, 63, 157n15
Inverness 98

Inverness-shire 79, 113
Ireland 4, 35, 62, 64–5, 72, 83, 91–3, 99, 107, 124
  Act of Union (1800) 83
  Great Rebellion 65
  Parliament 64–5, 83
  Society of United Irishmen 65, 83
Irish 65, 83, 93–4, 99, 114
Irvine, Alexander 88–9, 93–5, 97
  An Inquiry into the Causes and Effects of Emigration 88–9
Islam 115, 134–6, 139, 142. *See also* Quran
  law 115, 119
  merchants in India 116, 135
  piracy 123
Isle of Mull 98
Isle of Skye 79, 96–7
Isle of Uist 79
Italy 1, 59, 63–4
Italian language 137
itinerancy 1, 3–5, 12, 16–18, 37, 55–7, 71, 80, 95, 98, 105, 153–5
  sign of immorality 16–18, 37, 57, 71, 105, 153, 155
  sign of lack of humanity 3, 16–17, 105, 153

Jacobites 88, 90, 92, 106
Jahan Shah. *See* Muhammad Khurram, Shahab-ud-din
Jamaica 6, 40, 62, 65–6, 68, 70, 72, 76, 83, 128, 133, 173n31
  Tacky's War 68
Jats 6
Jefferson, Thomas 40–1, 43, 50, 67, 69
  Notes on the State of Virginia 40, 50
Jeffrey, Francis 39, 169n62
Johnson, Samuel 23, 80, 94–5, 100
Jones, William (Sir) 21, 110, 121–2, 125, 186n34
Judaism 110
  merchants in India 116, 135

Kames, Lord. *See* Home, Henry
Khair-un-Nissa 131
King of Clubs (London) 129, 137
Kings College (Aberdeen) 51, 107
Kirkcaldy 21

Kirkpatrick, James Achilles 131
Kirkudbright 82, 84
Knox, John 90, 98, 111
  Tour through the Highlands 98
Kyllachy 98

Lafitau, Joseph-François 25
  Moeurs de Sauvage Américains, comparés aux moeurs de premier temps 25
Lambert, William 130
Lansdowne Marquis of. *See* Petty-Fitzmaurice, Henry
Latin 110, 148
Leclerc, Georges-Louis (Comte de Buffon) 33, 40
  Histoire Naturelle 33
Lee, Arthur 34–5
  'An Essay in Vindication of the Continental Colonies from a Censure of Mr Adam Smith, in His Theory of Moral Sentiments' 34–5
letters 3–4, 11–12, 14, 49, 63, 106, 116, 121, 124, 127–30, 133, 136, 143–4, 151–2, 160n56
liberalism 12, 15, 39
  belief in European supremacy 12
  liberal imperialist thought 15, 39, 121
Linneaus, Carl 33, 168n23
  Systema Naturae 33, 168n23
Lisbon 66
Locke, John 46, 52
London 12–14, 39, 107, 115, 118, 137
Louis XVI 111
Louisiana 83
Low Countries 92
Lunar Society 63
luxury produce 6–7, 12, 14, 43, 65, 70, 115–17

Macaulay, Catherine 49
Maciel da Costa, João Severiano 66
MacGillivray family 107, 131
MacGillivray, Lachlan 131
Mackenzie, Henry 10
  Man of Feeling 10
Mackenzie, William Gordon 1, 10
Mackintosh, Catherine (née Allen) 113, 124, 128–30, 133–5, 137, 143–6, 148, 151–2

'A Political Epistle to Sir J on his return to Bombay from Point de Gaulle' 129, 143–4, 146
  Biographical summary 129, 151
Mackintosh, Catherine (née Stuart) 129
Mackintosh, Catherine 'Kitty' 127–8, 133–4, 136, 138, 141
Mackintosh, Elizabeth 'Bessy' 136
Mackintosh, Frances 'Fanny'. *See* Wedgewood, Frances
Mackintosh, James (Sir) 13–14, 18, 25, 39, 63–4, 103, 106–25, 127–34, 136–44, 148, 151, 184n14
  autobiography 184n14
  biographical summary 106–8, 129
  contends European superiority to non-Europeans 117–20, 123–5, 142–3
  contrasts British values with Indian 117–20, 138–9
  critique of European imperialists 112–13, 117–18
  defence of British rule in India 113, 117–18, 123, 143
  family 18, 106–7, 113, 129–30, 133, 134–5, 137–8, 143, 147, 149, 154
  'Observations relating to the population of India' 122
  Recorder of the Court of Bombay 103, 113, 115, 117, 129, 132–3
  'On the Law of Nature and Nations' 108, 110
  use of Hindustani 136
  views on Indians 117–18, 121–2, 129–30, 138–40, 142, 149
  Vindiciae Gallicae 107, 111–12
Mackintosh, Maitland. *See* Erskine, Maitland
Mackintosh, Marjory (née Fraser) 106
Mackintosh Mary. *See* Rich, Mary
Mackintosh, Robert James 129, 134, 137
  use of Hindustani 137
Macpherson, James 91
  The Works of Ossian 91. *See also*, Ossian
Madras 114–15
  Great Mogul 140
Mahayr, Fatima 142
Mahayr, Shabab o'dien 140, 142
Mahim 145

Malabar Hill 145
Malcolm, John 123
Malthus, Thomas 13, 80, 87–8, 129
  An Essay on the Principle of Population 87–8
Marathas 6
Marchand, Sehoy 131
masculinity 10–11, 18, 20, 30–1, 68–9, 91–3, 98, 101–3, 119, 143
Mazagong 133, 135
McEarchen, Angus Bernard (Father) 100
medicine 5, 26
merchants 4, 14, 23, 55, 82, 91, 103, 114–16, 120, 130, 135–6
Mexico 70
Middle East 5, 116, 137
migration 4, 79–80, 87–90, 94, 101. *See also* British empire, migration within
Mi'kmaq 79, 83, 84, 100. *See also* Americans indigenous
Mill, James 39, 143
  History of British India 39, 143
Millar, John 16, 38, 47, 54–7, 60, 94
  The Origin and Distinction of Ranks 54–6, 94
Milton, John 133
MintoEarl of. *See* Elliot-Murray-Kynynmound, Gilbert
missionaries 15, 25, 120–1
Modena 137
Moir, John 145–6
  Female Education 145–6
Monboddo, Lord. *See* Burnett, James
monogenism 7
Montesquieu (Charles-Louis de Secondat) 35, 40, 108–9
  Spirit of the Law 108
Montgomery, James 73
  'The West Indies' 73
Moore, George 116
Moore, John 113
moral philosophy 15–16, 20, 22–4, 26, 39, 49, 51, 53, 57, 60–1, 64, 67, 86, 107, 110
morality 3, 5, 7, 10–11, 15–20, 27, 33, 35, 37, 41–5, 47–8, 51–4, 56–7, 59–61, 66–8, 71–3, 76–7, 87, 90, 105, 108, 116, 118–19, 124–5, 130, 133–4, 138–9, 141, 142–6, 153–4
More, Hannah 49, 60

mortality 5, 87
Mughal empire 6, 104, 109, 112, 114, 132, 141
    legal code 111–12
Muhammad Khurram, Shahab-ud-din (Shah Jahan) 109
Murray, John 64, 74
Muthu, Sankar 12
Mysore 111

Napoleonic wars 80, 93
national identity (British) 3, 5, 10–11, 15, 17–18, 60, 89, 98, 101–3, 106, 116, 126, 128–9, 176n94
National Library of Scotland 1, 129
neoliberalism 21
New Brunswick 83
New York (State) 83
Newfoundland 14
newspapers 12, 99
Newtonian Club 38
Niger River 40
non-Europeans 7, 11, 15–16, 20, 21–3, 25, 33–4, 49–50, 57, 86, 131, 138
    Africans 4, 6, 8–9, 15–17, 19–20, 23, 30–2, 34–7, 40–5, 50, 57, 59–63, 65–9, 71–7, 82–3, 85, 96, 100, 105, 109, 141, 151–4
    Indians 4, 45, 63, 103–4, 109, 114–16, 118–20, 125, 131–2, 135, 138–43, 154
    indigenous Americans 6, 17, 22, 25, 32, 54, 65, 70, 79, 83–4, 86, 100, 103–5, 117, 112, 131, 141, 154
North America 4–6, 14, 17, 19, 23, 25, 40–2, 54, 70, 79–80, 84, 86–7, 89, 91, 92–4, 103, 128, 131, 154. *See also*, American colonies, Canada, United States of America
    British-French wars 92
    Indian wars 92
Nossa Senhora da Luz (Bahia) 75
nostalgia 12
Nova Scotia 83, 85
novels and short stories 3, 10, 12, 16, 26, 39, 63–7, 75, 99, 151

occidentalism 11
Olinda 59, 74
orientalism 39, 63, 109–11, 120–2, 132, 139–40, 192n34

Orissa 104
Orme, Robert 109
    'A General Idea of the Government and People of Indostan' 109
Ossian 44, 91
Ouseley, Gore (Sir) 127
Ouseley, Harriet Georgina (Lady) 127, 138
Oxford 21
Oxfordshire 62–3
Oyster Club 21

Pacific Islanders 86, 139
Pacific Ocean 21, 84
Palgrave Academy 80
pamphlets 2–3, 13–14, 17, 34, 81, 95, 129, 141
Parel 135
Park, Mungo 37, 40
Parsis 5, 115–16, 133, 135–7
patriarchy 2–3, 7, 10, 16, 38, 56, 62, 75–7, 128, 133, 149, 153–4
Payne, John Howard 2
    'Home Sweet Home' 2
Pelham, Thomas (2nd Earl of Chichester) 83
Penalves Rocha, Antonio 66
Pennant, Thomas 94, 98
Pernambuco 59, 70, 74
Persia 5, 127, 137
    language 110, 137
    poetry of 21
Persian Gulf 137
Peru 70
philosophy 3, 7–10, 12–16, 18, 20–2, 24–6, 28–9, 32, 35–40, 44–5, 47–54, 57, 60–1, 63–4, 67, 74–5, 82, 86, 106–8, 110, 121, 129, 151, 153
Philosophical Society 38
Pinkerton, John 91
Pitt, William (the Younger) 82, 114
plantations 4–5, 7, 14, 19, 35, 40–1, 60, 65–7, 70–3, 75, 84
Pliny 108
plunder 6, 17
poetry 1–3, 16, 38–9, 49, 60, 74, 79, 81, 99, 101, 143–5
Poker Club 21
political economy 49, 64, 68, 86, 89–90, 94, 122, 139
polygenism 7
Portugal 65–6, 70

empire 59, 65–6, 70–1, 73, 76
Portuguese 59, 65, 71, 73–4, 76, 134–5
Postans, Marianne 142–3
postcolonialism 20, 140
power 3, 6, 8, 13, 19, 24, 30–2, 43, 55, 60, 66, 73, 89, 96, 104, 107, 111, 113–14, 116–18, 120, 122, 141, 152, 155
Priestly, Joseph 82
Prince Edward Island (Epekwitk) 79, 83–5, 95–6, 100
Prince, Mary 77
property 9, 24, 27–9, 31, 54–6, 59, 69, 75–6, 82, 93, 97, 101–2, 104, 106, 153
   marker of 'white' and 'black' 9
protestantism 5, 60, 64–5, 82, 135, 145–6
   Anglicanism 5
   dissenters 65, 82
   evangelicalism 60, 145–6
   presbyterianism 65
providence 27, 38, 47–9, 52–3, 69, 117
Pune (Poonah) 146–7

Quran 21

race 7–11, 35, 45, 56–7, 71, 90–1, 102, 109, 111, 123–4, 132, 134, 138–9, 143–4, 152–3
racism 7–9, 11, 36, 42, 56–7, 61–2, 69, 72, 106, 128, 134, 146, 154
   justification for exploitation 8, 57, 62, 69, 72, 106
   perceived anatomical traits 8
   perceived phenotypical traits 8
   'race science' 57, 61
   skin colour 8, 9
Rajputs 6
Ram Mohan Roy, Raja 21
Rao, Baji II 138
Raynal, Abbé 12
Red River 96
Reid, Thomas 38, 47–8, 51–2, 57
   biographical summary 51–2
   'common sense' philosophy 51–2
   An Inquiry into the Human Mind on the Principles of Common Sense 47–8, 51–2
Rennell, James 110
   'Memoir of a Map of Hindostan' 110

Revolutionary wars (French) 80, 82, 93
Ricardo, David 13, 129
Rich, Claudius James 122
   Memoir on the Ruins of Babylon 122
Rich, Mary (née Mackintosh) 127, 134, 137, 143, 147
Rio de Janeiro 66
River Amazon 105
River Ganges 152
River Plate 105
River Thames 137
Robertson, William 38, 109, 125
   An Historical Disquisition Concerning the Knowledge Which the Ancients Had of India 109
Roma 154–5
romantic movement 11–12, 91, 98, 101
Rome (Ancient) 24, 31
Roscoe, William 74–5
   'Mount Pleasant' 74
   'The West Indies' 74–5
Ross-Shire 79, 96, 98
Rothiemurchus (Strathspey) 98
Royal Society of Edinburgh 38. *See also*, Philosophical Society
Russell, Henry (Sir) 137

Said, Edward 140
Saint Domingo 72
St John's Island 84
St Kitts 14, 83
St Mary's Isle (Scotland) 82
St Vincent 40
Salsette 122
Sancho, Ignatius 23
Sanskrit 21, 110
Scandinavia 92
science 16, 26, 42, 53, 57, 61, 63–4, 109, 111, 122
Scotland 4, 21, 24, 35, 91, 94, 99, 107, 123, 141. *See also*, Highlands, Highlanders
   Gaelic language 91
   history 11
   independence movement 82
   Jacobite rising 88, 90, 106. *See also* Jacobites
   Lowlanders 17, 90–1

Lowlands 17, 98–100
traditions 11
Scots 1, 6, 83, 91, 95, 106, 113–14, 123. *See also* Highlanders
identity 91
Scott, Henry (3rd Duke of Buccleugh) 21
Scott, Walter (Sir) 91
Waverley 91
Scottish Enlightenment 2–3, 8, 10–13, 15–16, 20, 23, 28–9, 32, 37–8, 41, 43, 49, 54, 56–7, 60, 62–3, 67, 69, 72, 74, 86, 90, 94, 106–7, 112, 138, 153, 166n5, 168n32
  characterisations of India 16, 108–9, 138
  'common sense' philosophy 51–2, 57
  emotional capacity 3, 28, 153
  essentialist understandings of 2–3, 16, 28–9, 37, 41, 47–8
  ideas of human development 2, 16, 20, 22, 32, 37, 40–1, 56, 85–6, 89–90, 111, 153
  materialist understandings of 2, 16, 29, 31, 37–8, 47, 54–6
  ideas of human difference 2, 7–8, 16, 20, 32–3, 40–3, 57, 90, 106, 153
  ideas of race in 32–4, 57, 153, 165n80, 168n32
  moral philosophy 8, 15–16, 20, 22–3, 37–9, 49, 51, 53, 57, 60–1, 64, 67, 86, 107, 110
  notion of moral superiority 3, 110–1
  political economy 49, 68, 86, 89–90, 94, 122, 139
  racialised 8, 15–16, 32–3, 37, 109, 111, 153
  sensibility 10, 22, 26, 30–1, 36, 41, 44, 54, 74–5, 141
Second Anglo-Maratha war 113, 151
Selkirk Earl of. *See* Douglas, Thomas
sensibility 10, 22, 26, 30–1, 36, 41, 44, 54, 74–5, 141–2, 144
Seven Years' War 107
sexuality 11, 26, 57, 67–8, 86–7, 114, 131–2, 138–9, 141, 145–6, 151
Shaftesbury, Lord. *See* Cooper, Anthony Ashley
Shah Alam II. *See* Gohar, Ali
Shakespeare, William 133
Sharp, Richard 13–14, 116, 122
Sheridan, Richard 111, 124

Sinclair, John (Sir) 89
Siraj-ud-Daula, Mirza Muhammad (Nawab) 104
slave trade 4–6, 9, 18, 20, 38, 40, 42, 60–2, 65–6, 69–71, 73–6, 85, 105, 152
  Act for the Abolition of the Slave Trade (1807) 73, 85, 99
  white slave trade 99
slavery 4–6, 9, 17–20, 23, 30–1, 34–5, 40–3, 45, 59–62, 65–6, 69–77, 82–3, 85, 96, 99, 144, 152–4, 176n89, 192n30
  abolitionism 17, 20, 23, 34, 38, 40, 42–3, 45, 59–62, 66–7, 69, 72–3, 77, 85, 154, 172n4
  gratitude, notion of 61, 69, 75, 172n8
  James Somerset (ruling of 1772) 9
  literary representations of 61–3, 66–7, 69, 72–5, 77
  manumission 42, 70, 72
  racist justifications for 8, 17, 42–3
  slave rebellions 6, 35, 45, 66–72, 74–5
  social death 197n4
Smith, Adam 12, 15–16, 18–38, 43–4, 47, 49–57, 60, 66–7, 69, 71–2, 74, 80, 85–9, 89–90, 104–5, 110, 112, 117, 141, 142, 152–3
  binary of 'civilised' and 'savage' 15, 20, 23–5, 28–32, 34–7, 44, 69, 72
  biographical summary 20–4
  critique of European conquest 15, 19, 34, 104–5, 112
  critique of imperial monopoly 15, 106, 112
  Dissertation on the Origins of Language 47, 110
  gendered exclusions in work 22, 161n16
  Lectures on Jurisprudence 23–5, 29, 31
  notion of 'sympathy' 15, 19, 22–8, 30–4, 36–7, 44, 49, 51–2, 89, 163n34
  opposition to slavery 15, 18–20, 30, 34–5, 43, 66, 72, 105, 153, 160n5
  stadial theory 20, 23–5, 33, 37, 91, 94
  The Theory of Moral Sentiments 15, 19–21, 25, 27, 29–32, 36, 44, 49, 90, 141, 152
  theories of human development 22–32, 42, 44, 47, 51, 54–5, 86, 153
  views on Africans 22–3, 33, 50, 60
  views on God 27

views on middle classes 32
views on racial difference 20, 23, 33, 42
views on women 20, 22–3, 28, 30, 33–4, 49
The Wealth of Nations 20–2, 31, 33, 86, 90, 104–5, 112
Smith, Cecil 144
Smith (née Douglas), Margaret 21
Smith, Samuel Stanhope 41–2
  Essay on the Causes of the Variety of Complexion and Figure of the Human Species 41–2
Society in Scotland for Propagating Christian Knowledge 90
Society of United Irishmen 65, 83
song 2, 99
South Africa 1
South America 1, 21, 60, 63, 66, 70
South Asia 4, 6, 137–8
South Carolina 107
Southey, Robert 70–1
  History of Brazil 70
Spain 65, 70, 73
Speculative Society 38, 82, 107
Staffordshire 2, 95
Stewart, Dugald 13, 15–16, 25, 32, 37–51, 53–4, 56, 57, 60–4, 67–9, 72–3, 77, 82, 85–6, 94, 107–8, 110, 121, 129, 139, 153, 166n5, 168n23, 169n62
  biographical summary 38–40
  'common sense' philosophy 51–2, 57
  concept of 'reason' 45–8, 50, 54
  'conjectural history' 25
  critique of Smith 16
  Dissertation Exhibiting the Progress of Metaphysical, Ethical and Political Philosophy 39, 54
  Elements of the Philosophy of the Human Mind 39–40, 45, 53, 63–4
  Lectures on Political Economy 86, 94, 139
  moral philosophy 15, 25, 37–9, 49, 51, 53–4, 57, 61, 64, 67, 86, 110
  notion of human difference 16, 25, 38, 40–6, 50, 56, 68, 110
  notion of human progress 16, 25, 37–8, 40–2, 44–8, 60–1, 153
  opposition to slavery 38, 40, 42–5, 67, 72, 85, 153
  Outlines of Moral Philosophy 40, 51, 53

views on Africans 40–4, 50, 60–1, 68–9
views on women 49–50, 56, 68–9
Stewart, Marjory 38
Stewart, Matthew (father of Dugald) 38
Stewart, Matthew (son of Dugald) 39
Strathspey 98
Surat 116
Sutherlandshire 98
Swift, Jonathan 2, 52, 124
  Gulliver's Travels 52
Switzerland 21
Syer, William (Sir) 115

Tacitus 63
Tahiti 54
Tamerlane 109
Tartars 24, 32, 109
Tehran 127
theology 26
trade 3–6, 12, 14, 21, 31, 70, 104, 115–16, 135, 137
Transactions of the Geographical Society 64
travel writing 1, 8, 12, 15–16, 21, 39, 59, 63–4, 69–70, 81, 88–9, 98–100, 109–10, 129, 142
Treaty of Utrecht (1713) 84
Turnbull, George 52

unhomely 15, 129, 149
United States of America 83

Vassall-Fox, Henry (3rd Baron Holland) 129
Virgil 137
Virginia 9, 34
Voltaire (Arouet, François-Marie) 2

Wadia Family 133, 136
Wales 151
war 3–4, 6, 68, 80, 82, 92–3, 104, 107, 113, 151
  British-French wars (North America) 92
  Indian wars (North America) 92
  Napoleonic wars 80, 93
  Revolutionary wars (French) 80, 82, 93
  Second Anglo-Maratha war 113, 151
  Seven Years' War 107
  Tacky's War 68
Ward, John William (1st Earl of Dudley) 40
Warwickshire 103

Webster, Alexander 89
Wedderton, Andrew 83
Wedderton-Colville, Jean 83
Wedgwood Archive 129
Wedgewood, Frances 'Fanny' (née Mackintosh) 135–7
Wedgwood, Josiah 2, 63, 95
    family 129, 151
Wellesley, Richard Colley (1st Marquess Wellesley) 120
Welsh 114, 129, 151
West Indies 14, 43, 104, 112. *See also* Caribbean
Western Isles 95
Westminster 83, 112
    House of Commons 119
    House of Lords 85
whiggism 13, 39, 82, 107, 129
Whishaw, John 112
white supremacy 3, 6, 9, 12, 15–17, 38, 57, 61–2, 69, 75, 77, 132, 153–4
whiteness 7, 9–10, 12, 14–15, 17–18, 22, 32–3, 38, 43, 57, 60, 62, 76–7, 85, 95, 99, 101–2, 103, 106, 111, 116, 121, 123, 125–7, 129–30, 133, 138, 143, 145, 148–9, 152–4. *See also* British empire, whiteness
Williamson, Thomas 131–2, 134
    East India Company Vade Mecum 131, 136
Wiltshire 72
Wise Club (Aberdeen) 51
Wiseman, William (Sir) 127–8, 133
Wollstonecraft, Mary 49, 111, 145
    Vindication of the Rights of Woman 111, 145
women 4, 6, 8, 12, 23, 29–30, 33–4, 38–9, 43, 45, 49–50, 54–6, 61–2, 64, 66–8, 70, 72–3, 76, 81, 97–9, 103, 128, 130–2, 136, 138–44, 146–8, 152, 192n24
    white womanhood 127–31, 134, 140, 143, 145–9
Wordsworth, Dorothy 100, 129
Wordsworth, William 98–100, 129
    'To a Highland Girl' 98–9

Zoroastrianism 5, 137

www.ingramcontent.com/pod-product-compliance
Lightning Source LLC
Chambersburg PA
CBHW072147290426
44111CB00012B/1997